STRATEGIC PREACHING

THE ROLE OF THE PULPIT IN PASTORAL LEADERSHIP

WILLIAM E. HULL

CHALICE
PRESS
ST. LOUIS, MISSOURI

Cover art: Fotosearch
Cover and interior design: Elizabeth Wright

Visit Chalice Press on the World Wide Web at
www.chalicepress.com

10 9 8 7 6 5 4 3 2 1   06 07 08 09 10 11 12

Library of Congress Cataloging–in–Publication Data

Hull, William E.

Strategic preaching : the role of the pulpit in pastoral leadership / William E. Hull.
  p. cm.
Includes bibliographical references and index.
ISBN-13: 978-0-8272-3467-3 (alk. paper)
1. Preaching. 2. Pastoral theology. 3. Church leadership. I. Title.

BV4211.3.H85 2006
251—dc22

2006028830

Printed in the United States of America

Contents

To
Duke K. McCall
Willis L. Meadows
Thomas E. Corts,

defining friendships of
a vocational lifetime,

models and mentors of
strategic Christian leadership

Preface

I have written this book primarily for pastors. I invite you to rethink the preaching task by linking it more closely to your leadership role in the congregation. I hope to convince you that the pulpit can become a crucial catalyst in helping your church to fulfill its mission in today's world. I call this approach "strategic preaching," sermons that move the people of God toward the goals defined by the promises of the gospel.

Why this focus on preaching in relation to leadership?

- Because a congregation searching for a pastor looks first and foremost for a leader.
- Because many congregations are concerned that the minister is not moving the church forward, resulting in an alarming rate of involuntary termination.
- Because few works seek to relate the core functions that pastors perform to their roles as leaders.

A lack of effective pastoral leadership has now become a serious problem in the churches. George Barna has reported that only 14 percent of senior pastors in the United States believe that they are effective at thinking and acting strategically even though most think that they are gifted at motivating people.[1] The Alban Institute has depicted "the prevailing sense of crisis" in terms of an acute clergy shortage, an aging ministerium, and a noticeable decline in the leadership potential of those entering church vocations.[2] In response, the Lilly Endowment is investing millions of dollars in a massive effort to help arrest "this sense of a downward spiral into pastoral mediocrity."[3]

I am convinced that preaching can enhance one's leadership and, conversely, that leadership can enhance one's preaching. Surprisingly, these two central functions of the pastoral office have seldom been integrally related. Studies of pastoral preaching seldom mention leadership. Similarly, pastoral leadership studies normally ignore preaching. Moreover, most seminaries and divinity schools keep these two aspects of ministry at arm's length in the curriculum. Denominational executives and theological educators are concerned with such pressing needs as clergy recruitment, retention, compensation, and morale. Thus they cannot or do not help pastors develop a holistic approach to ministry that unifies all of their essential functions in support of effective leadership. So let us pave the way for pastors to understand leadership as a distinctive way of doing what ministers have always done, not as one more responsibility added to the many others already expected of pastors.

Of the many clergy duties, why focus on preaching as one way to lead a congregation?

- Because preaching is by far the most visible thing a pastor does on a regular basis with the greatest number of church members.
- Because congregations give pastors almost complete freedom to prepare and proclaim whatever they feel to be most relevant and urgent, permitting a high degree of creativity and innovation.
- Because preaching in the spiritually charged atmosphere of worship sets the tone for the life of the church throughout the week.

Of all the settings for ministry, the pulpit is the one place where pastors are encouraged to declare their deepest convictions, to take courageous stands on important issues, and to call on others to act on the claims of the message that has first claimed them. A free pulpit offers the minister unique opportunities to function as a leader. But how can a pastor reconceptualize the preaching task in this fashion? Seminaries and divinity schools have not taught homiletics in this way. Standard homiletics textbooks say nothing about preaching as leading. The best-known writers of published sermons do not approach their craft from this perspective.

This admittedly groundbreaking venture will follow a relatively simple path. Two introductory chapters will show the need for a new homiletical praxis and a biblical-theological framework in which to set it. Then the book's two main parts will seek to balance our twin concerns for preaching and leadership. The four chapters of Part 1 track the preaching task from start to finish; that is, from its beginning with a biblical text to its ending with the act of proclamation. The four chapters of Part 2 then trace how to lead in such a way that the sermon becomes "strategic"; that is, how to make the weekly pulpit utterance crucial to the shaping of those plans and priorities by which the congregation seeks to fulfill its God-given mission. Two concluding chapters assess the relevance of this approach for contemporary life and present case studies of strategic preaching in a variety of settings.

You may be wondering what qualifications I have to guide you over unexplored terrain. I spent a half-century in full-time ministry (1951–2000) divided almost equally between pastoral and educational pursuits. Twenty years were spent as a pastor of everything from a one-room country church to a tall-steeple, historic "First Church." I also spent twenty years as a New Testament teacher in a theological seminary, the last six involving leadership responsibilities as dean and provost. I later spent nine more years as provost and four years as a teacher of religion and leadership studies in a Christian university. These numbers add up to more than fifty years because I often carried overlapping assignments. I continue to divide my time equally between service in a church as theologian in residence and in a university as a research professor. I have spent all of my adult life mediating between the two worlds of teaching and preaching, theory and practice, scholarship and leadership.

This book has no bibliography because, as best as I can tell, no one has written at any length about the relationship between preaching and leadership. To compensate for this absence I have included extensive notes. These not only document my direct dependence on published sources, but also indicate some of the reading that has contributed to my exploratory treatment of this subject. However, writing as a "reflective practitioner,"[4] no more than half of the material has come from my study and teaching; the other half comes directly from my experience in the practice of ministry. Having pursued a kind of boundary career, I have tried to learn as much from people as from books, from the world as from the church, from the laity as from the clergy, from failure as from success.

This book seeks to be useful to three kinds of readers. First are working pastors deep enough into the vocational trenches of ministry to know what it is really like to preach—yea, to *have to* preach—to the same people week after week for years on end while, at the same time, seeking to facilitate the institutional life of the church. Second are teachers of preaching willing to consider a somewhat contrarian approach from outside the guild, which contends that homiletics needs to sustain a closer working relationship with leadership studies. Third are theological students who have not yet experienced what it means to be responsible for the constant care of a congregation but who are willing to prepare for that eventuality by becoming leaders-in-the-making.

This is not a quick-and-easy handbook with five simple steps to strategic preaching. Some sections of the book will seem a bit scholarly, much like the academic approach that you received in seminary. I have included this material because I want both preachers and their teachers to understand more clearly the underlying reasons for the innovations I am suggesting. Be assured that everything I have included is intended to contribute to a more effective ministry of preaching in a pastoral setting.

I freely admit this is not the last word on the subject. It is a first word that seeks to address a critically important but neglected issue: How may we preach and lead at the same time? Charles Templeton told of a man lost in the Burmese jungle who hailed a passing inhabitant and asked if he would lead him out. The guide said, "Follow me," as his machete hacked a path through the tangled undergrowth. Fearful of getting lost the man called ahead, "Are you sure this is the way?" His leader paused a moment and then answered, "There is no way. I am the way. Follow me."[5] Homiletics has never gone this way before, but I shall do my best to lead you as far as I can go. My greatest hope is that, when our journey together is ended, you will be able to travel much farther on your own.

Acknowledgments

This book began modestly and grew slowly. On July 29, 1997, I was asked to lead a workshop for the Samford Pastors School sponsored by Beeson Divinity School. I entitled the workshop "Strategic Preaching." During this informal presentation I introduced the idea of plotting a sermon trajectory that would guide the hearers from wherever they might be on their spiritual pilgrimage (Point A) toward that horizon of promise defined by the gospel (Point B). Jerry Batson, associate dean of Beeson Divinity School, urged me to develop these ideas more fully. With the concurrence of Dean Timothy George, he soon implemented this suggestion by inviting me to teach a number of Master of Divinity classes and Doctor of Ministry seminars on strategic preaching and the related area of pastoral leadership. Thus began my efforts to shape a coherent and comprehensive understanding of an emphasis that had been forged almost entirely on the anvil of pastoral experience.

As the material gradually took shape, it was greatly strengthened by interaction particularly with my D.Min. students, all of them already serving as pastors in diverse and demanding congregational settings. Two groups contributed most directly to the development of a manuscript that would be useful to practitioners of ministry. The 1999–2000 seminar reacted to the first draft and offered many valuable suggestions for improvement. My thanks to Russ Dean, Scott Fowler, Bob Hatfield, Bobby Hopper, John Johnston, Patricia Outlaw, Bill Russell, Chip Starnes, and Steve Traylor. The 2002–03 seminar wrote critiques of the second draft, which led to yet further useful revisions. Appreciation for these helpful evaluations goes to Bob Ehr, Mark Goodman, Alan McBride, David Richardson, James Rumph, and Ralph Wooten.

In addition to this important input from advanced students and full-time parish clergy, I also received wise counsel from a number of academic colleagues. Those who offered detailed responses of great help when preparing the third draft include Jim Barnette here at Samford, Larry McSwain at Mercer/Atlanta, and especially Walter Shurden at Mercer/Macon. Here I gladly acknowledge the great stimulus received from delivering Part 1 of the book as the William L. Self Lectures on Preaching at the McAfee School of Theology of Mercer University. Every courtesy was extended to my wife and me on this occasion by Dean Alan Culpepper and by Professor Peter Rhea Jones as chair of the lecture committee, both former students whose distinguished careers have brought great joy to my life.

Closer to home, our son, David W. Hull, kept me abreast of cutting-edge developments in congregational ministry while he served as pastor of the First Baptist Church in Knoxville, Tennessee. Now even closer by as pastor of the First Baptist Church in Huntsville, Alabama, he has begun to share with me the offering of D.Min. seminars in this area, providing students with a much appreciated clinical dimension of how strategic leadership is currently being implemented at the parish level. With the completion of this book, I pass the baton to him for any future writing from our family on congregational life, an area in which he now has greater aptitude, insight, and experience than his father.

In my immediate working environment, this book was made possible by the creative role that President Thomas E. Corts provided for me as a research professor at Samford University following my retirement as provost and university professor. In addition to the essentials of office space, library privileges, and a parking permit, the University has generously allowed me to retain the services of Joellen Henson as research associate, office manager, copy editor, engagement coordinator, travel planner, and—most important—time-saver extraordinaire! The two of us are the only ones who fully realize that this book would not have been possible without her help.

As the manuscript began its journey toward publication, I was fortunate to secure the services of Trent Butler as editor in addition to his duties as vice president and editorial director of Chalice Press, thereby renewing a cherished relationship going back to seminary days. At the most labor intensive point in this process, his office and home were thrown into disarray by a devastating tornado—even the cat went missing for a month!—but Trent scarcely skipped a beat in sending me his valuable suggestions. In the midst of this confusion, the production staff lost its publishing assistant, Sarah Tasic, to graduate school, but Carla TenBroek and her colleagues stepped into the breach and, again, the work moved forward without delay. To say the least, a great deal of tedium accompanies the birthing of a book, but I was encouraged to stay the course by the disciplined example of those with whom I worked at Chalice Press.

Why do authors almost invariably end such acknowledgments with a word of appreciation for their spouse? It is because they are so keenly aware of just how much time, attention, and energy the project has diverted from the one with whom they live. For a half-century and more of marriage, Wylodine has often seen me disappear behind the study door when she might have preferred my more immediate companionship. Yet her strong support and good cheer have been unfailing even during this project, which, because of its interdisciplinary nature, took longer than most. I only hope she realizes how much I appreciate the way she has willingly shared the sacrifices necessary to get the book written and will derive some measure of satisfaction should it prove useful to others.

INTRODUCTION

CHAPTER 1

Strategic Preaching in Contemporary Homiletics

The term "strategic preaching" is unknown in the literature on homiletics. I begin with a working definition that will be further clarified and enriched as our journey unfolds. Strategic preaching is the kind of Christian proclamation that is *designed to guide a congregation in the fulfillment of its mission.* On this understanding, one primary purpose of a sermon is to lead its hearers from Point A to Point B, that is, from where they are now to where the imperatives of the gospel call them to be. In short, the sermon is to *help God's future happen* in the lives of its hearers. Strategic preaching is a call to be pulled forward by God's unfinished agenda in this world. It invites us to live out of that vision Jesus called the kingdom of God, indeed to claim the life of the "new age" here and now "on earth as it is in heaven" (Mt. 6:10). In pointing the way to God's tomorrow, the preacher not only gets out in front of the congregation as a leader but thereby opens up a path that invites the congregation to undertake the journey with its pastor.

The Absence of an Emphasis on Strategic Preaching

Over the past seventy years, 6,484 titles have been catalogued in the three standard bibliographies on homiletics.[1] A close look at the title as well as the description, abstract, or review of these entries failed to turn up a single work which dealt primarily, or even directly, with the role of preaching in providing a congregation with a strategy to fulfill its mission. All three of the bibliographies are organized by subject groupings, none of which cover such areas as leadership, purpose, and planning. This bibliographical survey leads to the conclusion that what we are calling strategic preaching has no place in the standard homiletical resources available to pastors.

To test the validity of this conclusion, I attempted three other soundings. First, since my readers study homiletics across an entire generation, I examined the most widely used textbooks over the past half-century[2] to see what they might say about the sermon as an effective instrument for moving a congregation to accomplish its mission. In the most recent period (1955–2005), five works have dominated the field, written by H. Grady Davis, George E. Sweazey, Fred B. Craddock, David G. Buttrick, and Clyde E. Fant.[3] On our agenda, Davis and Fant are silent. Buttrick briefly mentions "in-church preaching," but is more interested in issues of identity than of purpose.[4] Sweazey emphasizes the importance of an explicit purpose statement for each sermon but does not relate it to the congregational planning process.[5] Craddock comes closest to our concern in his discussion of "the pastoral context," but limits his treatment to the importance of congregational involvement as an influence in sermon preparation.[6] Once again we come up empty-handed, this time in our search for guidance from the most widely used manuals of homiletical instruction.

William H. Willimon and Richard Lischer's *Concise Encyclopedia of Preaching* presented the opportunity for a second sounding.[7] One searches the two hundred alphabetical entries in vain for any mention of such topics as purpose, mission, strategy, planning, or visioning in relation to the pulpit. The Preface contains a listing of articles in several tracks "for those who wish to read the *Encyclopedia* systematically,"[8] but these topical groupings show clearly that the editors do not conceive of the leadership agenda as a part of the preaching task. I find it ironic that these two editors, in particular, should neglect a discussion of the role of preaching in the exercise of pastoral leadership. It would be hard to think of a preacher more intentional than Willimon about pointing the church in new directions as a strategic imperative,[9] while Lischer recently wrote a prize-winning study of Martin Luther King Jr., who was perhaps the best exemplar of strategic preaching in his time.[10]

My third sounding used a recent work by John McClure to look at the cutting edge of homiletic theory. Rebecca Chopp lauds McClure's volume for including "one of the finest histories of modern preaching ever written."[11] This probing philosophical analysis of every important work on homiletics from Broadus to Brueggemann shows how the leading thinkers in the field have been concerned almost exclusively with finding an epistemology that can overcome the fact/value split the Enlightenment bequeathed to us rather than with how preaching can help build strong churches that are centers of spiritual and ethical transformation for their members and for the communities in which they are located. Pastoral leadership in the pulpit is never identified as a concern of any of the works cited. Indeed, the implication of McClure's own thrust is to be wary of traditional leadership roles because of their tendency to become "hegemonic," i.e., authoritarian or domineering.[12]

From the practical side we can point to significant practitioners of "strategic preaching," particularly since the turbulent decade of the 1960s. One thinks immediately of the prophetic preaching by Martin Luther King Jr. and his fellow African-American pastors on behalf of civil rights, of the social justice preaching by William Sloan Coffin Jr. at Yale and Riverside, as well as of preaching from the margins by advocates of liberationist and feminist theologies.[13] But a close look suggests that these currents of transformative proclamation emerged more by intuition than by design, more in spite of than because of the ways in which their spokespersons had been taught to preach. The great host of pastors do not possess the creative insight and courageous tenacity of these high-profile pacesetters. How can they learn how to exercise a similar ministry on a more modest scale?

Dynamics behind the Neglect

In light of the growing attention being devoted to pastoral leadership in theological education,[14] how are we to explain this strange silence on the leadership aspect of preaching? Three dynamics seem to have subtly influenced teachers of preaching to neglect its strategic function.

First, homiletics lost its place as the prince of studies among pastors. This ancient and honorable discipline dominated the "practical" portion of the curriculum in Protestant seminaries and divinity schools until the twentieth century. After World War I and then accelerating after World War II, homiletics lost ground in the competition for required hours and electives in the curriculum to a host of newer disciplines such as religious education and church administration, pastoral care and counseling, evangelism and church growth, plus a variety of applied social ministries. As a seminary dean and provost in the 1960s and 1970s, when American theological education moved away from the classical approach embedded in the Bachelor of Divinity degree to the more professional approach of the Master of Divinity and Doctor of Ministry degrees, I well remember the pain and frustration associated with the downsizing of the preaching curriculum to make room for these newer emphases.

For more than a century homiletics professors tended to be more aligned with faculty in the classical trivium of Bible, church history, and theology. Some of them, such as Broadus and Craddock, held joint appointments in

Preaching and New Testament. In the sixties and seventies, homiletics languished under the enormous popularity of the pastoral care movement. Its historical place with the classic disciplines and the growing "competition" with new disciplines made homiletics hesitant to build its approach directly on the empirical realities of congregational life.

Second, most faculty members do not function as leaders responsible for unifying their institution around a shared sense of mission. Presidents and deans do that. Professors who presume to venture outside their disciplinary specialty and begin to talk about the strategic direction of the institution are immediately cautioned by their colleagues not to act like "administrators." Such clear-cut roles inhibit any exercise of institutional leadership by those supposed to be teaching their students how to become congregational leaders!

How different it is in congregational life. The seminary graduate just beginning to preach in a small church with only a hundred or so members is expected to exercise far more institutional leadership than a tenured full professor who may have written several books on preaching. Thus theological faculty have been slow to introduce courses on leadership studies into the curriculum or to include such emphases in their own courses despite the prodding of their accrediting agency.[15]

Third, most homiletics professors are enormously talented and highly trained scholars who preach frequently, thereby practicing what they are teaching others to do. But virtually all of their pulpit assignments are as a visitor, either to substitute for an absentee pastor or to speak on some special occasion. They use the same sermons again and again until they polish their biblical insights and rhetorical flourishes to a high gloss, thus earning the plaudits of the pew for delivering a "pulpit masterpiece." (I speak as one who has functioned in this role for more than fifty years!) On these brief visits to faraway churches, one can hardly gain any profound knowledge of where the people have been or where they are trying to go on their spiritual pilgrimage. The visiting preacher cannot speak with any urgency or specificity to their strategic goals or function as the acknowledged leader of those being addressed. The act of proclamation becomes an end in itself rather than an attempt to move its hearers toward a mutually chosen destination to which both speaker and hearer are committed.

Related to this is the "great preacher" phenomenon that continues to attract a fair amount of attention. All such lists, as Kenneth Woodward shrewdly observed about Baylor University's survey to determine the twelve "most effective preachers" in the English-speaking world, reflect those who did the choosing. Most of the choosers and the chosen are academics whose reputations are based more on what they have published *about* homiletics than on the actual results of their pulpit performance in building a community of faith.[16] Even the sermons homileticians publish are often limited in their strategic impact: strong on biblical exposition, stylistic elegance, and cultural perception, but weak on what is at stake for the hearer in a particular context. It is difficult to determine what such sermons are trying to accomplish in the life of the congregations to which they are addressed or what the hearers should actually be doing in response to what they have just heard. Inexperienced pastors read such sermons from "the masters" and suppose that these are the models of "great preaching" to which they should aspire. In actuality such sermons are more often literary and exegetical gems than they are marching orders for a battle-weary congregation struggling, not only to survive, but to prevail in an indifferent and even hostile climate.

Strategic Preaching and Traditional Pulpit Approaches

The strange silence of homiletics on strategic preaching rests on more than the vocational dynamics that influence those academicians who define the discipline. The long history of preaching itself bequeaths to homileticians a starting point for their own study. As a practicing sermonizer, not as an academic specialist, I find three emphases that have dominated the understanding of preaching. I shall call these the biblical, the rhetorical, and the relational.[17] Each of them has, in different ways, served to minimize the strategic aspect of preaching.

The Biblical Paradigm

The biblical paradigm of preaching has long predominated in my own ministerial tradition, which may be broadly defined as "free-church evangelical." Every sermon should have a text whose truths are expounded by closely adhering to the chosen passage both in form and content. Some in this tradition continue to emphasize that "proclaiming the word" or "declaring the gospel" is synonymous with "preaching the Bible." Anchoring the sermon firmly in Scripture confers on it an authority, a boldness, and an urgency that it would not otherwise have. In other words, a "high" doctrine of Scripture is used to undergird a "high" doctrine of preaching. The sermon somehow partakes of the inspiration, the uniqueness, and the compelling power of the text it proclaims.

In this paradigm the exegetical focus of preaching places enormous importance on a sound interpretation of the text. For some, to preach a sermon and to expound a text become the same thing. These preachers seem to operate on the premise that, because a message is the mouthpiece of Scripture, it should be received with the same reverence that one accords to the Bible itself.

But this homiletic is hardly adequate if its hermeneutic is flawed. For example, the Southern defense of slavery before the Civil War was waged directly from the pulpit by its clergy. Moreover, "the southern churchman's major argument in defense of human bondage was biblical in nature. He contended relentlessly that the master-slave relation was explicitly sanctioned in both testaments of the Bible, and that consequently to denounce that relation as sinful per se was to impugn God's word."[18]

A deficient hermeneutic has often led even those most committed to biblical preaching sadly astray. Protology (i.e., "creationism") and eschatology (i.e., "dispensationalism"), in particular, offer a happy hunting ground for homiletical misadventure.[19] But the problem is more subtle than these egregious examples of pulpit malpractice would suggest. I gladly affirm that the biblical paradigm of preaching holds rich promise for anyone with a high view of Scripture. But the promise is difficult to fulfill because its interpretation requires a more carefully considered hermeneutic than many pastors are willing or able to master. From beginning to end, Scripture was designed to move the people of God ever closer to their divinely intended destiny. But until recently, those who preached from it most earnestly did not read the Bible that way. Instead, exposition became a self-contained exercise.

How can we explain this misappropriation of Scripture? The strategic considerations that first called the biblical writings into being are largely hidden from all but the most highly trained reader. Not until well into the twentieth century did learned scholars began to probe the original thrust of the text in its own context. Most commentaries on the Bible written before 1950 provide little guidance to the preacher in search of the underlying sense of purpose that impelled a particular passage of Scripture to be written in the first place.

The exposition of the text should be a means of discovering the kinds of changes God was inspiring the biblical writers to attempt in their day, and then using this finding as the basis for considering the kind of changes God would have us make in our own day. Unless we learn to discern the strategic import of the scriptural text, we will not use the Bible effectively to do strategic preaching today. Chapters 3 and 4 will consider how that might be done.

The Rhetorical Paradigm

The rhetorical paradigm of preaching gained emphasis partly because of the difficulties of biblical interpretation and partly due to the demands of the electronic church for "pop rhetoric." Here the divine aspect of the sermon as a compelling word from above is balanced by attention to its human aspect as a persuasive word from below.

In my own seminary training, we read John A. Broadus's textbook in homiletics. Broadus was chiefly indebted to the classical work of Aristotle, Cicero, and Quintilian on rhetoric.[20] In subtle ways, this paradigm tends to stress form more than content, artistry more than authority, semantics more than hermeneutics, communication more than confrontation, convincing the skeptic more than confirming the believer.[21] The pervasiveness of the electronic church with its celebrity preachers has subtly redefined the sermon as religious performance, even entertainment, and driven parish clergy to compete by utilizing verbal pyrotechnics, dramatic illustrations, and flamboyant delivery. In my region of the country, this striving after pulpit eloquence is often wed to the old tradition of southern oratory in an effort to satisfy the criterion of enjoyability as decreed by our medium-as-message culture.[22]

Clearly the rhetorical paradigm offers much of value. If the Christian life is a work of divine artistry (Eph. 2:10), then pulpit discourse is deserving of our finest craftsmanship. But if we go no further, the sermon again becomes an end in itself, inviting the hearer to admire its vivid imagery as one might view a beautiful painting, or relish its creative design as one might follow the movements of a great symphony. Indeed, advocates of the "New Criticism" would insist that any work of art is autonomous and that we violate its integrity as a finished work by inquiring into the intentions that prompted it.[23] But a sermon, while it may certainly be artistic, is not just a work of art.[24]

The sermon does not turn inward upon itself as an autonomous work of art but outward to those whom it would seek to challenge. In one sense the sermon, like its Lord, is kenotic, that is, it "empties" itself into the life of the world rather than seeking to protect its prerogatives as a self-contained creation (cf. Phil. 2:5–8). In a paradoxical sense, some of our most effective preachers speak of dying to great preaching understood as the expression of their rhetorical skills. The apostle Paul, who would later pen an exquisite poem on love in the same letter, first set theological limits on the use of rhetoric with his confession to the Corinthians:

> When I came to you…I did not come proclaiming the mystery of God to you in lofty words…My speech and my proclamation were not with plausible words of wisdom, but with a demonstration of the Spirit and of power, so that your faith might rest not on human wisdom but on the power of God. (1 Cor. 2:1, 4–5, NRSV)

The Relational Paradigm

The relational paradigm emerged afresh in the second half of the twentieth century as an effort to help the preacher escape from the lonely pedestal erected out of inflated claims the other two paradigms made for the sermon. Both the biblical and the rhetorical approaches to preaching tend to isolate the preacher from the congregation in the act of sermon preparation. The biblical paradigm encourages a mystique of the sermon as a message shaped in a solitary struggle with Scripture and, ultimately, with the God who inspired it. It views the act of biblical interpretation as an individual effort that would somehow be compromised if others were to interfere. The rhetorical paradigm shifts the stress to the preacher as a creative artisan toiling alone to shape a verbal masterpiece. The isolating tendencies of both paradigms place the sole burden for sermon preparation on the preacher, whereas the strategic approach would view the pastor as delivering a shared proclamation imbued with the highest aspirations of those whom it addresses.

At least three antecedents contributed indirectly to the relational paradigm's growing importance as a homiletical option. The first was psychological, given early impetus by Harry Emerson Fosdick, the master of "preaching as counseling on a group scale."[25] As the pastoral care movement grew in influence, its therapeutic sensibility introduced more "non-directive" and "client-centered" assumptions into preaching.

A second source of conceptual underpinning came from the social sciences with their concern to understand the dynamics of congregational culture, particularly as regards its diversity.[26] For example, the very concepts of Black Preaching[27] and Women's Preaching[28] say as much about the matrix as about the messenger of the preaching event.

A final contribution may be traced to communication theory, which directed fresh attention to the importance of listener response and to the relationality inherent in oral/aural presentation.[29] Roger Van Harn draws a useful contrast with the earlier paradigms:[30]

PREACHING IS CENTRAL	HEARING IS CENTRAL
1. The preacher is the focus of the action.	1. The congregation is the focus of the action.
2. The congregation comes for the sermon.	2. The sermon comes for the congregation.
3. The minister speaks the sermon and listens for response.	3. The minister listens and speaks a response in the sermon.
4. The minister finishes the sermon.	4. The congregation finishes the sermon.
5. The test of value lies in what is said.	5. The test of value lies in what is heard.

In the mid-1960s, David James Randolph named these converging emphases "The New Homiletic."[31] Preaching on this understanding is not proposition-centered, attempting to prove the truth of the text by rational-istic argumentation; rather, it is person-centered, seeking to reproduce the action of the text in changing the lives of its original recipients. The eventfulness of proclamation means that when a sermon is preached something happens that changes the situation of its hearers.

Randolph's emphases fell on wrestling with the intentionality of the text rather than abstracting topics from it, confirming the truth of the text in the concrete situation of the hearer, and constructing a sermon whose form is consistent with its content. These themes soon received powerful reinforcement in the work of Fred Craddock, especially in his advocacy of the methods of induction and indirection, which offer the hearers a chance to draw their own conclusions and determine the actions that they require.[32]

In the last quarter of the twentieth century, approaches loosely identified with the New Homiletic came to dominate teaching and writing on preaching. So clearly did this thrust move beyond rationalistic modes of argumentation, both on the propositional model of biblical preaching and on the philosophical model of rhetorical preaching, that Richard Eslinger defined our third approach as nothing less than a "paradigm shift."[33] The crux of the change lies in relocating the central concern of preaching from the speaker to the hearer, i.e., from the pulpit to the pew. The old paradigms focused on content: *what* was said and *how* it was said. The new paradigm focuses on context: *who* the audience is and *why* it has come. Responding to the postmodern suspicion of certainty, control, and closure, the goal of preaching is here redefined, not in terms of proclamation or persuasion, but as creating an experience for the congregation.[34] If the biblical paradigm of preaching is content-oriented and the rhetorical paradigm is speaker-oriented, then we may say that the relational paradigm is hearer-oriented.

Building on the work of the New Homiletic yet seeking to move beyond it, the current generation of homileticians is focusing on preaching as "conversation," particularly in the work of John S. McClure, Lucy Atkinson Rose, and Leonora Tubbs Tisdale.[35] In a brief but brilliant survey of this convergence, McClure identifies the scholarly ferment that is shaping such an approach: "In an age of theological pluralism, in which themes of 'contextuality,' 'otherness,' 'relationality,' 'perspectivalism,' 'solidarity,' and 'community' are increasingly significant, *conversation,* or the give-and-take of face-to-face interaction between those who, by definition are *different,* has become an important cross-disciplinary category."[36] He then describes how preaching may be understood as a multi-perspectival dialogue through which the gospel emerges both within and across the varied "lifeworlds" of its hearers. The goal is to achieve, not consensus based on domination, but solidarity based on community, "what Levinas calls 'coming to terms,' i.e., making proposals for action that holds together often contradictory premises and perspectives."[37] That kind of "coming to terms" is, of course, what mission and strategy are all about, learning to move forward together despite our inherited differences.[38] The payoff from this line of thought deserves an extended quote:

> The Word of God arrives, not as a decisive judgment or as a personal insight, but as an emergent communal reality. Hearers discern God's Word as a new reality in the community that is emerging piece by piece through the give-and-take of an open, ongoing, homiletical conversation. The Word is a significant communal hunch…that provokes open-ended thought, reflection, and experimentation.
>
> I take this to be a call to relate preaching to congregational leadership—to the realities of transforming the "reality" of congregational life into a closer approximation of God's Reign.[39]

Nor is McClure timid about implementing this vision of preaching in practical fashion. Building on the "roundtable ecclesiology" of Letty Russell in her book *Church in the Round,* he describes a process of active collaboration involving listeners both inside and outside the congregation who meet regularly with the preacher to participate in sermon strategizing.[40] Such sharing of pulpit responsibility in a conversational context means that the sermon will be responsive to input both from the congregation and from the wider community that it seeks to serve. The great breakthrough here lies in the willingness to identify and probe the "actual differences" that may exist in the preaching situation, believing that wisdom for the way ahead does not reside exclusively on one side of the pulpit. Clearly the pulpit is moving in the direction of furnishing leadership when the preacher becomes a listener as well as a speaker.

The relational paradigm offers much to build on; however, even in McClure's formulation, it does not go far enough. Despite all of the emphasis on dialogue, little or no attention is devoted to mutually determined purposes, priorities, and plans. The minister enters into conversation with one diverse group after another to sense the variety of personal needs that each represents, but not to talk about how the sermon can help to guide the implementation of a vision for which both parties have accepted responsibility. A strange dichotomy seems to exist according to which the listeners function as those with needs to be met while the minister functions as the one seeking to meet those needs. But what about the opposite: If we are going to practice reciprocating authority, the congregation also bears responsibility to help meet the minister's "felt needs," many of which, I suspect, would be assuaged if clergy sensed a solidarity with laity in moving the church forward toward agreed-upon goals. If the pew is forever "feeling needs" and the pulpit is forever "meeting needs," we have just reversed rather than escaped the domination-trap inherent in the earlier paradigms.[41]

Toward an Enriched Homiletical Paradigm

Elton Trueblood once argued that Sunday worship is not the climax of the Christian week as many preachers try to make it. Rather, the sanctuary is a staging area where the people of God gather to receive marching orders for their primary work in the world as a "fellowship of penetration."[42] Some may not care for the military metaphor, but it nicely captures the strategic dimension so often missing, even in the relational paradigm, when the audience is viewed as a collection of autonomous individuals gathered to have their needs met[43] rather than as a company of those committed to changing the world because Christ has first changed their lives. Even the uncommitted who may be present for worship usually come either to understand what difference Christianity claims to make or to test whether it is actually making such a difference in the lives of believers gathered for worship. Unless the sermon becomes one instrument for implementing those changes mandated by the imperatives of the gospel, then the very nature of the congregation will subtly shift from being a community of purpose to being an audience of consumers.

My discussion of these three dominant approaches is not intended to imply a repudiation of any of their valuable features but only to suggest the revision of each of them by the introduction of a strategic dimension. The biblical paradigm offers a powerful vehicle for strategic preaching when undergirded by a hermeneutic that knows how to discern the intentionality of the ancient text and its relevance for today. Likewise, all of the arts of persuasion in the rhetorical paradigm provide needed motivation to move a company of believers from complacency with the status quo to a venturesome engagement with authentic risk. The relational paradigm ensures that pulpit and pew move together, each prodding the other in a dialectic of shared decision-making. In other words, elements of strength in all three paradigms are valuable if infused with a sense of where the congregation is trying to go and what it is trying to do in response to the beckoning of the gospel.

When preaching becomes strategic, it enriches congregational life in at least three ways. First, it provides clarity and adds urgency to the most basic questions of the group's existence: *Why* are we here? *Where* are we going? *How* are we going to get there? *What* will be required to make this venture?

Who will commit to join us for the journey? The church that has not reached a consensus in answering these utterly simple questions is already in deep trouble.

Second, this approach permits the integration of preaching and program into a unified expression of pastoral leadership. If strategy is a way to accomplish a church's mission, then it should involve everything that a church does. But most congregations see no connection between what happens in worship on Sunday and what the church does during the remainder of the week. On the approach being proposed here, pastor and people decide where they are going, and the sermon contributes to this end just as much as does every other activity of the church.

Third, anchoring the sermon in the total effort of the church to accomplish its mission gives it added purpose and direction. The problem with many sermons is not that they lack biblical content or careful organization or congregational rapport. The problem is rather that they do not seem to be going anywhere. The preacher takes a text, explains its meaning, and suggests its pertinence for the chosen theme; but the congregation is not quite sure what is supposed to happen next. Very often the unanswered question is, "Where do we go from here?" because that question has been neither asked nor answered in the preparation and presentation of the sermon.

Strategic preaching seeks to address this problem by focusing on what is at stake in hearing the sermon. It insists that no sermon is ready to be delivered until the preacher is clear just how it will help the hearers to press on in their pilgrimage of faith without being waylaid by hostile forces when passing through enemy territory. The sermon itself takes on movement precisely because it is designed to elicit movement from the congregation. In this movement toward God-given goals, pastor and people participate together in the life-changing mission of the church.

CHAPTER 2

A Biblical-Theological Framework for Strategic Preaching

Strategic preaching represents an effort to enrich the current paradigm of the pastor's pulpit ministry, as we saw in the previous chapter. While innovation is usually welcomed in areas such as technology, novelty is less readily embraced in regard to a function that the church has been fulfilling for two thousand years. Strategic preaching will avoid the suspicion of faddism only if it is grounded in a theology built directly on the central insights of Scripture. In this chapter, therefore, I hope to show that the assumptions underlying strategic preaching are both congruent with and contributory to the understanding of Christian existence as reflected in the New Testament.

If one master image or presiding metaphor lurks behind this discussion, it is that of the church as a pilgrim people journeying in hope toward a goal defined by the promises of God. This controlling assumption consists of three components: (1) The church lives by its ceaseless movement *from* an old age of frustration *to* a new age of fulfillment; (2) this forward thrust across unexplored frontiers is prompted, not only by divine deliverance from bondage in the past, but by the disclosure of God's intentions for his people in the future; (3) these great expectations nourish a lively hope sufficient to sustain the wayfarers against guardians of the status quo determined to block their journey to the promised land. Let us now consider each of these perspectives in turn.

The Church as a Pilgrim People

Our inquiry begins with the church because its "congregating" for worship is prerequisite to the act of preaching. Quite simply: no gathered congregation, no sermon! This means that the identity of those assembled should profoundly influence the way in which they are addressed. The nature of the church determines the nature of preaching because the purpose of preaching is to transform the world through the witness of the church. Since the church was called into being by the life, death, and resurrection of Jesus Christ, let us focus on the new situation those events created.

Strange as it may seem, the New Testament consistently affirms that, in Christ, the new age of salvation has now dawned but the old age of sin has not yet disappeared. This is a key point of Christianity's difference from Judaism. The parent faith cherished a hope that the present evil age would be replaced by a future messianic age in decisive, even catastrophic, fashion that would define the two eras as radically different and discontinuous. The daughter faith, by contrast, saw the new age as invading the old age without thereby displacing it, so that Paul could say that Christians live where the two ages impinge and, in a sense, overlap (1 Cor. 10:11). In Romans 5—8 the apostle Paul argued that we are now free from wrath, sin, law, and death. And yet, because their waning powers are still operative, we, with the help of Christ, must struggle to overcome those threats even though they no longer rule over us.

The elliptical shape of Christian existence in the New Testament may be described in many ways. After World War I, the dialectical theologians of the 1920s—Karl Barth, Friedrich Gogarten, and Eduard Thurneysen— found Europe in such chaos that they coined the phrase "between the times" (*Zwischen den Zeiten*) to describe both the New Testament situation and their own.[1] After World War II, Joachim Jeremias used a very precise German phrase (*sich realisierende Eschatologie*), for which we have no exact English equivalent, to describe Jesus' proclamation as "eschatology becoming actualized,"[2] not catastrophically but modestly after the manner of his own ministry. Recently, James Dunn gathered up a half-century of work on the theology of Paul in describing the "eschatological tension" that lies at the heart of his understanding of salvation.[3]

Of all the modern efforts to explain this paradoxical nature of Christian existence, none is more insightful than that of Rudolf Bultmann in his *Theology of the New Testament*.[4] Bultmann used the concept of "betweenness" to express the creative tension linking the "no longer" of the old age to the "not yet" of the new age. The Christian stands between the past of a salvation already achieved and the future of a salvation yet to be received (Rom. 5:1– 2; 13:11). This situation is not seen merely as a chronological interval of waiting. Rather, it is a time when by faith the believer sees God's redemptive work both in the past and in the future shaping the human present. This distinctive structure of existence results in a dialectical relationship between the indicative and the imperative according to which Christians are ever exhorted both to *become what they already are* and to *become what they are yet to be.*

Bultmann explained the first of these paradoxes linking our present existence to salvation in the past as follows:

> though Christian existence can, on the one hand, be described by the indicatives—we are sanctified, we are purified—nevertheless, so long as it moves within this world, it stands under the imperative. Though, on the one hand, it is separated from its past and its environment, yet this separation must be newly made again and again.[5]

Jürgen Moltmann helpfully supplemented this understanding. He described the second of these paradoxes linking our present existence to salvation in the future with these words:

> The imperative of the Pauline call to obedience is…not to be understood merely as a summons to demonstrate the indicative of the new being in Christ, but it has also its eschatological presupposition in the future that has been promised and is to be expected— the coming of the Lord to judge and to reign. Hence it ought not to be rendered merely by saying: "Become what you are!" but emphatically also by saying: "Become what you will be!"[6]

Writing from a recent feminist perspective, Sandra Hack Polaski concludes:

> Paul very carefully places the present time not in the eschatological time but in the "waiting in eager longing" for it. Another way to say this is that Paul understands his present time as standing *between* creation and new creation. The new creation is not yet fully expressed, not yet quite born. This is not, it should be said, the difference between living in evil and living in good. The original creation is the good gift of a good God, distorted and battered though it is by sin. Still, Paul's metaphor means that all that is promised in the new creation is not yet fully accomplished. Thus Paul can be honest about his own situation, his weakness, his foolishness, his "thorn in the flesh," and so forth, without denying the power of God or the reality of new creation. These, rather, are simply expressions of the first, distorted creation not yet replaced by the reconciled, new creation.[7]

Because the church ever lives in a betweenness that is not mere temporariness, it is always on the move: from darkness to light (1 Pet. 2:9), from hostility to peace (Eph. 2:12–14), from death to life (Rom. 8:2–11). The sense of a "walk" or a "journey" from the old to the new pervades many New Testament descriptions of the church. Here I select four closely interrelated examples of this central theme.

1. The earliest designation of the Christian movement was "the Way" (Acts 9:2; 19:9, 23; 22:4; 24:14, 22). The concept had deep scriptural roots as the most inclusive image of God's dealings with Israel.[8] Old Testament confessional recitals pictured life as a journey, especially from Egypt to Zion, during which God went before his people as companion and guide so that he himself defined the route that they traveled (Ex. 15:1–18; Deut. 6:20–24; Josh. 24:2–13; and Ps. 77; 78; 99; 136). Torah was a signpost along the Way, sin a turning aside from the Way, repentance a turning back to the Way, obedience a walking in the Way. The Old Testament bequeathed to the New Testament this sense of dealing with God in dynamic categories of movement and advance rather than in static categories of thought and contemplation.

Jesus came once "the way of the Lord" had been prepared (Mk. 1:2–3). He built his ministry around the way that he must take to Jerusalem (Lk. 9:51; 13:33). When there, he revealed to his disciples that he was their true and living way to the Father (Jn. 14:6). This suggests that, for him, discipleship was not a place to stand but a road to walk, what Paul would later call "a still more excellent way" (1 Cor. 12:31) and Hebrews would describe as a "new and living way" (Heb. 10:20).

This imagery incessantly presses upon us the sense of movement involved in a new beginning, an open-ended journey, and a final destination. The commitment to Christ cannot be implemented in an instant but involves "entering" a gate where one must choose between a way that is easy and a way that is hard (Mt. 7:13–14). The road ever forks into "Two Ways" and those who travel *the way* that leads to life (Mt. 7:14) are instructed in "*the way* of the Lord" (Acts 18:25) which is none other than "*the way* of salvation" (Acts 16:17). Bunyan had it right: the Christian life is the story of a "pilgrim's progress" in which the operative words are the prepositions: from…through… toward…at.

2. This central imagery of "The Way" prepares us for a specific model of discipleship viewed as "following" Jesus.[9] In the Old Testament, Elijah described this relationship in terms of divine adherence: "If the LORD is God, follow him; but if Baal, then follow him" (1 Kings 18:21). Jesus differed from the rabbis of his day in taking the initiative to recruit his own disciples with the sovereign claim, "follow me" (Mk. 1:16–20). This formula "acquires in Jesus' mouth a potency which is quite simply miraculous and which abruptly detaches those called from their previous obligations."[10] Eduard

Schweizer summarized the characteristics of the unique relationship established by "following Jesus" in this fashion:[11]

a. It is *the* decisive act of allegiance to his person.
b. It is a sovereign act of divine grace that begins something so new that it changes all things.
c. It leads to togetherness with Jesus and service to him.
d. It entails giving up all other ties.
e. It leads to rejection, suffering, and death, and thereby to glory.

To conclude:

the disciple who follows Jesus never expects to cease following him and to become a master himself, and to gather disciples round him, as the disciple of a rabbi was wont to do. He has followed Jesus in such a way as one can only follow Baal or Jahveh, a would-be Messiah or the Messiah. From the very beginning his faith has been such that he has expected complete salvation from Jesus.[12]

What does it mean for the New Testament to define the Christian life as "follow[ing] in his steps" (1 Pet. 2:21)? It means that discipleship is viewed, not as a noun, but as a verb. We are not called to *be* followers but to *do* following. Again, for the one so summoned, the offer is empty of human content. The command to follow conveys no ideas, arouses no feelings, describes no activities. Rather, everything depends upon what the leader will do next, which makes the imperative "follow me" entirely future-facing. It sets the respondents in motion, turns their lives in a new direction, and invites them to a succession of surprises. Further, it is only in such a venture that the follower discovers who the leader really is.[13]

3. Just as the exodus from Egypt to the promised land became a defining event for the people of God in the Old Testament, so the church in every generation recapitulates each stage of that pilgrimage over spiritual terrain. Exodus imagery dominates the letter to the Hebrews from beginning to end.[14] At the outset, the writer warns against hardness of heart, which led to rebellion in the wilderness and denied the generation of Moses a chance to reach its intended destination (Heb. 3:7–19). Instead, the readers are exhorted to claim God's promises which are offered to all who seize the moment called "Today" while it lasts and who "strive to enter" his Sabbath rest in a spirit of obedience (4:1–13). By the time the letter nears its conclusion, the company of the faithful "have come to Mount Zion and to the city of the living God, the heavenly Jerusalem" (12:22), having reached this point by "looking to Jesus" in his role as pioneer and pacesetter on every step of the way from start to finish (Heb. 6:20; 12:2; cf. Acts 5:31).

In a suggestive study of Hebrews called *The Wandering People of God,* Ernst Käsemann has shown how this "principal motif" of the letter, especially in its final section, is energized by verbs of motion.[15] Repeatedly the readers are urged to draw near to God (4:16; 7:25; 10:22; 11:6; 12:18, 22) by "going forth" to Jesus "outside the camp" (13:13). Their conduct is to be worthy of emulation for its courage (10:33; 13:18; cf. 13:7), strengthening weak knees (12:12) and making straight paths (12:13). The notion of receiving what was promised (10:36; 11:13, 39) is viewed in spatial terms as a prize to be claimed at the end of faith's journey. Indeed, Hebrews 11 is an extended homily, filled with an abundance of related verbs, which compares Israel's exodus journey to the Christian's seeking of a heavenly homeland (11:13–16, 22, 27–31). Here faith is understood primarily as perseverance on the pilgrimage through an alien wilderness until one reaches the land of promise.

4. The exodus motif in Hebrews prepares us for our final image of Christian existence, that of marathon runners. Because the readers were now surrounded by the Old Testament heroes of faith as a "great cloud of witnesses," they were to live as runners in a long-distance race, strengthened both by the example of their predecessors and by the trailblazing victory of Jesus in his own earthly life (Heb. 12:1–2). In Philippians 3:13–14 Paul gave vivid expression to this analogy of the Christian life as a race by utilizing the temporal categories of past, present, and future.

a. In regard to the past, Paul was prepared to forget "what lies behind," (Phil. 3:13) even though it included his conspicuous achievements both as a Jew (vv. 4–6) and as a Christian (vv. 7–11).
b. In regard to the present, Paul was ready to expend every energy in running his race with radical intensity.
c. As regards the future, Paul filled his horizon with a compelling picture of "what lies ahead," the goal where God's prize awaited him at the finish line.

Here time and space are united because the temporal dimensions of yesterday, today, and tomorrow correspond to stages in the race from its beginning, through its running, to its ending.

What the casual reader may miss in this familiar description of the Christian life is the dynamic sense of change at work in all that Paul says. His single sentence in Philippians 3:13–14 abounds with six prepositions that convey a strong sense of motion or direction. An overly literal paraphrase of the passage might read: "I do not reckon that I have gotten it all *down* as yet…so I turn *away from* that which is behind me and stretch *toward* that which is before me, bearing *down* on the finish line by reaching *out* for the prize that is waiting there, which prize is a calling that draws me ever *upward* to God in Christ Jesus." If anything, the participles in this passage are even more vivid than the prepositions: "*relinquishing* my hold on the trophies of the past, and *stretching forward* with empty hands to claim the even greater promises of the future, I run with every nerve and sinew taut, determined to make an all-out effort with every ounce of energy at my command" (author's paraphrase). With this vivid picture of racing to reach "what lies ahead," we come to the heart of the New Testament understanding of the Christian life.

What all these characteristic biblical images suggest is that one essential characteristic of the Christian life is *movement* impelled by the call of God. That is why a central purpose of strategic preaching is to set the people of God in motion as the gospel takes effect in their lives. The first systematic exposition of Christian preaching was Augustine's *On Christian Doctrine,* which appeared at the beginning of the fifth century. In book four of this famous treatise, the Bishop of Hippo described preaching as enabling those who hear "to be *moved* rather than taught, so that they may not be sluggish in putting what they know into practice." The congregation "shows *by its motion* whether it understands" what is being proclaimed.[16] Strategic preaching is not a summons to frenetic activism; rather, it is a bracing challenge to keep moving from the "no longer" to the "not yet" of God's redemptive journey.[17]

The Future as a Horizon of Promise

Motion as such is neither good nor bad. Everything depends upon the direction taken and the destination to which it leads. Note from the four expressions of movement discussed in the previous section that: (a) the exodus from Egypt would lead to "a good and broad land, a land flowing with milk and honey" (Ex. 3:8); (b) following Jesus would allow some to "see the kingdom of God come with power" (Mk. 9:1); (c) those who made straight paths for their feet (Heb. 12:12–13) as followers of the Way would come at last to "the heavenly Jerusalem, and to innumerable angels in festal gathering" (Heb. 12:22); (d) those who run the race toward the goal would claim "the prize of the upward call of God in Christ Jesus" (Phil. 3:14). Always the pilgrimage is sustained by the promise of what lies at its completion. What might this mean for strategic preaching?

1. No earthly leader generated or can generate these expectations for the future to motivate laggard followers. Instead the biblical Deity who makes promises that cannot be broken guaranteed these expectations (Heb. 10:23; 11:11).[18] So axiomatic was this understanding that we sometimes fail to realize how sharply it contrasted with the prevailing view of gods in the ancient world who often demanded that humans make pledges to them

or to one another but would make no such binding commitments themselves. By contrast, the biblical God agreed to accept responsibility for an unfinished agenda, thereby voluntarily limiting the free exercise of divine sovereignty by becoming obligated to do a "new thing" in the future (Isa. 43:19) and to accomplish such changes in the context of historical contingency. God never made these promises as a reward for human achievement, nor did the Deity ever withdraw the divine promises as the result of human failure. Rather, God confirmed them by an oath sworn as an autonomous Sovereign. This means that the promises expressed the unchangeable character of the divine purpose (Heb. 6:13–18).

If it is in the very nature of God to be bound to the building of a new future by making "precious and very great promises" (2 Pet. 1:4), then the Christian life is inherently provisional: "it does not yet appear what we shall be" (1 Jn. 3:2). Futurity is not just a matter of more time but of transformed time. Life now has both a background that records God's faithfulness to those promises in the past, and a foreground that anticipates their even greater consummation in the future. For example, we look backward to the first coming of Christ in whom "all the promises of God find their Yes" (2 Cor. 1:20), but we also look forward to the final coming of Christ when all that he won by his cross will be crowned with glory. Because we can already anticipate this eventual victory through the experience of the Holy Spirit (Eph. 1:14), life now has a horizon that is the source of a vision rooted, not in human optimism or in utopian thinking, but in the promissory character of the gospel.

In response to this perspective, strategic preaching is concerned primarily with God's unfinished business. As long as sin, guilt, and bondage remain part of human existence, we have something to preach because God has promised salvation, forgiveness, and freedom. As long as people experience alienation, division, and discord, we have something to preach because God has promised reconciliation, unity, and peace. As long as the world suffers under injustice, oppression, and retaliation, we have something to preach because God has promised righteousness, protection, and acceptance. Because these promises reflect the intentions of the divine will, the people of God have certain entitlements that they may dare to claim when emboldened by a courageous pulpit.

2. One problem arises as we rely on these promises as the ground of our confidence: their fulfillment seems to take so long. Scoffers abound who attribute such delay to God's preoccupation with other priorities or to divine procrastination rooted in deliberate indifference. But progress is often slow because God is patient with those who continue to cling to the status quo (2 Pet. 3:3–4, 8–9). God is willing to wait on those who are hesitant to change. Divine longsuffering results in God's people receiving providential

care during the sometimes lengthy interval between the inauguration and the consummation of the promised blessing.

For example, the exodus from Egypt led to seemingly endless wilderness wanderings, but during this time God not only provided a pillar of cloud by day and a pillar of fire by night but also gave the people quail and manna to eat. But note the stern prohibition against hoarding these blessings, which would have betrayed a lack of reliance on God's future (Ex. 16:13–21). Divine providence is not merely the predictable maintenance of an orderly universe. It is also a provision for our needs when the promised future is slow in coming.

What this pattern suggests is that God does not merely dangle a promise in front of people to lure them along toward an intended goal. Rather, the Sovereign chooses to be intimately involved in our struggle to claim a better future. By filling the interval between the inauguration and the consummation of promise with the divine presence, God actually provides a foretaste of the future that is still to come. Paul used many images to describe the anticipatory character of this experience. God's Spirit in our lives is likened to the "first fruits" of an eventual harvest (Rom. 8:23), to the earnest money or down payment that guarantees the completion of a legal transaction (2 Cor. 1:22; 5:5), and to the "seal" that identifies God as the owner and protector of our lives (Eph. 1:13; 4:30). This religion of the indwelling Spirit, in contrast to a religion of the sudden theophany, means that God does not come to us in a few blinding flashes of revelation that are an end in themselves. Rather, the Eternal One abides with us continually so as to foreshadow the future, thereby moving us through meaningful time instead of trying to make time stand still (Jn. 16:13).

Strategic preaching should never give the impression that claiming the promises of God is a quick and easy fix for current problems. After all, as we shall have many occasions to notice throughout this study, enemy forces hold the route to the promised land for which we are bound. We must overcome them if we are to claim this frontier for God (1 Cor. 15:25). Entrenched power structures do not yield ground without a fight. Our confidence in the promises of God does not come from our ability to claim them whenever we may wish. Our confidence in God's promises comes from the way that God strengthens us in our determination to live "as though" the divine promises are certain to prevail when "the form of this world" passes away (1 Cor. 7:29–31). Admittedly, the dynamics of change include a combative dimension that may lead to setbacks and even defeats (1 Cor. 4:8–13; 2 Cor. 4:7–12). But if God is willing to be patient, let us determine to be patient as well!

3. Knowing how hard it is to challenge the status quo, God sent Jesus to show us in tangible terms what it means to live out of the future and its

promises. Everything he said and did was dominated by the expected Kingdom that was "near" but had not yet fully arrived. For him, the whole point of prayer was to petition in the most urgent terms imaginable that what was "then and there" in heaven become "here and now" on earth (Mt. 6:9–13). Nothing in the status quo could lay a hand on him, whether family loyalties, ethnic prejudices, political passions, or religious customs. Instead, he kept talking about how things of apparent insignificance, such as a handful of seed, could have incredible consequences if only given time and opportunity to grow (Mk. 4:1–9, 26–34). Even his tragic death in Jerusalem would be the harbinger of a bright new day (Mk. 9:1; 14:62).

This is why Jesus was called the trailblazer (Acts 5:31) and pioneer (Heb. 2:10; 12:2) of our faith, the pacesetter who dared to venture into a whole new age of the Spirit and then call others to follow him there. We often refer to him as "the man for others," but he was also "the man for tomorrow" because that promised future toward which we press was actually present in his life long before we were ready for it to be present in our lives. Because he was the most utterly hopeful person who ever lived, those who accept him as Savior and Lord may learn to hope in his indomitable hope. They may have faith in his unshakable faith that every promise of God will finally be fulfilled. To be sure, that faith was impaled on a cross. That means the future for which he hoped would come only from the God of promise and not from the custodians of the status quo, only by travail and not by theophany (Rom. 8:18–25), only in God's good time and not in our own (Mk. 13:32–33).

Because Jesus uniquely embodied God's future, strategic preaching is profoundly christocentric, not so much in terms of the static categories that defined Patristic orthodoxy, but in terms of the way in which both the earthly life and the resurrected life of Jesus mediated that futurity to others.[19] Those first disciples became captive to his claims by faith. They learned to transcend even their most sacred inherited traditions. Though recruited from a provincial culture, they soon began to have a transformative impact on the wider world of their day. The literature they produced within a single generation is simply amazing in its breadth and depth. The only adequate explanation for these incredible changes is that the disciples had begun to live out of God's future in such a way that they experienced its promises being fulfilled in the present. Strategic preaching exists to replicate that life-changing orientation to the future in our day.

4. God defines promise in terms of a prize that we see even before reaching the finish line (Phil. 3:14). Our reward is to "gain Christ" (v. 8) and thereby attain his maturity (v. 15), which is not yet ours (v. 12). Paul gave classic expression to this aspiration in Ephesians 4:13, which may be paraphrased: "Let us join with all believers in a lifelong pilgrimage whose

final destination is to meet God's Son, the Messiah, and to share fully in the faith and knowledge that were the hallmarks of his perfect manhood."[20] In a word, all of life is given purpose by the possibility of attaining *Christlikeness,* a possibility that we have already begun to experience but which we will not fully achieve until we see him face-to-face at the finish line of life (Rom. 8:29–30; Phil. 3:20–21).

What do these four reflections tell us about the way in which strategic preaching seeks to shape our orientation to the future? That God is with us in *promise* when the journey begins, with us in *providence* when the journey is delayed, with us in the *person* of his Son when the journey grows wearisome, and with us in the *prize* of Christlike maturity when the journey ends. The one thing common to all four of these emphases is that God is always out in front of us setting a new future before us. As Stephen saw so clearly in his one recorded sermon, God cannot be contained even in sacred space, hence the Holy One is better worshiped in a portable tabernacle than in a stationary temple (Acts 7:44–50). God is much more than a static deity of unchangeableness, immutability, and impassibility. One defining characteristic of the biblical God is not just motion but *movement toward an intended goal.* God is the restless one. Our forward thrust is impelled by a divine beckoning from the Beyond. If we fail to move forward in response to that call, we will, like the exodus generation that died in the wilderness, be left behind (Heb. 3:16–19)!

The Resilience of Hope

When Gilbert Murray sought to characterize the Hellenistic Age in the ancient Greco-Roman world, he pointed to its "loss of self-confidence, of hope in this life and of faith in normal effort; a despair of patient inquiry, a cry for infallible revelation," a sense of pessimism that he called "the failure of nerve."[21] This mood was nourished by manifold failures: of Olympian theology, of the free city-state, of Roman government to foster a good life for mankind, and of Greek education to civilize a barbaric world.

By contrast, when Peter Gay sought to show how the Enlightenment of the eighteenth century gave rise to modernity, he rooted it in "the recovery of nerve," which he described as a willingness to embrace innovation, an obsession with improvement, a recovery of confidence, "a rational reliance on the efficacy of energetic action."[22] This new mood was the result of many forces, the dominant one being science and its offspring, technology. A host of intractable problems remained, but the sense of promise was so palpable that the heirs of modernity "built their house of hope less on what had happened than on what was happening, and even more on what they had good reason to expect would happen in the future."[23]

The nineteenth century seemed to fulfill the expectations of the eighteenth century by developing a dogma of irresistible progress.[24] But the twentieth century proved devastating to this unbridled optimism.[25] Three global conflicts, two of them hot wars and one a cold war, were all spawned in the very bosom of the Enlightenment. With its unleashing of nuclear energy, science showed its potential to contribute to the suicide of civilization. By the time the new millennium dawned, our belief in progress lay in shambles and with it has come yet another "failure of nerve."

As a result, many who hear our preaching now live with an attenuated will. Fearful of what the future may bring, they refuse to engage in consequential thinking, preferring to "make out" as best as they can with whatever each day may bring. The torpor of our time is perhaps best seen in the mood of acquiescence to whatever happens next. Jacques Ellul diagnosed the source of this lethargy as being "future-sick," and then spent 150 pages describing its pathologies.[26] A sample: the feeling of being caught in a snare, anguished by self-inflected absurdities, confronted by inevitability presided over by incoherence. "Never has man possessed so many means for making history, and for making his own history, yet never has he felt so completely determined, so subjugated."[27]

Strategic preaching provides one antidote to the inertia of a defeated will by mobilizing that abiding reality of the Christian life called hope (1 Cor. 13:13), which we may define as *a reaching for God's future*. Hope bridges the temporal chasm between the "no longer" and the "not yet," between the inaugurated and the consummated, between promise and fulfillment. Hope means living by anticipation with such a passionate sense of the possible that a foretaste of the promised future is already proleptically present in its anticipation.[28] Because of its openness to transcendence, hope is not tyrannized by the status quo. Ellul hammers away at the point: "The challenge of hope is the introduction into a closed age, into a tight security, into an autocephalous organization, into an autonomous economic system, into totalitarian politics, of an opening, a breech, a heteronomy, an uncertainty, a question."[29] Stated more simply: "The revolutionary act of hope is, and can only be, the opening up of situations that want to stay closed."[30]

Because hope is not of our making but is grounded in the promise of God's future, it is not a religious form of human optimism. It has no doctrine of inevitable progress based on ideologies of utopianism. It allows itself no apocalyptic or gnostic dualisms and guards itself against every form of fantasy and faddism. Just as Bonhoeffer taught us to repudiate the "cheap grace" that forgives sin without changing the sinner,[31] so every effort to escape from the duties of daily life in the real world is to be avoided as "cheap hope." Unlike the technologically driven cult of originality that neglects the problems of the present because of its obsession with newness,[32] hope refuses to live in a man-made future because it knows that the tyrannical structures of this world will not yield their sovereignty over the human spirit without a fight. Therefore, far from ignoring "the realities of human frailty, finitude, fallibility, and sin,"[33] hope arises precisely out of our realization that all is not well, that there is a better kingdom to be had if only we will let God give it to us (Lk. 12:32).

This means Christian hope is eschatological.[34] But the eschaton has now been relocated from the end to the midpoint of history. This creates a bipolar situation in which Christians do not wait passively for some catastrophic upheaval to usher in a discontinuous future. Rather, they become participants in the actualization of an eschatological event that stretches from the resurrection of Jesus to his return. Hope, therefore, is not merely a wistful yearning for "the sweet by and by" but is a living in openness to the transcendence that has already begun to invade time to redeem it (Col. 4:5; Eph. 5:16), not only because God is at the end of it, but because his Spirit is active within it as the anticipation of that end (2 Cor. 5:5; Eph. 1:14). This kind of hope enlivens and energizes us, while its absence as hopelessness weakens and paralyzes us.

Since true hope is eschatological, how does it come to us so that we "may abound in hope" (Rom. 15:13)? The clue is found in the way that the verse begins, "May the *God of hope* fill you" (italics added). The key phrase can mean that God is the *object* of our hope; that is, we have found God to be so beneficent that this causes us to hope. But it can also mean that God is the *source* of our hope; that is, we are the recipients of divine hope just as we are of divine grace. In either case, if hope comes from God, it must be because God is hopeful. But why should a self-sufficient Sovereign need to hope for anything? Because, in giving us freedom, God became voluntarily limited by our choices. It is always an open question whether we will ever learn to use our freedom responsibly, but God is hopeful! Because "God is love" (1 Jn. 4:8) and because love "hopes all things" (1 Cor. 13:7), our Maker keeps on hoping that we will finally live up to the potential for which we were created.

If it seems a bit daring or even speculative to speak of God in this fashion, consider the incarnation of divine hope in Jesus Christ. Has a more hopeful person ever lived? His Kingdom proclamation, his seed parables, his "third day" predictions were all manifestations of an indomitable hope. And where did he get this sense of expectancy that could not be shaken even by a cross? Surely not from his contemporaries, who were a dispirited lot at best (Mk. 10:32). Clearly his hope sprang from communion with God, which is why Paul said that it is "by the power of the Holy Spirit" that we "may abound in hope" (Rom. 15:13). The presence of the risen Christ within our lives enables us to hope with the God-given hope that filled the life of Jesus! Elsewhere Paul explained how a realistic hope groans in travail as God's new day of freedom struggles to be born (Rom. 8:21–23). Realistic hope is never content with the "seen" things that are transient, no matter how impressive they may be. Rather, realistic hope looks for the "unseen" things that are eternal (Rom. 8:24; 2 Cor. 4:18). It is willing to forego immediate gratification and "wait…with patience" (8:25) for God to honor the divine promises on God's own timetable because hope knows that, in everything that happens, God is already "working for good with those who love him" (8:28, author's translation).

This trinitarian structure of hope fortifies the preacher to take what Glenn Tinder calls a "prophetic stance" in today's world. To him, the word *prophetic* denotes "an unconditional willingness to enter into the future— the future inscribed in one's destiny—in spite of the darkness obscuring it."[35] The word *stance* suggests the posture of one with "an eschatological disposition, the bearing of one who lives in history with hope that anticipates the end of history."[36] Hope opens us to the truth of time, namely that the best is yet to be as a gift of transcendence, that life can be a story with a meaningful "sense of ending."[37] Then we are freed from feeling like a pawn of circumstance and are ready to respond to the possibilities implied by promise. Tinder well frames the issue at the heart of strategic preaching: "to resist all change is to fail in hope…If the meaning of history lies in its eschalogical momentum—its movement toward the end—then denial of the movement is denial of the end."[38]

The People of God and the Preaching Task

Alfred North Whitehead once wrote, "The task of a University is the creation of the future, so far as rational thought, and civilized modes of appreciation, can affect the issue."[39] We might adapt that wording to define a basic assumption of strategic preaching as follows: "The task of a church is the creation of the future, so far as the promises of God, acted upon in faith and hope, can affect the issue." In light of the biblical and theological perspectives undergirding that assumption, I draw three conclusions about the people of God that shape my conception of the preaching task.

1. The bipolar nature of Christian existence produces a creative tension at the center of the church's life, which provides the dynamic by which the church journeys on pilgrimage. Christian existence is a tension between the old age of sin and the new age of salvation, between Christ's first coming in humiliation and his final coming in exaltation, between the race to be run and the prize to be won. Christian existence is a tension between past and future that fills all time, as well as a tension between earth and heaven

that fills all space. This dialectic is inescapable because the church, by its very nature, "is the community of those who live here and now, in this sinful present age, in the light and by the power of the final consummation of all things in Christ. It is the community of the interval between His first and second coming."[40]

2. Because of this essential duality, the church lives not only in memory of what God has already done but in anticipation of what that same God is yet to do. A strong sense of futurity should pervade the life of the church because it is precisely among these "people of tomorrow" that the powers of the "Age to Come" have been foreshadowed. The poet Ranier Maria Rilke once said that "the future enters us...in order to be transformed in us, long before it happens."[41] The church is where God's future enters human life in advance, like seed growing secretly in the soil long before the harvest is ever seen (Mk. 4:26–29). This reaching out to pull the future into the present takes place especially in congregational worship, which, in the New Testament, was eschatological to the core.[42]

3. The distinctive character of the church means that *motion in an intended direction* is the hallmark of its life. Those who constitute its membership are a company of pilgrims on an unfinished journey—as the old hymn puts it, "bound for the promised land."[43] The congregation may best be understood as a *community of purpose*, a people on mission, possessed by a vision, haunted by a dream, reaching for a goal. It gathers for worship to hear afresh the imperatives that challenge each member to fulfill the indicatives of a salvation already received. Preaching becomes strategic when it moves the people of God *from* the Egypt of their discontent *through* the wilderness of their fears *toward* the Canaan of their deepest longings.

For preaching to serve this kind of church, it must become *proleptic*; that is, its purpose is to disclose in advance what is still to come. The task of the sermon is to describe God's unfinished agenda in such compelling terms that the hearers become permanently dissatisfied with the status quo. The mission of the preacher is not to relax but rather to intensify the tension between the good work that God has begun in his people and the greater work that he yet intends to bring to completion (Phil. 1:6). The pulpit is like Melville's prow of a ship that cuts a new path into tomorrow for others to follow.[44] The sermon is where the future is first put into words so that it can then be put into deeds. Such preaching is catalytic, precipitating a congregational response to *become* more fully what, in Christ, it already *is*. It is a beckoning of God's people to take a resolute step forward on the way that leads to the fulfillment of that hope in which we are being saved (Rom. 8:24).[45]

PART I

PREACHING

CHAPTER 3

A Hermeneutic of Strategic Preaching: Biblical

The primary purpose of strategic preaching is to set a congregation in motion toward its intended goal, as we have just shown. Since most Christian proclamation is based on Scripture, we begin Part 1 by asking how we may approach the Bible in such a way that its goals become the goals of the congregation.

The Text's Trajectory

We start by asking of the passage selected to undergird the sermon: *Where is this text going?* Every text has a trajectory, as does every congregation. The pastor's task as leader is to help these two trajectories coincide in moving toward the same target. The analysis of a text's momentum is more complex than might at first be apparent. In describing what he aptly calls "a redemptive-movement hermeneutic," William J. Webb identifies at least four thrusts or progressions of a text implied by his model:[1]

a. Movement begins when a prophet or apostle inspired to challenge the status quo offers a better understanding or application of some idea or practice in the wider world (Ancient Near Eastern World for the Old Testament, Greco-Roman-Jewish World for the New Testament).

b. Movement continues when this person addresses the people of God (Israel in the Old Testament, the church in the New Testament) with an appeal to implement the desired changes in their common life even before the society at large is willing to do so.

c. The movement becomes canonized and incorporated into Scripture when the church recognizes the validity of this appeal. In this way the appeal continues to function as a leavening force both in the believing community and in the wider culture, thereby prompting calls throughout church history to carry the process of change even further as new opportunities arise.

d. The movement toward the goal of the original appeal makes only fitful progress even after many centuries, and the ultimate intention of the text still remains to be fulfilled. The canonized Scripture summons each contemporary generation to narrow even more the gap between the real and the ideal by taking the same kind of courageous initiatives that have partially fulfilled the text ever since the prophets and apostles first raised the appeal.

Webb applies his redemptive-movement hermeneutic to a number of troublesome ethical issues, particularly to the rights of slaves and women. In the case of the former, he traces the way in which the relevant texts on this subject moved:

a. from an ancient culture with harsh abuses,

b. to a biblical culture that sought to create better conditions with fewer abuses, especially for slaves who shared faith in Christ with their owner,

c. to our modern culture in which slavery has been abolished,

d. and on toward the ultimate goal of working conditions that offer respect, fair wages, and purposeful relationships to all who labor.[2]

Obviously this fourfold analysis may be applied to other issues with which the Bible deals because all of Scripture was written to offer its readers God's plan for a better way of life than that found in the social or religious status quo. So: to ask where a chosen text is going is to ask what kind of trail it has blazed from the moment it was first inspired to the moment when today's preacher invites a congregation to join its trajectory toward a chosen target.[3]

When we ask why it should require so much effort over so many centuries to repudiate a practice as reprehensible as slavery, Webb replies that the reluctance of human nature to change necessitates a slower process.

> Alongside the human authors, God functions as a seasoned pastor who gently shepherds his flock, as a skilled teacher who instructs his pupils in ways that they can learn the best, as the imminent-transcendent One who speaks within a fallen world and yet draws us to other worlds beyond this one, as an experienced missionary

who infuses our lives with passion for the lost, as an informed sociologist who knows completely the makeup of our social worlds, as a father who lovingly talks to his children in ways that they can understand and as a leader who wrestles to find the delicate balance between realism and idealism.[4]

Textual Movement and Strategic Preaching

This hermeneutical concept of textual movement introduces three emphases central to the understanding of strategic preaching developed in this book.

a. The first is that such preaching deals with the art of the possible. In its most literal meaning, strategy is a plan for moving an army forward toward its assigned objective in light of the foes arrayed against it. Applied to the pulpit, strategic preaching begins on ground God's people have already taken in earlier generations and asks: What is the next battle to be fought? Instead of berating the troops for not having won the whole war, it shows them how to advance to the next hill so as to keep the enemy in retreat. This sense of maintaining the momentum launched by Scripture over the sweep of redemptive history makes strategic preaching deliberately incremental.

b. A steady focus on the forces that produced the text, and then were produced by the text, helps to remind the preacher that God's people have already employed many strategies to bring the text to its present level of fulfillment. The biblical writers themselves were master strategists in crafting their message, often for a reluctant readership. For example, the apostle Paul used all of the arts of persuasion—what scholars today call rhetorical strategies—in an effort to reshape the culture of a troubled church in Corinth. So effective was he in this regard that his approaches were repeatedly adapted to new situations throughout church history.[5] To see in the movement of the text how the church has actually applied it in a variety of settings gives the preacher confidence that the wheel does not have to be reinvented in designing strategies for the use of the text today.

c. To approach a text in terms of its movement means viewing it, not just in terms of what it *says,* but also in terms of what it *does.* The shift from a static to a dynamic understanding of Scripture involves a considerable broadening of the hermeneutic used to interpret its meaning. No longer is it adequate just to clarify the content of a text, as if an accurate translation of the vocabulary and syntax of what Isaiah said to Jerusalem in the eighth century B.C.E. will tell me what I need to say to Birmingham in the twenty-first century C.E. Instead, I must ask how Isaiah's text first took root in his own mind, then in the community to which it was addressed, then how it subsequently functioned first in Judaism and then in Christianity on up to the present day. To do this, the interpreter needs to become skilled, not only in the exegetical analysis of a text, but also in the cultural analysis of the world to which it spoke.

In this chapter I shall seek to flesh out a biblical hermeneutic for use in strategic preaching by utilizing the criteria of contextuality, intentionality, and potentiality, all of which are especially important in tracing where an ancient text was originally trying to go. Then in the next chapter I shall turn to a contemporary hermeneutic designed to keep scriptural truth "on the move" in our very different day. Taken together, these two chapters are intended to help the preacher trace the trajectory of the text and preach a sermon that contributes to its forward movement.

Utilizing the Criterion of Contextuality

As studies of leadership emphasize, the strategic stance is ever looking outward to what might be called its "surround,"[6] that soil in which a church plants itself to make the gospel indigenous. Because of an inseparable connection between the message and its matrix, we may not limit our hermeneutical task to that of discovering the content of a biblical text and then attempting to proclaim it in a contemporary form.[7] Rather, the biblical revelation cannot be stated adequately apart from its historical setting. We must seek to make that message meaningful for our situation in light of the way that it first became meaningful in its original situation.

What does this mean for strategic preaching? It means the preacher must pay more attention to the setting of the biblical text than preachers often do as they prepare sermons. Rather than merely gaining a general understanding of the "background" of a chosen scriptural passage, the preacher needs to devote careful attention

a. to the specific situation that the text sought to address
b. to the ways in which this particular setting shaped the strategy that impelled the text
c. to the results that the message of the text sought to achieve in the lives of its recipients

These three probes are central to the contextuality characteristic of strategic preaching.

Since about 1850, scholars have devoted as much attention to the biblical world as they have to the biblical text. Indeed, many of the most significant advances in the interpretation of Scripture have come as the direct result of a better understanding of its historical setting made possible by archeological discoveries and the recovery of such ancient sources as the Dead Sea Scrolls and Nag Hammadi Library. Literature abounds on the world of the Bible, designed to illumine almost every conceivable aspect of the milieu out of which our Jewish and Christian Scriptures emerged. Even after a century-and-a-half of remarkable progress, findings in the field continue to expand at a rapid pace, making it difficult for any but specialists and advanced students to keep abreast of recent developments.

Most pastors with only one seminary course in this area, and with limited reading on the subject since then, will feel insecure about making informed judgments because they do not have enough study time to gain confidence in working on this agenda. But do not despair! You have a number of economical shortcuts readily available to help in fulfilling this initial step of a strategic hermeneutic. Multi-volume Bible encyclopedias contain a wealth of compressed articles that provide the essential information needed.[8] If they prove too detailed for regular use, a one-volume Bible dictionary may suffice.[9] Beyond this, the more extensive recent commentaries will likely contain an introduction that sketches in some detail the setting of the entire book as well as notes that indicate specific environmental factors at play in particular parts of that book.[10]

Until fairly recently, most surveys of the biblical world tended to focus on what may be called macro-history, those major events that helped to define an era and the dominant leaders who shaped its pivotal transitions. While some knowledge of kings and dynasties in the Near East, or generals and rulers in Greece and Rome, may be useful in constructing an historical framework, most writers and readers of Scripture, especially in the New Testament, were largely uninvolved with these movers-and-shakers. What we really want to know is how ordinary people understood human existence in their daily life. What were the economic hazards, the political insecurities, and the social stresses that preoccupied believers and nonbelievers alike? Behind the spiritual symbols that they used, both verbal and material, what frustrations, anxieties, aspirations, and convictions were seeking to find expression? In particular, how were they coping with changes over which they seemed to have no control?

Fortunately, in the second half of the twentieth century the study of the past began to broaden to include not only macro-history but micro-history, not just institutional history as seen "from above" but also social history as seen "from below." Balancing the traditional interest in public history, fresh attention began to be devoted to the history of private life, especially individual and family life at home, at work, and at leisure. After

1970 the social science disciplines of sociology, anthropology, and ethnography were utilized extensively to reconstruct the world out of which each of the biblical writings emerged, the ways in which that environment influenced both the form and content of a particular writing, and how its recipients understood that literature in light of their political, economic, ecological, and cultural circumstances.[11]

Let me mention only a few of the many relevant topics the newer historical approach to biblical times is illumining. Because the Old Testament covers the people of Israel over many centuries, a number of studies have focused on the ways in which family and community life were affected by the successive shifts from a tribal confederacy to a centralized monarchy and then to a vassal state.[12] Or on the social settings out of which the prophetic, apocalyptic, and wisdom literatures emerged and the groups to which these traditions ministered.[13] By contrast, the New Testament covered only a few decades during which political, economic, and cultural conditions were relatively stable, thus permitting more detailed in-depth studies of such things as urban and rural life; social stratification and class status; domestic relations of male/female, parent/child, and master/slave; patterns of assimilation, marginalization, and alienation; voluntary associations and table fellowship; codes of honor/shame; property rights and taxation requirements.[14]

This brief listing only hints at the riches that are rapidly becoming available for a study of the biblical world, but these topics suggest that scholars are moving toward those "real life" issues that can contribute to what one of the leaders in this field, Wayne A. Meeks, has called "a hermeneutics of social embodiment."[15] Our first task is to relate faith to the history surrounding the text. That includes the history of the setting lying *behind* the text, the history of the believing community lying *in* the text, and the history of the intended recipients lying *before* the text. By taking all of these historical forces seriously, we combat the theological docetism that would turn Christianity into an abstraction or an ideology. To be sure, this approach magnifies the many dissimilarities between the biblical world and our world and so raises what scholars call the "problem of incommensurability," but it is precisely these differences that we must squarely face. Otherwise, we risk using the gospel to try to turn the twenty-first century into the first century.

The most common strategy preachers follow when they encounter the strangeness of the ancient past is to ignore those parts of the Bible that seem dated and search instead for texts that seem to enshrine timeless truths valid at any time or place. Thus we get no sermons on the food laws of the Levitical code or on meat offered to idols, on the sacrificial practices of the temple or the ritual purification of the priesthood, on fasting or foot washing, on speaking in tongues or veiling women, and a host of other ancient practices. In addition to its sheer arbitrariness, this approach hides at least two problems. First, the better we come to understand the details of daily life in the biblical world, the stranger it all becomes, thus lengthening the list of excluded texts that do not seem to "fit" our day. Second, the Bible's message is more often most strategic when it engages the distinctive agenda peculiar to its own day rather than when it deals somewhat abstractly with what seem to be timeless ideals. If you would like to see a practical application of how this approach made the biblical teachings on the ancient practice of circumcision relevant to the life of the church today, turn to the case study at the end of chapter 4 (pages 56–66).

Utilizing the Criterion of Intentionality

Because early Christians were committed to a strategy of actualizing the New Age in the midst of the Old Age, it is not surprising that their literature breathed a burning sense of purpose. They lived as a transformed and transforming remnant on the frontier of change from death to life, from bondage to freedom, from darkness to light. So passionately were the New Testament writers concerned to achieve greater Christlikeness in the totality of their existence that everything they wrote sought to accomplish this mission (Jn. 20:31). Therefore, as we ponder their words, our primary goal is to discover how they went about shaping in the lives of their readers a greater "measure of the stature of the fullness of Christ" (Eph. 4:13). Defining the hermeneutical task in this fashion is what I call utilizing the criterion of intentionality.

To be sure, the New Testament message was a uniquely new utterance that ever remains normative for our pulpit proclamation. But this miraculous endowment of speech gushed forth because lives were impelled by new purposes. Words, even holy words, were the coin of the realm, lying ready at hand to be used by Christians or non-Christians alike. Numerous so-called "parallels" in the religious literature of the first century amply prove this. Scripture is not unique because of the distinctiveness of the words and concepts used. Scripture stands unique because of the distinctive intentions that these words expressed. Even the most spontaneous word (e.g., "Help!") arises to serve some controlling purpose: "Human words are like arrows, deriving their meaning from the goal at which they are directed and from the purpose which they serve."[16] Regarding the biblical gospel, therefore, we must ask not only *what* was said but *why* it was said.

One way to do that is to take advantage of the maturing discipline called "form criticism." Begun early in the twentieth century, this methodology at first attempted to classify and trace the history of each unit of Scripture in light of the "form" in which it was transmitted orally before being incorporated into a literary document. To discern the earliest use to which each unit might have been put, form critics next tried to reconstruct its original "setting in life," often identified by the German phrase *Sitz-im-Leben.* Then they took all of these separate "settings" of the individual units of oral tradition and began to coalesce them into an inductively constructed picture of community life in which they functioned. This reconstruction was then correlated with everything we can know deductively about that religious community from other available sources.

At first, these techniques were applied primarily to the Psalms in the Old Testament and to the synoptic gospels in the New Testament. But in the latter half of the twentieth century the approach was extended to other biblical writings because of the growing realization that much of the material found there, even in the letters of the New Testament, had first functioned orally in a religious community before being included in a literary document. The pioneering form critics had a particular interest in trying to reconstruct the earliest form in which material may have circulated in its pre-literary usage so that they could then classify the various oral units by comparing them with nonbiblical forms circulating at the same time. But these efforts at comparative typology are now seen to have been excessively speculative and of little value to the interpretative process. As a result, form criticism has now become more of a mood than a method, a perspective from which to ask important questions about the text, questions which had long been neglected.

The internal logic of its method drove form criticism to concentrate on the *intentionality* of each text as it functioned in a particular life setting. The focus was on *why* the passage was written in the first place and not just on *what* was said or *how* it was said. Admittedly, this method is inferential or even hypothetical in arriving at some of its conclusions. Still, we can introduce a measure of control by the need to make the separate pieces fit into a coherent picture of all that we know about early church life at a time when the transmission of the tradition was moving from oral to written form. Now, tested and refined for almost a century, form criticism's results are used by scholars of virtually all theological persuasions in writing the kind of biblical commentaries that pastors may use in the preparation of sermons.

For our hermeneutical methodology this means that good recent commentaries, far more than their predecessors, pay close attention to the intentionality, or strategy, that a particular text employed in addressing its life situation. This may be illustrated by a quick look at the many commentaries on the gospel of Mark. At the beginning of the twentieth century, the standard commentary of Henry Barclay Swete (1898)[17] was a treasure-trove of close linguistic analysis, patristic parallels, and astute exegetical insights; but the reader learns almost nothing about the kerygmatic character of the text, about how Mark was being written as a gospel and what issues that gospel sought to address. The initial impact of form criticism was just beginning to be felt in Rawlinson (1925) and Branscomb (1937), becoming an explicit methodology in the massive commentary of Vincent Taylor (1952) but still not being utilized to bring out the full kerygmatic implications of the text.[18] Only in more recent treatments since 1970 has form criticism, supplemented by redaction criticism, enabled the exposition to become more life-centered.[19]

Pastors should turn to newer commentaries written from a life-setting perspective and supplement them by occasionally studying a sound popular treatment of the motives and purposes underlying the biblical literature as revealed by form and redaction criticism. These resources will go a long way toward providing a grasp of the strategic moves already embedded in the texts on which sermons are preached. Fortunately, the more recent exegetical emphasis on *intentionality* in interpreting the biblical text goes hand-in-hand with the parallel historical emphasis on *contextuality* in interpreting the biblical world. Each undergirds and strengthens the other, partly because both are united in understanding the text in terms of a reciprocating dialogue in which meaning emerges from the movement that takes place when the message engages the lives of its readers.

Utilizing the Criterion of Potentiality

In terms of determining where a text is going, most traditional hermeneutical approaches assume that movement stops at the point when the author has reduced the text's intention to writing. Once a message becomes written, it is as if its truth is frozen in literary form even though history continues to change. A dialogue designed for one context soon becomes dated as altered circumstances call forth new issues to be addressed. The familiar biblical phrase "it is written," found in the perfect tense with the force of "it stands written," seems to suggest that the message has now dug in its heels and adopted a form that is final with only one meaning. The fluidity of the text as an event in history is replaced by the fixity of the text in a document that is no longer in the hands of its author.

The sense of finality that attaches to a written text, particularly when it is gathered up into a collection that eventually becomes Scripture, may explain why scholars have devoted far more attention to what came before the text was composed than to what came after it. Form critics, in particular, have expended enormous effort in digging behind written sources to discern what influences may have shaped the sources and text in oral tradition, but paid limited attention to the way in which texts subsequently shaped the situations to which they were addressed. Even though a high degree of conjecture is involved, the preacher must attempt to determine both the causes that led to and the effects that led from a particular text. I would urge that sermon preparation devote attention to reconstructing both the prehistory of a passage and its posthistory as well. Once we have gained some idea of the context in which a text was formed and the intention of the author in addressing that context, it is not impossible to infer what outcomes the text was seeking to achieve in its literary expression.

Biblical scholars are now beginning to correct the imbalance that probed only the roots of a text and not its fruits. Not surprisingly, the Germans have come up with a technical term for the needed methodology, *Wirkungsgeschichte,* which unfortunately lacks a precise English equivalent. This word, which may be translated literally as a "history of effects," is being used to describe efforts to determine the ongoing influence of a particular scriptural text in the life of the church as seen from such sources as its sermons, hymns, and art as well as in the lived-out response of its members.[20] This is not merely the old "history of interpretation" approach (*Forschungsbericht*) that traces the various positions taken on a passage throughout church history. Rather, it is an effort to discover what effect the text actually had on those who implemented it in their lives. Viewing a scripture passage in terms both of its inputs and of its outputs permits one to practice a hermeneutic of the trajectory between them.[21]

Scripture itself presents at least three perspectives that undergird the emphasis on what I am here calling the potentiality of the text to impact its readers. Each of them not only enriches our understanding of hermeneutical theory but also provides abundant illustrations of how to apply that theory in hermeneutical practice.

1. The coming of Jesus inaugurated a new age of eschatological fulfillment (Mk. 1:14–15). As the Sermon on the Mount makes clear, one aspect of this transformation was to bring "the law and the prophets," our Old Testament, to a whole new level of completeness (Mt. 5:17).[22] The prophets themselves had long anticipated the day when the law of God would be internalized and the knowledge of God would be universalized (Jer. 31:33–34). To illustrate how this promise was being fulfilled, Jesus chose six antitheses that contrasted the traditional interpretation of texts with his interpretation designed to bring out their deeper meaning (Mt. 5:21–48). For example, in suggesting that the ultimate intention of the commandments against murder and adultery was to prohibit anger and

lust (Mt. 5:22, 28), Jesus was probing the potentiality of those texts (Ex. 20:13, 14) in ways that had never been adequately explored in the thousand years since they were written.

As the early church began to reflect on the significance of this eschatological hermeneutic, it came to realize just how meaningful it was to view Scripture through the lenses of the life, death, and resurrection of its Lord. At least a dozen times in both Matthew and in John, this experience was given theological expression in the formula, "this event fulfills that Scripture," i.e., some aspect of the life of Jesus served to disclose as never before a truth that had long been latent in some ancient text.[23] For example, descriptions of the righteous sufferer in the Psalms (e.g., Ps. 22; 69), or of the Servant of the Lord in Isaiah (e.g., Isa. 42; 53), took on incredibly deeper meaning once Jesus actualized their anticipations in his crucifixion. The risen Christ also empowered his followers to claim as never before the unrealized potential that lay dormant in their Scriptures. For example, the writer of Hebrews viewed the promise of Sabbath rest in Psalm 95 as only then coming true for the people of God (Heb. 4:1–10). The many and varied uses of the Old Testament by the New Testament[24] provide abundant case studies in how the subsequent unfolding of God's redemptive activity offers new possibilities for drawing out the potentiality of texts written in an earlier era.

2. The New Testament texts themselves have a potential for divine disclosure beyond that grasped by their writers who had already begun to experience the new age inaugurated by Christ. The gospel of John dealt directly with this issue, especially in the upper room discourse of chapters 14—16, with its five Paraclete passages.[25] Here Jesus promised that the Holy Spirit "will teach [the disciples] all things" by bringing to their remembrance all that Jesus had said to them (Jn. 14:26). An ongoing hermeneutical role was assigned to the Paraclete, not because Jesus had failed to explain God's truth (Jn. 14:6), but because the disciples were not yet able to bear the truth that he wished to disclose (Jn. 16:12). The very fact that the disciples needed to be *guided* into all the truth (Jn. 16:13) meant that the revelation they initially received had a latent potentiality that would need to be appropriated over time on a pilgrimage of discovery.

The Fourth Evangelist was not content merely to record this hermeneutical breakthrough promised by Jesus. He went on to illustrate its application in the subsequent experience of the disciples. For example, in John 2:21 Jesus spoke of "the temple of his body" in connection with the cleansing of the temple. Then John added that the disciples did not come to understand this saying until after the resurrection when they "remembered" that Jesus had spoken it and they "believed the scripture." A regular pattern recurs throughout this gospel. Sayings of Jesus that would eventually become Scripture texts are said to have been understood, not when they were uttered, but only as the Spirit of the risen Lord guided the disciples to remember the words of Jesus and to discern the relevant Scriptures that they fulfilled.[26] Indeed, the entire gospel of John is a monument to the ongoing capacity of Christian tradition for creative adaptation, representing as it does a dramatic recasting of the story of Jesus from that found in the synoptic gospels.

3. This way in which the Bible itself updates its own texts as a testimony to their potential for enhanced understanding prepares us for the extension of this hermeneutical process throughout the long sweep of subsequent church history. Nowhere does Scripture hint that the end of the Apostolic Era or the closing of the canon was meant to prohibit the quest for fresh insight into the biblical texts. The first disciples were not ready to "bear" much of the truth that would cost Jesus his life on a cross. In like manner their successors required more than eighteen hundred years to bear the moral and economic burdens of abolition and so come to a radically different understanding of the biblical texts on slavery. Even now, in the midst of a struggle over gender equality, we are discovering heretofore unrealized potential for insight that comes when women themselves are encouraged to interpret the texts. In a sense, biblical passages are like a bundle of promises that, far from being exhausted in antiquity, still await fulfillment as timid interpreters finally find the courage to implement them.

That courage may come not only from new urgencies, such as the modern collapse of serfdom and the rise of egalitarianism, but from the collective witness of those who have wrestled with the claims of Scripture in the centuries before us. The heroes of faith did not end with those catalogued in Hebrews 11. Ever since the New Testament was written, the pages of Scripture have been overlaid with a rich deposit of experience that deepens our perception of their meaning. Who can read Romans today without thinking of Martin Luther, or the great commission without remembering William Carey, or the Beatitudes without seeing Francis of Assisi? The Bible has not been quietly gathering dust for twenty centuries. Rather, it has taken on a rich patina from the blood of martyrs, the sweat of apostles, the tears of prophets. And yet it is filled with the unfinished business of drawing out the full *potentiality* of texts whose relevance will not be discovered until their ultimate *intentionality* has been tested in terms of the *contextuality* both of their time and of our own. Admittedly the well is deep and, with the passing of the years, is getting deeper all the time, but still it gushes with an inexhaustible supply of fresh truth every time we pay the price to let down our buckets![27]

We began this chapter with a search for movement in the text for one simple reason. If you don't think the text is going anywhere, then you probably won't think a sermon based on it is going anywhere either! A second reason is like unto it: if the congregation doesn't think the sermon is going anywhere, then it probably won't be going anywhere either! Here, then, is another law of strategic preaching: *a static text produces a static sermon, which produces a static congregation.* We have seen in this chapter how movement is at work in the inspired desire to change one's world, in the translation of that desire into a plea for action by the people of God, and in the ongoing response that such a plea prompts. Find the movement of the text, let the sermon move with it, and soon the congregation may begin to move where God is going as well.

CHAPTER 4

A Hermeneutic of Strategic Preaching: Contemporary

Why does "great preaching" often seem dated? In 1971, Clyde Fant and William Pinson published a thirteen-volume anthology, *20 Centuries of Great Preaching,* which included sermons from more than ninety pulpit giants of the past.[1] Since its appearance, I have consulted this encyclopedic resource with profit even though I often found material that would not be called "strategic" if preached today. This limitation is obviously not due to any lack of ability or spiritual depth on the part of the authors, for every sermon is a carefully selected masterpiece. Nor is it due to the absence of the preacher's personality, for sermons can be gripping even in written form. My conclusion is that many of these sermons lack sparkle and punch today precisely because they were written for another era.

Fant and Pinson launched their vast enterprise with these words, "Great preaching is relevant preaching."[2] I could not agree more. In making their sermons relevant to an earlier age, these masters utilized different exegetical methods and rhetorical styles. Their words carried nuances and suggested allusions that set off associations unfamiliar to us today. Most importantly, they responded to different urgencies, aimed at different targets, grappled with problems defined by different contexts. To be gripping, their message had to be, not timeless, but timely. In some cases, the very language in which they preached required that the sermon be translated, from Greek or Latin or German into English; but it is not possible to translate for our day the living situations that they addressed. I consider it a compliment that these sermons were so carefully crafted for their own time that they no longer resonate with the temper of our time. If the greatest preaching in

Christian history is dated to its own day, should not that be true of our sermons as well?

The Sermon in Its Time

At least three important reasons make it difficult to recast the ancient biblical message for a modern audience.

Peril of Objective Biblical Study

Many of the biblical scholars who have the time and expertise to study scriptural texts most thoroughly bend over backward to avoid being influenced by contemporary developments, even those—or especially those—in which they have a personal interest. After a long history of allegorical, dogmatic, and mystical approaches that read the views of the interpreter back into the text, scholars since the Enlightenment have sought to be scrupulously objective in following a critical methodology that seeks to reconstruct the past without regard for the present.[3] Krister Stendahl provided a famous formulation of this rigorously descriptive approach. He split the question of meaning into two tenses, assigning to the biblical scholar the determination of what the text originally *meant* and to the theologian and philosopher the determination of what it *means* today.[4] Rather than a fusion of past and present horizons as in Gadamar,[5] this bifurcation of function interrupts the trajectory of the text and leaves the preacher caught between interpreters with different frames of reference.[6]

A German Jew, Tania Oldenhage, brilliantly analyzed an especially haunting illustration of the problem in her reprise of parable scholarship in light of the Holocaust.[7] She focused on Joachim Jeremias' classic work finished in its first German edition just as World War II was ending. Jeremias gave no hint of the monstrous genocide that had engulfed the German nation for almost a decade. He included a section on "The Imminence of Catastrophe," treating those parables intended "to shock into realization of its danger a nation rushing upon its own destruction."[8] Even there, one finds no mention of the Holocaust. Although Oldenhage's immediate problem is the lack of resonance between Jeremias' comments on the "blinded people of Israel" in the first century and the agonies of European Jewry in the twentieth century,[9] her constructive plea is for biblical scholars to overcome this problem by a return to the history of their own time. She bases this plea on an insightful essay by Elisabeth Schüssler Fiorenza and David Tracy who

> ...argue that the nineteenth-century rise of historical conscious-
> ness...paradoxically led to a retreat from the history of our own
> time...With all its scientific vigor and critical potential, historical

criticism did not return into history. "The gains of the historico-critical method…are plain for all to see. But the loss—the loss of concrete history itself under the paradoxical cover of 'historical consciousness'—was a loss whose full impact we are just beginning to realise."[10]

Understanding Contemporary Life

Most seminaries offer no in-depth study of contemporary life anywhere in the theological curriculum.[11] Standard textbooks on homiletics are largely silent on strategy questions of how to engage the modern mind with the gospel. The wider literature on preaching in books and journals may contain a few scattered references of an inspirational or hortatory nature but very little solid analysis of the current *Zeitgeist*.[12] Nor do continuing education workshops on preaching devote any significant attention to this issue. One of the weakest links in present efforts to equip ministers to preach is the almost complete lack of resources to help them understand the world to which they witness.[13]

Both the magnitude and the irony of the problem may be glimpsed by comparing the training ministerial students receive to help them understand the biblical world with the training they receive to help them understand the contemporary world. Before attempting to interpret the New Testament message, for example, students are given a rather comprehensive introduction to the historical dynamics of the Hellenistic world, including the impact of exile and resettlement, conquests of Alexander and subsequent rule by his Ptolemaic and Seleucid successors, rise of the Maccabean revolutionaries and the Hasmonean dynasty, and the intervention of Rome and Herodian rule. They will know clearly such religious movements as Pharisees, Sadducees, Zealots, and Essenes; institutions such as temple, synagogue, and Sanhedrin; cultural trends such as Hellenization; philosophical trends such as Stoicism; and political trends such as emperor worship. They are taught to distinguish apocalypticists from gnostics and to talk intelligently about the significance of the fall of Jerusalem in 70 B.C.E. More crucially, they learn how these developments impacted the ways in which the New Testament message was formulated and proclaimed in such a world.

Yet when they cross over twenty centuries and study how to hammer out a message for today, they are left to understand their own world presumably by intuition or osmosis from watching television and reading newspapers, thin fare indeed. Even the best-trained students who leave seminary often do not understand the impact of the wars in Vietnam, Afghanistan, and Iraq on the American mind as well as they do the corruption and collapse of the Hasmonean dynasty on the Jewish mind.

They do not know the religious assumptions of the postmodern Echo Boomer generation as well as they do those of the ancient gnostic movement. They cannot explain the social causes that gave rise to American dispensationalism as well as they can explain the rise of Jewish apocalypticism. They have not analyzed the shifting patterns of church-state relations since the emergence of "New Right" religion in the 1970s as carefully as they have traced tensions between the Tobiads and the Oniads in the Jerusalem high priesthood. I hope the point is clear: students of preaching need as much training in the twenty-first–century world as students of New Testament need in the first-century world, but that training is not being provided to most future pulpiteers.

If seminaries are able to employ one or more specialists to offer courses on the ancient world, sometimes called "biblical backgrounds," why are they not able to employ specialists, perhaps with a master's or doctorate in American Studies, to offer courses that teach students to exegete the contemporary culture? Or, if that is not financially feasible, could they not assist a teacher of homiletics to gain needed skills in this area through a sabbatical leave program? Is there really any theological or homiletical justification for ministers knowing more about the world *from* which they preach than they do about the world *to* which they preach? Think how much it would sharpen the target at which a sermon aims if the preacher were trained to engage in cultural critique informed by the imperatives of the gospel. As one who taught seminary courses on "the world of the Bible" for two decades, I would have welcomed the chance to develop a team-taught course with a colleague specializing in contemporary American life on "the world of the preacher."

Fear of Being Relevant

Lacking any theological orientation to such study in seminary, some pulpiteers actually resist the challenge of understanding the world in which they live. Their fear is that to be "relevant" is to risk accommodating or even compromising the gospel to contemporary thought. In the name of integrity, they refuse to tamper with the traditional language of the pulpit, choosing rather to glory in the *irrelevance* of their message. Yet, to their chagrin, the forceful idiom of one generation becomes the tired cliché of the next. Static formulations become increasingly impotent as the times inexorably change. Finally they find themselves speaking in a language that is no longer fresh, about concerns that no longer matter, to a generation that no longer exists!

The risk of restating the gospel is neatly summarized in a somewhat sardonic comment of Dean Inge, "If you marry the Spirit of your own generation you will be a widow in the next."[14] Two clarifications are in order. First, our preaching task is not to embrace the modern mood but to contend with it on behalf of the claims of Christ. The urgent issue is not whether the church will capitulate to contemporary culture but whether it will address that culture with a proclamation that makes unmistakably clear the demands of the gospel upon the totality of human existence as it is lived today. Second, the good Dean appears to have overlooked the fact that we are not eligible even for widowhood in the next generation. He is correct that the spirit of our age will die, but he seems to forget that we will die with it. Mercifully, we are not required to anticipate what may meet the needs of future generations, since only God knows what tomorrow may bring (Mt. 6:34). Rather, we are to take up the task that never changes, that of fashioning our finest understanding of the biblical faith for the one and only generation that we are given to serve.

Those preachers who like to ignore the contemporary world often do so in the name of fidelity to the Bible. However, as the previous chapter sought to show, when we go in search of the meaning of the Bible's message, we are helped immeasurably by an awareness of its interaction with its own world. This understanding of the historical background does not provide the *content* of the biblical message but it does provide the *context* that enables us to clarify both its distinctiveness and its strategy. Just so, a study of contemporary backgrounds is not undertaken to find our gospel there. Rather, the purpose of such probes is to shed light on the strategies needed to address our world today with the biblical gospel. Dietrich Bonhoeffer expressed the need to take our world seriously in this way:

> A word can only be authoritatively and convincingly spoken to me when it springs from the deepest knowledge of my humanity and strikes me here and now in the total reality of my human existence. Any other kind of word is powerless. Hence the *church*'s message to the world, if it is to be authoritative and convincing, must be declared with the deepest knowledge of the world's life and must concern the world in the full scope of its present reality.[15]

A Proposal for a Preacher's Study Time

So what is a preacher to do who lacks the training needed to study the present age preparatory to offering a Christian critique? Begin by setting priorities that permit you to devote as much attention to modern life as you do to biblical life. A good rule of thumb might be to divide your study time equally between the biblical message and your modern message, in each of these two areas devoting about half as much time to a study of the world as you do to a study of the Word. Resolve to work on the gaps in your learning until you honestly feel that you understand the contemporary world *at least as well* as you understand the biblical world. With this commitment firmly in place, set up a systematic program to understand the contemporary context that you are trying to influence by your preaching. You can probably find help by talking with a good journalist, especially an editorial page writer at your daily newspaper; with a good reference librarian specializing in regional and local studies; and with academics in nearby colleges and universities whose disciplines in the social sciences are focused on current events. Once you gain an overview of your task, begin reading the books, periodicals, and newsletters that will contribute to the perspectives that are missing in your understanding.

Obviously space does not let us outline all of the components in such a study or to identify a basic bibliography, but I will suggest a few leads that may prove promising. Pollsters such as Gallup, Roper, and Yankelovich issue trend reports that usefully sample public opinion, but personal subscriptions are often expensive. Many newsletters take the contemporary pulse; one of the more insightful from a Christian perspective is *Context,* a somewhat miscellaneous "commentary on the interaction of religion and culture" written by Martin E. Marty. Periodicals that may be counted on to have something of worth in most issues include *The Atlantic Monthly* and *Harpers.* Faith traditions inform cultural critique from an Evangelical perspective in *Books & Culture,* from a Mainline Protestant perspective in *The Christian Century,* from a Catholic perspective in *America* and *Commonweal,* from a Jewish perspective in *Commentary,* and from an interfaith perspective in *First Things.* Most of the better books on contemporary life intended for the general reader rather than the specialist are reviewed, advertised, or mentioned in these periodicals as well as in the *New York Times Book Review* and the *New York Review of Books.* Pastors stay so busy that they must be very selective in their reading. I would suggest that you browse these sources in a public or academic library for a few weeks, then decide on the three or four for regular reading that best meet your needs.

Admittedly the field of study is enormous, and I have barely hinted at the resources available. Doubtless many preachers are daunted by the prospect of self-study in so vast an arena—it seems almost like teaching oneself to swim in the middle of the ocean! Yet we do not neglect the New Testament world simply because thousands of books have been written on first-century Judaism and Hellenism. Surely the better course is to be highly selective in choosing works on both worlds that provide a broad overview and integrate insights from many specialized disciplines.

Discerning the Signs of the Times

The preacher does not become intimately familiar with the contemporary world to deliver learned discourses on American culture any more than the New Testament expositor studies the first-century world to become an expert on ancient history. In both cases, this contextual perspective is used to determine both how the gospel message was originally proclaimed and how it can be proclaimed today so as to accomplish the same results. The ideal is for the preacher to keep one foot in the biblical world and the other in our own world so that the strategy that shaped a message to the former is consistent with the strategy employed to address the latter.

Here let me offer seven guidelines for understanding the modern world as the context in which our hearers live out the message we proclaim.

1. Set the contemporary era in a spacious context of past and future. We usually define the "present" in terms of a generation involving thirty or forty years, but it is unwise to wear blinders that restrict your purview to that time frame. Understanding our nation today is still profoundly influenced by insights from Alexis de Tocqueville's *Democracy in America,* published 1835–40.[16] The Civil War (1861–65) and the two World Wars (1914–18, 1941–45) unleashed forces that are still working beneath the surface of public life. Likewise, we are already being influenced by developments that will not come to fruition for several years into the future, such as microtechnology, robotics, space travel, genetic engineering, and globalization.

2. Within the present generation, look for studies that probe the underlying meaning of social change rather than merely chronicle the most prominent current events. For example, no Southern preacher can escape the influence of the civil rights struggle on this era, a story well told by Taylor Branch in his three-volume study, *America in the King Years.*[17] Equally important is the rise of the "New Right" in the late seventies, its ascendancy in the so-called "Reagan Revolution" of the eighties, and its triumph during the presidency of George W. Bush.

3. In addition to tracking the time-line of the present era, give equal attention to the meaning of place. Begin at home by learning what resources the public library has on the history and demographics of your city, county, and state. While census reports and metropolitan planning studies are important, move beyond such demographic analyses to learn the lore of your community as reflected in the work of local poets, novelists, and artists. Dare not neglect wider regional studies, especially if you happen to live and work in Dixie![18]

4. In approaching the culture of a particular time and place, be sure to look for the level in which most of the people to whom you are preaching live. Some academics who write books on contemporary life seem to operate on the principle of "the higher the culture the better" and so write at length about a rarefied intellectual climate that may be found in pockets of New York, London, and Paris, plus a few large university cities such as Berkeley and Cambridge. These writers may refer condescendingly to "mass culture" or "pop culture." The preacher must remember that this "mass culture" is a perfectly legitimate area of study, especially for those working at the grass-roots level where local congregations flourish. In particular, focus on such mass media as television, cinema, and musical recordings that so powerfully influence the symbol-systems by which many people shape their values. Also be aware that cultural differentiation takes place not only geographically but also generationally, such as between cohorts that came of age in relation to quite different defining events in American life.

5. Balance your study of contemporary culture, not only between high and low as well as between young and old, but also between public and private. Clearly the preacher needs to struggle with that elusive reality called the American character. The profoundly personal nature of religion also demands a special focus on the understanding of individual selfhood that comes from studying private life in its historical, psychological, sociological, and cultural aspects.

6. Since contemporary culture involves so many complex dimensions, look for integrative studies that approach significant change from a synoptic viewpoint. One of the best ways to draw all of the relevant strands together is through the continuous study of biography, since the whole spectrum of cultural dynamics is assimilated and acted upon one life at a time.[19]

7. Finally, once you have gained a unified understanding of American culture from top-to-bottom and inside-out, look for recurring patterns by which historical parallels illuminate the present. History does not repeat itself, but does reveal discernable rhythms or cycles by which the pendulum of change swings in corrective fashion.

Learning to Tell the Church's Story

Of all the worlds that interest the pastoral preacher, the one of greatest concern should be that particular context in which each congregation lives out its earthly existence. The target at which the sermon aims may be likened to a series of concentric circles that include the global, the national, and the regional; but the "bull's-eye" is the local. The minister should seek to understand most intimately that narrow slice of life that the pulpit seeks to address with the gospel on a weekly basis. In one sense, the sermon is a meeting place of the human and the Divine. Until the preacher has sat among the people to discover the dynamics of their own life-situations, it is premature to shape a message for them from God (Ezek. 3:15).

Fortunately, the interdisciplinary field of congregational studies is emerging to help us give greater depth and precision to this task by utilizing insights from historical, sociological, anthropological, and ethnographical methodologies. The pioneering work of James Hopewell[20] launched the field, but his premature death limited its reach and influence. Still, congregational studies remains one of the more promising probes. It is beginning to gain substance and a measure of maturity especially as a result of the work of projects at two centers. The first is the Congregational History Project at the Institute for the Advanced Study of Religion in the University of Chicago Divinity School.[21] The other is the research team led by Nancy Ammerman at the Center for Social and Religious Research in the Hartford Seminary.[22] We have every reason to hope that in the near future the impact of this movement will be felt in theological education and that congregational studies will become a valued part of the curriculum for future pastors.[23]

A key category in the effort to discern the meaning of congregational culture is that of each church's "story." The Bible, of course, is one long story of the people of God knit together by that familiar phrase, "And it came to pass…"[24] It is not surprising, therefore, that we should begin to see a renewed emphasis on "narrative theology"[25] and on "narrative preaching"[26] as we move beyond "modernism" with its Enlightenment preference for rational, analytical, universal, timeless, and abstract categories toward "postmodernism" with its Aristotelian preference for oral, particular, local, timely, and concrete categories.[27] In other words, many converging insights are helping us to see that the richly textured nature of reality is best captured when we begin with, "Once upon a time…" and tell an unfinished story.

In like manner, only a "narrative ecclesiology" is adequate to convey the identity and ethos of congregational life. Why should this be so? Because stories, by their very nature, link isolated events together in a meaningful sequence that provides continuity between past, present, and future. That is, they serve the essential human need to live and learn in all three temporal spheres through the use of memory, experience, and anticipation. But more: by a process of selection and emphasis these stories build a "plot-line" that "frames" the transitoriness of our earthy journey within a defining "whence" and "whither," in the midst of which is set the dialectic of suspense and denouement.[28]

As the storyteller sorts out what really matters in the interaction of challenge and response, priorities begin to emerge that describe the group's impelling sense of purpose. Gradually these commitments are contextualized by being set within the larger stories of the city, region, nation, and world. Nor is the story finished: In light of where and why the group got started, how is it seeking to write the next chapter in its odyssey? Is it chasing the dream of an Omega that will answer to its Alpha and make sense of all that happened in between?

In their own way, stories inevitably talk about purpose, context, and vision—the three essentials of a strategy for accomplishing mission, which will be discussed in Part 2 of this book. But they talk, not in terms of biblical texts or of leadership theory, but in the language of concrete events that focus attention on the roles of heroes and villains, on the interplay of chance and circumstance, on the ambiguities of motives and methods, and on the consequences of roads both taken and not taken. Stories carry within themselves an inherent drive to discover meaning, which is why they reach out to utilize symbols from the larger sagas of the human struggle that will give a sense of drama and destiny to what might otherwise seem to be an insignificant adventure. For Christians, this search for a "mythic" dimension to existence does not end until they learn to set the "Local Story" of their congregation within the "Universal Story" that is the Bible and sense that all of life is being lived, not just moment-by-moment, but *sub specie aeternitatis* ("under the aspect of eternity").

How does a church learn to tell its story? Listen to charter members talk about humble beginnings, or to participants talk about how the congregation weathered a grave financial crisis, or to veteran Sunday school teachers talk about how a squirming kid grew up to bless the community, and you begin to get the makings of a story. The tales that really matter are often told when former members return for some "homecoming" occasion, or when a resident raconteur steeped in the lore of church life is asked to talk about the congregation's pilgrimage in an orientation session for new members. The church library needs an oral history section in its archives to record the reminiscences of those who led the church through a great building program or a pivotal stewardship campaign or a major evangelistic effort. When the time comes to write a church history in celebration of a major anniversary, challenge the author to provide a narrative of God's providential guidance rather than just a chronological listing of activities and a compilation of statistical achievements.

Every good story needs one or more heroes. The people of God have their share of stalwarts who provide models of discipleship worthy of emulation, as Hebrews 11 makes clear. When a great saint of the congregation dies, those who gather for the family visitation often recount anecdotes that illustrate how the deceased embodied the very character of the church. An attentive pastor can weave these heartfelt tributes into the funeral eulogy in ways that contribute to the growing edge of the church's story without unduly glorifying the one being memorialized. It is often difficult to identify a congregation's heroes while they are still living, if only because it would offend their modesty. But death permits and even prompts a more candid assessment that can be used to install those who deserve such a role in their rightful place as pacesetters whose lives will continue to challenge their successors for as long as their story is remembered and told.

Beyond these informal, even spontaneous, expressions of the remembered story lie more systematic, even scientific, ways to analyze the story as the ongoing life of the congregation currently narrates it. Here I shall mention two such efforts by scholars who understand the importance of the church's story for pastoral leadership and the task of preaching. In doing so, I confess to a divided mind about conducting a formal process to analyze the story of what, to the minister, is a beloved spiritual family. The academic side of me relishes such an exercise, but the pastoral side of me hesitates to objectivize, and thereby "freeze," even for a moment, the complex unfinished saga of a congregation by turning it into what is often a set of social science constructs. I leave it to my readers to assess both their enthusiasm and their competence to work with these methods.

One of the most comprehensive and penetrating efforts to elicit a congregation's story and interpret its meaning appears in James F. Hopewell's pioneering book *Congregation*. He began by suggesting that a church's story should *not* focus on

1. the *contextual*, how it moved out to serve its world
2. the *mechanical*, how it achieved internal growth through program effectiveness
3. the *organic*, how it bonded its members into a caring fellowship

Rather, a church's story should focus on the *symbolic*: its sense of identity, personality, and character.[29] Building on the recognition of Northrop Frye that most tales are either comic, romantic, tragic, or ironic,[30] Hopewell constructed a typology of four possible religious worldviews, correlated with Frye's literary genres, to which he gave the somewhat misleading names of Canonic (tragic), Gnostic (comic), Charismatic (romantic), and Empiric (ironic).[31] His hypothesis was that one of these worldviews will become dominant in most congregations. To identify which one is most meaningful to the members will help to explain how the church deals with crises, the skills that it utilizes to accomplish its tasks, the way it nurtures its pervasive mood, and the purposes or goals that it pursues.[32]

Utilizing standard techniques of field research, Hopewell then proposed that these four worldview categories be probed by means of participant observation, guided interviews, and a test instrument.[33] After offering helpful suggestions on how one might analyze parish culture and question informants when conducting interviews, he provided twenty-seven multiple choice questions designed to measure the strength of each of the four worldviews among the respondents.[34] The answers may be scored on a graph with a horizontal x-axis holding the Canonic and Gnostic tendencies in opposition while a vertical y-axis does the same for the Charismatic and Empiric tendencies. This quadripolar analysis has the advantage of providing a more nuanced picture of congregational attitudes than a bipolar categorization that might, for example, distinguish a "liberal" from a "conservative" parish based on responses to questions about doctrine or denominational distinctives.

I find it frustrating to study Hopewell because some of his insights are original and brilliant while others are obscure and impractical. When preparing to write *Congregation,* he began to offer an intensive midwinter seminar for pastors who could come to Emory University and learn his methods under personal supervision. They would then implement these methods in their congregations before returning in late spring for a follow-up evaluation session. Under the expert tutelage of Hopewell, plus disciplined interaction with a pastoral peer group, the project might well have been carried through in effective fashion. Unfortunately, all of this soon ended with Hopewell's death, which also cut short his chance to write subsequent books that would have benefited both from scholarly critique and from parish feedback. Despite these unavoidable limitations, this one book by Hopewell will enlarge every pastor's understanding of the importance of the church's story and will define the richness of that story in ways that transcend the shallow stereotypes of church life to which we have long been accustomed in anniversary histories.

Of the several scholars who have built on Hopewell's work, Leonora Tubbs Tisdale has related story directly to sermon in her book, *Preaching as Local Theology and Folk Art.*[35] After first establishing that each congregation has a distinctive subculture, which may differ in significant ways from the subculture out of which its pastor has come,[36] she defines her goal as "contextual preaching" shaped by the "local theology" of that particular congregational subculture.[37] This is best done when the preacher learns to "exegete" the congregation in light of its contemporary world, just as exegesis of the biblical text is done in light of its ancient world.[38]

Regarding these and other social science methodologies that might be mentioned, I offer two words of caution. First, if you choose to utilize such techniques in your congregation, try to minimize reference to their scientific terminology lest the people begin to think that they have become guinea pigs on whom you are conducting an experiment. Second, if you wish to use these procedures but feel unqualified to implement them yourself, do not suppose that an outside expert can solve your problem by conducting a congregational survey for a few days and then filing a written report. The kind of profound knowledge we are after here comes only as both pastor and people learn together to tell their story, a task of many months and even years.[39]

In one situation, a trained consultant *can* be especially helpful in guiding a congregation to rethink its story. A contentious period in a church may result in two or more versions of the church's story. Those on each side may well develop competing versions of the congregation's story to vindicate their position in the conflict. As one of my students shared from his own painful experience:

> All too often…the past holds such hurt and emotion [that] the real story of what happens gets clouded in the misperceptions of what happened. Then the pastor is confronted with the prospect of speaking the truth into the life of the congregation of what happened or waiting until a generation passes to effect the needed change. The problem here is that congregations tend to recreate themselves and so the "mis-story" is passed on from member to member. I have found myself in these quandaries and felt somewhat helpless as I tried to speak strategically as a leader to a congregation confused and divided over its own history.

I know a congregation that went through a prolonged period of dissension so severe the pastor resigned, causing a great deal of divisiveness within the membership. Before trying to call a new pastor, the church engaged a mature ministerial advisor to lead it through an intentional interim designed to overcome the tensions that had erupted. One of the first things he did was to get all sides to recount their understanding of recent events for the benefit of a transition committee that then worked to meld these divergent perspectives into a coherent story on which all could agree. The very act of listening to so much heartbreak on all sides helped everyone to realize that what the church needed was not for one version of events to triumph but for the whole story to be embraced. First, the people came to an honest realization both of *what* had happened and of *why* it had happened. After this realization they discovered that they had gone a long way toward being ready to reunite and call a new pastor who would help them to begin a new chapter in their unfinished saga.

Learning to tell your church's story is crucial for our purposes because *those who would preach strategically can never know too much about their congregation, and that knowledge needs to be both broad and deep!* When preaching to the contemporary world, the pastor needs such an intimate understanding of the congregation's story that the sermon will voice the congregation's distinctive "idiom" or "dialect." This story is open-ended and may even be at a critical turning point, "between chapters" as it were. In a very important sense, one task of the pulpit is to help the congregation write the next chapter of its ongoing journey and to do so in ways that carry forward the chapters already written.

The pastor who does not know the church's story, or who tries to replace it with another story imported from elsewhere, is asking for serious trouble because it is primarily through this story that a congregation identifies itself, integrates itself, and invests itself with meaning. A congregation communicates through its own story just as God communicates through the biblical story. When both stories meet and merge in the sermon, then the gospel has begun to take root in the real world of time and place.

APPENDIX TO CHAPTER
A Hermeneutical Case Study

Now that we have sought in chapters 3 and 4 to describe a hermeneutical methodology suitable for strategic preaching, this may be a good point at which to insert our first case study illustrating how one might build a bridge connecting the world of the Bible with the very different world of today. When I searched for some important feature of the New Testament message that has disappeared completely from our contemporary proclamation, one obvious example was what early preachers such as Paul had to say about circumcision. Consider: In the modern world, this elective surgical procedure is nothing more than a discretionary medical matter to be discussed between parents and pediatrician following the birth of a male child. Thus we get no sermons on circumcision, not only because of the inherent delicacy of the subject matter to our modern tastes, but because it does not seem to "speak" to our spiritual needs in any meaningful fashion.

But is a dismissive solution really that simple? Circumcision was the most explosive issue in Paul's pivotal letter to the Galatians (e.g., 2:3–9,11–13; 5:1–12; 6:12–15). It recurred as a key theme in several later Pauline letters (e.g., 1 Cor. 7:17–19; Rom. 2:25–29; 3:30; 4:9–12; Phil. 3:2–3; Col. 2:11; 3:11; Eph. 2:11–13; Titus 1:10). Most important, it was the central controversy prompting the Jerusalem Conference (Acts 15:1–5), which became in many ways the watershed event of the apostolic era. Are we free to ignore so important an issue in our preaching just because it now seems dated?

What if we were to begin, not with our world that ignores circumcision as religiously irrelevant, but with the New Testament world? What if we were to ask how circumcision functioned then in the lives of those who were turning to Christianity? The first thing we would learn is that circumcision was not an optional hygienic technique, or even a medical concern for the population at large. Circumcision was a profound sign of Jewish identity developed over centuries of religious usage. The Book of Jubilees makes clear its decisive importance in the New Testament era:

> And every one that is born, the flesh of whose foreskin is not circumcised on the eighth day, belongs not to the children of the covenant which the Lord made with Abraham, but to the children of destruction; nor is there, moreover, any sign on him that he is the Lord's, but (he is destined) to be destroyed and slain from the earth, and to be rooted out of the earth, for he has broken the covenant of the Lord our God (15:26).[40]

Next we would learn how circumcision was so repugnant to the Greek and Roman masters of Palestine that, during the Hellenistic Age, Jews were under intense pressure to renounce the practice and surgically remove its mark (1 Macc. 1:14–15). This operation, called *epispasmos,* became common among the urban upper class, but Josephus viewed it as forsaking Jewish national customs to adopt a Greek way of life (*Jewish Antiquities*, XII, 241). To refuse to remove the offending mark resulted in ostracism from the gymnasium, the public bath, and the athletic contests, in all of which males participated in the nude. In some instances, to practice circumcision could lead to punitive taxation, loss of citizenship, or even death, as when Antiochus Epiphanes slaughtered those families who circumcised their children and hung the infants from their mother's necks (1 Macc. 1:60–61; cf. 2 Macc. 6:10). By the middle of the first century, circumcision had become the battle line at which Jews were preparing for a fight to the finish against extinction as a distinct people through cultural assimilation into Greco-Roman culture.

It should now be obvious that the view of circumcision in America today is completely "incommensurable" with the view of circumcision in first-century Judaism. What this means is that, unless we begin with a clear understanding of the dynamics at work in the biblical world, we will not get anywhere when trying to interpret the New Testament texts on circumcision. For us, circumcision is never even discussed as a religious issue, being relegated to the private realm of family preference. But for those on all sides of the circumcision debate in the first century, it was an intensely public issue, thought to be the very crux of Jewish survival in a hostile world. Indeed, for its defenders, circumcision divided the whole human race into two camps, one called "the uncircumcised" (Gentiles) by the other who styled themselves as "the circumcised" (Jews).[41]

Nothing that happened in the apostolic age was more crucial in determining the eventual nature and destiny of the Christian faith than its separation from Judaism. Precisely in those supposedly quaint texts on circumcision we are, if I may use a pun, on the "cutting edge" of that fateful issue! But once we discover this by applying the criterion of contextuality to the biblical world, how may we then interpret the relevant texts as the basis for our message today?

As in most explosive situations, two extreme groups within the early church contended for an either/or decision. On one side, a group of Judean Jewish Christians belonging to the party of the Pharisees insisted that circumcision was necessary for salvation (Acts 15:1, 5). After all, the practice was clearly commanded in the Law of Moses, was sanctioned by centuries of observance going back to the venerable Abraham (Gen. 17:1–17), had more recently had its claim on the conscience sealed by the blood of martyrs, and continued to be administered to Gentile proselytes who wished to convert fully to Judaism.

On the other side, a group of Hellenistic Jewish Christians represented by Stephen began with the same Abrahamic covenant of circumcision (Acts 7:8) but argued that it had failed to circumcise the heart and ears of the people. Such failure caused them to resist the Holy Spirit as proved by their brutal rejection both of their own prophets and of Jesus (7:51–53), thus rendering circumcision invalid. No wonder Stephen was accused of undermining "the law…and…the customs which Moses delivered to us" (6:13–14).

Caught between these extremes were three key leaders of the early church. Peter was sensitive to the rising tide of Jewish political passions that would soon erupt into a suicidal war with Rome. But he could not forget that the Holy Spirit had fallen on the Roman centurion Cornelius, thereby confirming his conversion, before any thought could be given to whether or not he should be circumcised (Acts 10:45—11:3, 17–18). James was sitting right on top of the powder keg in Jerusalem. Any sign of pro-Gentile sympathies could result in a riot (Acts 21:27–31), yet he knew that the church at Antioch was already flourishing (Acts 11:27–30) without ever having had any prerequisite of circumcision imposed upon its members (Acts 11:20–24). Paul had already encountered bitter opposition from Jews on his earliest missionary journey (Acts 13:45–50; 14:2–6, 19). Still, he knew that many Gentiles would never accept his message on the condition of circumcision. Their refusal came not, as we moderns suppose, because they might view it as a painful intrusion into their privacy, but because it would entangle them in a cultural and political agenda with which they wanted no part.

The earliest effort to address this impasse involved a compromise according to which Peter would lead a mission to Jews that included circumcision while Paul would lead a mission to the Gentiles that excluded circumcision (Gal. 2:7–9). This "two spheres" solution was valuable in clarifying that a Gentile did not have to become a Jew to become a Christian and, likewise, that a Jew did not have to become a Gentile to become a Christian.[42] As Paul would put it, "Was any one at the time of his call already circumcised? Let him not seek to remove the marks of circumcision. Was any one at the time of his call uncircumcised? Let him not seek circumcision" (1 Cor. 7:18), a position that nicely balances the "two age" tension of Christian existence. The great difficulty with this approach was that the church had no way to keep the two spheres separated in cosmopolitan cities such as Antioch. Thus in no time Jewish and Gentile Christians were enjoying table fellowship together there, which "the circumcision party" in Jerusalem could not accept (Acts 11:2–3), leading to a heated confrontation between Paul and Peter (Gal. 2:11–13), which effectively ended the "two spheres" strategy.

The circumcision problem was finally resolved, not by reaching some consensus in the early church, but by the catastrophic forces of history. Once the Jerusalem Conference reaffirmed the already prevailing practice of not requiring circumcision as essential to salvation (Acts 15:22–29), Jewish Christianity found itself on a collision course with its wider Jewish culture that could not be avoided. As Dom Gregory Dix put it, the refusal to make circumcision mandatory meant that "the Jewish-Christian Church chose to be rejected and to die that this 'Gospel' might continue, once it was sure that 'the Gospel preached among the Gentiles' was identical with 'the Gospel to the circumcision.' The end was swift. Jewish Christianity vanishes into obscurity with a startling suddenness in the sixties, and thereafter dies obscurely in the shadows."[43] With the disappearance of "the circumcision party," Gentile Christianity quickly gained the ascendancy, literal circumcision was abolished for all Christians (Eph. 2:15), and its meaning was spiritualized as something done to the heart rather than to the flesh (Rom. 2:28–29; Phil. 3:3; Col. 2:11).

What have we learned from this brief survey about the intentionality of the New Testament texts on circumcision? At least three conclusions are obvious:

1. they affirm that the gospel addresses persons in their own distinctive culture and seeks to honor the traditions of that culture insofar as possible.

2. nothing in one's culture may be allowed to compete with Christ as the sole and sufficient basis of salvation.
3. when cultures clash within the church over conflicting traditions, the claims of both contending parties must be subordinated to the supremacy of Christ regardless of the cost (Gal. 5:6; 6:15).

As we reflect on the relevance of these principles hammered out in the struggle over circumcision, the testimony of an observant Jew is best able to help us grasp their radical import, an importance most Christians have completely forgotten after two thousand years of living in a Gentile culture. Listen to Daniel Boyarin, a professor of Talmudic Culture, comment on the heart of what is at stake here:

> The true cultural issue dividing Christians from Jews by the second century was the significance of body filiation, membership in a kin-group, for religious life. As long as participation in the religious community is tied to those rites which are special, performed by and marked in the body, the religion remains an affair of a particular tribal group, "Israel in the flesh." The fraughtness of circumcision (almost obsession with it) of all of these people is not to be found in the difficulty of the rite to perform but in the way that it is the most complete sign of the connection of the Torah to the concrete body of Israel.[44]

Now we are clear from our biblical study that identity issues and political passions within Judaism thwarted its willingness to forsake ethnic and cultural distinctives so as to offer a universal expression of the faith to all peoples as called for by Jesus and Paul. Since circumcision had served as the supreme symbol of Jewish identity for centuries, it became the rallying cry for separatist practices that would have restricted the full acceptance and equality of Gentile Christians with Jewish Christians in the early church. This means that, as we begin the attempt to anchor our message in the modern world, we look first for those features of contemporary life that could threaten the universal offer of the gospel to outsiders who are perceived as the enemies of our ethnic purity or of our national way of life.

America, and even American religion, has long had a strong tradition of nativism with its frequently violent expressions of xenophobia, or deep hostility to anything foreign.[45] This separatist impulse has asserted itself particularly in response to major waves of immigration beginning in the 1880s, to fears of racial integration in the 1950s and 1960s that would "mongrelize" our dominant Anglo-Saxon stock, and to the threat of communism that prompted a half-century Cold War with the Soviet Union from the 1940s through the 1980s. To this day, a host of hate groups continue the tradition of fascist fear-mongering: some against African Americans, such as neo-Nazi white supremacy groups; others against political and economic elites, such as armed patriot militias; others against "internationalism," such as radical isolationists bitterly opposed to the United Nations, the Trilateral Commission, and the Council on Foreign Relations. The list seems to grow longer with each passing year, as a search of the Internet will quickly disclose.

Sad to say, religion has often been in the forefront of these strident efforts to sanctify sameness and demonize differences. Strange as it may seem in light of the long history of anti-Catholic animus in America, one of the most popular crusaders for nativism in the twentieth century was a Canadian-born Roman Catholic priest, Father Charles E. Coughlin.[46] Shrewdly using radio to rally the disaffected of the Depression Era, Coughlin first fulminated against Hoover and the WASP Eastern elites, then turned against Roosevelt and the New Deal "liberals." After shifting to a quasi-fascist attack on Jewish-Communist conspiracies reminiscent of Hitler, he was finally banished to enforced retirement during World War II when he could find no more scapegoats to blame. His Protestant counterpart, Gerald L.K. Smith,[47] was best known as an organizer of Louisiana Senator Huey Long's Share-Our-Wealth clubs. Smith was attracted to Long while serving as pastor of the King's Highway Christian Church (only a few blocks from the church I served in Shreveport!). After Long's assassination in 1935, Smith, like Coughlin, drifted into anti-Semitic, quasi-Nazi extremism and ended his ministry in obscurity.

In light of the strength of religious nativism, especially in the South, it is not surprising that organizational expressions of this impulse have often included a "churchly" component. This is especially apparent in the Ku Klux Klan with its Bible-thumping tirades against Catholics, Jews, and Blacks; its ritualistic use of "white" robes of purity; and its obscene use of fiery crosses as symbols of terror. After failing to halt the civil rights movement in the 1960s, the Klan lost credibility as nativism receded. A renewed emphasis on globalism as the twenty-first century dawned saw the advocacy of anti-alienism shift, not surprisingly, to groups with names such as "Christian Identity," "Aryan Nations Church," and "Phineas Priesthood." As the Catholic-Protestant struggles in Northern Ireland make heartbreakingly clear, religion can become a prime factor in defining "enemies" worthy of violent conquest rather than sensitive compassion in the name of God.[48]

I have cited some of the more extreme examples of religious nativism to show just how explosive it can become when combined with nationalistic zealotism, whether in the first or the twenty-first century. Lurking behind the overt fanaticism of this paranoid style of "theological politics" lies a mindset that can limit and even oppose the universal expression of the Christian gospel even when it does not resort to violence. At first, diversity is seen as merely "strange," but soon an excessive concern with differences causes it to be viewed as "alien," a competitor and threat to one's own familiar sense of identity. Under the influence of a charismatic leader, those who feel powerless to deal with this intrusive complexity develop a compelling sense of being chosen to protect their promised land from corruption by "outsiders."

Based on a sense of alienation, these radicals soon erect barricades to keep the wider world at bay, whether in the form of secret societies or loyalty oaths or third party politics or predictions of apocalyptic doom. We allow sameness to suppress otherness. We divide up the fullness of the divine creation into that which is superior and that which is inferior based on ethnicity or gender or nationality or class or ideology. We let a human or group of humans become foreign to us. Once we have done any of these, then our sense of sharing a truly universal faith with all the world is seriously compromised. Missionary activity may continue unabated; but, when infected with nativism, it carries condescending overtones of cultural imperialism that would link Christianity to the "American way of life." This does not mean that heartfelt patriotism today is somehow wrong any more than circumcision for Jews in the first century was inherently wrong. It does mean that patriotism must not become part of the "excess baggage" of the gospel to be required of those with other political loyalties or cultural orientations who would come to faith in Christ.

Now let me summarize what this case study has contributed thus far to our understanding of a hermeneutical methodology. In the ancient world, Judaism made circumcision the supreme symbol, not only of its religious identity, but of its political, cultural, and ethnic identity as well. For this reason, Jewish Christians faced enormous difficulties in separating their religious beliefs from the practice of circumcision in order to be able to offer the gospel without restriction to non-Jews. Today, circumcision remains a key issue for Jews in their struggle against assimilation,[49] but is no longer an issue in Christianity because of the church's separation from Judaism for almost two thousand years. In other words, the *context* in which we now consider the biblical texts on circumcision is completely different from the life-setting in which they were written, and it is crucial for the interpreter to recognize the full extent of those differences.

But this does not mean that the circumcision texts of the New Testament are no longer relevant today. We face contemporary pressures to tie our faith so tightly to one nation, one ethnic grouping, or one ideology that the sole sufficiency of Christ to save those of other nationalities, ethnic groups, and ideologies is thereby compromised. Indeed, one of the great unanswered questions of our day is whether "New Right" religion, which has gained such prominence since the late 1970s, will link God and country so closely together that Christianity in its American expression will be unable to function as a truly world faith.[50] The preacher will do well to follow these developments closely because the ways in which nativism complicates the universal expression of our faith today parallels, or is analogous to, the ways in which circumcision did the very same thing for Christians in the first century. In a word, the two historical contexts are in no way *identical,* but the challenges that they offer the gospel are in every way *comparable.*

Unlike the later case studies, I shall not conclude here with a specific sermon that I preached in this area, because we have not yet treated homiletics as we will do in chapters 5 and 6. Instead, let me talk more generally about how I approached this agenda when I served as pastor of the First Baptist Church in Shreveport, Louisiana, 1975–1987, which will help to prepare us for Part 2 on leadership.

Shreveport, with a metropolitan population of 350,000, had long been the leading city of the Ark-La-Tex area (meaning south Arkansas, north Louisiana, and east Texas). Its history since its founding in 1835 had often been marked by vigorous and even violent expressions of nativism instigated by such groups as the Know-Nothings, Knights of the White Camellia, Ku Klux Klan, John Birch Society, and White Citizen's Councils. Our congregation had long had ties to a planter subculture in which such influences were especially strong. During the years of my ministry there, Shreveport was a deeply religious town, often called "the buckle on the Bible Belt." It was also a passionately patriotic town whose largest employer, Barksdale Air Force Base, was the second most important Strategic Air Command center in the world. Week after week our citizens poured into a host of churches to worship in record numbers while B-29 bombers and KC-135 refueling tankers ceaselessly soared aloft to maintain the "balance of terror" by providing nuclear deterrence. This combustible mixture of traditional Southern evangelicalism and Cold War fervor offered veterans' organizations and local politicians abundant opportunities to champion the nativism that had been so recently exacerbated during the enormous upheavals of the civil rights movement.

Shortly after my arrival as pastor, I sought to counter the classic nativist agenda of anti-Catholic, anti-Jewish, and anti-Black by forming fast friendships with Monsignor Joseph Gremillion, a former parish priest returned to Shreveport after rendering distinguished service to his worldwide communion in the field of social justice; Rabbi Emeritus David Lefkowitz and Rabbi Richard Zionts of B'Nai Zion Temple in our neighborhood; and the Reverend David Matthews, pastor of Antioch Baptist Church, the most historic African American congregation in our city. These relationships resulted not only in collaboration on a number of community projects but in my speaking at their churches and synagogue and inviting them to our church for discussions of interfaith cooperation. The strategic move here was to counter nativism by showing our congregation how Baptists can be, not stereotypical critics, but best-of-friends with Catholics, Jews, and Blacks.

Attitudes in the area of international relations were more difficult to influence. Included in my support provisions as pastor was sufficient time away and travel funds to participate each summer in meetings of the Baptist World Alliance (BWA), which involved representatives from national conventions and unions in some 115 countries. Because of the congregation's investment in this activity, I made an annual report on the state of the Baptist world to our people. I also sprinkled my sermons with illustrations, gleaned from BWA meetings and publications, of the courage and sacrifice on the part of fellow believers laboring in hostile cultures or under oppressive political regimes. Once every five years our church sent a sizable delegation to the BWA World Congress, a large inspirational meeting often held overseas. This meeting provided attendees with abundant opportunities for personal fellowship with those of other cultures in breakout sessions, prayer groups, and home hospitality. The point here is that we regularly afforded our people a chance to meet and appreciate Christians from what were then politically "hot button" countries such as the U.S.S.R., China, and Cuba.

Let me provide one specific example of this strategy at work. At the height of the Cold War in the 1980s, with our President calling the Soviet Union an "evil empire," deep tensions in Russian Baptist life suddenly surfaced in this country. For years the communist rulers had required all religions to register with the government. In 1960 this policy led to a split between those Baptists willing to be legally recognized by the government and a dissident group that refused to register with a regime that it rejected as atheistic, choosing rather to function as an underground movement submissive in religious matters to God alone. In 1979, the most outspoken representative of these breakaway churches, Georgi Vins, was released from Siberian exile in a prisoner exchange for KGB spies and sent to America. Here he promptly began to accuse the "registered" Russian Baptist representatives of being KGB agents trying to seize control of the BWA. Soon the irascible Carl McIntyre jumped into the fray. Before long a delegation of Russian Baptists arrived at the Atlanta Airport to find a picket line of fundamentalist Christians protesting their "communist" affiliation.

As those who play cards might put it, what we had here was nativism in spades!

The susceptibility of Shreveport to such negative media attention led me to invite to our church Alexei Bichkov, General Secretary of the "registered" Baptist union, and Michael Zhidkov, best-known as pastor of the Moscow Baptist Church. Both men stayed in our home where we could extend Christian hospitality. Both spoke freely to our congregation in an open forum about the relation of their churches to the U.S.S.R. Ministry of Religion. Each "registered" leader took questions from the congregation and granted an interview with local reporters. Most importantly, both demonstrated in words of testimony and in the spirit of their lives that what we Americans shared in common with them through Christ was infinitely greater than the serious political differences that existed between our two countries.

At this point you might be protesting, "Why are you telling us all of this? I thought you were going to talk about how to prepare sermons." My response would be that these are exactly the kinds of things to work on when preparing to preach strategically. We shall develop this in Part 2 when discussing the components of organizational life. If we assume that the *purpose* of the church is to share a universal gospel, then a church that privileges its own nation or race or culture compromises this universal imperative. When that happens, then the *mission* of the sermon is to overcome such nativism so as to realize the *vision* of one worldwide fellowship of equals in Christ regardless of their earthly citizenship. As Part 2 will detail, this involves the shaping of a congregational ethos receptive to and supportive of this strategic imperative as it is given voice from the pulpit. In Shreveport, for example, the First Baptist motto was "The whole word for the whole world," expressed by a logo depicting an open Bible superimposed upon a globe. By utilizing this verbal and visual symbol of our identity on all of the church's printed matter and publicity materials, we were constantly reminding both our congregation and our wider community of the kind of "story" we were trying to write in the last quarter of the twentieth century.

The great advantage of this approach was that it enabled my individual sermons on this agenda to be undergirded by a pervasive emphasis throughout the church calculated to give the message what communication experts call "resonance." The Deacons and Missions Committee felt a sense of ownership by virtue of their promotion of BWA activities. The choir became "partners in proclamation" as they presented a choral version of "In Christ There Is No East or West." Even the children were involved as they carried "foreign" flags in the Parade of Nations on World Missions Sunday. To put it negatively, the pulpit itself, taken in isolation, was not expected to carry the whole weight of changing people's minds on one of the most explosive issues in American religious history. Instead, its sermons represented one climactic articulation of a comprehensive strategy designed to call the people of God from the constricting provincialisms of this old age to the worldwide witness and worship of the age to come (Mk. 11:17).

We began this case study by selecting a subject so "dated" to the first century that it is completely ignored in the twenty-first century despite its prominence in Scripture. We then utilized a hermeneutical method able to build a bridge from what the Bible *meant* in its own time to what it *means* in our time. As we reach the end of this exercise, I hope that it has helped you to see how to take the circumcision texts of the New Testament out of the pediatrician's office and back into the pulpit. By understanding their role in the biblical world, you can relate them to the universalism of exilic Isaiah, Ruth, and Jonah as they struggled to enlarge the paticularism of Ezekiel, Ezra, and Nehemiah. You can link them to the radical inclusivism of Jesus who welcomed "publicans and sinners," Samaritans, and Roman centurions in ways that scandalized the separatism of the scribes and Pharisees. You can feel them struggling with the fateful decision of Jewish Christians to risk political alienation by accepting uncircumcised Gentiles as full partners in the covenants of Israel.

Furthermore, with this biblical understanding firmly in place, you will be in a position to apply such texts to our modern world, where religion is often politicized to serve a limited national, ethnic, or cultural agenda. Once you grasp what these seemingly obscure texts meant in their original context, you will be able to develop a strategic initiative responsive to the challenges of your immediate context. Such an initiative will make the intentionality of these texts an integral part of the way your church understands its ongoing story, the "plot line" of its pilgrimage as the people of God in a particular time and place. After you have exercised the pastoral leadership needed to give these texts the kind of "social embodiment"[51] in your congregation that they sought in the New Testament church, then—and only then—will you be ready to move from hermeneutic to homiletic. How this may be done in terms of sermon preparation and presentation will be the subject of our next two chapters.

CHAPTER 5

A Homiletic of Strategic Preaching: Preparation

How can a pastor make preaching more strategic? This chapter will address that simple question as it seeks to supplement traditional homiletic approaches by suggesting ways that the pulpit motivates a congregation to fulfill its mission. Let us look now at how this may be done in sermon preparation, followed by a look in the next chapter at sermon presentation.

Planning a Year's Pulpit Work

A year is the most fundamental unit by which we number our days in an effort to give time itself a measure of regularity and recurrency. The annual revolution of the earth around the sun, involving two solstices and two equinoxes, further suggests that the year be divided into four seasons. In some churches, this cycle is viewed as a liturgical year beginning on the first Sunday of Advent, in others as an organizational year beginning when elected leaders take office, in yet others as a fiscal year beginning with the implementation of a new budget. Here, for the sake of convenience, I shall consider the calendar year as the basic framework in which to plan the work of the church and the ministry of its pulpit. This approach seeks to counter the all-too-common practice of planning sermons on a week-to-week basis.

When many churches project another year of work, they tend to limit this task to what they call "calendar planning." Members of the lay coordinating body and church staff gather, each with a list of dates of when they would like to schedule events in their area of responsibility. Often the meeting is dominated by efforts to limit competition and resolve conflicts, usually refereed by a somewhat beleaguered pastor. Once all of the dates have found a resting place somewhere on the church calendar as the result of necessary compromises, the group is then ready to adjourn, satisfied that everything possible has been done to accommodate the wishes of everyone within the necessary constraints of time and space. The problem, of course, is that a set of dates penciled in on a projected calendar does not add up to a coherent strategy and thus cannot serve as the basis for strategic preaching.

My suggestion is to place the kind of calendaring task just described at the end rather than at the beginning of the effort to plan another year in the life of the church. Start instead by seeking to design the year as an extension of the church's story. Pay close attention to the strategic imperatives that surface as a result of the planning process that will be described in Part 2 of this book. Encourage the group to discuss its best understanding of what the whole congregation would most like to accomplish in the year being planned. Ask how these aspirations are linked to successes and failures in recent years. Consider whether any proposals might need to be deferred so as to avoid trying to make too many changes within a limited time frame. In other words, give the year being planned a sense of movement toward defined goals rather than treating it as a self-contained unit that is not going anywhere. Capture at least a part of the church's vision by writing down two or three ways in which the planning group would like for the year under review to *make a difference* in the lives of the members and how what is done will contribute to the strategic objectives on which the church has agreed.

With these core insights in focus, seek consensus on a few key initiatives, usually no more than one a quarter, that will facilitate these hopes. For example, do changing demographics point to a certain age group needing special attention? Does a stagnant leadership pool need to be freshened by training events designed to identify and enhance the spiritual gifts of emerging pacesetters? Is the wider community in transition, prompting the need for innovative outreach or social ministries to newer residents? In answering questions such as these, the intentionality of the congregation will need to be balanced by the contextuality of its many constituencies. Agree first on a handful of "breakthrough" projects that deserve the highest priority during the year under review, discuss the optimum sequence in which they might be attempted, and try to anticipate when each would fit best into the rhythms of the congregational year.

Only then, after conceptualizing how to create a distinctive year that does not merely mark time by repeating the patterns of the past, will the group be ready to start putting dates on blank calendar pages. Begin by listing the greatest events of the Christian year, the two most central being

Christmas preceded by Advent and Easter preceded by Lent and Holy Week. Some will wish to add such major celebrations as Epiphany, Pentecost, and All Saints' Day. Then enter those highlights of the civil calendar sure to influence the congregation, especially the Sundays nearest New Year's Day, Memorial Day, Independence Day, and Thanksgiving Day. While Mother's Day and Father's Day may be said to come from the commercial calendar, these observances do frame a suitable context in which to emphasize the Christian home. Once these more public emphases whose timing has already been predetermined are in place, decide next where to locate activities specific to your congregation. These will include (1) major initiatives that will highlight the congregational year, (2) recurring events such as stewardship promotion and mission projects, (3) program emphases brought by representatives of Sunday school, women's ministry, youth ministry, etc., and (4) emphases from denominational and ecumenical calendars that the church has chosen to support.

The point in collecting all of these dates is to recognize that your members live in many temporal frameworks of meaning: the Christian year, the American year, the denominational/ecumenical year, and the congregational year, in addition to their own family and personal year defined by such dates as birthdays, anniversaries, and school holidays. From the pulpit you have no way to give even passing attention to more than a small percentage of possible emphases from these several sources. For example, *The Book of Common Prayer* of the Episcopal Church lists 152 entries in its Calendar of the Church Year, with seventy-five Major Holy Days to be observed annually.[1] Americans seem to have a boundless appetite for public holidays, with at least thirteen currently being observed nationally, many of them on Mondays to the detriment of Sunday attendance. Each year I receive a denominational calendar with approved national and state emphases printed in red that cover every week, indeed almost every day, of the year! Add to all of this the desired meetings relating to the congregational agenda, and soon the poor church calendar is hopelessly clogged with dates!

Clearly a great deal of selectivity must be exercised, or each new congregational year will be shaped by "calendar overkill."[2] Strange as it may seem, some churches seem so addicted to what I suppose is the Protestant work ethic that they try to cram the calendar with one activity after another, as if "more is better," until no time is left either for sufficient preparation or for adequate follow-up of the few really important initiatives that deserve highest priority. No sooner is one project completed than the congregation must race on to the next one because there it is on the calendar where it was placed many months earlier in an effort to fill in all of the blanks. Preaching to implement that kind of calendar makes the pastor little more than a circus barker announcing the next attraction on the church midway. The preacher has no opportunity to provide biblical and theological underpinnings for the sometimes risky but essential strategic moves that the congregation needs to be making. Soon the leader becomes immobilized, like Gulliver, by a swarm of Lilliputian duties![3]

To be sure, the church office needs to maintain a careful record that lists every meeting of every group (and whether child care will be provided!) if only for the benefit of those who unlock the doors and turn on the lights. But do not confuse a comprehensive activities calendar with planning the congregational year. To gain perspective on the shape of this new year, try to express in a single paragraph what you hope will have happened to the church once the year has been lived. If someone in the group has artistic talent, ask that person to sketch the year as the next leg of the church's journey, providing visual symbols of key turns in the road that the congregation is being asked to take. Or attempt to graph an EKG of the church's heartbeat during the year, tracing both those emotional high points of climactic engagement as well as those quieter fallowing times when the people renew themselves for their next great thrust. In your imagination, seek to dramatize or choreograph the year rather than viewing it as an endless succession of clutter on a calendar. In whatever way works for you, make every effort to *see* this new year steadily and see it whole.[4]

By now the impatient reader may be protesting this extended attention to the church's calendar. After all, except for those in a liturgical tradition, what does any of this have to do with sermon preparation? I know many churches in which the construction of the church calendar is viewed as nothing more than a clerical process. I would argue, on the contrary, that the work just described provides the single most important point of departure for planning a year's pulpit work. Indeed, strategic preaching may be understood as an impassioned effort to help the congregational year happen as planned, to call its deepest dreams into being, to transform time itself into what is truly *anno Domini*, a year of our Lord.

When pulpit work is based squarely on the congregational year as conceptualized above, then its attention to the historic Christian festivals renews our remembrance of those unique events—such as incarnation, atonement, and resurrection—that nourish that new life in Christ that the church exists to express. Mindfulness of the key celebrations of the civil calendar, so easily corrupted by excessive commercialism, gives voice to the deeper aspects of those commonalities that bind all of our citizens together in what Lincoln called "the mystic chords of memory."[5] The focus of the church calendar on those carefully chosen congregational initiatives that attempt breakthroughs to a higher level of commitment and maturity puts the pulpit in strategic alignment with a host of laypersons working to the same ends through the various organizations and programs of the church.

Without the guidance provided by a coherent and challenging congregational year, the pulpit is in danger of flying blind. The sermon may be based on a striking idea that the pastor has found in someone else's sermon addressed to a quite different situation. Or the sermon may be sparked by a problem shared in a counseling session and so have immediate appeal only to the one who voiced that need. Or a book that impressed the pastor, which no one else in the congregation has read, may prompt it! But if the lure of a new year is so vivid that the pastor can *see* it every time sermon preparation begins—with the result that the message seeks to point the way, wrestle with the problems, and provide the motivation for courageous action—then pulpit and pew are, as they say, singing from the same page. Synergy begins to work, and clergy and laity alike truly become a priesthood of believers. So ask yourself: Where do my sermons really come from? The contention here is that the most effective sermons come from a concerted effort to guide the congregation in achieving its God-given destiny one year at a time.

Now for the practicalities of this approach. Here I shall assume only one sermon responsibility per week on Sunday morning, even though many ministers preach twice a week if there is a regular Sunday evening service, or even three times a week if there is also a midweek worship hour. But even preparing to preach some forty-eight sermons per year cannot be planned effectively at one time, hence I would break the year into four seasons, as does nature. The units that I have found most effective extend from New Year's to Easter, from Easter to Memorial Day, from Memorial Day to Labor Day, and from Labor Day to Christmas. For most church members, especially families with children in school, these divisions correspond roughly to winter, spring, summer, and fall. For the minister, they break up the planning for a year's Sunday morning preaching into four clusters of about a dozen sermons each.

Like most pastors, I vacationed primarily in the summer, and thus used this most extended absence to reflect on my pulpit work of the past twelve months. By this time of year, usually in late July or early August, our church would have completed a design of the next congregational year so that it could be used during the early fall for leadership recruitment by the nominating committee and budget preparation by the finance committee. Thus the priorities incorporated in this plan were uppermost in my thinking as I plotted my preaching trajectory for the next twelve months. Within this wider context, my immediate task in midsummer was to decide on specific sermons for Labor Day through Christmas, which included at least a title, text, Scripture reading(s), strategy statement, and worship suggestions regarding music, lay participation, and special features such as baptism, communion, or parent-child dedication. I would then repeat this projection in November for the Sundays from New Year's to Easter, in February for Easter to Memorial Day, and in April for Memorial Day to Labor Day.

This seasonal approach to sermon preparation offers several advantages, three of which may be mentioned here. First, it encourages variety in the use of the Bible. The fall naturally lends itself to Old Testament preaching in preparation for Advent. From Christmas to Easter is the obvious time to preach on the life and teachings of Jesus from one or more of the gospels. Likewise, Easter to Pentecost reminds us of Acts and the letters when the early church began to grow in the power of its risen Lord. Summer is often refreshed by devotional preaching from the Psalms and more personal sections of Scripture. Some creative spirits have even sought to describe a seasonal spirituality correlated with this use of the Bible,[6] notably the contrast developed by Karl Rahner between a wintry and a summery sort of spirituality.[7] Distinctions such as these tend to influence the tone and mood of preaching more than its content.

Second, as I planned individual sermons on a quarterly basis, I would set up a file folder on each sermon, preprinted to enter not only the title, text, scripture, and strategy statement but also the way in which the sermon was classified by its purpose, the sources utilized in its preparation, and any places where it might be delivered again. These sermon folders were always at my fingertips in hanging files that filled one drawer of my study desk. Every time that I got an idea or read something pertinent to an upcoming sermon, I would jot it down and drop it in the file. By the time that each Monday morning came and I pulled out the appropriate file to start work on next Sunday's sermon, I faced, not the dreaded blank sheet of paper or empty computer screen, but a number of leads with which to begin.

To be sure, it takes additional effort to plan sermon strategies two or three months in advance, but the momentum already underway in the preacher's mind when final preparation begins more than recoups the time spent in advance planning. Just as marinated crab claws are a favorite Louisiana appetizer, I allowed sermon ideas to "marinate" for several weeks in my mind and heart rather than depending on last minute "microwaving" to produce tasty pulpit fare. To change the metaphor, pastors who do not even begin to conceptualize a sermon until the week when it is due will often be forced to resort to a forceps delivery on Saturday evening if their pulpit offspring is to be alive and kicking on Sunday morning!

Third, I would write up my projections for the next quarter's preaching in outline form and circulate them to ministerial staff and key lay leaders a month in advance of the beginning date. This not only provided an opportunity for reaction and dialogue, which was immensely beneficial to me, but it also had a number of practical consequences. It gave the minister of music time to search for appropriate musical resources and, when necessary, to order new choral works for the choir to rehearse. It gave the minister to children time to prepare a kit for youngsters attending the worship service, which was also helpful to the one presenting the children's sermon. It gave the editor of the weekly church newsletter time to prepare articles on worship emphases, particularly when a series was about to begin. Our church stressed lay participation in each service, and this approach gave us time to recruit the best persons whose contribution would reinforce what the sermon was seeking to accomplish. None of this long-range preparation is possible if the pastor's sermon is not known until only a few days before Sunday. But advance planning permits the sort of collaboration that makes lay and staff leaders feel that they are partners with the pastor in proclamation.

Soliciting Congregational Input

In a sense, the sermon planning process just described is primarily "top-down"; that is, it is shaped partly by ecumenical, denominational, and public leaders responsible for scheduling major events throughout each year and partly by local church leaders with heavy responsibilities for guiding congregational activities. For this reason, I suggest that you work to balance such influences with "bottom-up" input from those to whom the sermons will be delivered. Unfortunately, many hearers have been made to feel detached from the act of proclamation as if responsibility for sermon preparation is something that only a pastor is uniquely qualified to discharge by virtue of divine calling and advanced theological training. The New Testament provides a powerful corrective to this view by picturing the entire church as a prophetic community (Acts 2:17–18). To lay a foundation for effective strategic preaching, I think it important to emphasize from the outset of one's ministry that pastor and people alike are to view the work of the pulpit as a shared partnership. Let me illustrate one of the ways in which I did this by quoting here a few paragraphs from a pastor's column I wrote for our church newsletter in Shreveport:

> Such a partnership in preaching represents a sharp contrast to the prevailing silence on this subject in many churches today. My observation is that most ministers never take their congregation "behind the scenes," as it were, to explain why they preach as they do, much as a physician feels no need to explain to the patient why a certain medicine is prescribed. But the sermon is not like a pill to

be swallowed in blind faith! The priesthood of the believer means that every person is competent to discover God's Word for himself or herself and to apply it to his or her own life. At Pentecost, the Spirit fell on "*all* flesh" so that, not just preachers, but "your sons and your daughters shall prophesy" (Acts 2:17). That means that my sermons not only speak *to* you but also *for* you and, in a profound sense, *from* you as we share those concerns and insights to which the Spirit gives utterance.

My basic premise, therefore, is that preaching is not monologue but *dialogue*. It arises out of, and returns to, the believing congregation that it serves. It is not that you have all the questions for which I have sermons with all the answers. Rather, we *both* have needs for which we together search for guidance from God's Word. To be sure, I am the one called and trained to voice the message from the pulpit on Sunday morning, but that sermon, far from being a soliloquy to which you have contributed nothing, should be the fruition of whatever God has said to *all* of us as you have witnessed to me, and I to you, in our common life together during the week. That is why the only true preaching is pastoral preaching, because it alone is shaped by its rootage in the life of its hearers, and it alone is uttered by one who takes full responsibility for implementing what has been said.

If preaching is to be truly biblical—that is, if it is to be "*of* the people, *by* the people, and *for* the people"—at least two things must happen. First, I must take you into my confidence, sharing with you just how I approach the preaching task, exposing the agenda which I try to address, admitting what I judge to be my successes and my failures, and explaining how all of this relates to where our church is going. Second, you, in turn, must take me into your confidence, indicating both the problems which you face and the insights which you have found, the points at which my preaching has been a help to you and the points at which something has been lacking, and the ways in which you want my sermons to relate to where your life is going.

I realize that this partnership approach to preaching is based on a definition of shared responsibility that could be intimidating to both pulpit and pew. At one extreme, preachers have used the valid concept of "the sanctity of the pulpit" as an excuse to preach on whatever they please, without any accountability to the congregation, rejecting lay input as meddling in an area where the preacher is answerable only to God. At the other extreme, laypersons have retreated into passivity by insisting that they have no competence even to comment on anything as sacred as a sermon. But both extremes are equally distorted! Beloved, *we are in the preaching task together!* I do not have the right to preach in a vacuum any more than you have right to listen in a vacuum. We each have the obligation to share our concerns with the other because, as Paul put it, "If *all* prophesy, and an unbeliever or an outsider enters, he is convicted by *all*, he is called to account by *all*" (1 Cor. 14:24 [emphasis mine]).[8]

Once the people begin to sense and accept their shared responsibility for what happens in the pulpit, it is possible to get them involved in the sermon even before it is delivered. Just how that might be done needs further exploration here since it is now in the forefront of homiletical discussion. In chapter 1, we saw that a relational understanding of preaching reemerged in the second half of the twentieth century. This approach places equal stress on the listener as a participant in the preaching event. This has resulted in a fresh emphasis on preaching as "conversation" by such homileticians as John S. McClure, Lucy Atkinson Rose, and Leonora Tubbs Tisdale.[9]

Since McClure is one of the most persuasive exponents of this position and since he has presented the most detailed plan for involving laity in sermon preparation, let me now enlarge on my earlier critique in chapter 1 of his approach by comparing it with the one proposed here. In *The Roundtable Pulpit,* McClure advocates "collaborative preaching [as] a method that involves members of a congregation in sermon brainstorming. Preaching becomes a 'rhetoric of listening' through which the biblical interpretations and theological insights of the congregation find a voice in the pulpit."[10] This collaborative homiletic calls for consultative rather than hierarchical leadership, relational authenticity in the life of dialogue, participatory persuasion by interaction, and inductive understanding of the Word as an emergent communal reality. With these processes at work, preaching can become "a focal point for congregational self-leadership and mission."[11]

McClure's plan for collaborative brainstorming involves the enlisting of a sermon "roundtable" to meet for one and one-half hours each week for three or four months. Each such group of no more than ten participants is carefully chosen to achieve a deliberate diversity of age, background, and religious commitment, including active members, marginal members, and nonmembers. The agenda consists of free and open discussion that engages both the biblical text for next Sunday's sermon as well as the participants' own diverse understandings of the issues raised by the text, its relevance for today, and how it might be applied to the life of the church and its members.

The pastor then prepares a sermon that seeks to "describe and imitate" this core conversation of the roundtable "so that all may hear the variety of ways in which the congregation is coming to terms with the gospel of Jesus Christ. Collaborative preachers bring into the pulpit the actual 'talk' through which the community articulates its identity and mission."[12]

Our first response must be one of appreciation for a serious attempt to form a partnership between pulpit and pew that reflects both profound theological reflection and a careful methodology for achieving its aim. The reader of McClure's book will quickly discern that its theoretical underpinnings resonate deeply with some presuppositions of the present study. I have often found it helpful to utilize sermon dialogue sessions to secure both feedback on completed preaching and "feedforward" on future preaching. Therefore, in a very sincere sense I can applaud McClure's methodology even while asking whether it goes far enough. While agreeing that his approach may be helpful to follow occasionally, I would question whether this is the best way to achieve collaborative preaching on a continuing basis.

McClure's starting point for roundtable conversation is the biblical text for next Sunday's sermon, probably because his preaching follows the lectionary, which provides each sermon with a predetermined Scripture text. I would agree that it is extremely important to help the people find their voice—or their many diverse voices—for expressing the gospel that they discern in Scripture, but would suggest that continuous participation in a Bible study class is the best setting for such an effort. In what some churches call Sunday school, a small group engages a chosen passage on a weekly basis under the tutelage of a trained layperson who is free from the often intimidating expertise of an ordained professional. The pastor should listen intently to the "web of conversations" in these many classes and try to coalesce them into a corporate "voice" that joins with his own voice in proclaiming the gospel. I found it very helpful to meet regularly with Sunday school teachers both to solicit their input as to the character of these ongoing conversations in their classes and to suggest some of the ways in which these conversations about Scripture-in-life can supplement what is being said from the pulpit.

In terms of strategic preaching, however, the pastor needs to listen, not only to the ongoing struggle of the congregation to understand the meaning of its Scripture, but also to the yearnings of the people for spiritual growth and how they want their church to assist in that regard. In Part 2 of this book I describe a process for using every constituency in the congregation to formulate a strategy that enjoys the widest possible consensus. The achievement of a shared vision is increasingly difficult both because of growing diversity in American life and because heretofore marginalized groups are more aggressively seeking empowerment than ever before. McClure is especially sensitive to both of these dynamics, and his homiletical strategies are most helpful in identifying and honoring these differences. But his approach does not seem to be aimed at uniting that diverse flock around a shared sense of mission and moving it forward to fulfill a strategic vision.

Somewhat as a balance to the emphasis of McClure, I would suggest a twofold understanding of preaching as a congregational partnership. From the side of the pulpit it means that the pastor takes so seriously what the people want to see happen on their Christian journey that this vision is translated into a passionate proclamation calling them forward toward its realization. From the side of the pew it means that the people take so seriously what the pastor preaches that they undergird it by developing strategies to implement its claims through their own intentional efforts. When sermons and strategies come together in this fashion, it is a beautiful partnership to behold.

Shaping the Strategic Sermon

A typical treatise on homiletics will devote the majority of its content to a discussion of sermon design. What I wish to add here are comments in three areas that seek to give greater strategic effectiveness to pastoral proclamation.

1. *The strategy statement.* I was taught, in the Broadus tradition, that every sermon should have, not only a title for publicity purposes, but also a subject, one central theme that gives unity and focus to all that is said.[13] Furthermore, that subject should be expanded by the addition of a predicate into a "proposition" summarizing the substance of what the sermon intends to say about its chosen theme. My teacher, J. B. Weatherspoon, took Broadus yet another step by distinguishing between proposition and "objective," the latter having "to do with the desired ends of the sermon in the character and conduct of the hearers."[14] As a result of this training, I have never felt ready to preach until I could state three things in simple, succinct, and specific terms: what I wanted to talk about, the main point I wanted to make, and what I wanted my hearers to do in response. Few things focus the preacher's mind like the exercise of writing out a subject, proposition, and objective for every sermon preached.

I wish to take Weatherspoon's "objective" to the next level by suggesting that the sermon be shaped on the basis of a clear, concise, and coherent statement of strategy. Here I am not unduly concerned either about its length, such as "twenty-five words or less," or its form, whether stated in a single sentence with several subordinate clauses or in a few short sentences each with a single assertion. Rather, I am concerned that, at the key point when study and reflection are finished and the actual work of construction begins, the preacher be able to identify the strategic agenda that the sermon intends to address. The four key components of that agenda may be determined in response to the following questions:

- Where are we now in terms of the situation that this sermon seeks to influence? In candor rather than criticism, with honesty rather than hostility, what is a realistic assessment of the needs that this message is being designed to meet?
- Where do we want God's people to go in the foreseeable future in response to the appeal of this message? What realistic vision of new possibilities is needed to encourage the confidence that this goal is attainable?
- What stands in the way of moving forward to realize the hopes awakened by this sermon? Where is resistance or opposition most likely to surface? Do attitudes need changing? Do priorities need reordering? Do social pressures need combating?
- What must be done to overcome those forces that would seek to thwart the claims made by this sermon? What resources of the gospel may Christians utilize in achieving the purpose that it seeks to fulfill?

Here I would offer three suggestions about working with a strategy statement for your sermons. First, as you think through the four components just listed, I hope you will realize that the primary purpose of crafting a strategy statement is to contextualize the sermon. Searching for answers to these four sets of questions helps to root the sermon deeply in the soil where the church is planted, delivering it from being a homily on pious generalities that are easy to affirm and then forget. When I preach a sermon that lacks a clear strategy, which is often the case when supplying someone else's pulpit, I seldom execute well because I really don't know where the sermon is trying to go. Having a strategy gives the sermon a game plan, which adds urgency and what I might call nuance to the act of proclamation.

Second, avoid plotting "grand strategy" for any one sermon as if it would vanquish every foe in a single battle. Better to be modest in designing a more limited offensive, not because the gospel lacks transforming power, but because human nature requires a great deal of guidance, incentive, and motivation to change. Usually my strategic objectives for one sermon are but a small part of what I hope to accomplish by preaching several sermons over several weeks or even months. That is why much of my pastoral preaching has been grouped in serial form, not necessarily in the classic sense of being united by a single topic or section of Scripture, but in the sense of being consciously clustered together as parts of a single strategy. Stated as a formula: meaningful congregational momentum is almost always the result of incremental preaching, hence a successful strategy is more often the result of many sermons rather than of a few.

Third, of all the steps involved in sermon preparation, the strategic statement is the part that I most need to talk over with others to get it right. To be sure, it is always helpful to discuss exegetical findings and rhetorical moves with fellow pulpit practitioners who are hard at work on the same task week by week. But the emerging sermon strategy needs the benefit of thoughtful response by those who will join me in advocating its implementation in the days ahead. I did not schedule regular meetings for this purpose but rather utilized my numerous contacts with lay and staff leaders throughout the week to ask these kinds of questions: Will this work? Is the timing right? Are the troops ready to engage this foe? Have I overlooked threats that could blindside us along the way? Have we assembled sufficient resources to see this venture through to the end? Laypersons are of limited value in helping with the more technical aspects of sermon preparation, but they are invaluable in helping to craft a realistic sermon strategy.

2. *The internal structure.* Once the preacher has a clear sense of what the sermon is trying to accomplish, then it is time to ask how its structure may be put in the service of strategy. Remember from our discussion of hermeneutics that there are two tensions that all strategic preaching seeks to resolve:

a. the tension between where we are in the world and where the gospel wants to take us in Christ
b. the tension between what it *meant* to embody that claim in the biblical world and what it *means* to embody it in the modern world

Let us look at a few of the ways in which these dialectics shape what is commonly called the sermon outline.

When the key need is to apply the truth of some strange biblical teaching that could easily be misunderstood, you may wish to begin with the biblical message and show how it made sense in its own world, after that moving into our world to find meaningful parallels, concluding with the kind of contemporary response that preserves the original biblical intention. Take for example the case study of circumcision in chapter 4 that we used to illustrate the hermeneutical process at work. In preaching on this subject you could first show how Paul passionately opposed circumcision in Galatians 5, then explain how this practice had come to function as the badge of Jewish identity in the years leading up to the war with Rome.

After clarifying Paul's intention to free his worldwide mission from the partisanship that would exclude or marginalize Gentiles, you could then search for the types of nationalism, nativism, and tribalism that restrict mission outreach today, ending with suggestions as to how the church may offer a salvation purged of any ethnic or cultural prerequisites. The structure of such a sermon might look like this:

I. The Crisis of Circumcision in the Early Church
  1. Paul's attack on circumcision in Galatians 5:1–12
  2. The role of circumcision in Jewish separatism
II. Hindrances to a Universal Gospel Today
  1. Cultural barriers in contemporary Christianity
  2. Proclaiming salvation for all in Christ alone

In that example, I began with the biblical situation simply because circumcision is not understood as a religious issue in American Christianity today. At other times you may need to begin in the past because some present issue is too controversial to receive a fair hearing. I well remember when many Deep South congregations in the 1950s and 1960s would not confront the evils of racial segregation realistically because they felt that outside forces beyond their control threatened their whole way of life. This became a good time to talk about the ancient Samaritans, contrasting the revolutionary attitude of Jesus (Jn. 4:1–42) with the prevailing Jewish hostilities of his day. That historical analogy could prepare the way to talk about contemporary Christian attitudes toward despised minorities in the ghettos of America. The structure here inverts the sequence in each section as compared with the previous example:

I. The Early Christian Breakthrough in Samaria
  1. The bitter history of Jewish-Samaritan hostilities (Lk. 9:51–56)
  2. The transformation wrought by Jesus (Acts 8:14–17)
II. The Gospel for Modern "Samaritans" in our Midst
  1. Patterns of ancient prejudice in our world today
  2. Learning to witness across barriers of cultural apartheid (Acts 1:8)

Not only may we reverse the order in which we treat text and context both in the ancient world and today, but we may also reverse the temporal sequence by treating the modern scene first and then the biblical scene. In this age of media saturation, some events so dominate the news that they occupy everyone's mind. For example, on the Sunday after the Berlin Wall fell in November 1989, I preached a sermon that first traced the ugly history of that barrier following its erection in 1961, then described the irresistible yearning for freedom that finally breached its defenses without a shot being fired. After asking the congregation to live behind the Iron Curtain during the first half of the sermon, I then turned to repressive structures in the first century that erected walls of hostility, showing how Jesus broke down all such barriers by his ministry of "peace" (Eph. 2:14).[15] Note how this approach rearranged the sermon structure:

I. The Wall Came Tumbling Down
  1. The Berlin Wall: an epitaph (1961–89)
  2. The triumph of freedom over bondage in the Cold War
II. The New Joshua as Wall-Breaker
  1. The wall-weary world of ancient Judaism
  2. Jesus as the reconciler of enemies then and now

3. *The introduction and conclusion.* Few things are more important to any public address than a good beginning and a good ending. Here let me first caution against two common approaches that almost always fail to be strategic. One is to introduce the sermon with some current issue or event designed to arrest the hearer's attention, then devote the body of the message to a biblical homily that never really addresses this modern agenda. In other words, do not "use" the modern world merely for illustrative purposes, as if you are borrowing from it but not really engaged responsibly in addressing it. The other dubious approach is to reverse the procedure and begin with a biblical theme, devoting the body of the sermon to its textual or topical treatment, then using the conclusion to "apply" your findings to modern life. The problem here is that such a move comes too late in the sermon for the hearers to work out a meaningful relationship between the several biblical truths that they have just heard and the many complex issues that they face today.

Instead of trying to tack the needs of the world onto either end of the sermon in ways that do not really engage the biblical text or the contemporary hearers, I offer two interrelated proposals, one for the introduction and the other for the conclusion, designed to give the sermon greater strategic thrust. To use terms central to our discussion, I suggest that you emphasize contextuality in the introduction and intentionality in the conclusion. Now let me hint at why and how this might be done.

From the very outset, give your hearers the sense that this sermon is going to take them to that boundary where two worlds, with their different ways of living, are in conflict, either because the status quo is being attacked by the gospel or because the gospel is being counterattacked by the status quo. In concise, concrete fashion indicate how those present will be called upon to choose between the options they face. Even though the sermon has not yet clarified either the issues to be decided or the consequences of the choice to be made, the congregation needs to realize that *something significant is at stake* in what they are about to hear. The situation the introduction poses may be drawn from ancient or modern life depending on how the sermon is about to unfold. In any case it should be described in such a way that those present will say to themselves, "This preacher knows what it is like to live in the real world!" Such an impression is better given at the outset when the approach can be inductive rather than deductive, when questions can be raised rather than answers provided, when dilemmas can be acknowledged rather than conclusions drawn.

Once a sermon nears its end, it is time to talk about intentionality and tell the people where the gospel wants them to go. Avoid giving away the plot prematurely in the introduction, but be sure that you reach its denouement by the time that you come to the conclusion. Many preachers save their most impressive rhetorical flourishes for the final moments by recounting a vivid illustration, quoting a snatch of beautiful poetry, or citing a purple passage from some pulpit celebrity. But this is a time to speak very directly in your own voice clarifying the options, appealing for a verdict, asking for a response. Do not merely recapitulate the main points of the sermon, for there is no movement in such a summation. Instead of leaving the people with a great idea or a great feeling, leave them with a great resolve: the courage to move beyond the status quo, the commitment to embody the claims of the gospel in the life of the believing community, and the confidence that God will be faithful to his promises as they venture forth in faith.

From the outset I have defined strategic preaching as helping to get the hearers from Point A to Point B on the pilgrimage of faith without being waylaid by hostile forces along the way. What I am proposing here is to put Point A in the introduction, a sense of how things are where we live when overtaken by the gospel, which is our contextuality in this world. Then, after declaring the transforming power of the gospel in the body of the sermon, put Point B in the conclusion, a sense of that horizon toward which we press when impelled by the gospel, which is our intentionality that yearns for a new world to come. When movement, however modest, has taken place to guide the people from Point A to Point B, then strategic preaching has fulfilled the assignment for which it was designed.

APPENDIX TO CHAPTER
Preaching and the Lectionary

Up until now it has not been necessary to consider the role of the lectionary in preaching. Our discussion of planning a year's pulpit work in this chapter forces us to face the issue simply because the lectionary is one of the most widely used systems for determining one's annual pulpit fare. Here my purpose is not to summarize the pros and cons of lectionary preaching, since comprehensive critiques of its strengths and weaknesses abound.[16] Rather, I wish to focus more narrowly on whether the lectionary is useful for the kind of strategic preaching being developed in this book. I realize that some of my readers have never used the lectionary and have no intention of doing so, while others are deeply committed to its use by personal preference or ecclesiastical directive. Let me plead with those on both sides of the question to step back for a moment and look at the lectionary in terms of its strategic potential.

Since some readers will know very little about this subject, I begin with a bit of background. A "lection" is a reading or lesson, hence a "lectionary" is a selection of biblical texts arranged for use in public worship over a prescribed period of time. Throughout the history of the church, many efforts have been made to construct an orderly cycle of Scripture passages on which a homily could be based, particularly in liturgical services structured by the Christian year.[17] Following the Reformation, the use of a lectionary in preaching became required in Roman Catholicism, recommended in Mainline Protestantism, and largely rejected in Free Church Evangelicalism. The great diversity both in lectionary patterns and in denominational practices tended to limit the prominence of its use in the American pulpit.

All of this began to change with Vatican II. Based on the Constitution on the Sacred Liturgy (1963), the lectionary was thoroughly revised and an Order of Readings at Mass (*Ordo Lectionum Missae*) was decreed to begin on November 30, 1969. This three-year Roman *Ordo* was soon adapted for use by most Mainline Protestant groups in the U.S. To achieve greater standardization, a Consultation on Common Texts was established which produced a Common Lectionary in 1983 and a Revised Common Lectionary (RCL) in 1992 that has now been widely adopted with only limited variations by English-speaking communions around the world.[18] With greater uniformity of pattern and practice across denominations in Mainline Protestantism has come an increased interest in lectionary preaching on the part of some Free Church Evangelicals who spurned it in the past. Growing sales of lectionary materials would suggest that its use in the pulpit may now be at an all-time high.

Let us note the main structural features of the widely accepted Revised Common Lectionary. The plan covers three years, designated as Years A, B, and C, beginning with the First Sunday of Advent. Each year is distinguished by a synoptic gospel: Matthew (A), Mark (B), or Luke (C), with John being distributed over the triennial cycle especially during the period from Advent to Easter. In accordance with the liturgical calendar, each year is divided into a Christmas Cycle from Advent to Epiphany followed by Ordinary Time, and an Easter Cycle from Lent to Pentecost followed by Ordinary Time. Usually the readings are topical or thematic (*lectio selecta*) during the festival times from Advent to Epiphany and Lent to Pentecost, and continuous or sequential (*lectio continua*) during the Ordinary Time after Epiphany and Pentecost. Each week has three stipulated readings, one each from the Old Testament, New Testament (besides the gospels), and gospel, plus a selection from the Psalms as a response by the people to the Old Testament lesson. The sermon may treat any one of these four passages, or it may deal with the relationships between them, such as the dialectic of promise and fulfillment linking the Old Testament and gospel lessons.

What is the potential of this plan for strategic preaching? In facing that question, the contribution of this venerable approach to worship is not at issue. Obviously any scheme for preaching the Bible with breadth and balance is of enormous value, and the lectionary has more than proved its usefulness in that regard. To adapt an old saying, some of my best friends would not preach any other way, and I have been helpfully instructed by their testimonies to its many benefits. However, the issue here is whether lectionary preaching offers the most effective way to fulfill a pastor's leadership responsibilities in the pulpit. After trying to hybridize "strategic preaching" and "lectionary preaching" in a number of seminars and workshops, as well as in my own pulpit ministry, I have concluded that the two approaches are not easily harmonized and therefore confront the preacher with a choice. Let me explain why I have found that to be the case in order to help you decide which approach is more fruitful for your own ministry.

In the extensive literature on this debate, about a dozen reasons are advanced in support of lectionary preaching, which boil down to three main claims. The first is that the lectionary itself has been carefully constructed through a lengthy process of revision by biblical and liturgical experts, resulting in a complex arrangement that pastors would have neither the time nor the competence to develop. In accepting this pulpit regimen, the minister is delivered from having to decide what to preach each week; indeed, one's pulpit agenda is mapped out for a lifetime, permitting publishers to issue handy guides full of sermon helps for every Sunday in the three-year cycle. As one advocate put it, "The lectionary gives me a sense of stability and continuity because now I know exactly what I'm supposed to do!" Stated negatively, this approach "can help protect the congregation from the whims and prejudices of the pastor," can force preachers to "deal with texts they had rather ignore," and can be "an antidote to that homiletical arrogance that says, 'I know what my people need.'"[19]

Response: As I hope the first section of this chapter demonstrated, I am deeply committed to intentional planning in the preaching task. The issue here is whether that planning should be done primarily by pastor and people in the context of the congregational setting or by academic and liturgical specialists who may know a great deal about the church in general but little or nothing about *my* church in particular. In regards to a ready-made agenda, I do not want pastors freed from the responsibility of deciding what to preach week by week because it is precisely in their unending *search* for the most relevant biblical texts that they learn to relate Scripture to the urgencies of parish life. Regarding those pastoral "idiosyncrasies" that the defenders of the lectionary so often deplore,[20] all I will say here is that the kind of pastors who wish to vent their "whims and prejudices" or their "homiletical arrogance" on the congregation will find ways to do so even when using a set of prescribed texts printed in a book imposed on them. I do agree that "subjectivity" can become a problem in the pulpit, although I have not found this problem to be any greater among pastors than it is among the scholars who scold them. My contention here is that the temptation to indulge in excessive subjectivity is better restrained by the challenge of providing creative leadership to an intentional congregation than it is by accepting the discipline of preaching as directed by lectionary experts.

A second claim is that the lectionary offers scriptural comprehensiveness that seeks to be as broad and balanced as the canon itself. Nor can it be doubted that to read four passages in each service, two from the Old Testament and two from the New Testament, gives the people a chance to hear more Scripture than is typical of most topical or life-situation preaching. Although the entire Bible cannot be covered even in a three-year cycle, which would require the reading of some two hundred verses in each Sunday service,[21] lectionary selections do attempt a christocentric summary of the scriptural metanarrative, which is reinforced by observance of the liturgical calendar. At a minimum, the lectionary seeks to exalt the primacy of Scripture in worship, while some would go so far as to hope that it will provide a basic framework for biblical understanding to those who faithfully follow the plan year after year.

Response: This second claim is essentially hermeneutical; that is, it insists that regular use of the lectionary results in a better appreciation of the Bible by the church than results from other types of preaching. Even so-called "textual" or "expository" sermons are thought to be opinionated because the subjectivity of the preacher comes into play when favorite passages are picked for treatment. But the lectionary has hermeneutical problems of its own.[22] Clearly it creates a canon-within-the-canon that relegates to obscurity and neglect some eighty percent of the Bible not included in its Sunday selections. By devoting the same amount of coverage to the New Testament as it does to the Old Testament when the Psalm selection is included, even though the Old Testament comprises 74 percent of Scripture and the New Testament only 26 percent, the lectionary makes it particularly difficult to give the Hebrew Scriptures the attention that they deserve.[23] One of the most common hermeneutical problems even for scholarly commentators on the lectionary is to discern the congruity of the Old Testament lesson with the two New Testament lessons to which it is attached. Even though advocates extol the rich "diversity" that the lectionary encourages, its primary interest often seems to lie in choosing those readings that reflect an obvious unity and to neglect those readings that do not seem to fit.[24]

The issue goes deeper than criticisms of this sort, which revision committees can continually work to correct. The key question is: How does the pastor help a congregation grasp the overall structure of the Bible and a wholistic sense of its meaning? Lectionary advocates seem to assume that this is primarily a task of the sermon, hence an orderly sequence of prescribed homilies is obviously superior to what they fear would otherwise become a "random" miscellany of "subjectively" inspired messages. But I would argue that this assumption puts far too much responsibility on the sermon, which, after all, is delivered in an ever shorter time frame, without benefit of dialogue, to worshipers whose mobility makes their attendance erratic at best. Gaining a comprehensive grasp of Scripture is better understood as a function of the teaching rather than the preaching ministry of the church. It requires an awareness of the historical, literary, and theological framework of the Bible, which is not well conveyed by pulpit exhortations designed to provide inspiration, motivation, and application based directly on a brief portion of God's Word.

What the New Testament calls being "devoted…to the apostles' teaching" (Acts 2:42) may be accomplished in many ways. The pastor may lead such a teaching ministry on Sunday evenings or at a midweek service. Special workshops may be covered in a weekend retreat setting or in study courses launched at church and completed in the home with the help of computer-assisted or audio/videocassette instruction. Regardless of the format, the learning environment needs to include the use of outlines, maps, and graphics, plenty of time for questions and discussion, plus well-chosen readings from the splendid secondary literature in this area that should be made readily available in the church library. Most importantly, the church needs to offer small-group Bible study on a weekly basis taught by mature laypersons who are guided not only by carefully planned curricular aids but by regular input from the pastor or other ministerial staff. In making these suggestions, my contention is that the "scriptural comprehensiveness" that we all desire for our congregations is best attained in a participatory setting of teaching and dialogue[25] that corporate worship is not best suited to provide.

To explore this issue adequately would require a closer look at the basic New Testament distinction between *kerygma* and *didache* since my suggestion is that searching the Scriptures to discern their interrelationships is better done in a didactic than in a liturgical context. If anything, I am pleading for a *more* comprehensive understanding of the Bible than I think lectionary preaching can provide. I do so well aware that this will call for major attention to the teaching office of the church and, in many cases, for a fundamental redefinition of the minister's role as "pastor-teacher" (Eph. 4:11d).[26] As an overall understanding of the Bible is mediated to the congregation through careful catechesis, each sermon is then freed to find its own unique expression within that spacious framework and to be more sharply focused than is possible when conforming to the artificial pattern of four prescribed passages.

The third claim for the lectionary, particularly now that it has received "common" expression, is based on its ecumenical character. Historically, it represents a growing consensus hammered out during more than a thousand years of ecclesiastical usage. Its widespread acceptance today makes it one of the most significant achievements of interchurch cooperation. Standardization permits groups of ministers and musicians to discuss how they will approach future worship assignments. As Americans move about with ever-increasing frequency, they experience less disruption when changing congregations if churches in all parts of the country follow a uniform worship pattern. Some enthusiasts have even dreamed of the day when a community-wide conversation would be generated each week because all of its churches sounded the same note at the same time from the pulpit.

Response: While we may applaud the "communal ecclesiology" which is the "singular strength" of the lectionary,[27] the New Testament demands that we balance the universality of the church with its particularity. The salutations of the Pauline letters emphasize that believers everywhere are "in Christ," but that these same believers are also *somewhere,* such as "in Corinth." As the letters to the seven churches in Revelation 2—3 dramatically illustrate, each church lives in a different setting and so needs to hear a different message. Each "letter" was sent to all seven churches, but none of the letters was interchangeable with the others. To state the matter in theological fashion, the unity of the church is eschatological, but the diversity of the church is historical. That is why we make a doctrinal distinction between the universal church and the local church. What this means in categories central to this book is that while every church shares a common intentionality defined by the gospel, each church also has a unique contextuality that must not be obscured lest the incarnational principle by which the Word becomes truly indigenous is thereby compromised.

As regards the lectionary, the key question here is whether its very uniformity encourages each preacher to exercise enough flexibility to engage with maximum effectiveness the specific challenges of the local situation. I am particularly interested in the way that Leonora Tubbs Tisdale has addressed this issue for two reasons. First, I was shaped by a denominational tradition that has long been indifferent to the lectionary, whereas she speaks not only out of a tradition that has long been in the forefront of supporting the lectionary but as a teacher of preaching in a seminary of that denomination. Second, her concept of "preaching as local theology" has as many affinities with my concept of "strategic preaching" as anything I have been able to find in current homiletical literature. Even though she claims to be one of the lectionary's "many fans," her reservations are damaging indeed:

> One of the values that may have been lost or devalued in the move from a preacher-designed lectionary to an ecumenically designed lectionary is a serious consideration of the local congregation itself in the process of text selection. Lectionary preaching, as valuable as it is, also needs to be tempered by congregational concerns in the text selection process. Indeed, slavish adherence to any preset preaching program—lectionary or otherwise—militates against genuine contextuality. The preacher who "hides behind" a text (lectionary or other) in order to avoid engagement with a crucial congregational concern is no more virtuous than the preacher who hides behind pet "topics" in order to avoid confrontation with troublesome biblical texts.[28]

The three advantages of carefulness, comprehensiveness, and consensus claimed for the lectionary obviously have persuaded many to adopt this approach to preaching despite the serious questions that may be raised about each of them. However, over against these potential contributions we must also consider at least an equal number of limitations before reaching a verdict regarding its suitability for strategic preaching.

The first is the control that the lectionary schedule exercises over the timing of proclamation. Even its most avid supporters concede that the recommended lesson may not be appropriate when great crises intrude upon our weekly routines, such as the assassinations of John F. Kennedy and Martin Luther King Jr., the Oklahoma City bombing, the Columbine shooting rampage, the 9/11 terrorist attack, or the New Orleans hurricane devastation. But what about the preaching needed to undergird the more predictable emphases of the congregational year? Take, for example, the need for stewardship development in a materialistic culture that increasingly competes for the church dollar with relentless advertising. The Bible is full of pertinent passages on the proper use of money, but they seldom if ever show up in the lectionary on those Sundays when the congregation is attempting to underwrite its annual budget. Some would opt to ignore the financial campaign in the pulpit and frame the issue as that of choosing faithfulness to Scripture by preaching on the prescribed passages rather than using the sermon for "promotional purposes" to raise money. But if the preacher divorces Pledge Day from its biblical basis, will not the congregational practice of stewardship gradually lose its theological moorings and become just another option among many for charitable donations?

Even more important is the need to time very carefully the pulpit support of those major strategic initiatives that a church will likely attempt during "Ordinary Time" not dominated by the major Christian festivals. Sermons are needed to prepare the congregation for the proposed change, to guide them through difficult transitions, and to consolidate gains once they are won (much like the pattern of exodus, wilderness wanderings, and conquest that recurs throughout Scripture). Even if some of the lectionary readings happen to be relevant to this effort, they obviously have not been scheduled to fit a local timetable that may need to be adjusted as it unfolds, due to unanticipated resistance. In executing any strategy, timing is of the essence, a timing that can be determined only by those in the thick of the struggle, which is the very opposite of the way in which lectionary timing has been determined.

A second limitation is rooted in the restrictive use of Scripture imposed by the lectionary. The very nature of the plan seems to assume that a sermon always springs from Scripture. However, often the pastor is gripped by a great insight from some other source that clearly meets the need of the congregation. It may have originated in personal prayer or Bible study, in a curbstone conversation or a committee meeting, in reading a novel or watching a movie. But because it did not come from any of the lectionary readings of the week, it is in danger of being orphaned from the pulpit. The pastor may discover that the Scripture passage on which the idea is based has been scheduled for treatment two years hence, so is the sermon shelved until the suitable Sunday rolls around? My guess is that, if the idea is really relevant and urgent, the pastor will soon figure out a way to include it in a sermon based on a Scripture passage that does not really fit, all to accommodate the requirements of the lectionary.

A variant of this problem is created by the desire to do series preaching. Some passages in Scripture are so pivotal that it may take several weeks to mine their riches. Doing so consecutively has the advantage of creating cumulative impact while allowing the pastor to tackle some of the central sections in the Bible with greater depth than would be possible in a single sermon. As the abundant sermonic literature indicates, this is often done for such passages as the Ten Commandments, the Beatitudes, the Lord's Prayer, the parables of Jesus, the "I am" sayings in John, the "Seven Last Words" from the cross, and the letters to the seven churches of Revelation. Very valuable series are also possible on a wide variety of doctrinal topics and ethical issues. Having preached dozens of series over a ministerial lifetime, I find that they are some of the best remembered and most frequently requested of all my pulpit offerings. However, the lectionary just does not cooperate either in selection, sequence, or schedule with any of the best-known ways to do series preaching.[29]

We have touched here on only a few of the many ways that the lectionary inhibits creativity in the use of Scripture for preaching. The artificiality of basing every sermon on some sort of triangulation involving Old Testament, New Testament, and gospel not only limits topical and life-situation preaching, as is often noted, but also limits biographical preaching on biblical characters, preaching through whole books of the Bible,[30] and preaching on the great words of the Bible that constitute the vocabulary of faith. On and on the list might go, but, instead of easing these restrictions, the lectionary moves in the opposite direction by proposing that preaching be based on the same readings every three years, which, in a lengthy pastorate, could be a half-dozen times or more. By superimposing this pattern of cyclical repetition, the RCL strikes at the heart of pastoral continuity, which involves the matching of text and context in a particular time and place. This may explain why, when I look in the anthologies that collect some of our most creative sermons, few indeed seem to have been based on the lectionary.[31]

A third limitation of lectionary preaching is its restricted sense of purpose. By an exclusive focus on biblical passages as the controlling paradigm for preaching, this approach tends to stress the importance of scriptural understanding for the life of the Christian. The accent falls on coverage lest any salient points of the story be neglected, on remembrance lest a unique past be forgotten, on insight that enables the modern mind to grasp the meaning of ancient thought forms. On this model the preacher becomes, not so much the herald of a new day, as the faithful interpreter of the "Great Tradition." The center of gravity of the preaching event lies more in the past than in the future. The congregation is called upon to reaffirm a faith "once for all delivered to the saints" (Jude 3). The sacred nature of the liturgical calendar suggests that time itself has been forever changed. In a word, lectionary preaching tends to make the sermon more sacramental than eschatological.

Here its difference from strategic preaching becomes most apparent. Lectionary preaching begins with the Bible and its answers, while life-situation preaching begins with the people and their questions. But strategic preaching begins with the vision of a New Age in which "it does not yet appear what we shall be" (1 Jn. 3:2). It goes to the Bible for a clear definition of that horizon because Scripture shows us both how to succeed and how to fail in claiming the promises that are yet to be fulfilled. On this basis it calls the congregation to balance remembrance with expectancy, understanding with courage, insight with action, fidelity to the Word with freedom in the Spirit. To be sure, the preacher can try to emphasize the strategic dimension when dealing with lectionary texts, but my experience is that such efforts will be limited rather than enhanced by this system because the two approaches are based on different understandings of what is to happen in the preaching event.

CHAPTER 6

A Homiletic of Strategic Preaching: Presentation

Your sermon is ready to move from the pages of the Bible to the modern pulpit. The strategy the sermon hopes to implement is clear. Still, the sermon's strategic effectiveness faces a major threat—a pervasive mood of disconnection. This mood of disconnection has three dimensions:

a. The feeling that the life of the church is disconnected from the life of the world, that the "sacred" and the "secular" spheres are not in honest dialogue, that worship is more often an escape from contextuality than an encounter with it.

b. The feeling that what the church does on Monday through Saturday in its programs of ministry is disconnected from what it does on Sunday in its proclamation of the gospel.

c. The feeling that what happens in the first part of the worship service led primarily by the musician is disconnected from the second part led primarily by the minister, as if each part were prepared independently of the other without any effort to be mutually reinforcing.

The best way to combat these cleavages is to make worship a unified experience more integral to the life of the congregation in today's world. As this suggestion implies, three main participants are involved with the pastor in strategic preaching: the gathered congregation, the worship leaders, and the outside world. Let us focus on each of these groups in the temporal sequence of the proclamation process, looking in turn at what happens before, during, and after the act of worship. One helpful way to relate the three groups to these three stages of worship is to utilize the process categories of input, throughput, and output made popular by the "Quality

Movement."[1] On this model we look primarily to the congregation for input before the sermon is delivered, to the worship leaders for throughput when the sermon is delivered, and to the world about us as the recipient of output after the sermon is delivered.

The Congregation as a Source of Input

In the previous chapter I discussed the importance of getting suggestions from all parts of the congregation before deciding on what to preach. But it is also important to engage your hearers even more directly as the time approaches for delivering a specific sermon. Throughout this book I have stressed the importance of movement in making our preaching strategic. Nothing contributes more to a readiness to venture forth than a sense of anticipation. If, when worship begins, the congregation is politely passive but essentially uninvolved in what is about to happen, it will be difficult indeed to build a spirit of responsiveness before the hour is over. But if the people bring with them a sense of expectancy that is contagious, it is far more likely that the sermon will be catalytic of significant stirrings within their midst. One way to stimulate expectancy is to get the congregation thinking about the sermon even before it is delivered. Here let me offer three practical suggestions designed to increase a sense of congregational participation in the preaching event.

The first is to use what I call "Voice from the Pew." Once or twice a year, particularly in early summer before I did major sermon planning, we would add a perforated tear-off to our Sunday order of worship. This provided a half-dozen lines on which to offer suggestions for future preaching. I encouraged the people to frame their input in any way they desired. Would they like to hear a sermon on a particular biblical text? On a life need that they were facing? On a theological or ethical issue? This kind of input could be put on any slip of paper, scrawled on a visitor's card, or even put in a letter at any time of year; but periodic use of the tear-off with "Voice from the Pew" printed across the top helped to focus and encourage widespread response. I would often begin my annual sermon planning with hundreds of these slips sorted in piles before me.

To assure the people that I had taken their suggestions seriously, I often mentioned these responses when previewing a sermon or announcing an upcoming series in the weekly church newsletter. At other times I would introduce a sermon by mentioning how it sought to deal with an issue that someone present had suggested was worthy of pulpit treatment. In a few cases the "Voice from the Pew" submission was so strikingly expressed that I included it in the printed order of service so that everyone present might reflect upon it as time for the sermon approached. Over the years I found that use of this approach helped even those who had submitted nothing to feel that the congregation was directly involved in sermon planning, and this added to their sense of expectancy.

The second suggestion comes from my daughter, who, during the years of her active pastoral ministry, would put what might be called a homiletical appetizer in the weekly church newsletter to arouse interest in her Sunday pulpit fare. Instead of merely listing the sermon title and text, which attracts little attention unless the wording is clever or sensationalistic, Susan would raise questions to provoke response. For example, in announcing a sermon on "Adam and Eve: Getting Beyond Blame," she wrote:

> A garden. A tree. A snake. A woman takes a sumptuous bite out of the golden banana and shares a good thing with her mate. Next thing you know, she gets blamed, the snake gets shamed, and they all get kicked out of the garden. From the word go, the relationship between man and woman has been touchy (no pun intended). A few hundred thousand years later, we are still pretty sharp at the blame and the shame. But will we ever get back to the garden? Do we really want to? I'm willing to ask some heart to heart questions this Sunday, if you'll be willing to come and share the problem.[2]

Sometimes she would write at greater length, such as when she juxtaposed headline events from her mother's home town of Wedowee, Alabama, with those in her immediate ministry setting of Charleston, South Carolina, which was struggling at the time with a court-ordered admission of women to a local military college that historically had been all-male. Notice how her pulpit preview was calculated, not only to prompt comment, but to heighten anticipation even before she stood to preach a sermon entitled "On the Way from Wedowee":

> Wedowee, Alabama, is a two-stoplight fishing town of 800 people which splashed, surprisingly to all, into national media attention this summer. The white-skinned principal with a twenty-five year tenure at the Randolph County High School tried to prohibit interracial dating at the school prom and got himself in a bind when a senior student (born to a black mother and white father) asked, "And what kind of escort would you like for me to bring?" Unfortunately, he allegedly responded by telling her that *she* was a mistake. Two weeks ago, the high school was burned to the ground by arsonists, even as the Ku Klux Klan and outraged protesters gathered to clash in the heat of this schism.
>
> Across the street from the ruins of the Randolph County High School is the house that my grandmother built; the house I visited

each year as a child and where I ate from her table garden feasts of fried okra, creamed corn, black-eyed peas, and sesame pie. Next door is my great-uncle R. C.'s house, and down the row, my cousin Sylvia. Wedowee is where my mother hails from, and her mother and her mother and on back…so, in some psychic map, it is where I hail from, too. And now it is burning in two.

The Wedowee story in our local paper was run next to a picture of Shannon Faulkner as she might appear, Citadel-style, without hair. The juxtaposition made me wonder about the schisms that run deep in the silence of our lives until someone speaks up. It made me think of the prejudices that are passive but potent until they are detonated by a word. In this case, two high school students, two young women, in two southern states, question two citadels of power. Both are shamed for doing so. Both erupted tensions held passive by power, tensions that cut to the bottom of our beliefs. What is it that they have exposed? What is it we do to the one who speaks up? What can we learn on the way from Wedowee?[3]

My final suggestion is that we begin to make greater use of technology to solicit congregational participation. For example, if your church has a Web site, post your sermon topic for next Sunday at least by Monday morning. Include a few "teasers" indicating some of the issues and questions that you hope to address. Encourage the viewers to identify concerns that they hope such a sermon will answer and to name life needs that they would like for it to meet. Or you might choose a group of lay leaders, such as deacons or Sunday school teachers. At the first of the week, either e-mail or fax them a digest of your sermon strategy for the next Sunday. Invite them to help you identify exactly what target the sermon needs to hit and how the message can best reach its intended destination. Again, you might set up a chat room on the Internet composed of compatible ministerial colleagues with whom you share pulpit strategies and solicit their reaction as the process of sermon preparation unfolds.

Having used my daughter's ministry to illustrate the previous suggestion, let me use my son's ministry to illustrate this suggestion. Here is a pastor's column in his weekly church newsletter:

Preaching should be a conversation instead of a monologue. Now, I realize that on Sunday morning I am the one doing all of the talking. Hopefully a sermon flows from conversations that have already occurred and will lead into many conversations after the worship service. In that sense everyone is invited to join in the discussions.

We have begun a new way of having a sermon conversation. Using the modern technology of Internet communication, we are going to try to create sermon conversations that lead us into worship on Sunday and that come from the message on Sunday. On the home page of our Web site at www.fbchsv.org you will now see a reference to MOSAIC. Let me tell you what that is all about.

In the beauty of a mosaic, a picture is seen when many pieces fit together to create an image. About fourteen million pieces of tile form the grand mosaic on the front of First Baptist Church in Huntsville. The image of Jesus is 43 feet tall, but each tile is the size of a thumbnail. Every small piece fits together with others to form the picture of Jesus.

The witness of the church is like that mosaic. We all join the pieces of our lives and our faith together so that others may see Jesus. MOSAIC is an effort for that very thing to happen by using the power of new technology. We have created this Blog (a new word in our language that is short for Web log) to make a way for us to create an online mosaic so that others can see Jesus.

On Thursday, Friday, and Saturday of each week I will write about the message that I will be preaching the following Sunday. On Monday, Tuesday, and Wednesday of each week I will reflect on the message of the previous Sunday. You are invited to join in the conversation that leads up to a message and that flows from the message. Share the pieces of your faith, your ideas, your questions, and your suggestions by writing your own thoughts on the site. Comments will be screened (to make sure that no one is abusing this site) and then posted on MOSAIC. As many join in the conversation, the pieces of the MOSAIC will hopefully lead us to see Jesus.

Let the conversations begin![4]

The key point underlying such proposals is that we are living through a communications revolution in both print and electronic media that permits almost instantaneous input from a host of sources both within the congregation and beyond. This means that sermon preparation can become a highly interactive process if the minister is willing to plan far enough in advance to make it happen. In suggesting this, I am aware that, for many ministers, sermon preparation is almost secretive in nature so that no one, not even the minister of music, has the faintest idea what the pastor is going to say until the time comes to stand and speak.

My own experience challenges the wisdom of this approach. I have found that laypersons have a remarkably clear sense of the kind of sermons that they need to hear if only the preacher will listen. When I struggle with real questions that they are counting on me to address, it motivates my preparation far more than when I ransack the commentaries and clipping files for "canned" ideas and illustrations. Some of the textbooks on homiletics emphasize the value of congregational *feedback* after the sermon is delivered, but I have come to value even more congregational *feedforward* while the sermon is still in gestation. The more the people are enabled to contribute to the making of the sermon, the greater will be their anticipation and readiness to hear it proclaimed.

The Worship Leaders as Enablers of Throughput

Worship practices differ greatly between denominations and even within denominations, all the way from prescribed content and sequence in liturgical traditions to almost complete spontaneity in charismatic traditions. Because of this diversity, which, if anything, is increasing as some churches move into newer forms of contemporary worship, I shall discuss here the kind of services with which I am most familiar, inviting you to apply whatever may be appropriate to your particular setting. My key concern is with ways in which worship leaders may infuse the entire service with a strategic thrust.

In my tradition, the preacher and the musician plan worship, more often than not working somewhat independently of each other. Contrary to this practice, I feel that the closest possible collaboration between these two leaders is essential to an effective worship experience. The pastor needs to interpret the proposed sermon subject and strategy well in advance so that the minister of music may select congregational hymns and choral works supportive of that sermon.[5] Together they need to plan a structure and sequence for the service that will build sufficient momentum to set in motion those changes in attitude and action designed to move the congregation toward its intended destination. Only when these partners in worship leadership have a deeply shared sense of direction for the service will the participants grasp its central thrust.

Beyond this crucial collaboration, I would encourage teamwork in worship planning that involves other participating staff and lay leaders. For example, our worship services in Shreveport regularly included a children's sermon that could reinforce the thrust of the sermon with a simple illustration or object. Those who offer prayers or read Scripture lessons must also be clear about the central emphases of the service. Because of our theological commitment to the priesthood of believers, we involved at least one layperson to lead some important part of every service. Utilizing a different lay leader each week gave us an opportunity over the years to involve hundreds of our members in a "behind-the-scenes" understanding of our strategic moves. When worship leaders become aware that each service is seeking to accomplish some particular purpose, they will find ways to undergird that effort in their assigned areas of responsibility.

Once the worship event is conceptualized in this interactive fashion, the results are usually translated into a printed order of service made available to the congregation. The strategic value of such a guide is enhanced by carefully planned artwork on the cover,[6] which is even more feasible to produce now that desktop publishing has come to the church office. In Shreveport, we regularly headed the entire order, or each of its main parts, with a striking saying that captured our strategic thrust, thereby giving the people something to ponder before the service started or as the offertory ended. Some churches also provide with the order of worship an outline of the sermon, or a list of questions that the sermon seeks to address, or blank space to take notes on the sermon, or a series of suggestions about practical ways to implement the sermon in daily life. The point is to design the order as an invitation to interact with the worship leaders rather than as a prescriptive list of activities that the worship leaders will ask the congregation to perform as the service unfolds.

Many churches prepare the order of service late in the week because they assume that its use is only for the worshipers on Sunday. In Shreveport we found that the printed order could be used more effectively if preparation followed an earlier schedule. On Monday the primary worship leaders would critique the previous Sunday service as to timing, sequence, and feedback, asking especially how well it accomplished its intended purpose. By Tuesday we would circulate a draft of next Sunday's order of service for review by all of those with platform duties. By Wednesday, copy for the revised order was ready for printing so that the sanctuary choir would know at its rehearsal that evening what to expect on Sunday and the pastor would have the same information when completing sermon preparation on Thursday and Friday. By following this schedule, we were able to build anticipation for the Sunday service at our midweek prayer meeting on Wednesday evening. Giving those with leadership responsibilities for worship a clear idea of the service at midweek helped to foster closer collaboration as well as to build momentum for what would happen on Sunday.

Once the Lord's Day arrives and the service is about to begin, most worship leaders engage in a time of prayer, which, in our congregation, usually involved the platform party, the deacons who were to receive the offering, and the choir. Having visited hundreds of churches as a "supply preacher," I have witnessed great variety in how these pre-service prayers are framed. Without wishing at all to be critical of so sacred a moment, I find most such petitions are typically vague and unfocused—of the "lead, guide, and direct" variety—the only exception being intercession by name for any seriously ill or bereaved persons just mentioned in the group. Most worship leaders do not appear to know how to pray meaningfully for a service about to begin because they have no clear idea what the service is trying to accomplish. Remembering our discussion of the strategy statement in the previous chapter, I would urge that worship leaders not enter the sanctuary until all share the same hope for the service and pray specifically for their part in its fulfillment.

The World as the Recipient of Output

If the great unanswered question *during* the worship service is, "What is at stake here?" the great unanswered question *after* the worship service is, "Where do we go from here?" With this question we are back to the key factor of *movement* toward a goal, which has already been discussed as the hallmark of strategic preaching. How may preaching propel the people of God into the world of today as those who live out of God's tomorrow?

My first suggestion is that the sermon itself clearly delineate where the church is now (Point A), where the preacher is convinced that God wants it to go as the next step in its journey of faith (Point B), and the changes that will be required to negotiate that transition. Particularly in the closing exhortation of the sermon, or in a final word before the benediction, offer specific examples of the desired response: plan a family worship experience, attend an upcoming prayer retreat, join a Habitat for Humanity work crew, accept an unchurched prospect for personal cultivation, vote in an upcoming public election, teach English language skills to a class of recent immigrants…the list is obviously endless. Regardless of the response requested or received, everyone leaving the sanctuary ought to be clearly aware of the claim that the sermon has laid on their lives.

A second suggestion is that the sermon not be ignored or forgotten as soon as it is preached. Revise the message in light of initial feedback and make it available either in printed, audio, video, or electronic form, especially for those who were absent from the worship service when it was delivered. Follow up in a future pastor's column with further suggestions for implementing its thrust. Pray about responding to its claims at the next midweek prayer service. Sponsor occasional dialogue sessions to solicit wider congregational input, especially when the sermon raises difficult and debatable issues. Ask relevant church groups whether the sermon was of help in fulfilling their ministry responsibilities. Listen attentively to community voices to discern whether church members are making a difference in the world around them as a result of the sermons being preached. In other words, establish a continuous feedback loop to insure accountability for all of the strategic initiatives undertaken by the congregation, which certainly includes sermons from the pulpit!

My final suggestion seeks to underscore a comment in the previous chapter, which urged that the pastor not attempt or expect too much of a single sermon. Pastoral preaching usually works slowly and incrementally, more like a tiny stream that eventually splits a great rock than like a tornado that uproots the entire landscape in a moment. The minister may enjoy a few watershed moments in the pulpit, but they are likely to be few and far between. History books that compress a major revolution into a few paragraphs on one page sometimes create the illusion that change comes rapidly, but human nature is not so malleable. Momentum is better sustained by consistently applying firm but gentle pressure than by dropping a bombshell from the pulpit when it is least expected. Therefore, rather than trying to critique a single sermon in isolation, it is better to track the overall movement stimulated by several weeks or months of preaching, asking how a cluster of sermons contributed to the larger strategic initiatives underway at the time.

One other aspect to this cautionary word may be added here. Do not put undue weight on preaching as the only or even the best way to move the congregation forward into God's future. To be sure, the sermon is crucially *important* as a catalyst of change. If I did not believe that, this book would never have been written. But nothing is gained by glorifying the sermon as the *exclusive* route to the renewal of God's people and, through them, of his creation. Books on preaching offer a lot of inflated rhetoric about "the primacy of the pulpit," and some ministers have misused such rhetoric to claim all of the credit for "making things happen" because of their bold utterances behind the sacred desk. The pulpit may indeed be the prow of God's ship as in Melville's analogy, but many faithful laypersons are toiling at the oars down on the waterline to move the ship forward. When evaluating a sermon's strategic thrust, be quick to recognize that many unseen and unsung allies have contributed greatly to its total impact.

As we come to the end of Part 1 of this book, I hope that you have been stimulated to consider how to make the sermon, not an end in itself, but an instrument for building purposeful churches on mission for the gospel. In summary, strategic preaching is a matter of making the sermon something that is *done* and not just something that is *said*. It is a matter of preaching intentionally rather than impulsively, holistically rather than haphazardly, contextually rather than theoretically about God's great agenda for the church in the world.

APPENDIX TO CHAPTER

A Homiletical Case Study

Now that we have completed our treatment of homiletical matters, this may be a good point at which to provide an illustration of the kind of analysis undergirding strategic preaching along the lines discussed in chapters 5 and 6. I do so by considering a sermon I prepared as these chapters were being written.

At that time, the church in which I serve part-time as theologian in residence was considering a major building program, the centerpiece of which was greatly expanded facilities for weekday childhood education. Congregational opinion was divided over the wisdom of a large capital expenditure for programs involving many children whose families were not in the church membership. My duties included preaching one Sunday morning each month, which, that month, was the Sunday just before the church conference when these somewhat contentious issues would be decided. As this assignment approached, I first analyzed the situation by asking the four questions identified in chapter 5 as having to be addressed in shaping a strategy statement.[7] After talking and listening to a wide spectrum of opinion both within and beyond the church, I reached the following conclusions:

- The church facilities had not changed significantly in nearly forty years, during which time patterns of family life in the community had been profoundly altered, with many more working mothers and single-parent families causing a rapid increase in the need for developmental ministries to preschool children. Every elementary school in the community was expanding its facilities due to increased enrollments, but preschool programs in the church had not kept pace with this expansion, resulting in a long waiting list for available daycare and kindergarten openings in our programs.
- If sufficiently challenged, the congregation could contribute the financial resources necessary to double its facilities for preschool ministries. Handled skillfully, this outreach to additional children in the community offered one effective way to reach many more young adult families for a congregation whose existing leadership was "graying." The church needed to realize that enhanced ministries to children could become a prime source of its generational renewal.
- The capital funds needed to underwrite this venture without reducing gifts to the current operating budget were concentrated in senior adults who would personally benefit little if any through their children, or even their grandchildren, from the construction of new facilities. Facing the uncertainties of the retirement years, as well as a volatile economy

that was then heading toward a sharp recession, some of the old-timers who had built and paid for the present buildings were muttering that if the younger adults needed a bigger building they should wait until they were financially able to pay for it themselves. Meanwhile, a number of median adults with teen-age children felt that a higher priority should be given to strengthening current programs for their youth than to starting enlarged programs for small children.

- To reach a stronger consensus of support, all groups needed to realize afresh the incredible importance that Jesus attached to little children and the social revolution that this caused in the ancient world. To embrace his example would strengthen acceptance of the servant role by which the church lives, not for itself, but for a world full of the insecurities and vulnerabilities well symbolized by little children.

Based on this assessment of our context, I developed a sermon with the title "On Receiving Little Children" based on the text in Mark 9:33–37. Expressed in separate segments, a strategy statement for that sermon might read:

- The desire of many families in our community for their preschool children to receive developmental guidance in a Christian context is not being met.
- Our church has the opportunity to provide an enlarged and enhanced ministry to children by providing additional facilities and expanded programs.
- A united effort to do this will require a deeper commitment on the part of all age groups to serve the needs of children both within and outside our congregation.
- The resolve to meet this challenge will come from giving the same priority to children that Jesus taught his disciples to demonstrate as a sign of his presence in their midst.

As I began to organize the sermon, I wanted to build several bridges between the world of Jesus and our world to show the profound meaning of Jesus' revolutionary teaching on children for today. It was not necessary to dwell either on the growing needs of our community for preschool education or on the various congregational concerns that had been expressed regarding the proposal to meet those needs. These matters had already been addressed at length in a series of hearings and church conferences leading up to the final vote. Instead, I chose to stay very close to the biblical text to clarify the nature and relevance of Jesus' teaching for the decision that we faced. Note the close juxtaposition of "meant" as reflected in the number 1 entries of the outline and "means" as seen in the number 2 entries. The following outline provided the skeletal structure of the sermon:

I. The Human Drive for Top-Down Greatness
   1. The ambition of the disciples to be greatest (Mk. 9:33–34)
   2. Our insatiable desire for competitive success
II. The Divine Paradox of Bottom-Up Greatness
   1. The redefinition of greatness by Jesus (Mk. 9:35–36)
   2. Status based on love shared rather than on power conferred
III. The Claim of the Child on Discipleship
   1. The significance of "receiving" children (Mk. 9:37)
   2. Responding to the needs of children in our world today

In this particular instance, it was not necessary to stimulate interest in the sermon since it addressed an issue that had been on everyone's mind for months. Nor was it difficult to solicit congregational input since almost everyone had accepted the invitation to speak freely on all sides of the issue at a number of informal forums convened to include all of the age groups and constituencies with a stake in the outcome of our deliberations. If anything, the need was to enlarge the common ground on which a consensus could be built as we moved forward with whatever decision the church reached. Helpful in that regard was a series of neighborhood prayer meetings held in the homes of members to which church families living nearby were invited. Building on all of these efforts, it was not difficult to engage in a very focused time of prayer before entering the sanctuary to deliver the sermon that follows.[8]

SERMON: On Receiving Little Children

A great difficulty in grasping the deepest import of Jesus' message is caused by our unwillingness to let it shock us. What was once revolutionary has now become commonplace. A lifetime of familiarity has blunted the sharp edge of originality, and we find ourselves nodding assent to explosive truths that once shattered the religious status quo. Indeed, many assume that the purpose of his teaching was to offer comfort and assurance, therefore it simply could not be provocative or disturbing.

Today we consider a text that is doubly difficult to treat as controversial because it deals with little children. Surely nothing in the gospel story has been sentimentalized more than the way in which the gentle Jesus welcomed little ones into his arms and blessed them. So let me give fair warning: *prepare to be shocked by what you are about to hear!* Mark 9:33–37 records:

> They came to Capernaum and, once they were in the house, Jesus questioned them by asking, "What were you debating as we walked down the road?" They responded with total silence because they had been arguing with one another along the way about who among them was the greatest. Sitting down, he summoned the Twelve

and said to them: "If any one of you wants to be first, let him be
last—servant of all!" Then taking a little child into their midst and
enfolding it in his arms, he said to them: "Whoever welcomes such
a child in my name welcomes me, and whoever welcomes me welcomes not only me but the God who sent me." (author's translation)

I. The Human Drive for Greatness

As Jesus reached the turning point of his ministry in Galilee, he began
to excite the ambitions of his disciples by predicting that some of them
would soon see the kingdom of God coming with power (Mk. 9:1). Shortly
thereafter, three of the twelve were indeed permitted to glimpse that eagerly
awaited glory on the Mount of Transfiguration (Mk. 9:2–8). As they turned
toward Jerusalem, Jesus spoke repeatedly of rising from the dead (Mk. 8:31;
9:31, 10:34), which would surely confirm his messianic credentials. No
wonder that his closest followers began to consider seriously what their
status might be in such a time of triumph. We can easily imagine how each
might advance his claim to preferment: Peter for his leadership of the Twelve,
James and John for their place in the inner circle of confidants, Simon the
Zealot for his revolutionary fervor, Levi the tax collector for his influential
connections, Judas for his role as treasurer of the group's common purse.

Because the very question of who is greatest is inherently competitive,
it is little wonder that the disciples were too embarrassed to recount for
Jesus this jockeying for position behind his back, which had quickly
degenerated into petty bickering. By definition, the only way to identify
someone as "greatest" is through comparison with others who are excluded
from that singular status. When those in a group compete to decide who
among them is "the greatest," that very process inevitably produces a
hierarchical community with a top-down structure, the "greatest" reposing
at the pinnacle of the pyramid while others occupy subordinate positions
somewhere beneath them. Regardless of how greatness is determined, there
is no way for someone to become "greater" without everyone else becoming
"lesser." In the greatness game, if you're not at the top, you're nowhere!
There is only one winner but many losers.

Like the disciples of old, we seem to have an insatiable desire to
determine "the greatest" in every field. This is especially true in sport. Think
of the elaborate computer formula used in selecting bowl contenders to
compete for the collegiate championship, or the endless playoffs designed
to identify each year's best professional football, basketball, and baseball
teams. An almost frenzied interest focuses on such events as Superbowl
Sunday, the NCAA Final Four, and the World Series because this is where
"the greatest" will be crowned. Elaborate statistics are kept over many years

to determine, not only the greatest teams, but the greatest players and coaches as well. For example, Bear Bryant became one of "the greatest" because he lost only 20 percent of his games (85 of 425). But think of what that statistic means. Combined, the coaches who opposed Bryant failed to beat him 80 percent of the time (340 of 425), a sure formula for being fired. In praising the man with the houndstooth hat, we never consider how many careers he may have wrecked in the process of reaching the pinnacle of his profession.

Our arguments over greatness extend to every area of life, even to who might be "the twelve best preachers in America."[9] The debate seems to have intensified as we approach the end of a century and millennium. Our newsweeklies have enlisted panels of experts to determine "the greatest" in every conceivable category. *Time* magazine, for example, recently identified the 100 "most influential people of the 20th century"—leaders and revolutionaries, artists and entertainers, builders and titans, scientists and thinkers, heroes and icons—with a special issue devoted to each of these five groupings.[10] Not content with this audacious effort at selectivity, *Time* is now trying to build suspense as it decides on the single most influential person in the entire century. As if that were not enough, someone will surely sponsor a contest to pick the "Man/Woman of the Millennium" before this foolishness is over. Like the disciples of old, we should also be embarrassed to tell Jesus just how obsessed we are with the question of greatness.

II. The Divine Paradox of Greatness

The aching silence of the disciples in response to Jesus' question was mute testimony to their realization that arguing over greatness was in flagrant contradiction to the spirit of his teachings. Jesus had linked his own destiny to a cross and had called the disciples to the same kind of self-denial: to save life by losing it (Mk. 8:34–35). Now he repeated the paradox of becoming first by being "last of all and servant of all" (Mk. 9:35). Then, in an effort to overcome their continuing confusion (Mk. 9:32), Jesus added a simple object lesson by setting a little child in their midst. Before providing additional explanation, he acted out his message by taking the child into his arms and clasping it to his bosom. Everything he was about to teach them would be reinforced by that living picture before their very eyes.

In a perceptive interpretation of this passage,[11] Judith Gundry-Volf has pointed out that in the Greco-Roman world of Jesus' day, children were the least-valued members of society. Being considered not yet fully human, they had no legal rights; a father was entitled to punish, pawn, sell, expose, or even kill his own child. Baby girls were especially vulnerable to rejection because of their limited economic potential. Typically, only women cradled the young in their arms; men thought it beneath their dignity to show such attention to a mere child, as the disciples would soon demonstrate (Mk. 10:13). Remember how baby Jesus is always depicted in the arms of Mary, never in the arms of Joseph? By this parabolic action, Jesus was assuming a stereotypically female role to show his shocked disciples what it means to be "greatest." Imagine, the Messiah of God's glorious Kingdom more interested in showing love to a helpless little child than in passing out political rewards to his loyal but impatient followers. Surely, they thought to themselves, hugging kids is no way to rule a Kingdom!

Let us stare at this scene in shocked surprise until we begin to see what it is saying to us in wordless profundity. Here Jesus is modeling a counter-community to the one that the disciples were trying to construct in their debate over greatness. They wanted a hierarchical community controlled "from above" by whomever among them was "greatest." But Jesus wanted an egalitarian community characterized by solidarity "from below," based on a discipleship of equals, a community in which the kind of "grunt work" done by women in caring for little children constitutes true greatness. Here one attains status, not through power conferred, but through love shared. Can you begin to see it now? Jesus was turning the social hierarchy of his day upside down, creating "a new kind of community in which service of the least counts the most."[12] As I warned you, his "bottom-up" rather than "top-down" view of greatness is just as shocking in our day as it was in theirs.

III. The Demand on the Disciples

Based on this breathtaking object lesson, Jesus went on to shock his disciples even further by spelling out two truths implicit in what they had just seen. First, he taught that "whoever receives one such child in my name receives me" (v. 37a). That is, Jesus not only embraced little children as the object of his affection, but he bonded with them so deeply that their destiny became his destiny. The thrust is reminiscent of the parable of the last judgment (Mt. 25:31–46), in which Jesus identified so completely with the marginalized members of society—the hungry, the thirsty, the stranger, the naked, the sick, the imprisoned—that those who served "the *least* of these" oppressed and helpless folk were thereby serving the King of all eternity (v. 40)! To incredulous disciples he was saying here, "If you want to be close to the center of my power, then take a little child into your arms!" After all, it would not be long until he became as vulnerable as an abandoned child when they nailed him to a cross. If the disciples were too squeamish to embrace a nameless child, they would hardly relish embracing a crucified messiah!

Second, Jesus compounded the shock even further by teaching that "whoever receives me receives not me but [the one] who sent me" (v. 37b). Here the significance of servant leadership is lifted to its highest level in the breathtaking assertion that the mightiest power in the universe is not on the side of greatness but of weakness. "Look at me," Jesus said, still holding the little child in his arms, "*God is like that*! He is not playing the greatness game. You will not find him at the top of the power structure but at the bottom. He is not in the business of competing and winning but of loving and serving. If you want to find God, then wrap your arms around a little child!"

The Prologue of the gospel of John begins with the affirmation that, in Christ, God spoke a decisive word to his world (1:1). It ends by telling us what was disclosed through the earthly life of Jesus, namely, that God is the kind of Father whose Son is in his "bosom" (1:18). Is it possible that Jesus here enfolded a child in his arms, and linked that action to "receiving" God, because he remembered what it was like to be in the bosom of his heavenly Father from all eternity? In any case, we may infer from the vivid picture in John's Prologue that the early Christians soon adopted the revolutionary understanding of God that Jesus taught here, daring to picture the Sovereign of the universe in a maternal pose of filial embrace.

Today we have made great strides in lifting the status of children, especially in affluent communities such as Mountain Brook. Stringent laws protect against child abuse. Welfare services are available when there is danger of neglect. Labor laws protect against economic exploitation. Child care has become an increasingly professionalized and regulated industry for those who can afford it. Grateful for these advances, and for the crucial role that Christianity has played in transforming the attitude of society toward its most vulnerable members, we still have far to go before every child feels the warm embrace of Christ. Many parents still give top priority to the ceaseless quest for success in the workplace, denying their children the time and attention they sorely need. Many churches still consider their children's ministry as little more than a baby-sitting service staffed by hourly workers so that members will not be bothered. Many politicians still refuse to make children's needs a legislative priority, favoring instead those special interest groups that can reward them with contributions before the next election.

Beyond these regrettable trends lurks a creeping "child crisis" in America of dangerous proportions. Note these shocking statistics compiled by the Children's Defense Fund for the United States: Every nine seconds a child drops out of high school. Every twenty seconds a child is arrested. Every twenty-two seconds a child is born to an unmarried mother. Every thirty-five seconds a child is born into poverty. Every four minutes a child is arrested for drug abuse. Every eight minutes a child is arrested for a violent crime. Every five hours a child or youth under twenty commits suicide.[13]

As heartbreaking as this diagnosis is, we dare not forget the desperate plight of children beyond our nation's borders. In Pakistan, ten-year-olds bend over soccer balls stitching seams for ten hours a day, earning just pennies per hour for their backbreaking work. Outside New Delhi, twelve-year-old Indians make eighty-five cents a day breaking rocks in eleven-hour shifts. In northern Thailand, ten-year-old girls are sold by their fathers to Bangkok brothels for $400. A ten cent packet of salt, sugar, and potassium can prevent a child from dying of diarrhea, yet every day in the developing world more than forty thousand children under the age of five die of such preventable causes. When a World Summit for Children was held in 1990, leaders gathered to grapple with "the plight of 150 million children under the age of five suffering from malnutrition, 30 million living in the streets, 7 million driven from their homes by war and famine."[14] Where, we cry, are those who will throw the loving arms of Jesus around the neglected children of America, the orphaned children of Kosovo, the starving children of Rwanda?

IV. How Shall We Respond?

The account of this incident in Mark focuses on the radical demands of Jesus, while the parallel account in Matthew 18:1–5 emphasizes how we as disciples should respond. To "receive" children as Jesus did requires nothing less than a complete "about-face," literally a "conversion" on the part of his followers (v. 3a). This redirection of attitude means that we no longer seek "greatness" as the world understands it but that we ourselves "become as little children" (v. 3b, KJV). Otherwise, we will not only fail to find greatness but will be completely excluded from the coming "kingdom of heaven" (v. 3c). Again, imagine how shocking it must have been for disciples caught in the act of trying to grab places of glory behind Jesus' back to be told, not only that they would have to *receive* little children, but that they would have to *become* as little children!

This startling image was not intended to idealize childhood as a time of openness, innocence, receptivity, dependency, or spontaneity. Matthew is nearer the truth in pairing this saying with one on humility (18:4). What Jesus was teaching is that we will never fully understand and accept little children until we realize that there is a child within every one of us. That is, behind the adult facade of reputation, prosperity, and power lurks a hinterland of vulnerability, where we feel threatened, lonely, and insecure. Psychotherapists increasingly recognize that we often repress the wounds of childhood and carry them with us until we die.[15] Those who mentor would-be artists often find that the creative impulse is like a fragile inner child that must be protected from the ravages of premature criticism.[16] Only as we get in touch with our own childlikeness will we learn, not only how to care deeply for children, but also how to be compassionate toward the hidden weaknesses of others.

Our journey ends where it began: with a paradox. The gospel is forever telling us to grow up (1 Cor. 3:1–3; Heb. 5:11—6:2), to put away childish things and become adults (1 Cor. 13:11; Eph. 4:13-15). But it is also telling us to be born all over again (Jn. 1:13; 3:3, 5, 7) and become as little children (Mt. 18:3; Mk. 10:15). Somehow it is as important to become a child as it is to become an adult, but how can both be equally true? The answer lies in the teaching of Jesus here on children. When we try to "find" life in the quest for "greatness," we will "lose" it in the competitive struggle with others seeking to snatch the same prize. But when we are willing to love and serve "the least" by becoming "the least" ourselves, we gain everything because that is precisely where we find our Savior and our God.

So we grow into true maturity, not by climbing up the power pyramid toward "greatness" at its pinnacle, but by climbing down that pyramid toward "childlikeness" at its foundation. That is why power is best entrusted to those who do not need it for themselves—to enhance their ego, status, or reputation—but to those who will use it to meet the needs of others. Amazing, isn't it, that the crucial test of whether we have experienced the "conversion" that will open the door to the kingdom of heaven is determined by what we think and do about our children!

On next Wednesday evening, a church conference will be held at our midweek service for the purpose of considering a proposal to greatly enlarge and enhance our ministry to children. An affirmative vote on the recommendation from the Church Council and Deacons will imply your commitment to make a substantial investment in the lives of preschoolers who are just beginning to learn whether our congregation has a personal interest in their future. But why should you accept such a responsibility if no member of your immediate family will benefit personally from these new facilities and programs? Not just to insure the future growth of our church by reaching more young adults who live at such a hectic pace that one of their highest priorities is to find a household of faith eager to partner with them in the spiritual development of their children. To become that kind of church, we need more than your vote and your eventual pledge to a capital campaign. Our hope is that you will use this challenge as a way to wrap your arms of love around the children of our community and bless them in the spirit of the Savior who said, "Let them come to me." Most of all, we pray that you will identify so profoundly with the well-being of our children that you will put yourself in their place, become one with them in spirit, and thereby, as Jesus promised, "enter the kingdom of heaven" (Mt. 18:3).

PART II

LEADING

CHAPTER 7

The Pastor as a Strategic Leader

Most preaching seeks to answer one simple question. For some it is, "What are we *thinking*?" as if preaching informs a worldview and instructs the congregation on how to understand the most basic issues of life. For others it is, "What are we *feeling*?" as if preaching provides the inspiration and emotion needed to cope with the challenges of life. Yet another option addresses the question, "What are we *doing*?" as if preaching motivates its hearers to act upon their spiritual convictions in a variety of helpful ways.

All three of these emphases are obviously useful in a contributory sense, especially when combined in balanced fashion; but they do not penetrate to the core of the strategic issue. As we saw particularly when sketching the biblical and theological foundations of preaching in chapter 2, the underlying question should be, "Where are we *going*?" This views preaching as pointing a direction in which to move, thereby giving the congregation a strategic stance in relation to its setting. On this model the desired result is not just thought, mood, or deed, but rather movement toward an intended destination, the preacher serving as a visionary guide calling the pilgrim people of God from promise to fulfillment.

Once the pulpit is viewed as contributing a sense of momentum or spiritual thrust to all that a church does, then the leadership role of the pastor becomes both inescapable and indispensable. Without such leadership, preaching strategically would be like starting an automobile, putting it in gear, and then allowing it to move forward without a driver! In an effort to avoid this calamity, Part 2 will deal, not comprehensively with all aspects of the leadership task, but selectively with those functions that become essential once the kind of catalytic preaching envisioned in Part 1 sets the congregation in motion toward an intended goal. One central imperative of this book is that strategic preaching on Sunday *requires* strategic leading throughout the week. Warning: do not try one without the other, or you will fail at both!

Toward a New Leadership Paradigm

Leadership is such a vast and vague concept that one study turned up 130 definitions of the word itself.[1] Clarity is further complicated by a significant shift in the approach to leadership over the past generation, leading to differing attitudes and confused expectations regarding the practice of pastoral leadership on the part of clergy and laity alike. On the one hand, many younger clergy have developed a strongly negative bias against making church leadership central to the pastoral task.[2] On the other hand, many older laity *are* insisting on the importance of strong pastoral leadership as never before. Indeed, the clash between these two mindsets is fast becoming a prime source of conflict in contemporary congregational life. Why should this be so?

The primary reason for this clash of perspectives is that a paradigm shift has been taking place in our views of leadership since the mid-sixties and has continued to polarize opinion ever since. This tension is best understood against the historical backdrop of two contrasting emphases as seen, for example, in the elitism of Plato versus the egalitarianism of Aristotle, in the cunning of Machiavelli versus the selflessness of Lao-tzu, in the "Great Man" theory of Thomas Carlyle versus the perception of leaders as "history's slaves" by Leo Tolstoy, and in the militancy of W. E. B. DuBois versus the "truth force" (*satyagraha*) of Mohandas Gandhi.[3] This dialectic has expressed itself for clergy in the "pastoral director" model of H. Richard Niebuhr versus the "wounded healer" model of Henri Nouwen.

Let us look at how this paradigm shift has played out in parish ministry over the past half-century.[4] After World War II, with its many heroic military leaders, came a rapid expansion of religion, especially in the suburbs, which seemed to confirm the need for decisive pastoral leadership to manage the burgeoning institutional expression of faith. The dominant paradigm became a democratic adaptation of the hierarchical model that had served European Christendom since the emergence of the Constantinian Church.[5] The professionalization of the ministry created clergy executives who administered multiple programs designed to build a cohesive community of believers. H. Richard Niebuhr called them "pastoral directors" who shifted the focus of church architecture from the altar and the pulpit to the office suite.[6] Pastoral authority was derived not so much from preaching the Word or dispensing the sacraments as from satisfying the needs of the people.

But the turbulent sixties, especially between 1963 and 1968, saw a conscious revolt against all forms of hierarchical authority. Most notable in the public arena were the student protests against entrenched academic elitism, such as at Berkeley and Harvard; the civil rights protests against segregation, such as the 1963 March on Washington; and the feminist protests against political disenfranchisement, such as pushing an Equal Rights Amendment through the U.S. Congress in 1972 (after being bottled up in the House Judiciary Committee for 47 years!). Applied to church leadership, the new paradigm shifted the minister's role from that of "pastoral director" to that of "wounded healer."[7] Now the emphasis fell on inwardness rather than on institutionalism, on servant leadership rather than on professionalism, and, with the loss of Protestant hegemony, on counter-cultural life in exile as "resident aliens" rather than on presiding over the WASP (White Anglo-Saxon Protestant) cultural establishment.

Today, after a generation spent implementing a "bottom-up" egalitarian approach instead of a "top-down" elitist approach to leadership, the limitations of the new paradigm have become as obvious as those of the old paradigm that it replaced. With the more recent enabler model has come a gain in freedom and diversity, but with it a loss in the stability and cohesiveness provided by the earlier executive model.[8] The resurgence of fundamentalism in this same generation, after dormancy and near-death in the previous generation, offers powerful testimony to the importance that many people attach to authority, order, and security in their religious life. As one whose ministry has spanned the ascendancy of both paradigms, I well remember churches in the earlier years trying to find pastors who were not "bossy, domineering control-freaks" and churches in the later years trying to find pastors who were not "passive, laid-back, and nondirective."

The tragedy of 9/11, which launched the war on terrorism, has served to reinvigorate the command-and-control type of leadership best known in a military culture. In a significant sense, the presidential campaigns of 2000 and 2004 were a national referendum on the two paradigms that we have identified, Bush emphasizing leadership as initiating decisive, even aggressive, action; Gore and Kerry emphasizing leadership as the building of voluntary coalitions among diverse groups. The verdict of those contests was that America is evenly and deeply divided regarding its leadership preferences, so what is a pastor to do? Many enter the ministry early full of youthful idealism, or later full of disillusionment with the authoritarianism of the business world. This tilts them toward the enabler model of leadership favored in most seminaries. But then they go to serve churches full of lay leaders who want their pastor to take charge and "make things happen" in ways that clearly favor the executive model of leadership.[9]

In a political analysis that closely parallels this religious analysis, David Brooks pointed out that the late twentieth century was profoundly influenced by a boom psychology that made it "seem that harmony and perpetual progress toward a limitless future were the natural order."[10] But with the twenty-first century came the predators: greedy executives in companies such as Enron, pedophile priests in the Roman Catholic Church, terrorists in hijacked planes on 9/11. And so the culture began to shift its priorities from permissiveness to protection, from freedom to authority, from the dispersal of power to the consolidation of power. And with this shift came a new leadership paradigm: "The age of harmony called forth leaders…who were flexible, charming, empathetic, cooperative, and tolerant…The era of authority calls forth leaders who…are often more solitary than social, who are stern, combative, contemptuous of self indulgence, fiercely loyal to friends, and persistently hostile to foes."[11]

My suggestion is to adopt a strategic approach to leadership that combines the best features of each of these paradigms but transcends them both. From the executive or authority model, borrow the "can do" entrepreneurial spirit that inspires confidence in others to believe that shared goals will be achieved.[12] Be willing to get out in front of the crowd and risk failure in chasing your dream wherever it may lead. Most of all, do not be reluctant to exercise power in effecting change for the benefit of others, which is exactly what Jesus did in his use of miracles.[13] From the enabling or harmony model, draw on the synergy of a shared vision shaped in collaboration with the laity. Be highly participatory in the decision-making process, especially in drawing on the insights of front-line workers and welcoming of input from those who may have concerns about proposed changes. Focus more on spirit than on structure, since minimum bureaucracy is needed when working toward a common goal.

The great value of the strategic approach advocated here is that it mandates the practice of participatory leadership. After all, what the theology of the Holy Trinity expresses is that even God functions as a team and thereby calls us to do the same.[14] Exclusive use of the executive model finally leaves pastors stressed and exhausted from carrying the decision-making load in lonely isolation, while exclusive use of the enabling model finally leaves the laity confused and frustrated from lack of a clear sense of direction. But team-based leadership energizes both parties as they accept shared responsibility for the initiating and implementing process.[15] On this interactive model the pastor plays a vital role, but the people are able to say, "We did it ourselves."[16] A serious problem thwarting the needed breakthrough in this area is the failure of many churches to make leadership training of the laity an essential part of their purpose even though it was a prominent feature of the ministry of Jesus, a neglect to which we shall return in the next chapter.[17]

Foundations of the Strategic Stance

Having introduced the nature of leadership, let us now look more closely at the meaning of its strategic dimension. To do this, I shall first define four concepts that are crucial to the life of any organization, especially to that of a Christian congregation and hence to the leadership of its pastor. Terminology is not consistent, and definitions are not precise in the vast literature on these concepts; but there is enough general agreement regarding the nature of these central realities that, when taken together, they enable us to define the strategic stance.

1. *Purpose.* We begin with what might be called organizational ontology, the *raison d'etre* or "reason for being" of a church. Why was it established in the first place? What must it do to be true to its very nature? What would be lost if it were to go out of existence? A congregation probes its ultimate foundations when it asks, What are the essential functions that our church is uniquely equipped to perform? This dimension is sometimes discussed in terms of the "characteristics" or "marks" of a church because purpose is the most important factor in determining the identity of any organization.

2. *Context.* Every organization exists for the purpose of serving some defined group at a particular time and in a particular place. The setting in which this service is rendered may also be called its matrix or medium or milieu. The constituency being served may be called its clients or customers or consumers, depending on the nature of the service rendered. Often a congregation will refer to this working environment simply as its "community" or its "church field" or its "parish." Every situation is different, thus an organization's particular placement contributes profoundly to its distinctiveness.

3. *Vision.* Precisely because a church exists to offer the fullness of life in Christ, it seeks to be a force for change both in the lives of its members and in their wider world. But what will life be like for individuals, families, congregations, and communities when these purposes are fulfilled? Every organization needs a compelling picture of how the future will be impacted as a result of the contribution it is seeking to make in the present. When this vision is clearly seen and widely shared, it motivates concerted action by the group to claim its unrealized potential.

4. *Mission.* In a very real sense, the interaction of these first three elements of organizational existence determine the fourth. To utilize the biblical

and theological understandings developed in chapter 2, we may say that the church is constituted as a "People of Tomorrow" whose *purpose* is to anticipate the life of the "Age to Come." But it does this in the *context* of an "Old Age" still dominated by the powers of sin and death. It is not distracted by "the fashion of this world" (1 Cor. 7:31, KJV), however, because in Christ it has already seen a *vision* of the new humanity that God is seeking to shape in a restored creation (Rom. 8:29–30; 1 Jn. 3:2). The church cannot change its nature, or ignore its setting, or renounce its future and still be the church! Taken together, these three givens shape its sense of *mission,* which may be defined as what a church does to fulfill its purpose in a particular context in such a way as to actualize its vision.

Let me offer three comments about these defining categories before I relate them to the nature of strategy. The first is that, by whatever name, all four elements need to be kept distinct and held in proper balance. Because of diverse terminology in the literature on leadership, inexperienced leaders tend to confuse or combine some of these categories, especially in an attempt at simplification. This effort should be resisted because each of these components refers to an important reality that should never be forgotten when providing leadership to an organization.

One way to grasp the distinctiveness of each component is in relation to temporal categories. *Purpose* is anchored in the past, mandated by the New Testament, which defines the nature of the church much like articles of incorporation or constitution and bylaws set forth the founding purpose of a new enterprise. *Context* is rooted in the present, subject to ever-changing circumstances with which a church interacts on a continuous basis. *Vision* is set squarely in the future as an incentive and aspiration that cannot be collapsed into the status quo. *Mission,* therefore, is the driving force by which a church plots a trajectory in time from its heritage in the past through its habitat in the present to its hope in the future. To conflate any of these elements would separate the church from the full sweep of God's saving history and confuse the effort to create its own story.

My second comment is that these four concepts seem so axiomatic that many ministers suppose that their meaning for the congregation is self-evident. Indeed, some pastors never struggle to hammer out clear statements, or to seek consensus regarding their validity, because they assume that everybody already knows and accepts what they are talking about. On the contrary, it is extremely difficult to gain a profound understanding of what these concepts mean and to share ownership of what their application would entail in a particular church.

Let me hint at why this is the case. The Bible itself is so diverse that interpreters may seize upon any number of emphases as the starting point to define purpose. Add to that the many theological perspectives that have developed over the centuries of church history, and we begin to see why hundreds of Christian denominations have emerged, each with its own distinctive understanding of the purpose of the church. As to context, H. Richard Niebuhr has given classic expression to the strikingly different ways in which the church may relate to the world depending on whether it sees Christ against culture, of culture, above culture, in paradox with culture, or as the transformer of culture.[18] As regards vision, think how divergent are the future scenarios painted by premillennialists, postmillennialists, and amillennialists, not to mention dispensationalists. To choose between various combinations of just these few options as regards purpose, context, and vision confronts a congregation and its pastor with literally hundreds of alternatives in shaping a coherent sense of mission.

My final comment is that, difficult as it may be, few tasks of leadership are more important than giving substance and significance to these four categories of organizational existence. It should not be surprising that the pastor of one of the fastest growing churches in America entitled his much-admired manifesto explaining this success story *The Purpose-Driven Church*.[19] Or that the doyen of management studies, Peter Drucker, should devote most of his final books to the rapidly changing circumstances in which we find ourselves today.[20] Or that Burt Nanus of Bennis-Nanus fame in the field of personal leadership studies should write his climactic book, *Visionary Leadership*, out of the conviction that "there is no more powerful engine driving an organization toward excellence and long-range success than an attractive, worthwhile, and achievable vision of the future, widely shared."[21] If the central task of leaders is to instill in their followers a shared sense of mission, we now begin to glimpse the three main components involved in fulfilling that task.

There is no way for a pastor to lead strategically until the congregation shares with its minister a sense of mission resting squarely on the three-legged stool of purpose, context, and vision, for strategy is concerned primarily with the *contextualization of mission*. It inquires into the steps that an organization should take if it is to flourish in its chosen ecosystem. Coming from a Greek military term (*stratagos*) for the commanding general of an army, strategy implies the charting of a course of action or battle plan to overcome those challenges that would thwart an optimal relationship with the territory that it intends to occupy. Stated less militantly, strategy plots the direction in which an organization should move to position itself to carry out its mission most effectively.

Central to a strategic approach is what might be called the ecological imperative.[22] It begins with the recognition that nothing lives unto itself (Rom. 14:7), that every living entity is shaped and sustained in some setting, and therefore that it is essential for the entity to understand and adapt to the soil in which it is rooted. A church is not a disembodied ideal that can somehow transcend the particularities of its time and place, all talk about the "universal church" or the "invisible church" notwithstanding.[23] Rather, a church exists in surroundings that present both opportunities for, and obstacles to, the fulfillment of its distinctive mission. Just as farmers must decide what kinds of crops will best flourish in their complex mix of soil and temperature and rainfall, so church leaders must determine the kinds of ministries that will produce the desired results in their complex ideological-cultural-social milieu.

More than any other factor, *context* locates the arena in which strategy is put into play. The church that lives strategically first positions itself on the boundary where its internal and its external constituencies meet and then takes a balanced look in both directions at the challenges and threats that they pose. Strategy insists that every mission has a matrix, with the relationship between its components as intimate as that between a lock and its key. The nature of the strategic response is profoundly synergistic. It does not suggest that an organization capitulate to its culture, or that it compromise by accommodating itself to the prevailing cultural mood. Rather, it facilitates an ongoing dialogue by which church and community interact with each other until they achieve a fit, a bonding, a symbiosis that leads to a living together in a mutually beneficial relationship of creative tension.

The strategic response of a church to its context requires what might be called "strategic thinking" on the part of leaders. They must ponder the question: In light of *who* we are and *where* we are, *how* do we get to where we want to go? They must then ask *when* can we get there, and *what* will it be like when we arrive? This kind of thinking becomes operational in the form of "strategic acting" as the congregation learns to risk meaningful change in response both to a deeper understanding of purpose from within and to a recognition of emerging challenges from without. Once a church adopts this strategic stance as its habitual lifestyle, then, and only then, is it ready to attempt strategic planning, which may be described as a continuous process of designing the most effective means to accomplish its mission. But let the warning be heard clearly: there is little value to developing strategic plans until a church has first learned to *live* strategically in response to its shared sense of mission.

The Strategic Dimension of Leadership

Now let us seek to combine what we have learned about leadership and about strategy as they relate to the role of the pastor. Warren Bennis has defined leaders primarily in terms of those who "master the context" rather than surrender to it.[24] Leaders move beyond the conventional learning necessary to maintain an organization within the framework of the status quo or to rescue it when overtaken by unexpected crises. Instead, they practice creative learning by listening intently to the wider world, by asking questions that expose new developments, and by imagining the new settings that are already being shaped and will soon emerge.[25] Bennis aptly describes these leaders as persons who:

- ask what and why, not just how and when;
- keep their eyes on the horizon, not just on the bottom line;
- innovate and originate, not just imitate and perpetuate;
- develop long-range perspectives, not just short-range viewpoints;
- focus on people and processes, not just on systems and structures;
- do the right thing, not just do things right.[26]

It is crucial, however, not to understand these characteristics only in individualistic terms, as if the leader were some solitary brooding genius, for inherent in any concept of leadership is the obverse concept of followership. It is no more possible to have leaders without followers than it is to conduct an orchestra without musicians. The essential nature of leadership is binary: it is not a noun but a verb, not a status but a function, not a quality but a relationship of reciprocity and interdependence. Leadership is not a personality trait sometimes called "charisma." It is a social role that enables a diverse group to act together with unity of will and purpose.

Here it is important to recognize that there are two basic types of leadership. Utilizing a distinction developed by James MacGregor Burns,[27] we may describe managerial leadership as transactional, and strategic leadership as transformational. Transactional leadership involves an *exchange* of value according to which the leader renders some desired service to earn the support given by followers; thus it is concerned primarily with maintaining the status quo. Transformational leadership, by contrast, involves a *change* of value by which leaders guide their followers to accept new challenges and adapt to altered circumstances; hence it is concerned primarily with modifying the status quo. Managerial leaders work with bureaucracy, while strategic leaders work with "adhocracy." Managerial leaders use administrative skills, while strategic leaders use catalytic skills. Managerial leaders consolidate, while strategic leaders innovate.

Before leaving this distinction I would like to put in a good word for the managerial role because it is often deprecated in studies of leadership. Warren Bennis, for example, has a section entitled "Leaders, Not Managers,"[28] in which he seems to denigrate the "manager" as a stolid plodder while glamorizing the "leader" as an intrepid pioneer. "To reprise Wallace Stevens, managers wear square hats and learn through training. Leaders wear sombreros and opt for education."[29] There follows a list of twenty-seven contrasts between "education" and "training" calculated to make the "leader" look good and the "manager" look bad. But every leader, especially a pastor, will of necessity spend a great deal of the working day on managerial tasks. Indeed, it is precisely in demonstrating effective management of existing programs that a pastor earns the confidence of the congregation to try something new. Such mundane failures as calendar conflicts, budget overruns, and neglected maintenance can quickly raise suspicions about the ability to carry out more ambitious strategic proposals.

In reaching a healthier understanding of managerial and strategic leadership, remember that life is one long dialectic between continuity and change, each calling forth the other in a never-ending process of dynamic equilibrium. Continuity without change leads to stultifying rigidity, while change without continuity leads to capricious anarchy. Much of our organizational entropy results from the failure to strike an effective balance between fidelity and flux, anchor and adventure, home and horizon. Some "leaders" innovate brilliantly but then fail to build those infrastructures needed to conserve their hard won gains. Conversely, some "managers" adapt creative breakthroughs to the needs of daily life but then allow these routines to become brittle and unresponsive to changing times. Clearly the effective pastor needs at times to be a "leader" and at other times a "manager."

In practical terms, the great danger is that managerial duties, which are so relentlessly daily, will crowd out the development of strategic competencies. Some pastors who become the senior minister in a multi-staff church try to delegate most if not all managerial tasks to associates to concentrate on strategy. This approach is seldom successful because strategic needs are more often discovered in dealing intimately with the nitty-gritty of daily church life than in detachment from it. To avoid an imbalance between the managerial and the strategic roles, apply the following typologies to your work in diagnostic fashion, noting those areas in either column that may need more attention or emphasis in your ministry. Rather than viewing the left column as inferior and the right column as superior, accept both groupings as descriptive of different but equally important aspects of your pastoral responsibilities.[30]

Managers	Leaders
• Emphasis on the enterprise	• Emphasis on the environment
• Oriented toward stability	• Oriented toward innovation
• Venture directed	• Vision directed
• Deductive and analytical	• Inductive and integrated
• Reactive and predictable	• Proactive and serendipitous
• Internal focus on inputs	• External focus on outcomes
• Extrapolates from the past	• Anticipates from the future
• Bias in favor of continuity	• Bias in favor of creativity
• Orientation toward efficiency	• Orientation toward effectiveness
• Avoidance of ambiguity and risk	• Acceptance of ambiguity and risk
• Reliance on quantitative data	• Reliance on qualitative intuition
• Builds on inward strengths	• Builds on outward opportunities

In functioning both as a manager and as a leader, pastors may limit their effectiveness as a strategist in at least three ways:

1. Many pastors become so preoccupied with meeting the institutional needs of the church and the personal needs of its members that they fail to discern what is happening around them in the wider world. The apostle Paul's burning desire was to "preach the gospel" to every person, but his formulation of that message in Colossians was breathtakingly different from that which he used a few years earlier in Galatians, obviously because his audience had changed. Just so, pastors who would be strategic leaders must be sensitive to paradigm shifts in the culture and to the spiritual issues these shifts raise in the wider contemporary environment.[31] Only in a relationship of dynamic reciprocity between server and served is the sense of mission saved from fatal inbreeding. The context does not determine the kind of arrows that we shoot, but it does determine the range of targets at which we aim. A pastor who leads a church to serve only itself will one day wake up to discover that there is no one else to serve!

2. In assessing success or failure, many pastors continue to judge their churches in terms of inputs received instead of outputs achieved. A "more-of-the-same" fallacy tempts them to suppose that progress lies in doing better what they have always done by having more members, more money, more staff, and more facilities at their disposal. This attitude is especially seductive because enhanced resources do almost always have a favorable impact in the short term, but they can actually become a burden in the long term. That is illustrated by a host of our best-resourced business enterprises that have been forced to downsize rather dramatically to return

to profitability. The problem was not just with bloated payrolls or excessive plant capacity or redundant layers of bureaucracy, but with the way in which a focus on asset accumulation as the key to shareholder value took their eyes off of the emerging needs and desires of their customers. Some churches respond to numerical growth by building more buildings and adding more staff only to find that debt service and payroll costs have become so burdensome that they can no longer respond quickly and flexibly to new needs in the community. Ironically, at the moment of greatest apparent strength measured by asset accumulation—i.e., by the size of the membership, staff, plant, and budget—they find themselves strapped by their own infrastructure. Lay leaders begin to wonder why they can no longer recapture the "glory days" when they were a young and struggling congregation meeting in a borrowed building with no "game plan" but to serve the new community growing up around them.

3. One of the hardest things for pastors to do is to lead their churches to phase out any program at all, no matter how tentatively it may have been begun or how reluctantly it may have been continued. Lantern-makers in the early twentieth century must have railed against those conditions that eventually cost them their jobs, chief of which was the harnessing of electricity, when they should have been retraining themselves to make incandescent lights instead. Likewise, church staff members and lay leaders often feel that their competence or commitment is being called into question by the suggestion that their program assignments be revised or eliminated when a changed context is mandating the need for change.

While strategic insight cannot lessen the threat of changing times for those determined to perpetuate the status quo, at least it can help to shift the focus from issues of inadequate personal effectiveness to those of emerging environmental challenges that must be met. Unfortunately, some ministers make every proposed change in church life a test of their "pastoral authority" when it would be much less confrontational to agree on how the context is changing and what new needs these changes call upon the church to meet. If the pastor's leadership style is highly interactive and collaborative, then everyone struggles together with the same challenges. This removes the full blame from the pastor who made changes mandated by the context when those most directly affected may not even understand the reason for and intention of the changes.

If this section accomplishes only one thing, I hope it will show that strategic leading must become a pervasive climate before it can become an operational method. Over many years my work has taken me into hundreds of churches of every type in an endless variety of locales. Some are shut off tightly from the world about them, offering their members an escape from the pressures and perplexities of everyday life. They seem to be heedless, even oblivious, of the onrushing future that threatens to sweep away their haven of safety and security until it is too late to change. In such a climate of isolation, strategy withers and dies, regardless of how many long-range plans are carefully devised and approved but then placed on the shelf to gather dust.

What strategic leadership is all about is taking off the blinders and opening the shutters to a wider world. It is about letting the present be influenced as much by the future as by the past. It is about taking seriously that most characteristic biblical phrase, "it came to pass," which means that God has made time to move on, bringing with it a closure to what has been as well as an opening to what is yet to be. Without this climate of expectancy, this palpable sense of the possibilities created by the gift of time itself, strategic leading and the strategic preaching built upon it cannot reach their full potential.

CHAPTER 8

The Priority of Purpose in Strategic Leading

In the previous chapter we learned that strategic leading must be built on an interaction with context in the present, upon a foundation of purpose from the past, and upon a clear sense of vision for the future. In coping with present urgencies created by the context, it is crucial for you to look backward to the past and forward to the future because these two foci correspond to a deep polarity embedded within the very nature of individuals and of organizations. Giving equal attention to purpose and vision helps life in the present to maintain a deliberate equilibrium between its past and its future. We are creatures both of memory and of hope, ever seeking to harvest from yesterday the wisdom needed for tomorrow. Note from the characteristics listed at right how each of these temporal dimensions is needed to balance the other.

In ancient Greece, two philosophers entertained diametrically different views regarding the nature of ultimate reality. Parmenides argued that all change is illusory, transitory, and imperfect. Heraclitus saw reality as a flowing river always in constant flux. The former was the apostle of the eternal and unchanging, the latter of the existential and

PURPOSE	VISION
Anchor	Adventure
Being	Becoming
Constancy	Change
Continuity	Contingency
Essence	Existence
Fidelity	Flux
Heritage	Hope
Home	Horizon
Nostalgia	Novelty
Order	Originality
Predictability	Promise
Permanence	Progress
Stability	Surprise
Structure	Spontaneity
Tradition	Transformation

evolutionary. So profoundly have both these approaches shaped our under-standing of reality that we dare not discard one of them for the other.

Look again at the two columns above. Strategic leading does not choose one side to the exclusion of the other but rather holds them both in creative tension so as to be open to both the past and the future. Stated ideologically, excessive preoccupation with the first column is called "conservatism," and with the second column is called "liberalism." What I shall be pleading for in this chapter and the next is an approach to leadership that avoids either of these extremes.[1]

Here we shall explore how to build strategic leading and the strategic preaching which articulates its goals squarely on the foundation of purpose, since this is the most basic and enduring guide to the reason-for-being of the church. From a scriptural standpoint, preaching is profoundly connected with the people of God. In its divine aspect, a sermon is the voice of God calling the church into being; in its human aspect, it is the voice of the church bearing witness to that new being. This means that the purposes of preaching are the same as the purposes of God for his people. The primary task of the pulpit is to help the church execute the purposes for which it was established. The sermon beckons and propels the people of God toward the actualization of their reality here on earth. How may a sense of purpose guide the life of the congregation and the leadership of its pastor?

Defining Purpose as a Foundation for Ministry

If strategic leading is nothing other than helping the church to become what it is, then the place to begin is learning to do ministry by an agenda based squarely on God's purposes for his people as revealed in Scripture. Pastors are exposed to an avalanche of urgent claims, both personal and institutional, all of them worthy of immediate attention. Those ministers who respond to whatever need surfaces next will always be both busy and useful, but they may never get around to some of the things that need doing most. In ministry, the great struggle is not between the bad and the good but between the good and the best.

A clear sense of purpose gives coherence to one's leadership responsi-bilities. It provides a set of priorities by which to organize one's time. In the midst of unavoidable pressures that threaten to overwhelm the decision-making process, a comprehensive agenda to be accomplished offers a checklist by which to make sure you are touching all of the bases. A carefully conceived agenda is the antidote to normless existence. It is like a template that can be superimposed over a typical slice of church life to evaluate its breadth and balance. The need for such an agenda is based on the self-evident axiom, *If you don't know where you are going, you probably won't get there!*

To determine your own understanding of the church's God-given purpose, go to the New Testament and look for the church's most distinguishing characteristics. You will find abundant help by consulting Bible dictionaries and encyclopedias, theological wordbooks, biblical and systematic theologies, as well as historic creeds and confessions of faith. Most of these works conclude by describing what are often called the essential "marks" or "dimensions" of the church. Make a list of these features and functions. Then use a topical concordance to identify the relevant scriptures that clarify each concept. Once you have completed the preliminary spadework, involve both staff and lay leaders in reaching a consensus as to the best way to define the life and work of the church for your particular congregation. I would strongly urge you to stay with this assignment until the core leadership comes to a working definition of the purposes that the word of God mandates your church to fulfill.

When we undertook this process shortly after I arrived in Shreveport, our workgroup concluded that any description of an authentic New Testament church includes six components:

1. *Worship.* The gathering of the "*congrega*-tion" as a demonstration of its essential solidarity, a visible realm where reconciliation is being realized through "the unity of the Spirit in the bond of peace" (Eph. 4:3). The proclamation of the Word and the celebration of the divine Presence as the energizing of the Body to experience renewal through the judgment and mercy of God. The anticipation of the Age to Come, which both nourishes the holiness of the people of God and empowers them for service in the present age.
2. *Outreach.* The guiding of persons to God through the saving work of Jesus Christ. The forthright declaration of the gospel message with a compassionate invitation to accept its offer of new life through repentance and faith. The evangelization of all who profess no personal relationship to Jesus Christ and the enlisting of unaffiliated Christians who need to reestablish a vital connection with the family of faith.
3. *Nurture.* The developing of believers into mature disciples through a study of the Scriptures, training in doctrine and ethics, and enrichment of life through such participatory activities as music and recreation. The growth of the inner spiritual life, the strengthening of personal and social ties, and the edifying of the congregation by the enabling and enhancement of each member's spiritual gifts.
4. *Fellowship.* The undergirding of believers in such struggles as the temptation to sin, the danger of backsliding, the ravages of disease, and the pain of bereavement. The offering of encouragement and counsel

in such major transitions as marriage, childbirth, retirement, and death. The sharing of a common life in bonds of mutual love.

5. *Service.* The prophetic role of the church in challenging evils entrenched in the collective structures of society, liberating the oppressed from exploitation, seeking to build a more just and humane world in which to live. The servant role of the church in extending benevolence to the unfortunate, encouragement to victims of injustice, and rehabilitation to those who seek to overcome a legacy of failure. The apostolic role of the church in the world, working directly and cooperatively to extend the gospel throughout the earth.

6. *Support.* The assembling, allocating, and administering of all the human and material resources of the church needed to facilitate the effective implementation of its essential ministries. The discovery, development, and deployment of a gifted and trained leadership, both formal and functional, to provide motivation, guidance, and support to the members. The inculcation of a sense of responsible stewardship in the use of one's time, abilities, and financial resources.

Obviously numerous scriptures could be cited in support of every phrase in these six components. However, in seeking to provide the congregation with a comprehensive overview of the entire analysis, I found a convenient summary in a single passage (Acts 2:41–47), which contains all of these emphases in integrated fashion. Most commentators see in this text an idealized summary of the earliest apostolic Christianity created at Pentecost, a sort of "protology" of the church to serve as a model of how things were "in the beginning." Just as Luke 1—2 provides an "infancy narrative" of Jesus that undergirded what he began to do in the days of his flesh, so Acts 1—2 provides an "infancy narrative" of the church that undergirded what Jesus continued to do through his Spirit-filled followers (Acts 1:1–2).[2] On this understanding, the summary in Acts 2:41–47 corresponds to the summary in Luke 2:52. "Like her Lord, the church 'waxes strong' and is 'in favour with God and man.'"[3] Notice how this normative portrait describes the six categories just presented:

1. *Worship.* The first Christians met constantly to pray (v. 42), gathered daily in the temple (v. 46), and continually offered praise to God (v. 47). In the presence of spiritual power demonstrated by "many wonders and signs," every soul was filled with the "fear" of the Lord, which we might describe as an abiding sense of reverential awe (v. 43).

2. *Outreach.* Not only were their lives turned upward to the presence of God but also outward to those being saved on a daily basis (v. 47). God "added" to their number those receiving the Word, but the church

could both invite them by proclaiming the gospel and then welcome them by administering baptism, even though the great number of converts threatened to overwhelm the tiny nucleus of believers (v. 41).

3. *Nurture.* From its outset the church provided a continuous program of teaching by the apostles (v. 42) designed to ground these newcomers in the life and work of Jesus (Acts 1:21–22). This was not merely formal instruction in the facts of his earthly ministry but also a sharing of his life of graciousness, so strongly emphasized in the gospel of Luke. This nurture resulted in a new lifestyle characterized by a joyous spirit rooted in exultation to God and a sincere heart rooted in singleness of motive in dealing with others (v. 46).

4. *Fellowship.* Most conspicuous was the way in which these converts, drawn from the diverse crowd of pilgrims gathered for Pentecost (Acts 2:8–11), quickly became a unified fellowship (v. 42) in which their bonding was based on having "all things in common" (v. 44). This essential oneness of mind (v. 46) was especially evident in their shared meals (v. 42), which took them into one another's homes (v. 46) after the manner of the table fellowship of Jesus while on earth.

5. *Service.* The harmony that prevailed in all of their relationships was given practical expression as they voluntarily "sold their possessions and goods" to assist "as any had need" (v. 45). So great was their love for one another that they refused to let personal misfortune create inequities that would disrupt their fellowship (Acts 6:1), as the generous example of Barnabas so abundantly illustrated (Acts 4:34–37). No wonder that such a caring community quickly gained "favor with all the people" (v. 47) despite having been accused at first of public drunkenness (Acts 2:13, 15)!

6. *Support.* Lacking any type of institutional infrastructure, these earliest Christians depended upon two types of undergirding to stabilize their rapidly expanding movement. First, they relied on the personal leadership of the apostles both to provide them with instruction (v. 42) and to energize them with divine power (v. 43). Second, in responding to the needs of others, they developed a system of distribution (v. 45) designed to apportion their available resources in equitable fashion rather than depending on the spontaneous generosity of individuals.

Before leaving this paradigmatic passage, let me try to convey in non-technical terms a nuance in the original Greek not adequately conveyed in English translation. As befits a concluding summary statement, the three verbal forms in v. 41 (those who *received* the word…were *baptized*…were *added*) are all in the *aorist* tense, a form that states in undefined fashion what happened. But as verses 42–47 summarize the nature of their life together, every single verbal form shifts to the present or imperfect tense, which, unlike the aorist, defines the action as continuous or repetitive. Note especially a present participle (*proskarterountes*) used identically in verse 42 and verse 46 that somewhat "frames" this portrait of the early church. The verb stem (*karter-*), meaning "to be steadfast," is intensified by the addition of a prepositional prefix (*pros*) so that the compound stresses the unwavering perseverance, constant diligence, and steadfast tenaciousness with which these new disciples went about living the Christian life. This emphasis on their firm persistence is accentuated even more by the addition of the verb "to be" (*ēsan*) at the outset of verse 42, i.e., "they *kept on being* faithful," and by the addition of an idiom (*kath' hēmeron*) in verse 46 suggesting that they stuck by these practices "day after day."

Here we have, in other words, not a "snapshot" of how the church acted in the first flush of enthusiasm following Pentecost, but a description of those distinguishing characteristics to which they held fast in every circumstance. Their unswerving devotion to this way of life is implied by the durative force of all the verbal forms. Awe *continued to* fill every soul (v. 43). Wonders and signs happened *again and again* (v. 43). The believers *kept on* having all things in common (v. 44) by *regularly* selling their goods and distributing the proceeds as needs *repeatedly* surfaced (v. 45). They were *constantly* breaking bread and sharing food together (v. 46), *ceaselessly* praising God, and ever *maintaining* a favorable public reputation (v. 47). It is no wonder that God *went on* adding new believers to their number (v. 47). All sixteen of the verbal forms in verses 42–47 hint at the enduring sense of purpose that animated the New Testament church.

Once a clear understanding of what the church should be and do is grasped from a careful study of Scripture, then a congregation and its pastor are ready to determine an agenda for their ministry together. This agenda should lead the church to express as fully as possible each of these "marks" or "dimensions" of the church in its contemporary setting. In Shreveport, we defined the essential components of our purpose statement as follows:

1. To conduct regular services of worship that express the unity of the members in one body, that lay the claims of the Christian faith upon every hearer of the word, and that provide an experience of the presence and power of the triune God to all who believe.
2. To seek out all persons open to the ministry of our church and encourage their acceptance of the saving message of Jesus Christ expressed through personal commitment to his lordship and active involvement in the fellowship of his followers.

3. To guide a process of Christian growth toward mature discipleship through experiences of study, training, and sharing that will deepen the belief and strengthen the behavior of each member in all relationships of life, thereby building up the body of Christ into the likeness of its Lord.

4. To guard the flock from threats to its well being by sustaining members in times of difficulty and encouraging them in times of opportunity through a caring fellowship equipped to bear one another's burdens.

5. To meet the deepest needs of humanity through worldwide missionary and benevolent service that combats those forces that thwart the intention of God for each individual, for society, and for the created order.

6. To provide the human and material resources needed for the effective fulfillment of all ministries of the church indicated above through the development of trained leaders and responsible stewards.

Having studied a number of purpose statements from a diverse group of churches, I find a high degree of consensus regarding this general understanding of the church's reason-for-being. Terminology may vary, such as using spirituality for what I have called worship, evangelism for outreach, discipleship for nurture, pastoral care for fellowship, mission for service, and administration for support, but these differences are more semantic than substantive. Almost every statement includes the first five elements, while some omit the sixth because it is viewed merely as the "housekeeping" necessary to undergird all of the other purposes, whereas I give it equal status with the other five because of the great importance that I attach to leadership training and stewardship development as key functions of the church. Regardless of whether it is included in the purpose statement or not, pastor and congregation will be required to devote major attention to the support function if only to enhance the effectiveness of everything else that the church does.[4]

To this point, it might seem our discussion has concentrated on the purposes of the church as a corporate entity but devoted no attention to those purposes that should animate the lives of individual Christians. Such an impression is misleading, however, because each member is called to fulfill the very same purposes as the whole body. As the apostle Paul put it in 1 Corinthians 12, there is a rich diversity of gifts and functions, but all are united by a common calling (cf. Eph. 4:1–6). Therefore the sixfold understanding of purpose developed above should be applied to every level of church life. In Shreveport we worked especially with deacons to relate it to the entire membership, and with Sunday school teachers to relate it to their small Bible study groups. But we also emphasized the importance of families and individuals being guided by these purposes, such as in the following ways:

1. Set aside a time to pray daily and to worship at least once each week.
2. Share your faith in a witness to at least one person each week.
3. Engage in daily Bible reading and participate in at least one small group devoted to scriptural study.
4. Be part of a group that offers undergirding to those struggling with the crises of life.
5. Volunteer for at least one ministry that seeks to serve those oppressed and vulnerable.
6. Accept at least one assignment that enhances the life of your church through the investment of your time, energy, and money.

Making Purpose Pervasive in the Life of the Church

In Shreveport, once we gained a working consensus regarding our sixfold purpose, I began working with our lay leadership to get the entire congregation committed to the claims that this purpose laid on our corporate and individual lives. To communicate it as simply as possible and to minimize competition between those favoring only certain aspects of our purpose to the exclusion of other aspects, I utilized the familiar illustration of the wheel to show how all six components cohere in unified fashion. This analogy proved particularly appropriate for a church because the wheel is a dynamic image suggesting motion toward a destination, just as the church is often likened to a pilgrim people "following" Jesus on "the Way." Basically, the wheel is an apparatus with three essential parts, each of which corresponds to certain dimensions of purpose.

1. At the center is the *hub*, the crux of the entire wheel, for here, at its axis, the driving power from the engine is applied. We may liken worship to the function of the hub, the center of a church's common life where power from on high moves the entire enterprise forward. Just as spokes radiate out from the hub causing the entire wheel to turn, so the divine reality must radiate out from worship to quicken and nourish every aspect of church life. Unless God is at the beginning of every purpose, at the end of every vision, at the cutting edge of every strategy, at the heart of every activity, the people of God labor without power.
2. At the circumference of every wheel is the *rim*, that inconspicuous but essential framework on which the tire rests. Our support structures are like the "rim" of a tire. They underlie the implementation of every other purpose rather than being one coordinate purpose beside the

others. If worship provides the integrating divine reality, support provides the integrating human reality. Each needs the other to succeed: power without structure cannot be disseminated, while structure without power cannot be animated.

3. Finally, resting on the rim is the *tire* itself, that part of the wheel that actually "hits the road" and so propels the conveyance forward. To be sure, a wheel can run for a short while "on the rim," just as a church may bump along merely managing its human affairs. But it is the ministry systems, based on the four other purposes, that, like the tire, give the wheel traction in its context of ministry. Interestingly enough, these four purposes have a circularity that corresponds to the shape of the wheel. Beginning with outreach, the church invites people to a saving faith, then nurtures them in that faith, then sustains them in the struggle to keep the faith, then sends them forth to serve by applying their faith. This "go" imperative of service, once it is rooted in the world of human need, leads to the "come" imperative of outreach, and the cycle by which the church moves "forward through the ages" begins all over again. I have included later in this chapter a diagram called the "Church Purpose Cycle," which seeks to represent these relationships in visual form.

Once these conceptual materials were refined and embraced, I began to preach on living by the imperatives of our God-given purposes. An introductory sermon based on Acts 2:41–47, utilizing some of the exegetical insights summarized above, provided the congregation with a comprehensive overview. A series of six sermons, one on each component part of our purpose, followed. These utilized a number of scriptures, both to show how these "marks" were essential to the New Testament church and to suggest how the early Christians carried out each of these mandates in a variety of circumstances. At the same time I used my pastor's column in the weekly church paper to explore what it might mean for us to take these purposes with the utmost seriousness in our daily lives.

We also moved beyond preaching and teaching to infuse our organizational life with the same strong sense of purpose. Here are a few examples of how that was done:

• Our church sponsored twenty-six ongoing programs of ministry, all of which were grouped into the six comprehensive ministry systems defined by the above purposes.[5] All weekly, monthly, and annual reports followed this format. All relevant data were collected and conserved in accordance with these categories, whether on computer or in the church files. Quite simply, we as a church thought in these terms when doing our work.

- Regarding staff personnel, all organizational alignments, as well as all supervisory relationships, followed this six-fold structure. All position descriptions were written to insure that each of the ministry systems was adequately supported in terms of staff assignments. Performance evaluations were based on effectiveness in achieving strategic goals as measured by key performance indicators in these six areas of responsibility.
- Program budgeting was used to identify the financial resources needed to undergird each ministry system and its component parts. A double chart of accounts permitted us to keep track of the various types of expenditures by line items (e.g. salaries, benefits, office support, travel), without thereby obscuring the more important issue of the total amount invested annually to help achieve each aspect of our purpose. Even the prioritizing and budgeting for capital projects were considered within this same framework.
- The organizational structure of the lay leadership was also determined by these six purposes. All standing church committees, councils, and boards existed as working groups responsible for the formulation of strategies to accomplish agreed upon goals. The decision-making flow involving lay leaders paralleled that involving staff leaders so that the efforts of both groups were interrelated at every level. Reports and recommendations to the Deacons and Church Conference followed this sixfold framework so that the order of business at those meetings accurately reflected the progress being made in each area of our agenda for ministry.

I hope that this swift sketch will hint at how a strategic leader can work systemically to relate every activity, every schedule, every expenditure, and every meeting to a coherent agenda for ministry determined by church purpose. Most important to the focus of this book is the need to base one's preaching on the purpose of the church because what the pastor does as a strategist and as a preacher is all an effort to help the congregation express the fullness of its being as a church. I am keenly aware that preachers are an idiosyncratic lot, each with a different approach to sermon preparation. Still, it may be useful to mention here four of the ways in which I approached that task in an effort to unify my agenda for preaching with the congregation's agenda for ministry.[6]

1. Whenever I got a sermon idea, whether from scriptural study or current reading or personal experience, the first question I asked was: What purpose will that idea help me to accomplish in my total ministry? Once I grasped that key point, I then jotted down both the idea and its possible

usage as a sermon. I then added the idea to a notebook with tabs organized in accordance with the six parts of our purpose statement. This meant that when the time came to preach on fulfilling a particular purpose, I was able to find all of my "sermon starters" on that aspect of the agenda gathered at the same place for ease of review.

2. When planning the larger units of pastoral preaching, which I have already suggested be done on a quarterly basis, I not only reviewed my previous sermonic efforts, but consulted with staff and lay leaders about those facets of church life that were in need of emphasis during that period. Obviously I had also been personally counseling individuals and administering programs that dealt with these same needs, thus my emerging pulpit strategy became integral to my total pastoral work. In other words, what I said on Sunday was shaped by the same dynamics that determined what I put in the church paper on Monday, or discussed in staff meeting on Tuesday, or prayed about at the midweek service on Wednesday, or authorized to be expended on Thursday, or considered in conference on Friday. All such activities were, in a very real sense, one form of sermon preparation because they helped to clarify my understanding of just what it was that we as a church and as individual Christians were striving to accomplish.

3. When the preparation of a sermon began, each step in the homiletical process was guided by the criterion of intentionality discussed in chapter 3. Every effort was made to insure that the hearers would see clearly the target at which the sermon aimed. To be certain that I was clear regarding just what was at stake in preaching the sermon, careful attention was devoted to the strategy statement, which sought to pinpoint the kind of impact that the message was intended to make regarding the agenda under consideration. Indeed, each sermon was classified, neither by the biblical text on which it was based, nor by the topical themes which it developed, nor by the methodology utilized (textual, expository, topical), but by the purpose that it sought to accomplish.

4. After the sermon was delivered, its effectiveness was evaluated in light of the thrust that it had given to the particular agenda addressed. Its physical remains were then interred in a filing cabinet with tabs that, again, corresponded to the six parts of the purpose statement. This meant that when preparing a new sermon or reworking material from a previously prepared sermon, I could place it in the context of everything else that I had preached on that aspect of the purpose. Each year's pulpit work was recorded by this same classification system so that annually I could evaluate whether balanced attention had been devoted to the church's strategic priorities for that period of time.

Over many years of following this process of sermon preparation in tandem with ceaseless efforts to clarify the church's essential purpose, I gradually developed an outline of what became my agenda for preaching, a sort of "table of contents" to all that I was trying to do in the pulpit. In addition to reviewing it periodically for revision, I also shared it with various staff and lay leaders to test both its breadth and its balance among those attempting to do the same things for our church in other roles. In the Appendix to this chapter on pages 141–44, I have placed a full outline of this agenda for preaching in the hope that it will provide you with a more detailed analysis of my understanding of the purpose of the church, that it will furnish some useful categories for organizing and analyzing your own sermonic materials, and that it will provide a helpful basis of comparison with your efforts to provide a balanced pulpit diet that nourishes the people of God.

Using Purpose to Audit Church Health

Of the three components that determine a church's strategic mission, we know much more about purpose than we do about context or vision. After all, the essential purposes of the church are clearly defined in Scripture, and we have had two thousand years to reflect upon this mandate in terms both of theory (theology) and of practice (ministry). By contrast, our contemporary context is like an ever-shifting kaleidoscope of onrushing events and developments that we often do not understand until after they have passed us by. Vision, of course, is the most difficult to verify simply because it has not yet happened, its plausibility depending on inferences that are anticipated but have not yet been confirmed. Therefore, it is in terms of purpose that pastors can best address the twin leadership tasks of assessment and accountability.

Of all the core functions of a leader, the evaluating role is the one most often neglected in the church. The minute the word *evaluation* is used, many people think of a personnel committee meeting to review the performance of the pastor as the basis for a salary recommendation in the coming fiscal year.[7] However, I am talking here about something entirely different, namely the responsibility of the pastor to guide the congregation in determining how effectively the church is fulfilling its God-given purposes. We might call this the prophetic role of the strategic leader since it was clearly the mission of the prophets in ancient Israel to call the people of God to account, as may be illustrated by the dramatic confrontation between Amos and Amaziah (Am. 7:10–17). In our day, however, the assumption seems to be that since the church, by definition, exists to do God's work, it would be presumptuous to subject its activities to human scrutiny.

What is at stake here is not whether God's purposes are in need of clarification or correction but whether we as his servants have become misguided or complacent in seeking to implement them. All human effort is subject to confusion and sloth, thus a key duty of leaders in every field is to help the members of their organization realize both the untapped potential that they are missing and how they might achieve it. This awareness is particularly important to a church because it ever lives under the imperative to become by faith what it already is by grace. But this will never happen until a church confronts its true condition and resolves to take corrective action. Ironically, some congregations spend so much time boasting about their exalted purposes that they never get around to facing the hard facts of how far short they are falling in an effort to reach them.[8]

How may the pastor function as a quality control officer guiding the congregation to assess its compliance with stated purposes without thereby becoming judgmental or censorious? One way is to adapt for church use a number of approaches developed by the Quality Movement as nonthreatening ways to monitor the effectiveness of any enterprise. Here we may mention only a few:

- constructing a continuous feedback loop that stretches from frontline workers to every level of the organization;
- utilizing statistical data to report objectively on what is actually happening at each point in the processes designed to accomplish purposes;
- carefully checking results while still at the startup or pilot project stage before making permanent changes;
- agreeing on "key performance indicators" (KPIs) to measure the extent to which desired outcomes have been attained; and
- benchmarking the "best practices" of representative peer group churches.[9]

Beyond these more general ways of opening up any organization to ongoing self-examination, a pastor may use the purposes of the church as criteria to measure its vitality much as a physician uses various diagnostic procedures to determine the health of a patient. Because these purposes are God-given and grounded in Scripture, their use as transcendent norms helps to guard against a smug sense of satisfaction with what the church is doing. A patient in the examining room seldom if ever expresses the need or desire for an operation, both because of a limited understanding of the body and because surgery is a fearful prospect. But the doctor has an intimate knowledge of diseases as well as many objective measures to diagnose symptoms that may not be indicated by the way that the patient feels, such as a blood pressure reading, EKG, X-ray, and MRI. Just so, pastors should have such a clear understanding of God's purposes that they know how a church is meant to function, which may lead them to recommend corrective action even before the congregation is aware of its need.[10]

How do we learn to "take the pulse" or "listen to the heartbeat" of the congregation in the key areas defined by its purpose? In recent years a number of approaches have been developed to do just that. The designer of one such instrument applied the medical analogy to congregational life with these words:

> The process suggested is more a diagnosis than an evaluation. The team that is leading the planning will act more as a physician than as a counselor. Doctors diagnose and prescribe. They do not make value judgments. Sometimes the prescription is a remedy, and sometimes it is preventative medicine. But never is this kind of assessment a value judgment about the persons involved. The same is true about the Ministry Audit. The task is not to make a value judgment about the congregation, but to make a diagnosis. The process ends with strategic recommendations about what church leaders can do to improve or remedy their ministry.[11]

Here let me mention five such tools that you may wish to consider in conducting the delicate task of church diagnosis:

1. The well-known pollster and committed churchman, George Gallup Jr., has produced a comprehensive introduction to the field of survey research, which those with limited experience in this area might wish to consult for orientation.[12] In clear, nontechnical language it explains how to define the project, plan its execution, secure a sample, collect the data, design the questionnaire, analyze the returns, report the findings, and act on the results. Although not focused directly on the purposes of the church, it contains ten sample surveys, each with several questions that could be used to gather responses relevant to this agenda.

2. More directly related to purpose as it undergirds the mission of the church is an assessment tool by Thomas G. Bandy called *Facing Reality*.[13] Even though it investigates eleven "subsystems" of congregational life, it is not difficult to relate them to the six aspects of church purpose analyzed above:[14]

Foundational:
   GENETIC CODE: The identity of the church
   CORE LEADERSHIP: The seriousness for mission in the church
   ORGANIZATION: The structure of the church

Functional:

CHANGING PEOPLE: How people experience God in the church

GROWING CHRISTIANS: How people grow in relationship to Jesus

DISCERNING CALL: How people discover their place in God's plan

EQUIPPING DISCIPLES: How people are trained for ministries

DEPLOYING SERVANTS: How people are sent into the world and supported by the church

Formal:

PROPERTY: Location, facility, and technology

FINANCE: Stewardship, budget, and debt management

COMMUNICATION: Information, marketing, and advertising

The assessment tool is designed to reveal how the church is actually functioning in these eleven subsystems of its life. It also reveals linkages with what Bandy calls "positive habits" utilizing the "Seven Cardinal Virtues" (faith, charity, prudence, hope, temperance, justice, fortitude) as well as "destructive addictions" utilizing the "Seven Deadly Sins" (pride, covetousness, lust, envy, gluttony, anger, sloth). This overlay of the health-addiction polarity gives to the diagnostic instrument a dimension of depth by allowing it to measure both attitudes and behavior as reflective of how well the church is living out its essential commitments.[15]

3. Closely related to the work of Tom Bandy is that of Bill Easum, the two having formed a well-known consulting team on congregational renewal.[16] Easum's survey instrument is called *The Complete Ministry Audit: How to Measure 20 Principles for Growth,* which is fairly comprehensive, although, as the subtitle indicates, the focus is on church growth.[17] The twenty principles under investigation in his audit, which touch in varying degrees on all six of our purposes, are organized as follows:

1 – 6   Meeting People's Needs

7 – 11   Worship, Leadership, and Ability

12 – 16 Space, Distance, and Visitors

17 – 20 Money, Planning, and Change

As with the tool by Bandy mentioned above, trained consultants are available both to help launch the study and to do follow-up interpretation of its results.[18]

4. The two probes by Bandy and Easum concentrate primarily on understanding the church as a collective entity, while *The Christian Life Profile* developed by Randy Frazee is a tool used to chart the spiritual development of its individual members.[19] Here 120 statements are used to assess Thirty Core Competencies of the Christian life (ten core beliefs, ten

core practices, and ten core virtues) organized around loving God and loving neighbor. The profile does not attempt to measure a person's maturity in comparison with anyone else's, but rather provides a self-assessment based on the model of discipleship set forth by Christ. As George Gallup Jr., with whom Frazee collaborated, put it, "It is not so much a tool for spiritual measurement as it is a tool to create spiritual movement."[20] This makes it especially suited for strategic use. Individuals score themselves, then choose three trusted peers to assess them, on which basis they identify strengths and weaknesses and develop a personal plan for spiritual growth.

5. One of the most elaborate efforts to discover how well churches are fulfilling their purposes is called Natural Church Development (NCD) led by Christian A. Schwarz.[21] Its survey instrument, based on research in one thousand churches located in thirty-two countries, seeks to measure actual performance as regards eight "quality characteristics": empowering leadership, gift-oriented ministry, passionate spirituality, functional structures, inspiring worship, holistic small groups, need-oriented evangelism, and loving relationships. The pastor and about thirty church members complete a questionnaire, and their responses are compared by NCD with some four million previously collected answers to create a "church profile" that indicates "minimum factors," those least developed areas needing the most attention.[22] Again, respondents are not asked to appraise the church but only to describe its actual behavior.

The pastor may wish to enlist a strategic task force to examine these and other tools to determine which one, or combination of several, is best suited for the particular church and its strategy and purposes. Remember, the tools are to assess, not how satisfied the church is with the status quo, but how well God's purposes are being achieved in the lives of its members. Obviously such probes are only diagnostic, not therapeutic. But remedial action is seldom taken until there is first a clear awareness of the areas that may need treatment. Even though it can be difficult, even painful, to face reality when a congregation has been in denial for years, these tools are designed to be as objective and nonthreatening as possible. Just as patients are often relieved to learn the causes of debilitating symptoms, even when their treatment may be difficult, so churches can gain incentive to overcome deficiencies once they are clearly understood. As Max DePree put it, "The first responsibility of a leader is to define reality."[23]

Peter Drucker insists that the first and foremost questions to be asked by any nonprofit organization are, "What is our business?" and, "How are we doing?" To be more precise, "What is our reason for being? Why do we do what we do? What are we trying to achieve? What specific results are we seeking?"[24] A steady focus on purpose is designed to answer foundational questions such as these. It is no wonder that Rick Warren made this category central to his incredibly successful book for pastors, *The Purpose Driven Church*, and the one for laity, *The Purpose Driven Life*.[25] Indeed, in his hands the term "purpose" becomes a contemporary synonym for the somewhat stereotyped word "salvation." You cannot become a strategic leader without making God's purpose for his people central to all that you do as a minister.

APPENDIX TO CHAPTER
An Agenda for Preaching

I. Worship

As a divine creation, the church lives in the presence and power of the triune God. Worship seeks to establish, maintain, and deepen that transcendent dimension so that the people of God will live out their calling radiant in his glory, courageous in his strength, and united in his love.

A. Public worship

1. The gathered church as the realm of reconciliation, where unity in the body of Christ manifests a solidarity beyond all human divisions
2. The proclamation of the authoritative Word that binds its hearers together in a common confession of faith
3. The celebration of the coming kingdom anticipated in the Lord's supper as an icon of the eschaton

B. Personal worship

1. The individual's need of God, hunger for God, and dependence on God
2. The practice of private prayer and family devotions in the development of a contemplative spirituality
3. The Spirit-filled life of consecration that nourishes God-centeredness rather than self-centeredness

II. Outreach

The experience of God in worship produces an eagerness to share God with others. Since faith cannot be inherited, the church lives from one generation to the next on the effectiveness with which it brings persons to God through Jesus Christ in the convicting power of the Holy Spirit.

A. The divine initiative

1. The loving concern of God to redeem his creation by calling all persons into a saving relationship with himself

    2. The urgent responsibility of the redeemed to serve as agents of God's salvation through a compassionate witness to those without faith

    3. The plan by which God has provided new life to all who will receive it through the redemptive work of Christ

  B. The human response

    1. Repentance from sin, commitment to Christ, and confession of faith as the way out of guilt, judgment, and condemnation

    2. Baptism as the central enactment of identification with Christ in his saving death and resurrection

    3. Incorporation into the body of Christ by new and unaffiliated believers as the context of a continuing experience of salvation

III. Nurture

Once a person has been assimilated into the household of faith, a steady process of growth toward spiritual maturity should result. This quest for Christlikeness is the goal both of each member and of the body as a whole.

  A. Growth in belief

    1. The place of divine revelation and of human inspiration in understanding spiritual truth

    2. The study and use of the Bible as the revealed word of God

    3. The central convictions of our faith: God, humanity, sin, salvation, church, creation, and consummation

  B. Growth in behavior

    1. Personal ethics: moral decision-making, virtues and vices, character development

    2. Parish ethics: relations between Christians within the familial, congregational, and ecumenical households of faith

    3. Public ethics: the Christian as a responsible citizen in but not of the world as regards political, economic, and social issues

IV. Fellowship

When spiritual growth is impeded by weakness, temptation, and opposition, the Christian is not left to struggle alone. The body of Christ functions as a supportive fellowship undergirding the embattled believer with resources to persevere.

  A. Protection

    1. The sources of strength and security in the never-ending battle with the forces of evil

    2. Admonishing the flock of God to overcome temptation by resisting compromise with sin

3. Reclaiming the "backslidden" by a ministry of inreach to the indifferent and apathetic

B. Encouragement

1. The cultivation of a caring fellowship that bears one another's burdens in bonds of love
2. The offer of comfort and courage in the face of loneliness and discouragement
3. Coping with the common crises of life: sickness, suffering, tragedy, death, grief

V. Service

The church nurtures and sustains its members, not as an end in itself, but in order that they may help others. In so doing, Christians balance the "come" imperative of outreach that calls people out of the world with the "go" imperative that calls them to responsible care for that world.

A. Benevolence

1. The obligation of individual Christians to be ministers of reconciliation across barriers that divide humankind into hostile camps
2. The servant role of the church in the world, offering mercy to the downtrodden and protesting injustices that demean human dignity
3. The prophetic role of the church as a change agent in society, liberating humans from oppressive structures to serve the common good

B. Mission

1. The universal mission of the church in its local, regional, national, and international dimensions
2. Cooperative missions in its denominational and ecumenical expressions
3. Relationships with other religions and with civic/charitable service agencies in fulfilling the mission of the church

VI. Support

Spirit requires structure to channel and conserve its enduring impact. Therefore, the church is to be not only a living organism but also an institutional organization giving visible form to its ministries in the world of time and space.

A. Human resources

1. The nature of the church as a priesthood of believers utilizing and distributing the spiritual gifts of all its members for mutual edification

    2. The organization of the church to facilitate the accomplishment of its tasks through the commitment of its members

    3. The leadership of the church in such roles as ministers and deacons

B. Material resources

    1. The place of tangible realities as aids to an intangible faith

    2. The financial stewardship of systematic giving through tithes and offerings

    3. The erection and care of facilities as a focal place to facilitate the ministries of the church

Church Purpose Cycle

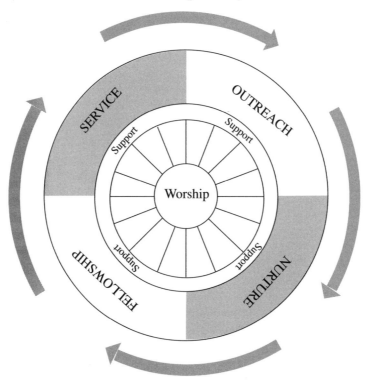

CHAPTER 9

The Vitality of Vision in Strategic Leading

Throughout this study, we have seen that guiding movement toward a goal is the essence of the strategic task. Just as a general deploys troops in battle to occupy enemy territory, so a pastoral leader mobilizes the congregation to journey toward that horizon of promise defined by the gospel (2 Pet. 1:4). The inaugurated eschatology of the New Testament makes clear: "it does not yet appear what we shall be" (1 Jn. 3:2). Thus one task of preaching is to challenge its hearers to claim more of that rich potentiality of life in Christ to which they are heirs by faith (Titus 3:6-7). But that is difficult to do unless you first have a clear sense of what the "not yet" will actually look like when it is revealed. When a consensus is reached regarding the shape of those legitimate aspirations that are attainable but have not already been obtained (Phil. 3:12), we call it the church's vision.

The key contention of this chapter is that strategy is best executed in the present when its agents are equally responsive to a sense of purpose from the past and to a sense of promise from the future. Go back to the twin columns at the outset of chapter 8. Note how balanced these two sources of input deserve to be. That chapter sought to suggest how pastoral leadership might make purpose a pervasive force in the life of the congregation. This chapter will seek to do the same for vision. Remember the quote from Rilke cited earlier,[1] "the future enters us...in order to be transformed in us, long before it happens."[2] That is precisely what Jesus was able to do for his disciples: he enabled them to claim a new and better future before others were open to such a possibility for themselves. Strategic leaders who minister in his name do exactly that today.

The Search for a Usable Future

I begin with three cautionary comments to protect the visioning process from misunderstanding.

1. Avoid what might be called the *predictive fallacy*—namely, the mistaken notion that Christians somehow possess clairvoyance to discern the course of future events. We have all seen the prophecy charts and heard the electronic evangelists expound "the signs of the times." Alas! Such efforts to detail a predetermined future are of no avail. Much as we might wish it otherwise, the Christian faith provides us with no preview of coming attractions. Jesus repudiated all attempts to make chronological calculations about what tomorrow may bring (Mt. 6:34) and claimed no special competence to predict the day and hour when heaven's timetable would supercede earth's calendar (Mk. 13:32). In light of the unpredictability of the future, his most urgent imperative was to "watch" because God's coming always involves elements of suddenness and surprise (Mk. 13:33–37). While Christians should be alert to what is happening around them, their ability to analyze data or spot trends will not necessarily be any better than that of the research department at the local chamber of commerce. If anything, the Christian understanding of the present age as transitory frees the church from futile attempts to speculate on its unfolding in the future.

An obvious source of skepticism regarding any systematic effort to plot the way ahead is the rapidly accelerating rate at which change is taking place in contemporary life, making it impossible to anticipate either the outcomes of present actions, which seem to obey the law of unintended consequences, or the causes of future events, which are full of surprises even for well-informed futurists. In such a frenzied atmosphere, it seems absurd to try to take the measure even of the next twelve months, much less the next five or ten years. The end of the twentieth century brought forth long lists of predictions made by experts over the past hundred years that utterly failed to materialize, further eroding our confidence in any form of prognostication.[3] Leonard Sweet draws the obvious conclusion: "There is no way we can plan for the future. We can't plan for the future because we can't predict the future... We can no more know how this day will end than we can know the end of our days or that final day of divine appearing."[4]

2. Avoid the *more of the same fallacy*. Recognizing our inability to predict the future, some make a second mistake of trying to perpetuate the present by crowning it with a halo of success, what might be called the "more-of-the-same fallacy." One typical response Christians often make when asked to dream about what they want their church to become several years from now is to wish for more money and more facilities to do what they have always done. The problem with this "shopping list" approach is that, if the

desired resources do not materialize on schedule, the visioning process itself is discredited. "See," say its detractors, "we sought to spell out in detail what was needed to insure a better future, but it didn't do us any good." Even more frustration may be generated if goals in terms of bigger budgets and buildings are actually met on schedule yet there remains a sense that the church is not really going anywhere but is still mired in the inherited routines of yesterday.

The problem with this approach is that visioning is not meant to be about incremental asset accumulation but about a willingness to conceive and to create in the foreseeable future a church that is fulfilling its essential purposes better than ever before. Even in the business world with its "bottom line" mentality, a more-of-the-same approach is seldom effective because it never thinks "outside the box." If all that a church's vision seeks to do is entrench the present state of affairs by means of securing enhanced resources, it will probably fail to do either. To put it plainly, visioning is neither a fancy name for fund-raising nor a way to justify a building program, not because those things are unimportant, but because they are a byproduct rather than a catalyst of God's tomorrow (Mt. 6:33).

3. Avoid the *angelic fallacy.* The notion that once a vision is defined everyone will embrace it because they prefer the future to the present is what I call the angelic fallacy. On the contrary, some of the strongest leaders in the church may well have more of a vested interest in the status quo than in transformational changes that might diminish their influence. Indeed, almost every great vision in the history of Christianity was initially viewed as subversive by the guardians of tradition. Today, for example, we enthusiastically endorse a vision of universal human freedom, but just 150 years ago the leadership of the Southern church bitterly opposed those visionaries who sought to abolish slavery. From the first to the twenty-first century, we have most often managed to reject pacesetters of the future in one generation, then live like parasites off of their courage in the next. If you still make generous allowance for original sin, then assume that God's people will often embrace God's tomorrow only reluctantly and in very small installments indeed!

All three of these fallacies are telling us that a true Christian vision is of God and not of us, that it is a matter of trusting in divine providence rather than betting on human circumstance. Vision jump-starts the future by daring to implement the imagination, allowing the heavenly to become earthly, the eschatological to become historical. In other words, constructing a vision does not involve deciding what we will do with more of the same kind of time (*chronos*) but rather deciding if and when we are willing to live out of a "New Age" of time (*kairos*). Vision is not the mere utopianism of wishful thinking or the building of scenarios based on contemporary trend analysis. Rather, vision is an effort to conceptualize and construct a whole new order of existence, what Jesus called life in the kingdom of God, and thereby to transcend the tired structures of our transient age. As Peter saw so clearly at Pentecost, the young "see visions" and the old "dream dreams" when God's Spirit is poured out on all flesh, thereby enabling the "last days" to arrive (Acts 2:17).

Precisely at this point the distinctive Christian understanding of eschatology described in chapter 2 comes into play. Unlike Judaism, which saw the eschaton coming at the end of time, as the term "*last* things" seems to imply, the New Testament viewed the eschaton as being inaugurated in the midst of ordinary time before its consummation at the end of time. In the ministry of Jesus, the future had already taken tangible form. His miracles, in particular, which were climaxed by his resurrection, unmistakably anticipated a transformation of human life that was yet to be revealed. Because the Old Age and the New Age now overlapped, the early followers of Jesus were, in a very real sense, more certain of the future than they were of the present, since the former was sure to witness the eventual triumph of Christ (1 Cor. 15:24–28) while the latter was already beginning to pass away (1 Cor. 7:29–31).

This bipolar perspective stands the human understanding of time on its head. Christians get their vision of the future from the past because it was never more clearly embodied than in the earthly life of Jesus two thousand years ago. So, for example, the ultimate destiny of the individual believer is defined in terms of growth in Christlikeness, which is described as being "conformed to the image of [God's] Son" (Rom. 8:29) or as "being changed into his likeness from one degree of glory to another" (2 Cor. 3:18). Again, the church is to grow into a spiritual maturity that will be attained when it reaches "the measure of the stature of the fullness of Christ" (Eph. 4:13). In other words, the *human* or temporal future is opaque and obscure at best, with many uncertainties beyond our ability to decipher (1 Cor. 13:12), but the *divine* or eschatological future is unmistakably clear because it has already been anticipated in Jesus of Nazareth and is ever being interpreted afresh to believers by his Holy Spirit (Jn. 16:13–14).

This means that the church takes a unique approach to its visioning process. On the one hand, it well understands the biblical warning that the future of this age is unpredictable because it is in the process of passing away. On the other hand, the church is also confident of its own manifest destiny, which is to actualize the fullness of life in Christ. Therefore, it ever seeks to fulfill God's plan of the ages "according to his purpose which he set forth in Christ" (Eph. 1:9), but to do so in light of the involvements of its members within the structures of the Old Age. This creates a tension between the church's *normative* understanding of its promised future given in the New Testament and its *provisional* understanding of earth's future shaped by contemporary circumstances. It is precisely the task of the visioning process to focus the aspirations and affections of the church on God's certain tomorrow even as it faces the many contingent futures that swirl about it today.

The paradox of finding a new future in the distant past is unknown in the secular literature on visioning. One writer has gone so far as to claim, "Not until around 1300 did people begin to think in terms of a future, a possible change ahead, in terms of the future as being potentially different from the present."[5] Apparently he never opened the New Testament, every page of which reflects a community riveted on a future so near at hand that its transforming impact was already beginning to be felt in the life of its members. While the future of the church is inescapably influenced by those current trends to which the planning consultants pay so much attention, its vision is not defined by these developments. If anything, the key threshold decision to be made when embarking on the quest for a usable future is whether the vision will be determined by the biblical understanding of God's New Age as disclosed in the first century or by our understanding of how "the present evil age" (Gal. 1:4) is likely to unfold in the twenty-first century.

The task of the strategic leader is to guide the church to implement the unique Christian vision of God's tomorrow rather than to conform to earth's vision of its own expected future. At times the two visions have been able to cooperate, as when the church's commitment to human equality taught by Jesus was supported by the abolitionists' crusade to end slavery. At other times the two visions have been strongly competitive, as when Christian compassion for the impoverished clashed with the obsessive consumerism of the market economy. At still other times the two visions have been in fierce conflict, as when the monolithic defense of segregation in the South during the fifties and sixties virtually foreclosed for a season the possibility of the church embodying its openness to all people regardless of ethnicity. Just as a general developing a battle plan must evaluate both the objective to be gained and the resistance to be expected, so the pastor seeking to be strategic must determine just what aspects of Christ's vision have not yet been actualized as well as to assess which of them the church may be ready to implement in its present circumstances.

Precisely here timing is of the essence in leadership. The issue is not one of timidity or cowardice in the face of opposition but of whether God's people are battle-ready in light of the amount of resistance they are likely to face. Even Jesus deferred a disclosure of "many things" to his disciples, not because he was fearful, but because they were not yet ready to "bear them" (Jn. 16:12). If, after two thousand years, we have been able to implement only a small part of that truth into which his Spirit ever seeks to guide us (v. 13), it is folly to think that the church will suddenly be able to actualize the entire sweep of his vision in only a few more years. So we practice the art of the possible, choosing our targets carefully, striking when the time seems opportune, daring to believe that, since the vision we chase is God's and not our own, delay does not mean defeat. As the prophet Habakkuk put it (2:3):

> For the vision still has its time,
> presses on to fulfillment, and will not disappoint;
> if it delays, wait for it,
> it will surely come, it will not be late.[6]

Creating a Climate of Expectancy

Regarding the future, we usually think that it is "coming, ready or not." As the hands of the clock and the pages of the calendar keep turning, who of us can stay what Andrew Marvell called "time's wingèd chariot hurrying near"?[7] But while the passing of earth's chronological time is certainly predictable enough, the arrival of God's eschatological time, which constitutes the church's vision, is conditioned on faith and therefore unpredictable. All too often, what we call the future is nothing more than a continuation of the present under slightly altered circumstances without anything really new about it. Rather than simply assuming the inevitability of the future as a matter of course, we need to face the crucial question of how a church can become truly open to God's tomorrow in the here and now.

In a general sense, this is the question of how authentic newness ever breaks through the brittle barriers of the status quo. Artists and writers struggle constantly to depict reality as it has never been seen before. Scientists brood for years in search of the breakthrough insights that will enable them to solve baffling problems. So-called "think tanks" experiment endlessly with proposals designed to help public officials improve the common good. Inventors are ever tinkering with new products to give their sponsors a competitive advantage in the marketplace. All around us, a host of people are pushing their intuition and imagination to the limit in an effort to introduce something truly innovative into human experience. Dare a church do anything less, especially when it is given a compelling vision of God's intention to "make all things new" (Rev. 21:5)?

I suggest three ways in which the strategic leadership of the pastor can help this to happen.

1. *Build a culture of creativity.* Rather than trying to produce a vision by depending on x-number of steps in a formula, begin by shaping the congregation into a corporate culture that might be described as porous enough to receive signals of transcendence. As used here, "culture" refers to a prevailing ethos of open-mindedness, a characteristic attitude of adventure, an instinctive way of responding to challenges by experimentation. We often associate the word *creativity* with the self-expression of gifted individuals, as in the phrase "creative genius," but I am using it here in the more basic sense of a group actually attempting to fashion something new by doing what it has never done before. Without this sense of being empowered to claim an unfulfilled but attainable potential, there is no possibility of vision.

Unless the very atmosphere of the church is infused with buoyancy and its mindset characterized by curiosity, God's future will have little chance to take root in its midst regardless of how much strategic preaching is done. Two words in vogue today are being used to describe what I mean by a "climate of expectancy." The first is *serendipity,* coined by Horace Walpole in 1754 to refer to unexpected discoveries made by accident, finding one thing when searching for something else.[8] The second is *improvisation,* referring to the cultivation of a playful mind that encourages the unpredictable to happen.[9] Both words point to the importance of spontaneity in preparing us for the arrival of that which is surprising, much like humor functions when its punch line elicits a sudden burst of laughter. Here are a few of the ways in which pastors may encourage this kind of creative openness in their working environment.

One is to practice a consultative rather than a controlling type of collaboration, in which everyone feels equally free to contribute in a partnership of shared learning.[10] Too often pastors think that they are facilitating the group process when they come to a meeting with a carefully prepared agenda and specific recommendations for consideration. While that approach may expedite action on routine housekeeping matters, it hardly encourages dreams to soar. Even to invite questions in such a context does little good because it tends to limit discussion to various reactions to the pastor's proposals. In searching for something as elusive as vision, it is better for everybody to begin on the same page—a blank page!—with the pastor primarily listening and encouraging freedom of expression. If the participants find it as hard as the pastor to break out of predictable role-playing based on their leadership assignments in the church, consider holding a vision retreat in a relaxed setting with enough "fun-and-games" to get folks relating to one another in fresh ways.[11]

A second suggestion that gets the creative juices flowing is to interact with those completely outside the leadership circle whose voices are seldom if ever heard in the formulation of church strategies. If those in traditional family units are dominant, then listen also to the unmarried, the divorced, and the widowed. If old-timers tend to prevail, talk also to new members about why they joined and to recent prospects about why they didn't. Ask some thoughtful outside observers such as educators, journalists, and civic leaders how they see the congregation and what they hope it will contribute to the community in the years ahead. Reggie McNeal goes so far as to recommend that you "rent some non-church people unfamiliar with the church to visit for two to four weeks, then debrief their experience."[12] The point is to introduce genuine diversity into the conversation so that the visioning group will begin to think "outside the box," looking at the church from a number of fresh perspectives.

Perhaps the most daring attitude adjustment I would suggest is to learn how to celebrate the creativity of failure. After all, what do we learn from success? Everybody pats us on the back and urges us to keep doing the very same thing. Indeed, a good way to lock something into the status quo and make it exempt from improvement is to call it a success. But failure, by contrast, when openly admitted and squarely faced, immediately causes us to say, "There must be a better way to do this. Let's try to find it." By forcing us to consider new options, failure brings us much closer to the threshold of creativity than does success. That is why almost every great discovery is preceded by a long string of defeats. Make the risk-takers your heroes, and you will begin to overcome the fear of failure that is a prime source of the rigidity and timidity that grips so many congregations.[13]

2. *Plead for God's future in prayer.* Consider for a moment the very nature of prayer. To talk to God presupposes two realms of reality variously called heaven and earth, the divine and the human, the world above and the world below. The central purpose of prayer is to establish contact between these two realms so as to appeal for more of the former to enter into the life of the latter. Note that we never pray for movement in the opposite direction. As the Lord's Prayer puts it, we are to plead for earth to become more like heaven but not for heaven to become more like earth (Mt. 6:10). In praise and adoration we value supremely the King of the universe, but in contrition and confession we abdicate every form of self-rule (Isa. 6:1–5). In petition and intercession we implore the Holy One to make major changes in our lives, but our thanksgivings and commitments contain no hint that we would change anything in the "Great Beyond."

In the language of this chapter, prayer is a way of breaking the grip of the "present evil age" (Gal. 1:4) upon our lives and allowing us to experience the life of the Age to Come. That is why prayer should be a prime source of that vision of God's tomorrow for which we yearn. And yet this dimension is missing from many of the public prayers that we hear today. Even praying people seem content to ask God to bless things just-as-they-are. Such expressions often take the form of thanking God for our free country (just-as-it-is), for the church we attend (just-as-it-is), and for the family we enjoy (just-as-it-is). Certainly nothing is wrong with acknowledging our gratitude for the blessings of a merciful Providence, but a steady diet of such acknowledgments may leave the impression that what we want most is for God to perpetuate and even sanctify the status quo.

What is missing in many of our prayers is a keen sense of just how much greater is what God yearns to do for us than what we ever request be done. As Paul put it, God is "able to do far more abundantly than all that we ask or think" (Eph. 3:20). C. S. Lewis once remarked, "We are half-hearted creatures, fooling about with drink and sex and ambition when infinite joy is offered us, like an ignorant child who wants to go on making mud pies in a slum because he cannot imagine what is meant by the offer of a holiday at the sea. We are far too easily pleased."[14] To be sure, we can thank God for letting us make mud pies, and can even ask God to allow us to keep on doing so, but such a prayer never nourishes a vision. The sense of a new kind of future comes only when we pray to be led from our spiritual slums and given a glimpse of the sea. How may a church learn to pray like that?

A first step is for the pastor to give careful thought to the leadership of prayer in public worship since these prayers may tutor the congregation in ways to address, and be addressed by, the Eternal One. When voicing the invocation, call upon God to come in surprising ways and assert fresh claims upon a waiting people. Name some of the promises of the gospel that you hope the congregation will claim before the hour is spent. Summon those present to be vigilant lest they miss the divine visitation amid the predictabilities of the service. Even an offertory prayer has rich potential as it consecrates the resources being gathered to undergird transformative initiates on behalf of human betterment. Guard the benediction from becoming a recital of requested privileges needed to produce a pleasurable week ahead. Instead, send the flock forth to grapple with the great issues of their life in God's strength. When Martin Luther King resigned his church in Montgomery to work for the cause of civil rights, he took a traditional benediction and infused it with a revolutionary dimension:

> And now unto him who is able to keep us from falling and lift us from the dark valley of despair to the bright mountain of hope, from the midnight of desperation to the daybreak of joy; to him be power and authority, for ever and ever.[15]

But most important is what is often called the pastoral prayer. Here the minister wrestles with God's agenda on behalf of the people. Many years ago I was invited to preach in a series of special services. One night a retired minister in the congregation led the evening prayer. Sensing a mood of complacency, he began, "O Thou perilous and untamed God…" Then, beginning with Abraham and moving swiftly through Scripture, he recounted how God had stirred the nest of patriarchs, prophets, and apostles by calling them to create a new future for the human spirit in their time. He concluded by asking God to do the same thing in our day as we respond to that call when voiced in the service for which we had gathered. By the time he finished, all of us were eager to have our names added to the roll call of faith in Hebrews 11. To hear the minister pray like that week after week will finally teach a congregation to ask God for more than business as usual.

Since guiding a church to pray visioning prayers may seem somewhat nebulous, let me offer an extended illustration of how I sought to do this in Shreveport on a very intentional basis. As often happens in older churches, our people were in danger of becoming content with inherited patterns of success. Beautiful facilities had been built, the budget had doubled and then tripled, attendance was the highest in years—and a mood of satisfied complacency was beginning to infiltrate our ranks. The feeling was abroad that, if we just kept doing more of the same, we were bound to flourish. Our dreams were more a replay of our past than a reach for God's future. Faced with the danger of becoming a self-sufficient church, I proposed a three-month prayer vigil designed to help our people "dream again."[16] The motto for this emphasis was "Our Church in the Hands of God: A Pilgrimage of Prayer." The logo depicted our church, symbolized by its steeple, enfolded within hands clasped to pray. Here, in brief, is how the project developed:

About a month before we began, I prepared for the emphasis by recounting from the pulpit the story of William Carey's "deathless sermon" of May 30, 1791, which launched the modern missionary movement. Using the "lengthened cords" and "strengthened stakes" of Isaiah 54:2 as a text, he developed two themes: "Expect great things from God," and, "Attempt great things for God." This watershed event enabled me to explain, not only how Carey's revolution of rising expectations transformed the Baptist movement of his day, but also how our church had the inalienable right to claim the divine resources needed to meet God's expectations for us in our day. Using a term then popular in the political arena, I began to spell out the "entitlements" Scripture promised to the people of God, and waiting there for us to possess through prayer.

Once the effort got underway in earnest, my primary pulpit thrust was based on the threefold promise of Jesus, "Ask, and it will be given you; seek, and you will find; knock, and it will be opened to you" (Mt. 7:7). This became our overarching text because here prayer is portrayed as the habitual lifestyle of the Kingdom disciple. All three of the imperatives are in the present tense, which makes their force repetitive: "Keep on asking…never weary in seeking…continue knocking over and over." In the next verse, the results are described as never-ending: "for those who perpetually ask and seek and knock are blessed again and again by God" (author's paraphrase). These words point to no impulsive religious plea but describe a continuous way of life lived in the expectant mood.

What is common to all three imperatives? *The inalienable right of God's people to expect more from him than they have yet received!* "Asking" implies many answers are already available, which we have not yet been given. "Seeking" implies that fresh discoveries are already in place waiting to be found. "Knocking" implies that many doors can be opened through which we have not yet walked. What an amazing conviction about God's grace undergirds these promises. According to Jesus, life is bursting with potential to be realized, with opportunities to be accepted, with surprises to be claimed. Reality, in other words, is far richer than it appears to be! Therefore, we must not limit our expectations to the status quo, for the realm of the unknown and undiscovered and unexplored is vastly greater than the tiny world of the familiar and predictable and commonplace that we now take for granted.

As I stressed in a series of sermons on each of the three petitions, we must be adventuresome and courageous and persistent if we are to appropriate these treasures God offers. After all, what good is a vast library if we never open a book? Or a great symphony if we never listen to a note? Or a rich museum if we never look at an exhibit? The summons to "ask… seek…knock" is an antidote to apathy, a challenge to overcome the fatalism, pessimism, and determinism that grimly assume that things will always be the same. Says Jesus: take a proactive approach to the promises of God. Seize the initiative, overcome your inferiority, dare to believe that the best is yet to be, claim the optimism of grace. Realize that these long-deferred blessings are now within reach, that they can be had simply for the "asking…seeking…knocking." After all, to "ask" means we do not need to figure out all of the answers but only to put forward the right questions. To "seek" means we do not need to invent any new discoveries but only to find the ones already there. To "knock" means we do not need to know how to open doors but only how to choose the ones ready to be entered.

With these biblical insights in place, we divided the journey into three parts, devoting a month to each of the following:

a. Praying Prayers of *Asking*. This involved an effort to loosen up traditional expectations and encourage boldness in actually wanting an even better future for our church than it had known in the past. While realism obviously was honored, the priority at this stage was to dream unfettered dreams and to uncover suppressed desires neglected by a capitulation to the status quo.

b. Praying Prayers of *Seeking*. Here the congregation focused on a plea for guidance in learning how to embody in its life together the dreams that emerged from praying prayers of asking. From this search came a list of changes that were felt to be needed in the life of the church. The spirit of prayer shifted the discussion away from criticism of the way "things had been" in the past to positive suggestions for the way "things could become" in the future.

c. Praying Prayers of *Knocking*. Here we reached the implementation stage, which involved making decisions, claiming commitments from members, and accepting challenging tasks never before attempted. Now was the time to pray prayers requesting the motivation, courage, and strength needed to translate insight into action.

Once the prayer campaign was structured on this timetable, steps were taken to lead all areas of church life to pray in these three distinct phases: each Sunday school class, board and committee meeting, worship service, midweek prayer meeting, men's and women's mission prayer group, staff meeting, as well as family and private devotions. The overarching purpose was to achieve a sense of oughtness "under God," that is, to give the membership a mandate undergirded, not by some complex study report and set of recommendations, but by a spiritual conviction as to the will of God for our congregation.

Three response cards were prepared corresponding to the three phases of the journey and were used to record individual and group impressions crystallized in prayer. This feedback was collected and then clustered into areas of concern that were used in listening sessions convened by the pastor on a periodic basis. In addition, several old-fashioned "cottage prayer meetings" were held somewhat spontaneously in the homes of members, to which staff ministers were invited. A sample of the three response cards will be found on the next page.

To mark the completion of our emphasis, I preached a sermon on the last Sunday entitled, "To Claim Our Church's Future." The sermon dealt more with the vision that I saw emerging from the prayers of the members

"Ask and it shall be given..."

In praying to God about the future of our church, I have been impressed to ask for the following gifts: _____

_____

_____

_____

"Seek and you shall find..."

In praying to God about the future of our church, I have been impressed to seek for the following discoveries: _____

_____

_____

_____

"Knock and the door shall be opened unto you..."

In praying to God about the future of our church, I have been impressed to knock for the following opportunities: _____

_____

_____

_____

than with any vision that I as pastor might want them to adopt. The style of church life was changing rather rapidly in our denomination, and I thought it important for the people to feel a strong sense of ownership of their own vision rather than feeling that it was based on borrowing some of the innovations that high-profile pastors were installing in their churches elsewhere. In this context, we did not move immediately to craft a new vision statement, although it may have been well to do so. We used the valuable input from the entire effort to enrich our annual strategic planning, which will be described in the next chapter. In retrospect, the greatest value of the project was to inspire our people to think more boldly, to not cling so tightly to the cherished triumphs of the past, and to be less fearful of changes that the future was sure to bring. That is the kind of human soil in which vision can grow and flourish.

3. *Base your vision on God's future in Scripture.* When Professor C. H. Dodd sought to find the foundation of the Christian faith, the "substructure" of that literary edifice that we call the New Testament, he isolated its earliest expression in the message (*kerygma*) that we call apostolic preaching.[17] After analyzing and comparing nine summaries of this proclamation in the Acts of the Apostles and the letters of Paul, he concluded that its core exhibits a consistent pattern that is characteristic of all the major theologies of the New Testament despite their great diversity.[18] These clarifications are crucial for our purposes both because this apostolic *kerygma* is the definitive declaration of God's tomorrow and because, once we know how to identify its controlling convictions, we will find it reflected on almost every page of the New Testament. How may we study the Bible to claim these treasures for our task?

According to Dodd's groundbreaking analysis, the primitive preaching had three main parts, each of which discloses the futurity that lies at the heart of authentic Christian vision.

  a. A new age of fulfillment had dawned "in accordance with the scriptures" (Acts 2:16; 1 Cor. 15:3–4).[19] Therefore, remembering our discussion earlier on the potentiality of the text,[20] begin by exploring the use of the Old Testament in the New Testament. Look for those promises in the former that are said to be coming true in the latter. Particularly important is the frequent claim that certain Old Testament prophecies have now been "fulfilled." A concordance check of this terminology (*pleroō* and cognates) will yield a list of the relevant passages, while entries in Bible dictionaries and theological wordbooks on such key words as *promise* and *fulfillment* will provide the needed conceptual framework.
  b. The life, death, and resurrection of Jesus had inaugurated this new age of fulfillment (Acts 2:22–24). This central affirmation of the apostolic

kerygma was linked to the first by attributing the entire ministry of Jesus to "the definite plan and foreknowledge of God" (v. 23). If Christ was God's future incarnate, then everything that the New Testament says about him is relevant to a Christian vision. Note especially what he claimed to have done of divine necessity to "accomplish" his mission on God's timetable, which the gospel of John identifies as his "hour." In the gospels, recognize components of this new age by using what scholars call the "criterion of dissimilarity"[21] to note where Jesus differed from the religious beliefs and practices of his day. See that in the letters his followers practiced these new age components in his name, such as abrogating circumcision, Sabbath observance, and temple worship.

   c. The resurrection of Jesus marked not only the end of his earthly life but the beginning of a vindication that included his exaltation to the right hand of God, the sending of the Holy Spirit to empower his church, and his triumphant return in glory (Acts 2:33–36; 3:20–21). We tend to think of God's future only in terms of the Second Advent; however, in the earliest proclamation, this threefold scenario was seen as "inseparable parts of a single divine event."[22] Therefore, in building our vision we look especially at what Christ is seeking to do in his heavenly reign, what the Holy Spirit is seeking to do in the life of the church, and what God will yet seek to do when the heavenly Kingdom is established on earth at the end of time. Because we already live in the "last days," our mandate is to claim the potential inherent in Christ's exaltation, his Spirit's outpouring, and his glorious appearing.

I hope that this summary of the apostolic *kerygma* has been sufficient to show the shape of God's tomorrow breaking into earth's today. At its heart the reality described was radically christocentric, since Christ fulfilled the Old Testament; Christ's "mighty works and wonders and signs" (Acts 2:22) made visible the kingdom of God; Christ's tragic cross would be transformed into a cosmic crown. With the help of a few good works on New Testament theology, you will want to use your teaching ministry as pastor to fill out the details of this vision so that the church will understand its centrality for the Christian faith. Unless a solid foundation is laid in the New Testament vision of what Christ came to do for human life, our vision today will lack spiritual substance and compelling power.

I mentioned above that this kerygmatic vision is implicit if not explicit on almost every page of the New Testament. Let me now test that claim with a case study to illustrate the kind of pastoral leadership needed to undergird strategic preaching. I have selected somewhat at random Matthew 5:17–48, the so-called "antitheses" passage in the Sermon on the Mount. The material is ethical rather than eschatological, didactic rather than kerygmatic, practical rather than theoretical; yet it breathes the sense of a whole new order of human existence entering an old and weary world that was hardly prepared to receive it. There is not space here to do a thorough exegesis of its verses, but let me highlight a few key features of the vision to which it contributes.

The passage is structured like a briefer sermon within the Sermon on the Mount. An introduction (Mt. 5:17–20) defines the problem being addressed, namely, that the revolutionary thrust of Jesus' ministry might tempt his hearers to suppose that he was bent on "abolishing" their inherited religion (v. 17a). This is countered by the insistence that they must never let such a thought enter their minds but should view his purpose as "fulfilling" the deepest intention of Scripture in the here and now (v. 17b). Based on this clarification, the key contention is then enunciated, somewhat as the "text" of this little sermon—Jesus expects his followers to exhibit a righteousness that "exceeds" even that of their religious leaders (v. 20). Six concrete illustrations follow this mandate. They show how the Kingdom ethic of Jesus, far from diminishing the religious legacy of the past, actually enhances it by showing his disciples how to do "more" than traditional morality ever demanded (v. 47).

The account is full of references to God's future, which Jesus was implementing in the present. The controlling category is "fulfillment" (v. 17), which is immediately reinforced by the promise that nothing given in Scripture will pass away until it is "accomplished" (v. 18). Faithfulness is now viewed, not just as obedience to the Law, but as seeking greatness in the "kingdom of heaven" (v. 19). The criterion of dissimilarity is enunciated strongly in the recurring formula, "You have heard that it was said of old...*but I say* to you" (vs. 21–22, 27–28, 31–32, 33–34, 38–39, 43–44, italics added). The demand for a righteousness that "exceeds" that of inherited religion (v. 20) is picked up at the end of the passage when the same root word (*perisson*) is used to insist that his hearers do *more* than others (v. 47). The sermon ends with a call to "be perfect" (v. 48), another term for the completeness or fullness of life expected in the New Age. Some Jewish groups expected a Messianic Age when a New Moses would mediate a New Torah,[23] but Jesus dared to suggest that this future scenario was already beginning to unfold before their eyes even as the Old Age continued.

With so many clues calling us to look here for glimpses of God's tomorrow, what is the vision to which this passage calls us? Space permits only a suggestive summary from each of the six antitheses:

1. In a world where rampant brutality had made human life cheap, Jesus not only prohibited murder but outlawed the anger that gives rise to

any destructive deed. Even the casual insults that demean the dignity of others are to be avoided at all costs (5:22). In their place, reconciliation is to be an overriding imperative of greater importance than participating in a climactic act of worship (5:23–24). Think what this attitude, which Albert Schweitzer called "reverence for life,"[24] says about such debated issues as abortion, gun control, suicide prevention, and capital punishment.[25]

2. Moving from the sixth to the seventh commandment in the Decalogue, Jesus then tracked adultery to its lair in the lustful look (5:28). In so doing he condemned not only the act but even the use of the imagination in secret to exploit a woman's sexuality for self-gratification. Again we think of the sweeping implications of this injunction for such pervasive practices as pornographic titillation in the mass media, prostitution involving even young girls, date-rape on campuses, and widespread sexual harassment in the work place.

3. Closely related to male exploitation of females was the unilateral right of a husband to divorce his wife. But Jesus would not countenance the rupture of the marital union by divorce or by the unchastity that could destroy it prior to divorce (5:32). As he taught more fully elsewhere, the marital bond is formed by God, hence nothing human is to put it asunder (Mark 10:9). Here we think, not only of the multiple divorces so common in the celebrity culture of Hollywood, some of which amount to little more than serial adultery, but to the huge increase in divorces among Christians, leading to a divorce rate that now equals that among non-Christians.[26]

4. In place of the deceptiveness that can corrupt not only marital but all other relationships, Jesus insisted on transparent honesty according to which one's word is one's bond (5:37). Since all of life is lived before God, we have no need to guarantee truthfulness by swearing a holy oath, as we might say, "on a stack of Bibles" (5:34–36). Yet how hard it is to practice complete candor when on every hand we encounter deceit: academic plagiarism, accounting fraud, specious political promises, inflated advertising claims, and innumerable "white lies" contrived in the name of public relations.[27]

5. Speaking to harassed people groveling under military occupation, Jesus quickly alluded to four familiar instances of offensive behavior: a slap on the cheek, a seizure of one's coat, a demand to shoulder another's load for a mile, and begging to receive a handout (5:39–42). Instead of retaliating in kind, Jesus suggested that the offended party seize the moral initiative by responding with undeserved kindness. Does not

our aggressively assertive society, with its road rage and endless shouting matches, provide abundant opportunities to practice this surprising strategy of returning good for evil?

6. The practice of nonretaliation was given climactic expression in the final antithesis when Jesus taught that even our enemies who persecute us are to be the object of our boundless love and compassionate intercession (5:44). After all, does not God shower the bounty of creation on friend and foe alike (5:45)? These words were spoken in a world much like our own, where passionate hatreds were directed against both insiders, such as Samaritans, and outsiders, such as Romans. Proof of the centrality of this radical response to evil was provided, not only by likening it to perfection (5:48) but by the fact that it explains exactly how Jesus achieved redemption on the cross and how his followers finally conquered the mighty Roman Empire without ever reaching for a sword. And yet, two millennia later, ours is a world in which many nations live in a perpetual state of warfare either internally or with others.

Stepping back to view the entire passage as a whole, what we have here are two lifestyles, two communities, indeed two worlds that could not be more different. One is characterized by a culture of competitiveness in which hostility abounds, in which the strong exploit the weak, in which privilege and pleasure triumph over sanctity and integrity. Duplicity toward friends and aggression toward foes is the preferred path to power that spawns animosity and alienation on every hand. While this was certainly a realistic picture of the world in which the hearers of Jesus lived, does it not also resemble the world in which we live today?

Over against that ever-present world, Jesus dared to depict another world in which all persons are so intrinsically important as created children of God that nothing should be allowed to violate the sacredness of their very existence, whether it be resentment or contempt, infidelity or intrigue, exploitation or rejection. In place of the self-centered will to dominate, Jesus focused on building relationships characterized by forgiveness, respect, fidelity, candor, compassion, and love. In stark contrast to the life of that day, he described a whole new realm of reality that they could "enter" as an alternative "kingdom" to the empires of earth (5:20). It was his way of saying, "Here is what God's future looks like, a future that you can claim here and now as my disciple." In making that offer, Jesus gave them a vision that they would never forget.

What shall we make of his challenge as we seek to construct a vision for our day? Clearly we are offered a choice: to accept life either as we know and live it or as Jesus knew and lived it. Obviously we have not yet made much progress in embracing the latter alternative. Think how far we are from achieving divorce-free marriages, or abolishing the genocide euphemistically called "ethnic cleansing," or instituting the rule of law rather than military conquest as the preferred way to settle international disputes. And yet there is hope. We have almost completely eradicated slavery and have at least banished dueling from respectable society. We are beginning to accord a measure of true respect to women in some parts of the world; and some governments are trying to outlaw fraud in the workplace. Despite these gains, however, few would say that we are even halfway toward actualizing the future Jesus described two thousand years ago. We do indeed live where the ages overlap!

I hope you have seen from this case study that one page of the New Testament provides far more than enough unrealized vision to engage one's ministry for a lifetime. I cannot tell you on what front to launch a new offensive to claim some aspect of its promise, for the circumstances in each situation differ in terms of where the enemy is entrenched. But the opportunities are endless to take new ground. For example, in just the last year or two I have worked with churches that help to sponsor adoption services as an alternative to abortion for unwed mothers, that staff well-run food and clothing closets to cut down on begging in the streets, that send mission teams to Cuba to help churches suffering as the result of repressive diplomatic relations with our country, that give women places of responsibility intended to enhance their dignity in the eyes of men, and that sponsor marriage enrichment programs with strong premarital and marital counseling designed to reduce the prevalence of divorce.

To be sure, some churches are ready and able to wage all-out war on the front lines, while others are prepared to do little more than consolidate the gains won by others. As emphasized earlier, it is crucial that the pastor be able to discern the strength and resolve both of the army to be led and of the enemy to be faced. But the whole point of this case study is that strategic preaching on God's tomorrow is reinforced by strategic leading to implement that future in the lives of the members. Few things frustrate a church more than gaining a compelling vision on Sunday that is then ignored on Monday through Saturday. The antidote to that frustration is found in Clarence Jordan's paraphrase of Hebrews 11:1, "Now faith is the turning of dreams into deeds."[28]

The Pastor as an Agent of the Future

Let me conclude this chapter by seeking to summarize how vision-oriented strategic leadership can undergird the role of the pastor as a strategic preacher. First and foremost is the importance of the minister functioning proleptically as a harbinger of hope, a pacesetter for change, a forerunner of the future that is yet to be. Just as a herald announces the coming of the king so that all may make ready, so the preacher anticipates God's unfinished agenda that the church is to address. In many of the well-established denominations of European background, the emphasis is on the minister as a sacramental agent of grace who helps Christians live in the present. At the heart of the New Testament is the concept of the minister as an eschatological agent of change who helps Christians live out of the future. The pastor has no ministry but that of the Master who was so full of the future that he seemed to belong to another world. This does not mean living far out in front of the congregation in splendid isolation, but rather calling God's people to join their pastor in facing that horizon where tomorrow's sunrise is already beginning to banish yesterday's darkness (Rom. 13:12).

Second, because Christians continue to live *in* this world even though they are not *of* it, the pastor must also determine to function intentionally as an effective leader of the church in its earthly existence. Competence in this regard will not come easily since the majority of theological schools that train pastors, and the majority of books that survey the primary pastoral tasks, largely ignore the leadership role.[29] It is almost as if pastors today must decide to become leaders in defiance of their seminary teachers and the ecclesiastical experts who define ministerial identity. But ask laity in parish life about their priorities for the pastor, and invariably leadership skills head the list. The institutional structures of the church have become so complex, the competitive nature of the religious environment so intense, and the expectations of church governing boards so sophisticated that most congregations simply will not flourish today without a high caliber of strategic leadership at least equivalent to that in a successful business of similar size.

Third, visionary leadership must be catalytic in the sense of precipitating out of an increasingly diverse and mobile membership a core agenda for change that will give the congregation both direction for the future and distinctiveness in its community. A church that does not know where it is going will soon try to go everywhere, resulting in stagnation and impasse. A church that does not know how to get where it is going will soon try everything, resulting in fragmentation and fatigue. The task of the pastor is to listen both to God and to the people, discerning where the will of God in Scripture and the will of the Spirit in the people converge, then guiding the congregation to develop a plan of action that will have both divine sanction and human ownership. The skill of the leader is especially crucial at two points in this group process: to design a strategy that, internally, builds on the strengths of the people and, externally, meets or exceeds the expectations of those who look to the church as a transformational force in the community.[30]

Fourth, visionary preaching dare not be neglected as a prime instrument of pastoral leadership. After all, according to the New Testament, worship should be the one recurring ministry of the church through which its eschatological orientation is most clearly expressed and passionately felt. Here more than anywhere else the community prays together for God's will to be done "on earth *as it is in heaven,*" thereby declaring its commitment to a world that is yet to be.[31] The proclamation of the gospel, which is the proper subject matter of the sermon, announces a New Age, thereby intensifying the tension between "Now" and "Not Yet." At a very practical level, this is where the pastor is most visible and where a challenging utterance on the life of the church can be heard in a spiritually serious setting. It is also where the greatest number of members gather with one another on a regular basis. John Ruskin once described preaching as "thirty minutes to raise the dead."[32] In that act of renewal the church finds fresh strength to continue its age-long journey looking "forward to the city which has foundations, whose builder and maker is God" (Heb. 11:10). If the tug of God's tomorrow is not felt in the preaching of the congregation's spiritual leader, pray tell where will it be felt?

But even when the church becomes a purposeful community impelled by a shared sense of vision with a transformational leader as its pacesetter, it is not easy for it to reach its intended destination. Like the children of Israel, it may wander in the wilderness for a generation, yearning for the fleshpots of Egypt while fearing the challenge of Canaan. Like the runner in a race, it may be distracted by former accomplishments (Phil. 3:4–13) or be tempted by besetting sins (Heb. 12:1). Why is the journey so difficult? Because the Old Age has not yet passed away; because the flesh which we still inhabit is the seat of a host of insecurities; because systemic evils, what Paul called "principalities and powers," continue to defy God and seek to keep his creation in subjection. By the very nature of Christian hope as incipient rather than instantaneous, its realization involves ceaseless struggle rather than easy victory.

There are, of course, many ways to dilute the eschatological urgency so characteristic of New Testament preaching. The seminary-trained pastor will know the sociological argument that early Christians were a marginalized underclass without any proud traditions or public power, hence they had no choice but to hope for a better lot in the future. Or the historical argument that, as the church began to be accepted in society, it shifted its focus from the eschatological to the sacramental, emphasizing the present rather than the future aspect of salvation. Or the theological argument that first-century expectations were tied to an apocalyptic literalism that failed to materialize in what was thought to be the last generation of history, hence it is unrealistic to try to maintain a lively eschatological tension after twenty centuries.

Arguments such as these overlook the fact that implementing God's vision of the future in the here-and-now was a central factor in biblical faith. The two constitutive events of Old Testament religion were exodus and exile, both of which were adventures in hope played out before the bright horizon of a promised land. The two constitutive events of New Testament religion were the ministries of Jesus and of Paul, both dominated by the conviction that an Old Age was dying and a New Age was being born. If the Old Testament was wrong in its understanding of exodus and exile and if the New Testament was wrong in its understanding of Jesus and Paul, then what do we have left at the core of the Christian faith? But if both testaments were right, how can contemporary preachers fail to give that same kind of futurity a prominent place in their pulpit work?

To be sure, many Christians in the pews are accustomed to think of their religion in static categories. They love the sentiment of the old hymn, "Change and decay in all around I see: O Thou who changest not, abide with me."[33] They want to see their pastor as the guardian of a "faith which was once for all delivered to the saints" (Jude 3). Their theme song is not, "I'm pressing on the upward way," but is rather, "I shall not be moved!"[34] Such folk want a sermon to be either the exposition of some Scripture passage that is finished when all parts of the text have been "covered," or the topical treatment of some religious theme which is finished when the standard "three points-and-a-poem" have been treated.

It never occurs to those with such a mind-set to view the sermon as finished only when its hearers have changed some attitude or position or direction in life. They agree with the ancient Greeks and Romans who viewed childhood as a time of rapid change discontinuous with adulthood, which was viewed as a timeless ideal existence with little or no change. But the New Testament transformed the meaning of maturity by viewing it, not as a goal already attained, but as a process toward which one continues to grow for a lifetime.[35]

To those with an aversion to the kind of changes called for by God's vision of life, at least three responses may be given. First, the followers of Jesus are promised that, through the teaching ministry of the Holy Spirit, they will be led to a fuller understanding of Christ's truth (Jn. 14:26; 16:12–13). As new light breaks from God's Word, the church is called to put away inherited notions and live by mature insight (1 Cor. 13:11). Second, new circumstances in the world around us teach the church new necessities. For example, at the beginning of the twentieth century American Christianity was forced to struggle with the impact of immigration, urbanization, and industrialization; but now it must face the equally great challenges of the twenty-first century: globalization, computerization, privatization. Third, with the benefit of hindsight we can see that the church has made many tragic mistakes in areas as diverse as science and slavery. The patience of God has extended the present interval as a chance to repent, to make needed course corrections, and to begin afresh on the basis of forgiveness and reconciliation.

But to experience such change, the church must first experience movement. The early church's conception of itself as a community of the end-time determined its distinctive sense of motion toward God's new future. This orientation transformed the way in which New Testament Christianity viewed all three temporal dimensions:

1. Everything in the *past* was viewed, not in terms of a tradition to be continued, but in terms of a promise to be fulfilled. This is seen in the breathtaking way that the earliest Christians suddenly and radically transformed the fundamental Jewish institutions of the Sabbath, the temple, and circumcision. Changes this dramatic could not have happened, almost without comment, in only a few decades if the church had not had its eyes on a new horizon.

2. Likewise, the sense of the *present* was infused with anticipation. Already the Holy Spirit was active in their midst as the living presence of God's tomorrow. This gave to daily life that quality of "as though" so vivid in 1 Corinthians 7:29–31. The present had already been invaded by the future, and thus the paralyzing grip of the status quo had already been broken for the believing community.

3. Finally, the immediate *future* was no longer seen as an extension of the present but rather was collapsed into the far reaches of eternity. What we call the imminent parousia expressed in the formula "the Lord is at hand" (Phil. 4:5b) meant that the future was no longer viewed as additional time in which to work out the incomplete agendas of the past and present, i.e., as more of the same kind of time to which the world had long been accustomed. Rather New Testament writers viewed the future as a new kind of time that would witness the consummation of the ages. Although the intensity of this experience diminished with the gradual institutionalization of the church, in our day the challenge remains to unleash the forces that accounted for this passion. Preaching in the spirit of the New Testament is a call to live out of the future, to be pulled forward by the future, indeed to claim the future "ahead of time" and thereby anticipate in advance the reality of the Age to Come.

CHAPTER 10

Strategic Planning to Implement Mission

Strategy plots a course of action designed to help a church reach its goals in a manner consistent with its deepest identity. Two basic insights have prepared us to understand strategy as *a plan for implementing mission*. The first is that the paramount task of leaders is to instill in their followers a shared sense of mission. The second is that mission is accomplished when purposes are fulfilled in such a way that vision is achieved.

The Problematic of Planning

Observant readers will be aware that I have thus far deliberately omitted any discussion of the planning process despite the fact that the words *strategic* and *planning* have become almost inseparable in popular usage. The reason for this is that the traditional approach to organizational planning is under attack today, nowhere more so than in relation to the formulation of strategy.[1] Instead of talking about "strategic planning," I have talked thus far about "strategic leading" because the latter is prerequisite to the former. Indeed, the greatest problem with many so-called "strategic plans" for the future is that the pastor and congregation have not first learned how to live strategically in the present. Usually "strategic plans" fail, not because the plan itself is faulty, but because those implementing it do not understand what it means to think and act strategically.

Planning Pitfalls

Let me warn you of a few planning pitfalls. Then we will turn to more promising ways to plan how a church may attempt to implement its mission. Central to the biblical understanding of humanity is the conviction that God created us for love, which, by its very nature, must be uncoerced. Thus God gave us the freedom to choose both whether to love and whether to be loved, options that some accept and some reject. One result of rejecting God's unconditional offer of love is what the New Testament calls "the sinful mind" (Rom. 8:7 NIV; cf. Rom. 1:28), which is characterized by a senselessness that has abandoned any pretext of living in purposeful fashion.

A single passage in Ephesians 4 is sufficient to suggest how the sinful mind functions. It is infantile and immature, tossed to and fro by every ideological wind that blows, deceived by the cunning and crafty scheming of others (v. 14). A futility marks this mindset (v. 17) for it is darkened in its understanding, ignorant of God and insensitive to others (v. 18), hard of heart and always greedy for more (v. 19). As Eugene Peterson put it in his colorful paraphrase, this is the lifestyle of those who go along with "the empty-headed, mindless crowd. They've refused for so long to deal with God that they've lost touch not only with God but with reality itself. They can't think straight anymore."[2]

What has all of this got to do with planning? It helps us to see that the human heart has more than enough rampant irrationality to thwart the best-laid plans of any individual or organization. Most planning models simply assume that everyone involved in carrying out the plan will be sensible, helpful, and exemplary if only because the group has carefully studied and approved the plan. In other words, the model makes no allowance for the sinful mind, for the stubborn fact of human perversity, for the frequency with which perfectly good plans are bitterly opposed by those who have no reason for doing so except to protect their vested interest in the status quo. Planners tend to be optimists, even perfectionists, which may explain why I have never seen in the relevant literature any discussion of the ways in which human waywardness introduces an unpredictable element into the planning process at unexpected times.

Let me illustrate how what I earlier called the "angelic fallacy" can sabotage the most careful planning process. H. Beecher Hicks Jr. became pastor of Metropolitan Baptist Church in Washington, D.C., one of the nation's largest and most prestigious African American congregations. Shortly after he came there, the church and all its official bodies developed and duly approved plans to replace the historic sanctuary with an enlarged worship center. The membership underwrote the plans financially. However, before ground could be broken, controversy engulfed the project. Controversy came from within, caused by a power struggle that featured character assassinations, accusations of fiscal mismanagement, and efforts to undermine the reputation of the church with lending agencies. For nearly five years the pastor struggled against hostile forces that threatened to destroy his ministry, none of which surfaced during the planning phase.[3] No wonder Paul warned his readers that they must no longer live with the sinful mind

(Eph. 4:17), for plans are as chancy as the hearts of those charged with carrying them out.

One of the most damaging criticisms of planning contends that it often reflects a covert attempt by a power elite to control the life of an organization. Henry Mintzberg is unsparing in his denunciation: "Perhaps the clearest theme in the planning literature is its obsession with control—of decisions and strategies, of the present and the future, of thoughts and actions, of workers and managers, of markets and customers."[4] Planners like to gain this control, not by contending for their preferred direction in open debate, but by incorporating their ideas in an "approved" plan expressing the collective will of the organization. They secure this legitimacy for a predetermined course of action by magnifying the threat of turbulence and minimizing the possibility of surprises, which leads the group to adopt their rational, coordinated blueprint for the future.[5]

In case this indictment seems a bit harsh, let me try to describe the way it plays out in a typical church situation. The pastor announces the need to develop a "long-range plan," either because he has recently come to serve the congregation or because the timetable of the old plan has expired or because major changes are taking place in the community. A "blue ribbon" committee is appointed, which, by that very description, is comprised almost entirely of longtime lay leaders with a vested interest in the status quo. They solicit input, which comes primarily from the committed cadre of workers who are generally satisfied with the way things are going, but who yearn for an expansion and enhancement of their efforts in the future. Little if anything is heard from that great host of largely passive members on the periphery of congregational life or from the many prospects who considered the church but chose for whatever reason to look elsewhere.

First the committee discovers some of the approaches "successful" churches are taking elsewhere, and that the pastor would like to try in this setting. Then the committee issues a report describing an optimum future for the church. A business meeting attended by perhaps 10–15 percent of the resident membership readily accepts the plan. After an initial flurry of publicity in the church paper, implementation is left to the pastor and staff working with appropriate church boards and committees. At times resistance begins to surface for one or more of several reasons. Perhaps the assumptions on which the plan was based have now changed. Or original projections of costs have proved unrealistic. Or some group not involved in formulating the plan has come up with different ideas. Whatever the reason for such resistance, the entrenched power structure moves to quell such opposition by pointing out that the plan was unanimously adopted by the church in conference upon recommendation of all the appropriate committees and boards several months or even years ago. This is one way to reinforce a "command-and-control" style of leadership, but it is hardly a suitable way to execute strategy!

Dealing with the Problem of Control

How can a pastor and church deal with the problem of control? First you must identify Christlikeness as the ultimate goal of Christian existence both for the individual believer and for the church. Second, you must describe sin as a self-centeredness that can thwart the freedom of others to respond to the claims of God. On the issue of control, these two approaches stand in the sharpest possible contrast to each other. On the one hand, Christ was entirely "a man for others," never seeking to dominate even his closest disciples or to exploit the crowds for his own purposes. On the other hand, those determined to maintain the status quo—especially when challenged by a marginal voice out of Nazareth—brutally suppressed Jesus for no good reason. A central issue in Jesus' ministry was whether the destiny of God's people would be controlled by the ideology of the religious establishment or whether it would be open to surprise by the unfettered voice of prophecy.

In reflecting on this issue, the early church quickly came to realize that Jesus embodied a new kind of servant leadership that was the antithesis of the desire to control. In a passage of poetic beauty and theological brilliance (Phil. 2:5–11), the apostle Paul pictured his Lord at the pinnacle of cosmic power, equal in every respect to God (v. 6). But Christ voluntarily relinquished those heavenly prerogatives; he "emptied himself" (v. 7), exchanging the "form of God" (v. 6) for the "form of a servant" (v. 7). Rather than divesting himself of divine status, Jesus embodied that status in the lowliest possible form by his death on the cross (v. 8). Note the scandalous implications of this central "metanarrative" of New Testament faith: sovereignty expressed itself in servanthood! Power was made perfect in weakness (1 Cor. 1:25)! For centuries it had been axiomatic that the business of God was to control. This religious axiom entitled religious representatives on earth to do the same. But now, once and for all, every impulse to control was destroyed by being nailed to a cross!

To summarize: we have identified three key problems with planning. Inherent in the very process of execution is (a) the problem of accelerating *change,* which may be addressed by adopting the kind of vision discussed in the previous chapter; (b) the problem of unbounded *contingency,* which may be interpreted in light of a realistic understanding of human evil; and (c) the problem of covert *control,* which may be countered by a Christian understanding of servant christology. These doctrinal perspectives do not somehow "solve" the problematic of planning, but they do provide insights that should help pastors and churches guard against some of the more common mistakes made in this area, which have discredited the enterprise in the eyes of many.

Thus we move forward with three principles clarified: (a) our task is not to predict the future of the Old Age, which is uncertain at best, but to actualize the future of God's New Age in the midst of the Old; (b) efforts to do this will be resisted because God's future challenges the status quo in which many have a vested interest, thus our plans will often fail, not because the plan is bad, but because human sin is strong; (c) the Christian way to overcome entrenched power is not to exercise authoritarian forms of control but to model a servant leadership that encourages even "the least" to find the freedom and fulfillment that come from being equal partners with all God's people in the divine "plan of the ages."

A New Paradigm for Strategic Planning

Having identified some of the main problems inherent in the traditional planning process and having offered correctives designed to counter their negative influence, we can now propose a positive approach to strategic planning congruent with the kind of preaching and leading advocated throughout this study.

Five-Step Model for Perennial Planning

I suggest a model of perennial rather than periodic planning, which involves five steps:[6] start with the future, look back to the past to discover the resources already available as foundations on which to build and the constraints this inheritance imposes, correlate these two understandings at the point at which they converge in the present, create a strategic plan, and create a continuous feedback loop.

1. Since many strategic planning efforts soon get bogged down in the "paralysis of analysis," surprise everyone by starting with the future rather than the past. Before becoming inhibited by a mass of historical trend data, ask leaders and followers alike to describe their understanding of the biblical vision that they would like to see the church implement at an appropriate point in the future, say five or ten years hence. Create a serendipitous climate in which the imagination can improvise, restrained only by "the art of the possible." Input should not be limited to a few key leaders on a "long-range planning committee" but should be sought as widely as possible by means of surveys, focus groups, vision retreats, and a host of informal discussions.

This is a prime time to help the "silent majority" in the congregation find its voice. In particular, solicit suggestions from potential stakeholders *outside* the church. Find out what kind of church your prospects, community leaders, and those in the supporting ecosystem feel that they want and need. In balancing feedback from insiders and outsiders, face early on the central question of the extent to which the church exists for those it has already reached and the extent to which it exists for those it has yet to reach.

At this initial stage in the process, try to avoid vague generalities and resist any attempt to reach a premature synthesis of what the preferred future should be. One way to do this is by suggesting that vision statements be linked to "key performance indicators" (KPIs), which may be defined as concrete, measurable descriptions of the changes that are desired.[7] The quantitative aspect should not be allowed to tilt the discussion toward a statistical rather than a spiritual agenda, but should be allowed to provide handles for determining how a specific aspiration might affect behavior and attitudes. For example, someone might suggest the following KPI: "In five years I would like for the number of members who report praying regularly in family devotional times to increase from 37 percent to 60 percent." Or even less tangibly: "In five years I would like for at least 75 percent of the deacons to feel that their service to the church is undergirded by the prayer ministry of the laity." The point is to describe each facet of the vision with enough specificity so that the group will know when and whether it has actually been implemented. The more components of a possible future that can be identified, even if some appear to be incompatible or unworkable, the more options will be available to consider when organizing and prioritizing to develop a preferred scenario.

2. As the hoped for "church of the future" begins to take shape, look back to the heritage of the past to discover both the resources already available as foundations on which to build and the constraints that this inheritance imposes. Internally, this could involve a study of the membership, the facilities, the finances, the programs currently in operation, the policies and procedures guiding the organizational life of the body, and the effectiveness of strategies recently employed. Externally, this could involve a close look at the community, its demographic trends, shifting residential patterns, employment and economic outlook, social and cultural tensions, and "competitor" churches in the religious marketplace. Planning manuals are full of helpful checklists in these and related areas.[8] Avoid, however, the temptation to spend too much time and energy amassing a complex database replete with charts and graphs that do little more than report the past without interpreting it or probing how the members understand it.

One way to break out of the "fact-trap" and struggle with issues of meaning is to utilize the data gathered in a "SWOT" analysis, an acronym standing for **S**trengths, **W**eaknesses, **O**pportunities, and **T**hreats.

Looking primarily at the internal data, ask:

a. What do we do best? In all of our programs, where are the centers of excellence? What has contributed most to our favorable reputation as a church?

b. Conversely, what are the constraints under which we now work? What are the sources of our greatest frustrations and failures as a church? What are the main reasons why people decide either not to affiliate with our church or to leave us for another church?

Then looking mainly at the external data, ask:

c. What trends in the community are creating needs that our church is best equipped to meet? What creative expression of the gospel offers us a distinctive niche because sister churches in the area are neglecting or ignoring it?

d. Conversely, what sources of support within the community are diminishing in size and strength? What social, cultural, and political dynamics are running counter to the ethos of our congregation? What popular religious trends, such as newer worship styles, are we as a congregation reluctant or unwilling to consider?

3. Once the net has been cast far and wide to gauge the perceptions of both insiders and outsiders regarding the direction they want the church to go in the future and where they think it has gone in the past, correlate these two understandings at the point they converge in the present. This is the most difficult and yet the most important stage in the strategic planning process. To facilitate effective dialogue on this assignment, the vision components may need to be organized into coherent clusters suggesting the three or four breakthroughs that the most insightful contributors want the church to attempt.[9] Likewise, the audit of past activities may need to be arranged in meaningful categories, such as the SWOT analysis just mentioned. This organizing and reporting task is best done by a small group, but the editing team should be careful to include as many diverse voices as possible so as not to circumscribe the ongoing conversation by superimposing prematurely its own priorities on the input received.

At this stage, when seeking to correlate heritage and hope, let the dialogue be as free and unfettered as possible. Hold brainstorming sessions with every major group that has a stake in the outcome. To avoid the politics of special-interest pleading, keep the discussion tightly focused on the question, "Granted where we have come from and how we have gotten to where we are now, what is the best way to get to where we want to go next?" A small task force can use the ideas generated by this dialogue to create a more careful correlation between KPI aspirations for the future and SWOT attainments in the past. This may be done by a "cross-impact" or matrix analysis according to which a realistic assessment is made of the church's ability to achieve its intended future in light of its inherited past. Obviously the desired outcome at this stage is to discover ways to maximize strengths, minimize weaknesses, optimize opportunities, and neutralize threats.[10]

4. The ideas that emerge from this interaction between the "whence" and the "whither" of the church's trajectory, once they are clarified and prioritized, become the building blocks of the strategic plan itself. Stated as a simple formula: *foresight* regarding the future, combined with *hindsight* regarding the past, leads to *insight* regarding the present. There are many ways to write out a strategic plan for popular consumption. Most begin with an enriched and updated statement of mission, perhaps with brief commentary on how this thrust is faithful to the enduring purposes of the church in light of its emerging context. Then they list several strategic imperatives to be accomplished within a reasonable time frame, either in priority order of importance, in chronological order of sequence, or in topical order corresponding to the organizational structure of the church.

Beyond these core affirmations, two schools of thought describe what else to include in a strategic plan. The first school argues that since an ad hoc group often develops the strategic plan, this group should provide only a skeletal outline to standing committees and boards for their use in determining implementation. The second school feels that such referrals usually result in a loss of focus and momentum. This group would create a standing committee on strategic planning, or ask some coordinating group such as the church council to function in this regard. This coordinating group, in consultation with relevant committees and boards, should develop detailed guidelines for implementing the strategic plan. Whether the church takes a more decentralized or a more centralized approach, your plan is not likely to have enduring impact unless leadership assignments are clarified, programmatic support organized, financial resources allocated, and an implementation timetable projected for each strategic initiative that is approved. In other words, the strategic plan must also include an operational plan.

5. Most churches seem to think that the strategic planning process is finished when the four steps just outlined have been completed. Such thinking may explain why so many strategic plans are never implemented or have only minimal impact on the congregation. To succeed, the church must take one more essential step: create a continuous feedback loop consisting of two parts—deployment and accountability. The former seeks to make the strategic plan pervasive throughout the congregation so that

everyone will feel a sense of ownership in what is being attempted. The church leadership will need to work in partnership with the frontline workers in each organizational unit to help it understand and accept the changes needed if the plan is to succeed. Deployment includes clear delegation of responsibility, but it also involves training in how to carry out assignments effectively and motivation to persevere when resistance to change makes the strategic objective difficult to attain.

The word *accountability* sounds harsh, even judgmental, especially in a voluntary organization such as a church; but it really means that the church must develop mutually agreeable procedures to insure that authentic feedback as to how effectively the strategic plan is actually working will be received in timely fashion. Because such plans are developed to accomplish God's will for the church, they are often written in explicitly religious language. Such language strongly inhibits any admission of failure lest it seem either that the church has failed God or that God has failed the church. In actuality, some flaw in the plan itself or an unexpected change in circumstances may have changed the context in which the plan was being implemented.

Some pastors are convinced that enthusiasm among the members can be maintained by talking only about success. They suppress any mention of setbacks as bad for morale. Such deliberate denial of difficulties may allow the situation to grow steadily worse. In such cases prolonged lack of attention may allow a problem that might easily have been corrected when it first surfaced eventually to become intractable. The solution is to create a climate of trust in which the messenger is not shot for bearing bad news, in which remediation is more important than placing blame, and in which the strategic plan is subject to continual revision in light of its demonstrated effectiveness as evaluated in the process of implementation.

Making the Strategic Plan Operational

All five parts of the strategic planning model just described are of equal importance and thus should receive equal attention. In actual practice, however, churches tend to focus on the earlier stages, to the neglect of the latter stages. A common pattern is to spend far too much time studying the past (step 2), resulting in a limited effort to conceptualize in concrete terms a desirable future (step 1). Facing self-imposed deadlines or waning interest in a project that has taken more effort than originally anticipated, the pastor and a few key leaders are asked to correlate the findings (step 3) without benefit of widespread dialogue and to come up with a set of recommendations (step 4) for church adoption at a poorly attended business meeting, all on a rushed schedule to meet predetermined deadlines. Everyone is so happy to have the report completed and approved that they soon move on to other matters, neglecting almost entirely the implementation process (step 5). Within six months or a year, the strategic plan has become little more than a report-on-the-shelf, consulted only occasionally by a few church leaders until the exercise is repeated again in five or ten years.

Let me be both explicit and emphatic here: there is no reason to attempt strategic preaching on the basis of that kind of strategic planning! The resulting sermons will have no greater impact on the congregation than the plan itself has had. The problem, however, is not that strategic planning as such is ineffective but that its usefulness was fatally compromised by following a faulty process. Unless the strategic plan becomes a pervasive influence continually shaping the life of the congregation, it does not deserve the support of the pulpit. Above all, it is imperative that any approved strategic plan become fully *operational* if it is to serve as the basis for strategic preaching. This means that it must function as a vital force guiding the ministry of its members in their efforts to fulfill a shared sense of mission. Therefore, we need to look more closely at how to take with great seriousness the neglected steps 4 and 5 of the overall planning process.

The key to making a strategic plan fully operational is to break it down into manageable units of implementation. Even with a conscious effort to be as concrete and specific as possible at each step identified by the model outlined above, most plans tend to become so general and comprehensive that they are useful only to a few churchwide leaders such as pastor, ministerial staff, and members of the official board. While a unified overview provides helpful background, most of the work of the church is done in smaller settings to which the plan never quite penetrates. Sometimes the very existence of the plan is known only to a small percentage who attend church business meetings and who sit on some committee or board. How can a sense of ownership of the plan be created among what Edmund Burke called "the little platoons"[11] that constitute the "front line" of the church's life?

Five Ways to Unpack the Plan

I suggest five ways of opening up or "unpacking" the plan so that it will become more accessible to the greatest number of church members.

1. Identify all the functional units of the church's ministry that you need to enlist in support of the plan. Beyond the boards and committees that constitute the "power structure" of church governance, do not neglect each Bible study class and discipleship group, choir and instrumental ensemble, evangelism and mission team, prayer and support group, sports and recreational teams, age-group organizations such as for senior adults, plus the many ad hoc affinity groups that spring up for a season in church

life. Why the stress on these diverse groupings that often get omitted from the organizational chart? Because they interface with the church's publics far more than official bodies ever do. In fact, support staff such as custodians, secretaries, child-care providers, and food service workers—precisely because their work is so people-intensive—need to have an especially clear understanding of the church's mission as well as the strategy for attaining it. Do not consider a strategic plan operational until an informed and enthusiastic advocate has met with every group in the church to explain the plan and sell its members on it.

2. Break down the underlying concept of purpose into its several component parts. In chapter 8 we described one such analysis, which organized purpose in terms of worship, outreach, nurture, fellowship, service, and support. Each of these six components can become the basis of an integrated "ministry system" supported by committee assignments, program budgeting, data collection, and organizational infrastructure. If the strategic plan is developed around the enhancement of each of these purposes, then those interested in and involved with a particular component can readily grasp how they might help to advance that aspect of the plan. Sometimes strategic plans are presented in such a way that all of the members are made to feel that they must work on every part of the plan. Such a presentation creates an intimidating burden. Many members would find it much more manageable to help achieve only one part of the plan that is important to the success of the whole.

3. Sub-divide each of the strategic imperatives into a set of objectives that break up what might become a challenge for several years into brief manageable tasks and so "incrementalize" the steps needed to achieve progress. In military parlance, objectives are the short-range tactics needed to accomplish a long-range strategy. Typically, in church life such tactical objectives are flexible, even experimental, seldom requiring more than a year to complete. Usually they involve an action plan comprised of only a few steps, which may be adjusted or even abandoned on short notice if they prove ineffective or if circumstances change. Many members who are reluctant to take official church jobs because they seem to be of endless duration will commit to work on some carefully focused objective if the assignment is of limited duration. Particularly, newer members may need to gain confidence by working in the church's "adhocracy" before they are ready for a more permanent position in the church's "bureaucracy."[12] A good strategic plan should offer many such short-term opportunities to those who are only marginally involved.

4. Broaden the understanding of inputs needed in the feedback process. Most strategic plans are excessively dependent on objective data of a statistical

nature, much of which can be provided by the office staff. Such trend-lines of performance data usually measure activities undertaken rather than results achieved. Of equal or greater importance are "soft data" designed to measure changing perceptions and feelings of participant satisfaction. A successful plan requires a great many people not in leadership positions to report and interpret how the life of the church is actually being experienced by a wide segment of its members.

Likewise, the church needs many "eyes and ears" outside its walls to discern both how the changes taking place in the community are impacting the congregation and how changes taking place in the congregation are impacting the community. Others need to be observing church life elsewhere, not only among nearby "competitor" churches but in "peer" churches in other cities, where they may have contacts through family members or business associates. A surprisingly large number of members would welcome the chance to discuss how they see things in the congregation, the community, and the wider religious world, but are seldom asked to do so. Instead, planning efforts are too often based on feedback from an inbred leadership cadre whose input is circumscribed by a defense of the status quo.

5. Once a steady stream of input begins to flow from the "grass-roots" of the membership, build into the church year a rhythm of review that is just as predictable as annual budget preparation by the finance committee, annual staff reviews by the personnel committee, and annual recruitment of lay leadership by the nominating committee. You do not need to review every part of a strategic plan on the same schedule. The understanding of purpose should be constantly enriched, but you may not need to reexamine it in depth more than once in a decade, or when a new pastor is called. Changes in the surrounding community influence the sense of mission, however, and so it needs a careful look at least every three to five years. Objectives should be reviewed annually prior to allocating personnel, financial, and facility resources. Specific action plans need almost constant review, either monthly or quarterly. The pastor should insure that these review cycles are imbedded in the duties of the appropriate church officers and planning groups and that the results of these reviews are promptly disseminated to all who have a stake in the outcome of the planning process. A strategy is like a "game plan" on which good leaders constantly "keep score" in low-key, nonthreatening ways.

These five suggestions, taken together, are little more than procedural moves designed to make the strategic plan as well understood as possible and to offer meaningful ways for everyone to participate. The more participation the plan elicits, the more likelihood that it will broaden a consensus regarding the future direction of the church. What we are really after here, however, is not just a lot of busywork intended to increase member involvement. We are reshaping the congregational culture into what Peter Senge calls a "learning organization."[13] By this he means a process of collective inquiry, of self-directed team learning, which enables and empowers all of the participants to contribute to a common fund of insight, thereby enlarging the group's capacity to conceive and create its own future.

The crux is to move from stereotypical illusions caused by leadership inbreeding to new conceptions of reality achieved through the openness and freedom fostered by dialogue. Four larger issues are at stake in this congregational learning process. These include the resulting ability to take a long-term orientation, to search for structural causes rather than to react to symptomatic events, to spot paradigm shifts in their early stages, and to invent new mental models when old ones become obsolete.

Pastoral Leadership in Strategic Planning

This chapter has sought to present as a process for guiding a church in the implementation of its mission. Even though this task should involve the entire congregation, the pastor has a unique responsibility to model how strategic planning may be done effectively. Therefore, let me conclude with a few comments on the kind of ministerial leadership that facilitates effective strategic planning. As Peter Senge has emphasized, the leaders' task is to design and guide learning processes whereby people throughout the organization can deal productively with the critical issues they face.[14] Here follows a decalogue of imperatives that I have found helpful in that regard.[15]

1. Listen both to your congregation and to your community with blow-torch intensity, resisting every impulse to proclaim answers before you gain a profound understanding of what the deeper questions really are.
2. Invite your members to live the life of dialogue with you as pastor, assuring them that your pronouncements, even from the pulpit, are not the "last word" on a subject but are intended to elicit a response that will lead to collaborative learning on your part as well as theirs.
3. Discover the rich diversity of viewpoint within the membership; however, at the same time, try to discern patterns of convergence, those points of commonality at which unity can support diversity. Adopt as your own the American motto, *e pluribus unum,* and learn how to fashion a singleness of purpose out of a plurality of interests.
4. Do not construct a defensive strategic plan like a spiritual Maginot line designed to insure institutional survival. Instead, dare to believe that if the church focuses on meeting the needs of people both inside and outside the congregation, survival will take care of itself.

5. Do not make your strategic plan a statement of what the pastor and church leaders want the members to do, but a statement of what the members want the pastor and church leaders to help them do together. The plan should encourage typical and even marginal members to believe that they can make an important difference in the life of their church.

6. Create coherent ministry systems[16] designed to stabilize and give structure to those dynamic processes that produce the incremental changes needed to reach the vision in small but steady steps. Remember: the future can be shaped, but it cannot be hurried.

7. Construct a vision open to perpetual *re*-vision, not because the original conception was flawed, but because new circumstances offer new opportunities. Celebrate the God of surprises who often confronts us with fresh challenges when we least expect them.

8. Show that you as a leader will not only accept changing circumstances, but that you are also willing to change as your understanding grows, as a new consensus emerges, or as unexpected crises arise. Do not change while pretending not to change, since this will eventually leave an impression that you are vacillating in response to covert influences.

9. Do not shield yourself from negative developments or ignore poor results; welcome them as early warning signs of weaknesses in the plan that need to be corrected. As Jay Forrester once remarked, the hallmark of a great organization is "how quickly bad news travels upward."[17]

10. Perhaps most important, do not be afraid of failure. Leaders always learn more from their failures than from their successes.[18] Nobody ever said that it is any fun to fail, but adversity is the anvil on which clarity, courage, and compassion are fashioned. So be quick, not only to admit your mistakes, but to legitimate a healthy "failure factor" among those with whom you work.

APPENDIX TO CHAPTER
Henry Mintzberg on Strategic Planning

Early in this chapter,[19] I alluded to the work of Henry Mintzberg when discussing the problematic of the planning process as traditionally practiced, but did not say more because of the complexity of his critique. Since old styles of so-called "strategic planning" are still widespread in many churches, I want to provide a more comprehensive summary of his contentions for the benefit of those willing to reconsider whether newer approaches might be justified. Mintzberg's major study of this issue carries an ominous title, *The Rise and Fall of Strategic Planning*. He insists with some vehemence that "the term *strategic planning* has proved to be an oxymoron."[20] By this he means that both the theory and practice of planning as it has developed into a major force shaping organizational life since the 1960s is incompatible with the very nature of strategic leadership and the tasks for which it is responsible. In more than four hundred pages of densely packed argument, Mintzberg both tries and largely succeeds in demolishing the planning orthodoxy found in the standard literature (which requires a bibliography of twenty-six pages just to list!).

Unfortunately, this pivotal work will not be easily used by most pastors. It is written almost entirely about the business world, with a few comments on government and education, but none on religious organizations. It interacts constantly with the technical research on planning, which will be unfamiliar to all but a few academicians. Later Mintzberg and two colleagues wrote "an easily accessible explanation of the fascinating field of strategic management,"[21] but my experience with advanced theological students suggests that even this popularization will prove difficult for most ministers to digest. Since Mintzberg has mounted the most formidable attack on the very legitimacy of what is called "strategic planning," we need to engage his concerns in ways relevant to our interest in pastoral leadership. Mintzberg admits that "a certain cynicism of tone pervades much of this book"; nevertheless, he concludes that "there are indeed ways to couple the skills and inclinations of the planners with the authority and flexibility of the managers to assure a strategy making process that is informed, integrative, and responsive to changes in an organization's environment."[22]

Mintzberg is writing primarily about the way in which planning was done for a quarter-century (1965–1990) in large businesses that employ full-time professional planners to guide the process of strategy formation. These specialists tend to constitute a separate subculture within the corporation. Mintzberg contends that this subculture has become inbred and divorced from the realities of managerial responsibilities. His book is really a frontal attack on the close-knit fraternity that controls the contemporary planning movement and on those scholars whose writings seek to justify its theory and practice.

Most churches make little or no use of professional planners, even as an occasional consultant. Rather churches depend on the pastor to function both as their chief leader/manager and as their chief strategist/planner, thereby overcoming the dichotomy that Mintzberg identifies as lying at the heart of the problem in the business world. For that reason, we shall concentrate here only on issues rooted in the very nature of planning rather than on problems caused by internal corporate arrangements not typical of congregational life.

The best way to grasp Mintzberg's complex argument is to focus on the sharp contrasts he draws between the way planners operate and the way strategists operate. He hammers away at the strikingly different mindset, methodology, and mission each party brings to the task of determining direction for an organization. We shall utilize these three categories to simplify Mintzberg's somewhat convoluted treatment of the issues.

1. *Mind-set.* From the initial stage of the process, at the level of preparation, planners seek to isolate their work in structural fashion as a distinct function unrelated to the daily operations of the organization. This deliberate detachment is viewed as the only way to be as objective and dispassionate as possible, free from the influence of the status quo. Mintzberg calls this "the fallacy of formalization,"[23] the mistaken notion that innovation can be institutionalized through a separate set of systems guided by planning experts with little or no "hands-on" experience in figuring out how to make the organization work. He contends rather that strategy emerges from "front-line" involvement in leading the troops, from insights fashioned in "hand-to-hand" combat with the enemies of success, i.e., from passionate subjectivity rather than dispassionate objectivity, however informal and unstructured the former might be.

Once the planners assume an impartial pose, they tend to do their work in rational, abstract fashion. They clearly favor deduction rather than induction, analysis rather than synthesis, hence a reductionistic rather than a holistic approach to problem-solving. To use psychological categories, planning is primarily a left-brain activity with its preference for the orderly, the linear, and the sequential, rather than an activity of the right-brain, which is more comfortable with the informal, the relational, and the simultaneous. To hammer the point home, Mintzberg quotes Wildavsky: "Key words appear over and over: planning is good because it is *systematic* rather than random, *efficient* rather than wasteful, *coordinated* rather than helter-skelter, *consistent* rather than contradictory, and above all, *rational* rather than unreasonable."[24] The problem, of course, is that this cognitive emphasis neglects the more creative sources of insight such as intuition, imagination, and instinct, which Mintzberg would insist are crucial to the discernment of strategy.

Consistent with the thought processes just described, it is not surprising that the resulting plan is usually tilted toward conveying information rather than stimulating inspiration. In form it is carefully articulated, more explicit than implicit, more detailed than suggestive, more in writing for "paper-to-person" communication than oral for "face-to-face" communication. In content, it is strongly data-driven, especially the hard data of "facts" rather than the soft data of "opinion," thus weighted more toward quantitative conclusions based on statistical trends than on qualitative judgments based on emergent needs. The whole way that the plan is conceived seems to be based on the assumption that thinking precedes action, that formulation is the key to implementation, that if the situation can just be delineated in enough detail, the solution will be obvious. Remembering our comments on the nature of strategy both in chapter 7 and earlier in this chapter, we are compelled with Mintzberg to ask, Where in all of this is a vision-driven plan based on dynamic interaction with the context?

2. *Methodology.* In terms of actual procedures, how is the kind of plan just described supposed to work? With clear "central vision" focused on the internal life of the organization rather than "peripheral vision" focused on the wider context, the plan is naturally more position-oriented than perspective-oriented. Its posture of deliberate detachment creates the likelihood that it will be more policy-driven than people-driven and thus must be implemented in hierarchical fashion, top-down rather than bottom-up. The typical model is more centralized than decentralized to achieve the efficiencies of "unity" and "coordination," which are almost always euphemisms for conformity and control. While a certain amount of standardization is useful when not unduly coerced, the practical question here is whether a pyramidal plan with the full weight of institutional authority behind it will become too rigidly programmed to allow for enough flexibility and diversity to cope with the rapid rate of unexpected change.

As implementation begins to unfold, it does so in accordance with a plan that seeks to be comprehensive, carefully scheduled, and therefore self-contained rather than open-ended. This design encourages a number of short-term incremental steps rather than a few long-term quantum leaps. The intention underlying this approach is to make change systemic rather than dynamic so that it will be as predictable and permanent as possible. The more carefully the planners do their work, the less room they leave for the surprising and the serendipitous. Close attention to logical sequence timed to unfold at a steady pace should eliminate any need for the provisional or the experimental. Over against this scenario of the organization sailing serenely even through white-water rapids, Mintzberg insists that true strategists "revel in ambiguity" because the very nature of strategy is to be "dynamic, irregular, discontinuous, calling for groping, interactive processes with an emphasis on learning and synthesis."[25]

Here we come to the heart of the problem. Planning's great attraction is its promise to provide stability and continuity in a time of rapid change, to maximize safety and minimize risk in the midst of turbulence, to achieve consistency and even a measure of certainty in the face of massive complexity. Thus Mintzberg's most surprising indictment is that "planning is fundamentally a conservative process: it acts to conserve the basic orientation of the organization, specifically its existing categories," which is why "planning itself breeds a basic inflexibility in organizations."[26] At bottom, planning is oriented to the past while strategizing is oriented to the future! The whole thrust of strategy is to be catalytic, not conservative, which is why it emphasizes boldness, inventiveness, and adaptability in the face of the unexpected that could never be factored into a plan.

3. *Mission.* What purposes does planning hope to accomplish by following the procedures outlined above? At the heart of the planning process lies an assessment of current strengths and weaknesses, often measured statistically by "hard data" and plotted on a trend line. Once this "objective" audit is completed, the future is essentially extrapolated from the past by eliminating the most egregious errors uncovered by the analysis of recent experience, all on the assumption that, having learned the lessons of history, the organization is no longer doomed to repeat them. In other words, the plan says, "let's keep doing what we've been doing, but do it better by benefiting from this careful review of our operation undertaken without bias by those who had no part in creating the situation that we are trying to improve." By now the contrast with a strategic approach will be obvious to every reader: Plans look backward to the past for guidance; strategies look forward to the future for challenges. Plans look inward to the organization to see what can be changed; strategies look outward to the context to see what changes are already underway. Plans seek verification based on objective calculations; strategies seek transformation based on subjective commitments.

Once the plan is written out in full, approved at every level of the organizational hierarchy, and issued as the roadmap to be followed on a prescribed schedule for the next few years, it becomes, in effect, another form of quality control. If the planners have done their work well, this blueprint should optimize the utilization of human, financial, and physical resources. Maximum efficiency should result from the coordination of activities on a common timetable by producing that near-magical effect called "synergy." Should a few laggards fall back into the bad habit of repeating the already identified mistakes of the past, the plan itself, with its carefully calibrated set of "action steps," should offer a mechanism for self-correction. But for strategists this prescriptive approach to an improved future has a fatal flaw because the plan has been devised in advance by detached thought rather than in retrospect by involved action. As Mintzberg put it:

> Strengths and weaknesses are situational: internal capability can be assessed only with respect to external context...[H]ow can we *know* that a strength is a strength without acting in a specific

situation to find out?…[T]he detached assessment of strengths and weaknesses may be unreliable, all bound up with aspirations, biases, and hopes…[T]he assessment of organizational strengths and weaknesses cannot be just a detached cerebral exercise. It must be above all an *empirical* one, in which these things are *learned* by being tested in context. Every strategic change involves some new experience, a step into the unknown, the taking of some new kind of risk. No organization can, therefore, ever be sure in advance whether an established capability will prove to be a strength or a weakness—ultimately a help or a hindrance in making that change.[27]

As we come to the end of the process and look back at what it typically means to plan, the contrast with what it means to strategize could not be clearer. Planning is more interested in means; strategizing, in ends. Planning moves deductively from general principles; strategizing moves inductively from specific contexts. Planning is more analytical ("hands-off"), strategizing is more entrepreneurial ("hands-on"). Planning seeks to clarify concepts; strategizing, to shape cultures. Planning is neat and orderly; strategizing is messy and unpredictable. On and on the list might go. Indeed, I went through Mintzberg and found at least fifty clear contrasts between strategizing and planning that he discussed, most of which I have sought to incorporate in this summary.

So the issue becomes how we shall deal with these differences. Some might prefer to be planners in a staff position while others would seek to be strategists in a line position, which is still the situation in much of the business world. But the luxury of having both roles in separate positions is really not an option in most churches, so must a pastor choose between the two? Although Mintzberg ends by assigning a modest legitimate role to planners, the cumulative impact of his argument is to underscore the "fall" of that function in its usefulness to organizational leadership. By my use of the word *strategic* in the title of this book, I may seem to be giving preference to that aspect of a pastor's work.

But is it necessary or even wise for the pastor to choose between these two tasks and the contributions that they are intended to make? My suggestion is that the pastor hold both roles in equal balance and fulfill each of them in such a way that, in the life of the church, the phrase "strategic planning" will no longer be the oxymoron that Mintzberg found it to be in the business world. To hint at how that might be done, let me ask you to turn back to the comparative typology of "managers" and of "leaders" found in chapter 7 on page 122. Notice how the twelve characterizations of managers listed in the left column correspond almost exactly to the approach taken by planners described above. Likewise, the attributes of leaders in the right column agree almost entirely with what has just been said about strategists. Which leads me to conclude that planning is an essential task of "managers" while strategizing is an essential task of "leaders." Just as I argued there that the pastor must be both a manager and a leader, so I would argue here, for many of the same reasons, that the pastor must be both a planner and a strategist. The key is to understand the difference between the two tasks and how they relate to each other.

In the hope that I have now allowed Mintzberg to say enough about the differences between planning and strategizing, let me conclude by asking how we may better understand their proper connection. For, as Mintzberg quips, if we do only planning we have "paralysis by analysis," and if we do only strategizing we have "extinction by instinct," since the danger is that planners will think before acting and strategists will act before thinking.[28] In response, he provides a premise on which a helpful linkage may be established: "Organizations engage in formal planning, not to create strategies but to program the strategies they already have…Thus, strategy is not the consequences of planning, but the opposite: its starting point."[29] Planning brings order to strategy, codifies and elaborates it so that it may be communicated to others, and insures that implementation will not fall between the cracks because of forgotten agenda, missed deadlines, and overlooked data.

Thus the pastor is forever switching hats to cover both the right brain and the left brain: one month charging up the hill to achieve a breakthrough and attempt something new, another month going on retreat to evaluate the fallout caused by innovation; one day listening intently to feedback through the congregational grapevine as to how "things are going," another day pouring over a computer printout of participation patterns in every age group; one Sunday preaching a sermon that is "prophetic" to challenge the status quo, another Sunday preaching a sermon that is "priestly" to consolidate hard-won gains. What this whole discussion is trying to say is so obvious and yet so difficult: true "strategic planning" will not take place unless the pastor is both a strategist and a planner who appreciates the value of each.[30]

CONCLUSION

CHAPTER 11

The Relevance of Strategic Preaching

Now that we have completed a methodological survey of how to do strategic preaching undergirded by strategic leading, let me try to assess its usefulness for a pulpit ministry. To practice this approach, you will need to change some well-established homiletical habits as well as train church leaders to collaborate more closely with you in the formulation of a pulpit strategy. So the question now is whether the results will be worth that effort. Remembering an imperative of strategic leadership, "Thou shalt know the enemy!" let me address the issue of relevance by selecting three ominous trends in contemporary American life that threaten to undermine or at least inhibit an intentional ministry, testing in each case how well strategic preaching is equipped to meet the challenges that they pose.

The Erosion of Community

The American experiment has always been a risky attempt to redefine civic connectionalism without those hierarchical structures such as monarchy, papacy, and patriarchy that had held European civilization together for centuries. In the Colonial Period, while still a loose confederation of states, the Puritans attempted to establish a theocratic society united around a particular belief in God, but this option soon proved too inflexible for an increasingly pluralistic population. By the time of the Civil War, the greatest crisis of concord in our history, Lincoln succeeded in substituting a deepened sense of nationhood as the center around which a shattered people could rally. But by the second half of the twentieth century, both of these symbol systems had lost much of their capacity to evoke a sense of transcendent unity, having been replaced by a possessive individualism that made autonomous selfhood the measure of all things.[1]

With amazing prescience, Alexis de Tocqueville anticipated this eventuality as early as the 1830s when he described this new breed as:

> an innumerable multitude of men, all equal and alike, incessantly endeavoring to procure the petty and paltry pleasures with which they glut their lives. Each of them, living apart, is as a stranger to the fate of all the rest; his children and his private friends constitute to him the whole of mankind. As for the rest of his fellow citizens, he is close to them, but he does not see them; he touches them, but he does not feel them; he exists only in himself and for himself alone.[2]

This fraying of the social fabric by a postmodern privatism has led to what Robert Putnam calls "the collapse of American community."[3] In a massive study of contemporary civic engagement, he traces how the sixties' generation is much less involved in those voluntary associations which Tocqueville so cherished than is the generation tempered by the Great Depression and World War II. It is not just that the numbers are down as regards both affiliation and participation; rather, the very character of the connection has changed. As Robert Wuthnow has shown, people today are joining groups more in a quest for personal fulfillment than out of a sense of obligation to contribute to the common good.[4] Their commitments are more tentative and short-term; their preferences are for ad hoc support groups rather than for hierarchical status groups. Those who do organize themselves to influence the public square are often more interested in enhanced advocacy than in building inclusive communities of character. As Putnam puts it, "Thin, single-stranded, surf-by interactions are gradually replacing dense, multi-stranded, well-exercised bonds. More of our social connectedness is one shot, special purpose, and self oriented."[5]

These trends have directly impacted the fundamental nature of the church as a fellowship. Parallel to the patterns of civic engagement described above, church membership has declined steadily over the past generation, roughly 10 percent since the 1960s; but church attendance has slumped even more, between one-third and one-half over the past half-century.[6] Disturbing as these aggregate survey statistics may be, the actual situation is likely to be even more serious. Sociologists have begun to find significant over-reporting of church involvements as survey respondents "misremember" to their advantage.[7] Growing churches that chase demographic shifts to the suburbs tend to receive disproportionate publicity, leaving unnoticed the high percentage of congregations, perhaps over 80 percent, that are stagnant or in steep decline. Denominational agencies are skilled at reporting overall numerical growth by comparing current levels with those in earlier years but neglecting to point out that membership is not growing as fast as the total population or that contributions are not increasing as fast as the gross domestic product.

Perhaps most deceptive is the way in which aggregate statistics disguise the trends in each generational cohort. True to the wider picture, those born in the 1920s and 1930s have remained much more loyal to the church at every stage of life than those born in the 1950s and 1960s, which means that overall averages will continue to decline as seniors depart the scene. As Putnam notes, "Wade Clark Roof estimates that two-thirds of all boomers reared in a religious tradition dropped out, while something less than half have returned."[8] Those in the minority who do return show a tendency to "surf" between congregations and denominations in an endless quest for greater fulfillment, while those in the majority who do not return seem to prefer a self-directed inward journey in search of subjective "spirituality" to be cultivated by reading religious best-sellers, watching the electronic church on television, and/or chatting with virtual congregants on the Web.[9]

These trends suggest that we live in a culture in which the church finds it harder than ever to fulfill the imperative of E. M. Forster, "Only connect!…Live in fragments no longer."[10] All the polls tell us that nearly 90 percent of Americans affirm core Christian beliefs, yet only a little over 40 percent actually participate at any given time in the life of a Christian community. In other words, there are now as many putative believers outside the church as inside! Half of these outsiders are on some membership roll but are either inactive or nonresident, while the other half have never even bothered to affiliate. And yet the Christian faith is profoundly relational, requiring incorporation into a body of believers for its authentic expression. Clearly we must learn to speak more compellingly of the need for community and of the unique benefits that such bonding provides to those who seek a robust spiritual life.[11] What does strategic preaching have to offer in that regard?

Think back over the approach described in this book. You will immediately realize that a dominant concern has been to root preaching as deeply as possible in the life of a particular community of faith. We began by emphasizing that the preacher's self-concept should be primarily not that of an exegete or rhetorician but of a leader. A leader is primarily a community builder, one who works to mold a somewhat amorphous collection of individuals into a cohesive group with a shared sense of mission. By giving voice to their common aspirations, the sermon points to what they can accomplish together that no one of them could do alone. But the sermon fulfills this pathfinding role only if the preacher first works closely with the people to decide just what goals God wants them to reach so that together they can plan a route to get from where they are to where they want to go.

In a very real sense, then, the sermon is not only *for* the congregation but is also *from* it, never fully formed without significant input from a continuous feedback loop involving lay leaders and followers alike.

This dialogical model of proclamation carries over to the way in which Scripture is interpreted in the sermon. Using the positive fruits of a mature form criticism, the biblical writings are viewed as community literature written, not by an isolated writer for an introspective reader, but fashioned by the people of God to address the urgencies of the life situation in which they found themselves. Indeed, much of this material probably took shape in oral form and was used for liturgical, kerygmatic, catechetical, paranetic, and apologetic purposes before being edited into the literary form that has come to us. This means that the pastor first asks of every biblical text, What kind of community life was this passage seeking to develop? With that clue in mind, the sermon attempts to express the same intentionality for today so that those being addressed will be guided to build a comparable community life for their own time and place. This corporate aspect of preaching is further emphasized by making the entire service of worship highly interactive. Pastor and people leave the gathering with a common conviction that what happened would not have been as meaningful if all of those present had not done their part.

But does this consistent emphasis on community somehow neglect the individual? Far from it, for what Christians need most when threatened by social conformity at one extreme, or by loneliness at the other, is a safety net woven out of that commonality with other believers called *koinonia*. Life in Christ is life in the body of Christ where each member, no matter how insignificant, is embraced as "indispensable" (1 Cor. 12:22). Today, people too often draw a sharp contrast between serving "the institutional church" and serving "the individual Christian," as if the two were competitive or even incompatible. Surely this sets up false alternatives. Although the institutional church has a history as checkered as that of any individual, at its best it seeks to give embodiment to what might otherwise be little more than "virtual" Christianity, offering relationships of mutuality and solidarity in which individual believers can find the encouragement and reinforcement so essential to the fulfillment of their calling.

In his important work on community, Robert Putnam has made use of the concept of "social capital" to describe those assets that voluntary associations create and accumulate for the benefit of both their own participants and the wider world which they serve.[12] Such resources, for example, create networks of trust that facilitate the resolution of collective problems. These same networks "also serve as conduits for the flow of helpful information that facilitates achieving our goals."[13] The very act of bonding strengthens the sense of identity both of the group and of its individual members, while the maintenance of these ties requires norms of reciprocity that shape and sustain patterns of conduct. Congregations are like holding companies for those forms of social capital, which Christian fellowship is designed to enhance. Strategic preaching is very intentional about increasing these commonly held assets as a reservoir on which those who feel isolated from the connective tissues of life may freely draw.[14]

In a word, what we are after in strategic preaching is the kind of sermon that creates *synergy* within a congregation. From a Greek compound referring to that which is done together (1 Cor. 3:9), this term assumes that a "multiplier effect" is at work when individuals mesh their separate efforts in a common endeavor. Stevens and Collins comment on this enhancement as follows:

> Mutual reinforcement, described by the term synergy, suggests that more can be achieved by a group than can be achieved by the total efforts of individuals within that group…Similarly, synergy describes the multiple impact members of a living system have when they work together. One plus one often makes more than two.[15]

Central to the intention of Jesus was the making of disciples through the building of a cohesive fellowship in which their relationships could flourish, a purpose that lies at the heart of all strategic preaching.

The Shriveling of Selfhood

Needless to say, legitimate reasons underlie why the quest for individuation has become so characteristic of our culture. Viewed historically, this struggle for greater autonomy represented a necessary effort to escape the clutches of oppressive collectivities that thwarted human freedom by coercing conformity. Even in our modern democracies we shall always need the witness of nonconformists to warn us against being stampeded by the herd instinct into mere "groupiness." The problem, rather, is that our Promethean reach for personal authenticity has resulted in an almost exclusive preoccupation with selfhood to the neglect of our wider responsibilities. The centrality of the self may be seen in the way that we couple it with our most cherished goals: *self*-actualization, *self*-assertion, *self*-consciousness, *self*-determination, *self*-esteem, *self*-expression, *self*-fulfillment, *self*-improvement, *self*-interest, *self*-reliance, *self*-sufficiency, *self*-understanding. The list of such compounds is almost endless.[16] No wonder that the reigning ideology of our day has been described as "selfism."[17]

One of the most popular categories used to analyze this obsessive concern with one's well-being is narcissism, from the ancient Greek myth of Narcissus, who, because he loved himself so much, died from endlessly admiring his own reflection in the water. Christopher Lasch[18] has stressed how the narcissistic personality lives only for immediacy viewed as an endless succession of unconnected episodes. What is important is each instant, not the line that connects them in time. Life has no real sense of beginning or of ending, but only of experiencing the now. After all, why bother with the past or with the future, since we live only in the present? Lacking any narrative undergirding of the life story, the narcissist lives by nostalgia rather than by memory, and by optimism rather than by hope. Isolated from any real engagement with, or appreciation of, human otherness, the only way to relate to the wider world is in exclusive lifestyle enclaves that celebrate the "narcissism of similarity."[19]

When meaning is limited so exclusively to the evanescent experiences of the moment, we may well ask how the expressive individualist tries to wring a measure of immediate gratification out of the present. The answer is hedonism, which, in our culture, means pleasure derived primarily from sex and money. Instead of achieving relational intimacy over years of ripening reciprocity, the selfist seeks recurring spasms of ecstasy limited to little more than what Andrew Delbanco describes as "the neurological effects of vascular congestion in the genitals."[20] Desire becomes appetite, and the commodification of life through relentless advertising shapes the narcissist into a perpetual consumer. As Erich Fromm put it, "The world is one great object for his appetite, a big bottle, a big apple, a big breast. Man has become the suckler, the eternally expectant,"[21] whose worth consists not in what he can create but in what he can devour.[22]

These trends are so significant that they have begun to coalesce into the making of a new mind-set that goes by the name of postmodernism. The prevalence of that prefix, as in *post*-industrial, *post*-Enlightenment, and *post*-structuralist, suggests that, thus far, we know more about what postmodernism is *not* than about what it *is*. As regards human personhood, however, modernism and postmodernism offer strikingly different understandings of the self as suggested by the following contrasts:[23]

The Modern Self	The Postmodern Self
1. Autonomous with inalienable rights based on universal truths.	1. Socially constructed identity shaped by local communities of influence.
2. Unique, bounded, consistent, self-defined authenticity.	2. Unstable, fluid, changeable, multiple potentials for being.
3. Rational, cognitive, introspective.	3. Emotional, intuitive, affective.
4. Inner-directed by character, optimistic, confident of progress.	4. Other-directed by context, skeptical, even suspicious of motives.

Confronted by the relativity, complexity, and ambiguity of postmodernism, especially in its more thoroughgoing deconstructionist mode, many selfists have responded by retreating into a quasi-religious stance that may be characterized as neo-Gnosticism.[24] The radical subjectivity of this ancient esoteric tradition offers the narcissist an ultimate experience of salvation, the divinization of the self. The central actor in this redemptive drama is not the God-Man entering into history but the man/woman-god fleeing from history! While the most conspicuous expression of this spirituality in our day is the New Ageism that flourished in the 1990s,[25] of greater concern to us is the way in which neo-Gnosticism has infiltrated mainline America religion and planted there its fateful legacy of egocentrism, elitism, and escapism.[26] In the ancient world, the ahistorical character of Gnosticism was best known by Christians for its docetic christology, whereas its influence today is more significant in shaping a docetic ecclesiology.

For our purposes, the key result of this pervasive trend is the way in which it has eroded a sense of the self as a responsible actor in human affairs.[27] Modernity, for all of its limitations, dignified the self as an active agent in control of its own destiny. With Decartes, the self became the starting point for the discovery of new knowledge. Kant made it the locus of autonomy and hence the wellspring of free decision. The scientific method launched by the Enlightenment bequeathed to it a sense of optimism in the possibilities for progress. By contrast, postmodernism has "decentered" the self as an active agent, emphasizing instead its "situatedness" in a particular social group, thereby making it almost a prisoner of the norms and rules constructed and imposed by its peers, fated to live out its existence as a victim of contextual pragmatism. So another urgent question that preaching must address is whether our listeners feel confident that they can actually shape a better future, or whether the best they can do is to help their advocacy group get the better of its competitors in a struggle to influence the present.

Throughout the presentation of strategic preaching in this book, a strong emphasis on building community inside the church has been balanced by an equally strong emphasis on addressing the outside world that the church exists to serve. In defining a leader, particularly in comparison with a manager, the stress fell on what Warren Bennis calls "mastering the context."[28] This involves not only a careful study of "the surround" but an ongoing commitment to honor the ecological imperative, which means discerning the deepest needs of the church's habitat and determining to contribute more to the environment than is taken from it. We then saw that strategy involves the matching of mission to matrix. Just as a general would never launch an attack without first reconnoitering the enemy-held territory, so the strategic sermon must be based on careful reconnaissance of the wider community if it is to confront effectively those foes arrayed against the gospel instead of merely tilting at windmills.

As we saw in chapters 3 and 4, this effort to contextualize one's pulpit message takes place at two levels. First, the interpretation of Scripture begins with an understanding of the life-setting in the ancient world that a chosen passage was seeking to address. A probing of this relationship is necessary to discern the kind of impact the text intended to make in dealing with the circumstances of its day. Second is the need to know our own world equally well if we are to identify the most urgent contemporary challenges and strategize how to address them with the gospel. As our hermenutical model emphasized, we cannot preach relevantly simply by repeating the message of Scripture in its ancient form because our world is now very different from the biblical world. But what we can do is attempt a translation that makes the same kind of impact in our day as the New Testament made in its day. What this conception of the preaching task implies is that Scripture is best understood by asking how it took root in human history: the friends it made, the enemies it fought, the influences it unleashed, the changes it wrought.

My guess is that the heaviest intellectual demand that strategic preaching lays on most preachers is this insistence that they become more intimately familiar both with the world out of which the text first came and with the world unto which it is now being sent afresh. Why this emphasis on mastering the two-fold context of preaching? Precisely in an effort to root the proclamation *in* history rather than allowing it to become an escape *from* history as the apocalypticists and Gnostics would have it. This kind of pulpit ministry invites the hearers to move beyond an exclusive preoccupation with self and engage in hand-to-hand combat with those foes who would try to capture God's kingdom for their own ends (Mt. 11:12). Put as simply as possible, strategic preaching is a call, not to ignore history or to flee history, but to *make history* and thereby recover a keen sense of agency as a responsible actor in human affairs.

One reason we stressed the importance of learning to tell the church's story[29] is that it adds a narrative line to the Christian faith that is missing in the spiritual odyssey of so many narcissists. It is a line drawn by the moving finger of history, which may encompass the trajectory of a single life, or of a congregation over several generations, or even of the sweep of God's saving history through the ages. Strategic preaching is designed to help write the next chapter in that story. It goes to Scripture asking, What history produced this text, and what history did this text produce? When the answers to those questions are incorporated into a sermon, its hearers are confronted with a cast of characters who faced down the challenges of their day and determined to make a difference for God. By "making history" in obedience to the will of God rather than living in conformity to the spirit of their times (Rom. 12:2), their story thereby became "holy history," the kind of history that we can make today if, in the power of the Spirit, we respond to our challenges with the same courage that they did to theirs.

The Wager on Chance

One of the most prevalent conditions of human existence has driven many into the enfolding arms of Gnosticism both in the ancient and in the modern world. This condition is a sense of the capriciousness of life. We experience a disconnect between cause and effect. Both individuals and groups tend to think of themselves as powerless to shape or even to influence outcomes. Indeterminacy seems to characterize the course of events. Under such conditions, those who feel alienated by the arbitrariness of life embrace a dualism of Manichean proportions. It sets their subjectivity over against this sinister world in which they are physically captive. Their response to the randomness of the daily round is one of apathy and anomie, often characterized as "numbness," "sleep," "drunkenness," and "oblivion."[30] To say the least, they are not meaningfully engaged in building a better life here on earth because their religion is a call to the world beyond, which, by means of *gnosis* (revealed knowledge), they can experience in the subjective world of the inner self.

Our twenty-first century is much like the first century in providing that climate of aimlessness in which Gnosticism often flourishes. Note how scientific trends have revised our understanding of the physical habitat in which we live. In place of an orderly world of purposeful creation, the foundations of modern physics are based on Albert Einstein's Theory of Relativity (1905) and Werner Heisenberg's Uncertainty Principle (1927), which suggest that the smallest units of matter and energy are unpredictable at best. In biology, Darwinism posits the evolution of life in response to such fortuitous factors as natural selection based on the survival of the fittest and genetic variation based on random mutations, or "mistakes," in the DNA molecule. As a result of recent findings, the scientific mindset has shifted from a mechanistic determinism to a tolerance of ambiguity grounded particularly in Niels Bohr's Principle of Complementarity (1928), which recognized that there is an ineradicable element of contingency in the very act of observation itself.

Although few in a typical congregation will be knowledgeable of these scientific shifts, I mention them here because comments by scientists in the popular media often challenge the comfort level of those accustomed to understand the world as governed by the providential care of a benevolent God. Of greater influence is the impact of current events that dramatize the erratic nature of our existence. In economics, when we approached the millennial divide astride a roaring bull, analysts were almost unanimous in predicting a new decade if not century of unprecedented prosperity.[31] Instead, we were greeted by a severe recession that cost many people their jobs or wrecked their retirement savings. In politics, the presidential election of 2000 ended in a disputed verdict that, after endless wrangling, was resolved in such chaotic fashion as to further confuse the outcome. In foreign affairs, the terrorist attacks of September 11, 2001, completely blindsided both our intelligence and military experts, redefining our geopolitical priorities in as sweeping a fashion as the Cold War had done in the twentieth century.

On every hand, a succession of surprises so haphazard that they appear to have no meaning or purpose bombard us. The future becomes more precarious as we feel ourselves caught in an undertow of irrationality beyond our ability to control. In response we come to rely increasingly on luck, viewing life more and more as a game of chance.[32] Think of how many important decisions are made by the toss of a coin or the draw of a lottery: the assignment of new gates at LaGuardia Airport, the distribution of donated organs to those desperate for a transplant, the selection of immigrants to receive a green-card visa.[33] Most prominent are the publicly sponsored lotteries that began in New Hampshire in 1963 to cover a budget deficit and have now spread to forty-four states where more than half the adult population participates. The Powerball multistate lottery of 1998, for example, had a $295.7 million jackpot with an 80 million to one chance of winning, equal to the odds of getting struck by lighting fourteen times in a single year![34]

This brings us to the more ritualistic expression of this growing addiction—legalized gambling in such temples of chance as casinos, racetracks, and bingo parlors whose New Jerusalem is Las Vegas. The statistics change daily, but these will suggest the trend: in 1962 Americans placed $2 billion in commercial bets, whereas by 2000 the nation was betting $866 billion, increasing the revenues of the "gaming industry," as it likes to be called, by 35,000 percent during this period.[35] Nor does the trend show any signs of abating. For example, "2 million gamblers patronize 1,800 virtual casinos *every week*. With $3.5 billion being lost on Internet wagers this year, gambling has passed pornography as the Web's most lucrative business."[36] A final comparison: "The sum total spent on tickets to all movies, plays, concerts, and live performances, plus all sports events, is only about $22 billion per year. Americans are spending three times as much on gambling as on *all* other kinds of entertainment combined."[37]

The ubiquity of the Internet is now making online poker games a particularly addictive form of gambling, especially for young males, some of them not yet in high school. Once the World Poker Tour was launched on the Travel Channel in 2003, high stakes betting became a favorite pastime on college campuses. Despite growing acceptance as a form of recreation, up to 10 percent of these youthful practitioners become pathological gamblers, a ratio three times higher than that in the general population. By 2005, with 1.8 million players per day and $2.7 billion in revenues per year, poker had become the third most popular "sport" on cable television after auto racing and football.[38]

Not only does the compulsion to gamble mirror the temper of our times, it also subtly influences our religious sensibilities. As Adam Wolfson put it:

> Gambling…raises an almost metaphysical challenge to our belief in an ordered cosmos, governed either by providence or a fundamental rationality…[W]hat is gambling—especially a pure game of chance like the lottery—but a rejection of the belief that there is a rhyme or reason to things?…In our postmodern times, too many of us tend to think that the cosmos is a kind of chaos—that we have been thrown into the world for no higher reason than to pursue our own pleasure-fantasies.[39]

But the issue goes even deeper than that. Jackson Lears, author of a major study on luck in American life, sees gambling "as part of a wider culture of chance—a culture more at ease with randomness and irrationality, more doubtful that diligence is the only path to success, than our dominant culture of control." He views this culture of chance as encouraging "the notion of grace as a kind of spiritual luck, a free gift from God," and suggests that "the most profound meditations on grace, from Blaise Pascal to Jonathan Edwards and Paul Tillich, have all led toward a refusal of anxious striving, a recognition that the dream of mastery over fate was a delusion."[40] Questions throng: Is the sermon to be seen as offering instant solutions, implying that the listeners are lucky enough to be given a golden opportunity, rooted in the grace of God, to get something for nothing? Will the call to faith be understood somewhat like the decision to buy a lottery ticket in hope of an ultimate payoff beyond one's wildest expectations? How can preaching in a "culture of chance" steer between the zeal for control characteristic of legalism and the impulse toward risk characteristic of antinomianism?

In responding to that challenge, note a third dominant characteristic of strategic preaching in the dynamic relationship that it establishes between the community of faith and its wider context. The key reality is that of motion, what we have called movement from Point A to Point B. We first saw that the thrust of the Christian life is described in Scripture by such metaphors as journeying on the way, following Jesus, retracing the exodus sojourn, and running a long-distance race. Next we saw that the most essential role of the leader is to foster a shared sense of mission, which becomes a driving force guiding the group on a trajectory toward the fulfillment of its vision. To accomplish this task, the leader must be "out front" as a pacesetter: a proactive, risk-taking innovator whose pulpit is like the prow of a ship cutting a new path into the future for others to follow.

Of all the vocabulary used to describe this approach to a pulpit ministry, perhaps the word *strategic* is most relevant because it implies the execution of a battle plan for invading the enemy's stronghold. In this analogy, a strategic sermon is a call to arms, an initiating moment designed to launch an offensive that will extend the reign of Christ over "every rule and every authority and power" (1 Cor. 15:24). The hermeneutic of intentionality used to frame such a message views the gospel, not only as a truth to be understood, but as an event to be reenacted, a story to be performed in such a way that "holy history" of old "makes history" again in our day. On this understanding, the proclamation of the gospel is both an utterance and an occurrence because it has the potency to bring to pass what it declares. The herald is not just explaining an ancient record or analyzing a religious idea but is calling into being a redemptive happening.[41]

When talking about the potentiality of the biblical text in terms of its ongoing impact or "outworkings" (*Wirkungsgeschichte*), we saw that this perspective has profound implications for the way in which those addressed are to face the future.[42] What it suggests is that we do not claim to know what the future holds *before* we act, as do those utopians who first embrace a theoretical ideology and then try to superimpose it on the course of history. Rather, we discover God's future only *as* we act upon his promises. This is what Jesus meant by describing discipleship as a life of asking, seeking, and knocking in which the giving, finding, and opening are provided, not by us, but by God (Mt. 7:7–8). If we shrink from taking risks until the way ahead seems clear, we will succeed only in perpetuating that part of the status quo with which we have become comfortable. But God's future always comes as a surprise, whether we are ready for it or not, because it offers the Lord of history the freedom to do a new thing (Isa. 43:19; Rev. 21:5).

This does not mean, however, that we go "flying blind" into the future, for the same gospel that calls us to that temporal frontier also discloses the kind of tomorrow that God is working to build. Rather, by understanding the sermon as a speech-act that has the power to bring God's future into existence through its "outworkings" in the lives of hearers who respond by faith, strategic preaching seeks to repair the broken linkage between cause and effect that has made life seem so aimless and capricious to many. When the sermon is only the analytical exposition of a chosen text, or the rhetorical embellishment of a noble topic, leaving the congregation without a clue as to what it should do about it, then proclamation becomes little more than a random ray of light in the darkness, a weekly "spiritual high" that becomes one emotional "blip" among many, with no story line connecting the blips. But when the sermon announces a strategy designed to achieve certain effects promised by God and prayed for by his people, then it not only tutors its hearers to think consequentially, it also restores their confidence that acting on the gospel can make a significant difference in human affairs.

This dimension of self-determination is referred to by scholars as "agency," meaning the release of individuals from traditional hierarchies to serve as self-reliant actors on the stage of history. In a masterwork on American history, James E. Block has traced the way in which a

> fundamental shift of the human role in relation to authority was effectuated as a new human character type: individuals shifted from being servants of God and society carrying out rigidly defined duties on behalf of distantly formulated but fully designated ends. They became agents, that is, individuals participating actively in shaping the worldly means to be employed for realizing divine and collective purposes.[43]

But more: Block sees the building of a nation of agents as the central metanarrative that best explains American identity. What this means is that, if Block is right, strategic preaching is not only compatible with the historic Christian faith but is congenial with the overarching story of what our nation is struggling to become.

What Block calls "agency" is what I have called "intentionality" throughout this study. Since I propose it as an antidote to the purposeless living so characteristic of our time, let me conclude this chapter with an analysis of how intentionality actually functions in human experience and then relate those findings to the preaching task. First, a look at the three components of intentional living:[44]

1. *Decision.* Caught in vast collectivist structures so characteristic of modernity, many persons suffer from a paralysis of will—unable to commit, much less to act, in decisive fashion.[45] This "failure of nerve"[46] resulting from a loss of will power may take the form of indifference, apathy, or procrastination. The result is frustration, even futility, which produces a feeling of impotence. By contrast, those who live intentionally are able to identify their options, define their priorities, and mobilize their resources to make clear choices even when the alternatives are ambiguous. This ability to focus the attention on what must be decided is the beginning of volition, which is itself a powerful form of cognition.[47] Such persons are proactive rather than reactive, willing to seize the initiative rather than be overwhelmed by circumstance. They cherish the confidence that they can change, and

thereby change their world, thus actively shaping the future rather than passively letting the future shape them.

2. *Direction.* The etymology of the *intention* word-group roots in the Latin *intendere,* composed of the prefix *in-* plus *tendere* or *tensum.* The latter means "to stretch," from which we get our word *tension,* which is why one definition of *intention* is a "stretching toward something."[48] The core word in this etymological history is *tend,* which implies movement toward something, as does the word *tendency.*[49] To say, "I *tend* to agree with you," means that my view is moving toward your position. Thus inherent in the concept of intentionality is a sense of movement in a certain direction. Decisions are not made in isolated fashion but together they plot a trajectory of purpose and so, taken cumulatively, become part of a larger design. Rather than living by opportunism or mere happenstance, what is popularly called living by "luck" or "breaks," the intentional person projects a pattern of meaning on what might otherwise be viewed merely as random circumstance. This determination to pursue an overarching sense of purpose, whether vocationally or religiously, is often referred to as following one's "calling."

3. *Destination.* The notion of direction set by a clearly perceived goal toward which one journeys implies an end, which makes the practice of intentionality both teleological and eschatological. Our very capacity to have intentions means that we are able to participate proleptically in the possibilities offered by the future, for we would not know how to intend something if it were not already present at least by anticipation. By this very act of intending something, we both express our confidence in the future and prepare ourselves to receive what it has to offer.[50] Rollo May has insightfully expressed this dimension of futurity inherent in intentionality:

> [T]he word "will," in connection with intentionality, is also the same word we use for the future tense in English. Will and intentionality are intimately bound up with the future. Both meanings— simple future, something will happen; and personal resolve, I will make it happen—are present in varying degrees in each statement of intentionality…Power is potentiality, and potentiality points toward the future: it is something to be realized. The future is the tense in which we promise ourselves, we give a promissory note, we put ourselves on the line. Nietzsche's statement, "Man is the only animal who can make promises," is related to our capacity to posit ourselves in the future.[51]

With this brief description of intentionality before us, I now offer three comments relating it to the homiletical approach for which this book contends:

1. Note the close correlation of intentionality with the biblical norms identified in chapter 2. To live intentionally is to focus and commit, much like Paul's "one thing I do" (Phil. 3:13). It is to live in tension, stretching and straining between the "now" of our fate and the "not yet" of God's future, what Bultmann described as the "betweenness" of Christian existence.[52] The epistemology of intentionality—cognition through volition—parallels the theological insight of Albert Schweitzer that we shall learn who Christ is only in our own experience of his toils, conflicts, and sufferings.[53] The movement generated by acting on our intentions propels us toward the finish line in the race of life. Most impressively, both the apostolic witness and the concept of intentionality have what might be called "eschatological thickness,"[54] a sense of the looming future so strong that we are permitted to anticipate and even participate in God's tomorrow before it fully arrives.

2. Next, note how intentionality is firmly rooted in the ministry of Jesus himself. Even before his followers began to heap upon him great titles of messianic dignity, the Master described his mission in terms of a transcendent design. The synoptic gospels contain striking sayings in which Jesus announced that he had "come" to accomplish certain purposes (e.g., Mt. 5:17; 10:34; Mk. 1:38; 2:17; Lk. 12:49). In the Fourth Gospel this self-attestation is even more frequent and is strengthened by numerous texts in which Jesus claims to have been "sent" to do the will of his Father (e.g., Jn. 4:34; 5:30; 6:38; 9:4). His unshakable sense of mission was grounded in an awareness that both his origin (Jn. 7:25–31) and his destination (Jn. 7:32–36) lay ultimately in God. Stated theologically, Jesus lived with radical intentionality because he knew *whence* he had come and *whither* he was going (Jn. 8:14; cf 3:8). Stated historically, this is why he "set his face to go to Jerusalem" and refused to turn aside (Lk. 9:51–53; cf. 13:33). The dominant picture of Jesus in the gospels is of a person utterly free from human control yet utterly bound by divine necessity.[55]

3. As persons attempt to accomplish their purposes on an individual basis, they soon realize the need for enrichment and reinforcement. Strategic planning may be defined as an activity by which a group deliberately seeks to pool the insight and support of its members so as to facilitate the realization of intentions that they hold in common. John Biersdorf edited a volume of essays on *Creating an Intentional Ministry* in which he identified the key components in achieving this goal as: (a) a shared consciousness of the possibility of change; (b) a collaborative approach to problem-solving; and (c) a willingness to negotiate the differences that inevitably arise to threaten the group consensus.[56] To utilize these dynamics in creating a strategy that reflects the shared intentions of the congregation is as important as the plan itself.

CHAPTER 12

Case Studies in Strategic Preaching

I was ambivalent about including case studies in this book because each of us has a distinctive style of preaching and a different situation in which to minister. To evaluate a sermon as an example of strategic preaching, one would need to understand, at a minimum: (a) the particular purpose that the message was attempting to achieve; (b) the forces that might try to thwart the changes needed to accomplish that purpose; (c) the way in which the pastor was leading the congregation to meet this particular challenge; (d) the specific aspect of the overall strategy that this one sermon was designed to accomplish in the context of other sermons before and after it; and (e) the results or "outworkings" that resulted from implementing the sermon, and the changes that they made in the life of the congregation.

Ideally, for you to grasp the strategic thrust of the sermons that I preached to the First Baptist Church in Shreveport, you would need to know the history of the city and of the church, both of which were 150 years old at the time. Even more important, you would need to know how both the city and the church were changing at just the time when these sermons were preached so as to understand how I was seeking to help the congregation write the next chapter in its ongoing story as a pilgrim people of God. Obviously you would need a candid appraisal of the lay "power structure" responsible to guide church governance, as well as a probing analysis of the interplay between the congregation and the denomination with which it had been prominently identified for many years, a relationship in considerable turbulence at the time. On and on I might go, but you get the point: every pastor realizes the cruciality of factors such as these to the way in which sermons are nuanced, yet there is no possibility of even hinting at all these vital perspectives here.

I could try to eliminate the contextual particularity of the sermons in an effort to turn them into generic messages that would fit in any pulpit; but to do so would, of course, strip them of their strategic dimension. The heart of the problem is this: the more a sermon is truly strategic, the more it is valid only for a particular place at a particular time in response to a particular challenge. Nevertheless, I do appreciate the usefulness of studying the sermons of others, the better to understand their methodology even if they are not directly adaptable to other situations of ministry. Therefore I offer here a few samples of my strategic preaching drawn from various areas of congregational life, each with a brief introduction that seeks to sketch the setting in which the sermon was delivered.

Hearing the Cry of Human Need

As we saw in chapter 8, serving God's world is one of the six central purposes of the church, of which global missions is a major component. In Shreveport we normally devoted the first three weeks in November to a primary focus on meeting this challenge. Several months prior to that time, our associate pastor, who had staff responsibility for the ministry system on service, would meet with the missions committee, the leaders of our men's and women's mission organizations, and the pastors of our three mission congregations to hammer out plans designed to get more of our church members involved "on mission" in terms of the familiar triad of action projects, financial giving, and prayer support. All of this work was mediated to me in such forms as committee minutes, staff discussion, publicity in the weekly church paper, and regular conferences with the associate pastor.

When I began to plan my preaching input for this emphasis, all of the preliminary work was before me. I knew everything from the theme that would appear on posters in the hallways to the decorations that would be used at the missions fair, which would be set up in Fellowship Hall with kiosks where representatives explained various mission opportunities to our members. My sermonic task was to infuse all of this preparation with biblical meaning, to provide contemporary insight into the world's desperate plight, and to fortify the will of our people to act courageously in the face of daunting obstacles. For this I would need not only sermon content, an obvious necessity, but even more a sermon strategy, a trajectory that would "lock-in" my message on the goals that we had defined for this effort.

Our church had a long history of mission support expressed primarily by generous giving to an annual World Mission Offering, by a program of mission education for all age groups, and by earnest prayer for missionaries on far-flung fields of service. We were weakest in hands-on mission involvement, even in our surrounding community, despite the fact that our members had many skills that would make a valuable contribution to human betterment. Some in our congregation were cautious about expressing a religiously aggressive lifestyle, which made them reluctant to intervene in the affairs of others, not from any lack of concern, but out of respect for their privacy. In this context we decided to devote one November emphasis to involving more of our people in direct mission action. Leaders of the effort worked with community and denominational strategists to select a host of challenging mission opportunities in Shreveport, South Louisiana, Mexico, and Zimbabwe. My assignment as preacher was to motivate participation by those who had long been sincere but passive supporters of the service imperative.

At this particular time, Robert Ballard's discovery of the sunken ocean liner *Titanic* was in the headlines, so I decided to use the story of that maritime tragedy as the "presiding metaphor"[1] for my sermon. Rather than focusing on the *Titanic* itself, I chose to draw a sharp contrast between the two ships most directly involved in responding to the disaster, the Cunard liner *Carpathia* and the Leyland liner *Californian*. In developing this sermon, the abundant literature on the *Titanic* tragedy made it easy to highlight the characteristics that caused one of these ships to be so responsive and the other so unresponsive to human need. [2]

The Bible contains many vivid passages warning about the dangers of the deep. We finally settled on Psalm 107:23–31 as our Old Testament lesson to be read antiphonally by choir and congregation. The New Testament lesson was Mark 4:35–41 on the terrors of the storm-tossed life, and the text for the sermon came from the poignant question in verse 38, "Master, carest Thou not that we perish?" (KJV). The central purpose of the message was to increase the sense of urgency that our people felt for a compassionate hands-on response to human need. I decided to entitle the message, "Rescue the Perishing!" because these words were applicable both to the desperate plight of the *Titanic* and to the mission of the church as evoked by an old gospel song with that title, which most of my hearers would remember.

With these basic elements in place, the minister of music and I began to look at all of the "water music" in the hymnal for suitable selections. We decided to use the Navy hymn, "Eternal Father, Strong to Save," early in the service both because of its thematic relevance and because of its robust trinitarian theology. As we moved toward the sermon, we sought more personal songs reminiscent of the Edwardian Era, which sank beneath the waves with its illustrious flagship, singing one stanza each of a medley with piano rather than organ accompaniment—drawn from "Jesus, Savior, Pilot Me," "The Haven of Rest," and "Peace Be Still." We did not sing "Rescue the Perishing!" because in our hymnal it was set to a tune not serious enough for the mood of the hour. The front of the order of service carried the drawing of an ancient boat on the high seas, a traditional symbol of the church through the centuries.[3] The major parts of the order were separated by selections from the Psalms on the spiritual significance of the sea.[4]

The sermon itself proved to be both probing and powerful because it illustrated how vulnerable is the voyage of life even under the best of circumstances, and how God yearns to come to our rescue by using earthly agents who are sensitive to signals of distress and willing to act boldly at the earliest signs of danger. And yet, having said that, I would insist that the sermon gained strength because it was undergirded by everything that a host of dedicated laypersons had been endeavoring to do for months. These selfless workers were my unseen pulpit allies in defining both individual and corporate needs, in proposing possible strategies for consideration, and in permeating the congregational environment with a readiness to hear what I had to say. At the same time, I was perceived by those mission leaders as their ally in summoning our church to a true sense of service. They saw me using the high visibility of the pulpit to put my office as pastor, my own personal concern, and my preaching of the word of God behind their planning efforts. This perception of a *mutually shared ministry* was very valuable both in overcoming the loneliness of the pulpit and in encouraging lay and staff members who might otherwise have felt that they were working in isolation from the pastor's influence and without benefit of the public platform that I enjoyed on a weekly basis.

What about results? Members were given opportunity, not only to pray, study, and give in response to our World Missions Emphasis, but also to sign up for training and involvement on one of several mission action teams. Soon we were sponsoring an after-school program for latch-key children in a low-income housing project near the church, replacing substandard housing in the downtown slums of Shreveport, holding back-yard Bible studies at South Louisiana mission stations, sending petroleum engineers to drill water wells in the Zimbabwe bush, and converting Airstream trailers into movable clinics where medical teams repaired the cleft palates of indigent Mexican children in rural areas. Did all of this happen because of a single sermon, or even because of a three-week emphasis during one November? Of course not! Changes of this kind result only from the reshaping of the church's culture over many years. But it greatly helped to bring the full resources of worship to bear directly on the accomplishment of this long-term goal, and such a connection gave relevance to preaching and worship that it would not otherwise have had.

SERMON: Rescue the Perishing!

Recently we were reminded of the sinking of the *Titanic* when a team led by Robert Ballard discovered its wreckage a thousand miles east of Boston on the ocean floor 13,000 feet below the surface of the Atlantic. Using an unmanned submersible robot to sweep the seabed by remote control, investigators came upon the great ship resting upright in two sections where it had settled on April 15, 1912, 2:20 a.m., with 1,503 aboard, one of the most tragic disasters in all of maritime history.

The story of the *Titanic* has long been told, especially in a 1955 book by Walter Lord, *A Night to Remember*, and by a movie based on it with the same title. But do you know, as Paul Harvey would put it, "the rest of the story," involving two other ships that played startlingly different roles in dealing with the stricken ship's cry for help? One was the Cunard liner *Carpathia,* the other the Leyland liner *Californian.* The way in which each responded to the plight of the *Titanic* symbolizes something urgently important about how we react to the desperate pleas heard all about us on the high seas of life. Climb on board each ship with me bound for a rendezvous with destiny.

I. The Carpathia

As the *Carpathia* steamed south from New York bound for the Mediterranean, the balmy breezes of the Gulf Stream were quite different from the frigid temperature where the *Titanic* lay stricken fifty-eight miles to the north. The moment the CQD (our SOS) emergency alert was received at 12:25 a.m., it was rushed to Captain Arthur Rostron, who turned the ship north even before taking time to plot a course. Most of the passengers and crew were bedded down for the night, and the ship was making a relaxed fourteen knots. Immediately word was flashed back to the *Titanic:* we are "coming hard." As every available stoker was mobilized to feed the furnaces, the old ship sped up to seventeen knots, arousing many of the passengers who were curtly told, "Get back in your room. We're going north like hell."

Without a moment's hesitation the Captain seemed to think of everything. The sleeping crew sprang to life and soon had swung out the lifeboats, rigged lights along the ship's sides, opened the gangway doors, set up the dining rooms as first aid stations, and converted the lounge and library into dormitories. Then came the hardest part: waiting as the ship sped forward, every plate and rivet shaking with the exertion. Second Officer Bisset noted Captain Rostron standing nearby on the bridge, holding his cap an inch or two off his head, eyes closed, lips moving in silent prayer.

At 2:45 a.m. the dreaded icebergs began to be sighted, but, with the help of extra lookouts, the ship dodged them on all sides without ever slackening speed. By 4:00 a.m., sooner than anyone could have predicted, they reached the site and began the delicate task of plucking survivors in their tiny boats from the sea. Once all 705 were safely on board, the *Carpathia* steamed slowly over the surface of *Titanic's* grave and, finding no sign of life, turned at 8:50 a.m. to race back to New York with its precious cargo, flags flying at half-mast.[5]

The first thing that this story of a heart-rending rescue tells us is that tragedy never chooses a convenient time to strike. The *Carpathia* was bedded down for the night, in a warm climate, headed east. But danger decreed that the crew wake up, forget their needed rest, and head north into icebergs and freezing temperatures. Just so, people still get into trouble at the most awkward times. Having worked hard all day, we want to rest at night, or to be left alone for the weekend; but when the SOS is heard, that is the only time that matters. It's now or never! Either drop everything and go full speed ahead, or forget it. Danger carries its own built-in deadlines that confront us with a sense of urgency. We do not like to act precipitously any more than did Captain Rostron of the *Carpathia*, but we have no choice. To delay is deadly when every minute counts.

The second thing that we learn is that all must be mobilized to meet disaster. Once the human cry is heard, there is no time for questions, debate, or indecision; it is a time for action. Just as the entire crew of the *Carpathia* participated in the rescue operation, so must all the members of a church do their part to be ready when the victims of life's disasters arrive. This may involve tasks as mundane as ushering, or keeping the nursery, or working in the parking lot. Captain Rostron alone could not conduct that rescue operation, nor can the pastor alone meet the spiritual needs of the community. The world is not waiting to see whether a church's ministers care about them but whether the members themselves really care about the world's needs.

The third truth dramatized by this event is that, however great the price to pay, it is supremely worth it to rescue lives from destruction. Is there any satisfaction quite like that of making the difference between death and life? Those *Carpathia* tourists would have enjoyed their Mediterranean pleasure cruise, but a chance to save the *Titanic* survivors became the thrill of a lifetime that they never forgot. Just so, we may try to keep all of our discretionary time free for pleasure, but that will never provide a joy like seeing someone we have helped find strength and purpose in Christ.

II. The Californian

On that "night to remember" in 1912, thirty-six ships were at sea in the North Atlantic, at least a half-dozen of them in the vicinity of the *Titanic*. Some of these ships were so close that their lights could be seen on that clear, calm night. To attract their attention, the *Titanic's* wireless operators continued to pound out the CQD emergency signal. When a Morse lamp failed to receive a reply, Quartermaster Rowe began to fire off powerful distress rockets toward a nearby ship at anchor drifting with the current.

Disgusted after no response to eight emergency flares, he left the four remaining rockets unfired to take charge of a lifeboat.

The greatest enigma in this entire episode is why not a single one of these "mystery ships" ever came to the rescue. The best explanation is provided by a closer look at the Leyland liner *Californian* that had twice warned the *Titanic* of ice so serious that it had stopped around 10:30 p.m. and now lay dead in the water some five or ten miles to the north. About 11:40 p.m., Third Officer Charles Victor Groves, standing on the bridge of the *Californian,* saw a ship stop and put out most of its lights, but assumed that it had stopped because of icebergs and had turned out its lights to encourage passengers to go to bed. Groves did not seek to contact the ship because his wireless shack had shut down at the regular 11:30 p.m. closing time, ten minutes before disaster struck the *Titanic.*

At 12:45 a.m., when the *Titanic* began sending up a flare every five minutes, Second Officer Herbert Stone and Apprentice James Gibson of the *Californian* saw the blinding flashes and thought it strange that a ship would fire rockets in the middle of the night. In fact, Stone and Gibson began counting the flares. When they reached six, they notified Captain Lord, who wondered if they might be some sort of company signals. As the *Titanic* began to sink, the observant Stone and Gibson, now studying her on the horizon through glasses, began to notice that her red side light had disappeared. By 2:00 a.m., her other lights were so low on the horizon that they concluded she must be steaming away. Promptly they sent a second message to the Captain that the ship was disappearing into the southwest after firing altogether eight rockets. Twenty minutes later, Stone concluded that the strange ship was definitely gone and at 2:40 a.m. so notified Captain Lord who, for the third time, ordered no response.

At 4:00 a.m., Chief Officer George Frederick Stewart relieved Stone, heard his story, saw the *Carpathia* arrive, and awakened Captain Lord to brief him on these developments. The Captain decided not to contact the *Carpathia* because she was not sending any signals. Finally, at 5:40 a.m., Stewart awakened Wireless Operator Cyril Evans to contact the *Carpathia* because it had begun to fire rockets. Two minutes later Captain Lord learned that the *Titanic* had sunk and so, for the first time, started his engines and headed for her last reported position, only to arrive after the *Carpathia* had completed its work. The *Californian* was perfectly set by circumstances not of its making to participate in the rescue of the century, but it left the scene without a single survivor on board.[6]

What does spending that night aboard the *Californian* tell us about the great issues of life? The first is that, when we feel safe, we tend to project our sense of security on others. The *Californian* was aware of the icebergs and so had stopped for the night. Having repeatedly warned other ships of the danger, why worry about them? Would they not be just as prudent and do the same? In like manner, those with a strong conversion experience may come to feel that their faith in Christ will protect them from destruction both in this life and in the life to come, so why would not any sensible person exercise the same caution? Regrettably, some Baptists allow their cherished doctrine of the "security of the believer" to dull their awareness of the insecurity of the unbeliever!

Second, we learn so poignantly that even the high and mighty of earth are not invulnerable to tragedy. When completed, the 46,000-ton *Titanic* was the world's most impressive showcase of human progress. It carried the elite of the world in its staterooms, the 190 families in first class being attended by twenty-three handmaids, eight valets, assorted nurses and governesses—in addition to hundreds of stewards and stewardesses on the ship's crew. By contrast, the *Californian* was a plodding 6,000-ton ship with rooms for only forty-seven passengers—all of them empty. It was simply unthinkable that the "unsinkable" *Titanic* could be in trouble. Even after its distress signals began to go out, its own passengers as well as other ships had difficulty grasping the gravity of the moment. Just so, when successful people begin to send out their SOS signals, we tend to dismiss them as the whining of a pampered class accustomed to having their way because we cannot imagine that anyone so fortunate could actually be in serious trouble. Does a shabby little church down the street really have something important to offer a Harvard or Yale graduate who drives a Mercedes or BMW in the fast lane of life?

Third, we tend to miss so many distress signals because of our reluctance to live with the crushing fact that life is filled with monstrous icebergs that can take even our friends and neighbors to a dark and watery grave! On every hand we hear hints of domestic discord, of job dissatisfaction, of emotional depression or even despair, but do nothing because the sensitivity of the situation numbs our nerve and the awkwardness of intervening immobilizes our initiative. We may listen sympathetically and express the sincere hope that a way will be found to solve these problems when what we are really being told is that their boat is taking on water, that they are bailing as hard as they can, and that they will soon sink unless someone comes to their rescue.

In any case, we will never learn what difference we can make unless we try! The *Californian* was so insignificant beside the mighty *Titanic*, but it was safe! If only it had inquired, persisted, even demanded to know the facts, hundreds more might have been saved. The problem was not indifference, for when finally confronted with the facts it did what it could to help. No, the problem was complacency: it just could not grasp the enormity of what might happen if it did nothing. The *Californian* obeyed every one of the maritime rules, but it lacked the initiative to go beyond what was required to discover how it could be of help.

III. Responding to Cries for Help

How hard it is to take on the troubles of other people, especially at inconvenient times and under difficult circumstances. After all, do not we have our hands full just looking after ourselves and our immediate family? Having experienced our share of misfortune and failure, who are we to be offering advice about how to solve problems that may trip *us* up one day? Are there not professionally trained experts to deal with this sort of thing? To come charging to the rescue might be seen by those who know our own weaknesses as intruding into matters that are beyond our competence and are none of our business. The litany of excuses for doing nothing are endless. Indeed, Captain Lord and the crew of the *Californian* spent the rest of their lives trying to justify why they made no response, but such explanations were of no value to those pleading for help on the *Titanic*.

As hard as it is to offer help to friends and business associates whom we know so well, it is even harder to offer help to those whom we have never met. When you visit our Missions Fair this evening in Fellowship Hall, you will find over fifty tables and booths, each offering a different opportunity to volunteer for service. Some, such as the Wilkinson Terrace Ministry, are in our immediate community, while others are in the "Cajun Country" of South Louisiana. A few stretch beyond our borders, such as medical mission in Mexico or drilling for water in Zimbabwe. But for all of their diversity, one of the things that all of these projects have in common is that they involve people you have never met, people who may not share your culture, speak your language, or embrace your faith. In fact, the only thing that you may have in common with them is that you all share the same basic human needs.

As you browse the exhibits, you may read a brochure, watch some slides, or talk to representatives familiar with those ministries that attract your attention. But will you hear in what is said the urgent SOS that they are trying to telegraph to your heart? Will you see in those pictures the flares that they are sending up against a darkened sky? Almost immediately the temptation will arise to say to yourself, "I can't do that, for I don't know those people or understand their situation." But remember: the crew of the *Carpathia* did not know those on the *Titanic*, nor did they have any idea what they would find when they arrived at its location. The only thing they knew was that help was urgently needed, which is about all that you may be able to learn about those to whom you will be introduced this evening. But because the *Carpathia* responded without a moment's hesitation, it was able to save every person found alive when it reached the scene.

In our New Testament lesson this morning, we remembered the time when Jesus and his disciples were suddenly caught in a "great storm" that threatened to swamp and sink their boat (Mk. 4:37). Exhausted from a long day of ministry to the crowds, Jesus was asleep in the stern as his disciples—some of them professional fishermen who frequently plied those waters—began to panic. Desperate for help, they aroused him with the cry, "Teacher, do you not care if we perish?" (v. 38). Instantly he responded, bringing peace not only to the raging tempest but also to their troubled hearts (vs. 39–40). In answer to that pivotal question, the gospel shouts, "Yes, he cares!" But only we, by our actions today, can answer the question of a needy world, "Do his disciples today still care for the likes of us?"

In a prominent position near the top of our baptismal window above and behind the pulpit is the image of a ship, one of the great symbols of the church throughout its history. Today's message forces the question: What kind of ship will we be, like the *Carpathia* or like the *Californian*? Are we ready to turn into risky waters as soon as the SOS of human need is heard, or are we content to lie at anchor and do nothing until a better day dawns? The world never forgot what Captain Rostron and his crew did on that fateful night: the survivors presented him with a silver cup, the U. S. Congress struck a special medal in his honor, and the Cunard Line made him its Commodore until his retirement with full honors. For what will you and our congregation be remembered? Will you dare to "rescue the perishing" as an agent of Christ so that someday, somewhere, someone will be able to say in the words of another gospel song composed in the very year that the *Titanic* sank:

> I was sinking deep in the sin, far from the peaceful shore,
> Very deeply stained within, sinking to rise no more;
> But the master of the sea heard my despairing cry,
> From the waters lifted me, now safe am I.[7]

Clarifying Leadership Expectations

When discussing the core purposes of the church, I emphasized the importance of including the support function. Though it is often omitted, we must include it because of the crucial importance of trained lay leaders in helping the congregation to fulfill its mission.[8] For the pastor to be the only one who leads strategically is as bad as an army general planning grand strategy back at headquarters without any captains and lieutenants who can execute those plans on the front lines. When Jim Collins probed why some companies become "great" and not just "good," he discovered, to his surprise, that transformational leaders "did not first figure out where to drive the bus and then get people to take it there. No, they *first* got the right people on the bus (and the wrong people off the bus) and *then* figured out where to drive it," referring not to customers but to the management team.[9]

What this means for the church is that strategic preaching is no stronger than the lay leadership infrastructure that undergirds it. It is obviously important to select and train those who are gifted, influential, and resourceful; but we must also take care to make the team *representative* of the people it would lead. Remember how often I have stressed the need to avoid the kind of inbreeding that causes those in positions of responsibility to become insensitive to input from groups with whom they have little or no dealings, resulting in those who are ignored feeling that they are not really partners in building a vision for the future. The very nature of representative governance in a democratic polity means that the committees and boards of the church should be a microcosm of the total membership.

When I arrived at the First Baptist Church in Shreveport, its official leadership was composed almost exclusively of median and senior adult white males, which was typical of the power structure in almost all churches of its type. The key committees and boards had no singles, soon to become one of the most rapidly growing segments of our membership. They included no women, even though they constituted a clear majority (53 percent) of our members. Committees and boards had no ethnic groups represented, even though we soon opened the membership to African Americans and sponsored a Chinese-speaking mission that reached a diverse group of Asian Americans, especially Vietnamese refugees. Nor were there any physically challenged persons, even though we sponsored the only deaf ministry in the city. Seventy-five persons served staggered terms on the board of deacons, a similar number on two other boards dealing with business affairs and a church-sponsored school, plus about fifty on a half-dozen key committees. This leadership core of some two hundred individuals had close contact with, and could speak on behalf of, well under half of those involved in the life of the congregation.

Let me hasten to say that there was no deliberate effort to disenfranchise any groups or to deny them a voice in church affairs. When I emphasized the importance of these leaders keeping in touch with all of their constituency, they sincerely tried to listen and to learn; but deeply set habits over many years made it difficult for them to break out of familiar patterns of involvement. As you would suspect, the heart of the problem was simply traditionalism—they had always done it this way! By recognizing that this created a problem which they could not solve themselves, the inherited officialdom led the congregation to adopt a major strategic objective of making our committees and boards more representative of the total membership; and they cooperated beautifully in the implementation of this goal, even though it would cost some of them their place in the regular rotation of elected leaders to make room for those who had never before served.

Because the deacons were the most respected and influential lay leaders in the church, I have selected for treatment here two very specific issues that we faced in relation to membership on that body:

a. Could a person who had been divorced serve as deacon?
b. Could a person who was a woman serve as deacon?

For almost 150 years the answer to both questions had been negative. The church did not have any by-laws with restrictive language on either point, but it was clear that candidates must meet all of the scriptural qualifications for a deacon, thus the issue in both cases turned on whether the congregation could reach a consensus as to how the Bible should be interpreted on these two debated issues. I inherited a situation in which the mind of the membership was divided, due more to generational attitudes than to theological differences.

The development of more inclusive leadership policies evolved over several years, but decisions in these two contested areas crystallized in a matter of months. Even though I dealt with each issue in separate years, the circumstances were sufficiently similar that I believe I can trace the context of both sermons together. Here, in summary, is how the strategic factors unfolded:

1. Before the deacon nominating committee began its work each year, the congregation was invited to make suggestions for its consideration. The chair of that committee informed me that they were receiving more and more recommendations of people who were either divorced or were women. There were at least two obvious reasons for this trend. First, divorce rates had begun to soar in the aftermath of the social turbulence launched by the 1960s. Hardly anyone in the church had not experienced divorce in their immediate family—either themselves, their spouse, parents, siblings, or children. Furthermore, as the feminist movement gained momentum, fewer and fewer women were willing to have men speak for them, especially if they were single, divorced, or widowed. Second, within the church some of our most godly men had once been divorced, often during the upheaval surrounding World War II, but had later remarried and exemplified Christian family life of the highest order for many years. Moreover, women were some of our most respected Sunday school teachers, several of them having more extensive spiritual responsibilities in the church than did individual deacons.

2. Because divorcees and women had long been excluded from the diaconate, some of our members in either of these groups increasingly felt

consigned to a sort of second-class church citizenship. A very distinguished pastoral predecessor had tried to solve the problem by establishing a bicameral system of church governance according to which some could serve on a board of directors dealing with temporal affairs without meeting all of the requirements for serving on the board of deacons dealing with spiritual affairs, but this arrangement also served as an unintended reminder of the first-class/second-class distinction. Older women who had worked in the home for years continued to accept church assignments related to child care, food service, and housekeeping matters without complaint; but younger women entering highly competitive professions such as law and medicine did not respond to such invitations so readily. I increasingly came to realize that the profile of the deacon group marching up the aisles each Sunday to receive the offering provided a powerful symbol of the kind of people that our church wanted to reach, but this symbol was entirely too restrictive for the growing diversity in our midst.

3. Rather than force the issue in an up-or-down vote at a business meeting, I began by involving divorcees and women in a wide variety of leadership roles unrelated to the diaconate. For example, I took a computer printout to a meeting of our all-male finance committee showing that the "head of household" (i.e., the person who usually filled out the pledge card) in almost five hundred of our homes was a woman, either because she was single, divorced, widowed, or married to someone not in the church. Needless to say, experienced businesswomen began to appear on the finance committee the very next year. As this kind of leadership involvement increased throughout the church, I began to ask committee chairs and ministry project directors to make reports at deacons' meetings and church conferences on significant phases of their work. Well before either of these sermons was preached or any new policies adopted, the deacons themselves, as well as the membership at large, had abundant opportunities to see divorcees and women "in action" and to learn to appreciate the contributions that they were prepared to make as spiritual leaders.

4. The situation just sketched called for sermons quite different from the one in our first case study. After all, no one doubts that Christian compassion mandates an all-out effort to "rescue the perishing." What was needed in that case was strong motivation to act in the face of obvious obstacles, a need that I sought to meet with the help of a gripping story. In this case, the congregation harbored plenty of doubt about whether divorcees and/or women should ever be given a leadership role as deacons. Therefore I chose to take a low-key approach by the use of "teaching sermons" that took a clear position but left plenty of room for each person to rethink the issues involved as they saw fit. The *Titanic* sermon had made only limited use of Scripture in a brief, climactic reference in the conclusion. These

sermons needed to be dominated by the interpretation of Scripture from beginning to end so that the issues would be resolved by biblical guidance rather than by inherited traditions or by current social trends. This approach made both sermons lengthier than usual, requiring us to abbreviate other parts of the service; but attention never waned because everyone knew that we were grappling with a potentially divisive agenda that needed to be resolved.

5. Because of the potential of these sermons for controversy, I provided the congregation with written copies of the message and scheduled a "sermon dialogue" that evening for an informal time of discussion. These well-attended sessions gave me a good chance to show that I was not going to be defensive or argumentative about the positions that I had taken in the pulpit. That, in turn, opened the door to a number of private conferences in which those on both sides of these issues could express strong feelings in more candid fashion. As might be expected, some thought that my positions on these two issues somehow compromised the plain teachings of Scripture as they had always understood them. This gave me the opportunity to show how the same charge was leveled against both Jesus and Paul when they introduced change into the traditional practices of their inherited religion. When the dust settled, a rather strong consensus quickly formed, which allowed us to take a more inclusive approach to leadership recruitment with a minimum of friction.

Before we turn to the sermons themselves, let me add a word here to pastors who feel that controversial issues such as these should not be taken into the pulpit for the sake of congregational harmony. Our worship services were televised by the local ABC affiliate throughout a region called the Ark-La-Tex (meaning southern Arkansas, northwest Louisiana, and east Texas). In addition, we offered a ministry of printed sermon distribution that was nationwide in scope, which meant that I got a lot of sermon feedback, often from strangers in distant places. I cannot recount here the many poignant letters I received from divorcees and women, or their family members, describing the subtle put-downs that they had endured for years because their church had avoided deciding whether to offer a level playing field for the exercise of one's spiritual gifts to those in their circumstance. My point is that sidestepping issues that touch the core of a person's identity seldom contributes to more than a surface show of harmony. Beneath the surface, the pain is already there. It will only grow worse unless it is openly faced in a spirit of compassionate candor that is truly strategic.

SERMON: The Deacon and Divorce

One of the most debated issues in Baptist life today is whether a divorced person should thereby be excluded from consideration as a deacon. In contrast to our lengthy arguments on both sides of this question, the Bible devotes only a single phrase to the subject by saying that deacons are to be "husbands of one wife" (1 Tim. 3:12). That simple, obvious rendering has been followed in most English translations since the time of the *King James Version.* We begin to move from translation toward interpretation in our two most important contemporary editions: the *Revised Standard Version,* which has "married only once"; and the *New English Bible,* which has "faithful to his one wife."[10] While either of these explanatory paraphrases may have been intended by the author, neither one of them is necessitated or even encouraged by the plain meaning of the three Greek words which were used. It will be less confusing to stick with the literal translation, "husbands of one wife," until we decide how to move into the task of interpretation.

Before doing that, an often unrecognized fact should be noted. This identical phrase is used not only of deacons in 1 Timothy 3:12 but also of bishops in 1 Timothy 3:2 and of elders in Titus 1:6. Furthermore, the converse phrase, "wife of one husband," is used of widows in 1 Timothy 5:9. So exact are the parallels that there can be no doubt that the same meaning was intended in all four passages. Since we are dealing with a concern applicable to more than deacons, we need not limit our attention exclusively to that one group in determining the writer's intention.

I. The Limitations of a Literalistic Interpretation

How shall we go about determining what our text sought to say? Many who begin with a desire to take the Bible *seriously* automatically assume that this is best done by taking it *literally.* There is an especially strong pull to do so here due to the simplicity of the monogamous ideal. The logic of that position is expressed in our familiar reference to a spouse as my "one-and-only." That is the implication of the original *Revised Standard Version* translation, "married *only once.*" Anybody who can count to one can apply the rule when so understood. It seems only natural to adopt this absolute sense in our text because its precept stands alone, unqualified by mitigating circumstances. So taken, it would admit to ordination only those men who are married to their "one-and-only" wife.

Before we jump to this simple conclusion, however, let us notice the difficulties, both exegetical and practical, that immediately arise. Only three may be mentioned here, involving the time before, during, and after a "one-and-only" marriage.

1. Such an approach, taken literally, would bar to the diaconate all of those who have never been married. One view of our text is that the apostle insisted on marriage as a prerequisite for office to combat the asceticism that was just beginning to emerge with such force that it eventually triumphed in the mandatory celibacy of the Roman Catholic clergy (1 Tim.

4:3–4). This position, however, stumbles over the practice of Paul himself. Although autobiographical details are intriguingly obscure, it is clear that the apostle viewed himself in the single estate and that he championed the freedom for ministry that such a condition permitted (1 Cor. 7:7–8, 27–28, 32–34, 37–38). Christian history, both within the Baptist denomination and beyond, is filled with magnificent examples of church leaders who were bachelors. In the light of the unmarried vocation chosen by Jesus himself (Mt. 8:20; Lk. 9:58), who was the supreme model of the diaconate as well as every other ministry (Mk. 10:45; Lk. 22:26–37), it would be unfortunate to exclude single persons from leadership positions on the basis of a literal application of our text.

2. Again, such an approach would also disqualify those persons who lose their spouse for whatever reason during marriage. It is curious how the literalists so readily assume as much in the case of divorce but not in the case of death. For death brings as decisive a rupture and as complete a loss of a marriage partner as does divorce. To be sure, divorce may have unfortunate moral connotations not associated with death, but of this distinction our text knows nothing. If it literally means only what it says, that the deacon must have one wife, then let us quietly remove a man's name from the membership roll of the diaconate on the day of his wife's funeral! Needless to say, widowerhood should not be any more of a bar to service than bachelorhood.

3. Finally, to take our verse at face value would also exclude remarriage for any reason, since obviously the emphatic "*one* wife" leaves no room for a second. As usual, we think immediately of divorce, but the restriction would apply equally to digamy, the taking of a second spouse after the death of the first. Our culture is so sympathetic to this latter practice that you may be shocked by the dominant interpretation of our text in the early church as a prohibition against widowers remarrying. In fact, to this day many of the standard commentaries consider this to be the primary thrust of the passage. While it is true that Paul can be cited elsewhere in support of such sexual continence (1 Cor. 7:8, 39–40), his basic emphasis in the pastoral letters is on remarriage, especially among those still young enough to accept its responsibilities (1 Tim. 5:14). Once abstinence becomes a virtue in itself, which begins to happen when a second marriage is viewed as a weakness barring ordination, then we have started down the road of viewing *any* marriage as inferior for church leaders. In our kind of world, where even young wives may die out of season from a tragic accident or a dread disease, we may applaud rather than punish the deacon candidate who marries again and finds in his second companion both solace for his loneliness and strength for the raising of his children so indispensable to his deepest fulfillment.

I have dealt at some length with the deficiencies of the literalistic approach for two reasons. To begin with, in showing what the text does *not* mean, we have tried to clear the ground for a better understanding of what it *does* mean. Further, to reach this better understanding we have established the necessity of finding a more adequate method of interpretation. If the literalistic approach is not to be applied to bachelors or widowers or digamists, then to whom shall it be applied? It is not for us to pick and choose according to our preferences or prejudices, for then we are relying on our own judgment instead of on the sanction of Scripture. Somehow we need to discover what the writer was driving at and then try to reproduce his intentions for our times. How may this be done?

II. The Contributions of a Contextual Interpretation

The only way to get inside our author's mind and be controlled by his convictions is to understand the context in which he was working. His intentions become clear from the changes he was trying to effect in the life situation that he addressed. His purpose was to put into words the will of God for God's people, to propose ways in which they could incarnate the gospel for their times. So viewed, our text has at least three settings, one in the pagan world, another in the Christian movement, and yet another in the particular book in which it is found. Let us now try to determine its transforming impact in each of these environments, attempting to be, not as *literal* as possible, but as *contextual* as possible.

1. Throughout the pastoral letters, we find a keen awareness of the widespread corruption that abounded in the first-century Greco-Roman world. Nowhere was moral decay more apparent than in the home. Divorce was commonplace; sexual depravity was rampant; promiscuity was flaunted; chastity was scorned. Against a dark backdrop of debauchery the letters to Timothy and Titus insist upon conduct that, as the introduction to this section says, is "above reproach" (1 Tim. 3:2). The specific injunction on marriage requires the Christian leader to protect and preserve that relationship in all its purity from such perversions as polygamy, concubinage, and incest. This stress on domestic fidelity is captured in the *New English Bible* rendering, "*faithful* to one wife." In our sensual society, where "new morality" often means *no* morality, this standard calls for an integrity of purpose and spirit among deacons that expresses itself in a tenacious loyalty to those virtues that honor the sanctity of marriage.

2. The pastoral letters also reflect a strong emphasis on faithfulness to that deposit of truth entrusted especially to Christian leaders (1 Tim. 6:20; 2 Tim. 1:12–14). Nothing could be more important in that tradition than the teaching of Jesus himself, with its rejection of divorce as having no

place in God's plan for creation (Mk. 10:2–12). The deacon is reminded that his Master called him to a "one flesh" commitment that transcends the marital obligations, not only in the pagan world, but in the Old Testament and in Judaism as well, a teaching that Paul was careful to distinguish as more authoritative than his own (1 Cor. 7:10–11). In our day of quickie divorces, which amount to polygamy on the installment plan, the difference that Christianity offers is best demonstrated in the lives of those couples who are so totally one in body, mind, and spirit that divorce is not even an option to be considered.

3. Finally, in the fabric of the book itself this guideline does not stand alone, but is integral to a composite list of qualifications that lift the church leader above criticism both within and without the church. Some suppose that these ideals reflect maximum requirements of morality applicable only to those holding office, but a closer look shows that they describe rather a minimum code of conduct for any Christian who maintains a reputation above reproach. There is no "double standard" beginning to emerge here according to which leaders must meet higher criteria than followers. The application of our text to widows (1 Tim. 5:9) is proof that the lives of church leaders are to be representative of, rather than an exception to, the lifestyle adopted by all parts of the congregation. Deacons today should be chosen not from those who pass some special litmus test, but from those who live exemplary lives that embody the moral qualities that should be common to all Christians.

III. Applying the Scriptural Intention to Our Deacon Selection Process

We are now in a position to ask how the results of our inquiry bear upon the concerns with which we began. We have already seen that the thrust of our text is much broader than the issue of divorce, that it was not intended simply as a mathematical formula designed to limit the diaconate to once-married men. Instead, it was meant to describe an important component of that "above reproach" character that every Christian should exemplify. Thus our understanding and application of these three words to the diaconate should reflect the kind of witness that we want our entire congregation to bear in a world so ready to undermine the stability of the home.

It is this issue of a strong and consistent witness in today's world, not that of a long-ago marriage that may have ended in divorce, which is crucial to the proper use of our text in the deacon selection process. Many active church members have never seen the inside of a divorce court, but their marriages are at best superficial arrangements of convenience. Although they may live out their years with only one companion, their union is neither nourished by Christian convictions nor does it bear clear witness to strong spiritual foundations.

On the other hand, many Christians have fought valiantly but to no avail in a desperate effort to save a marriage that was flawed from the first. Emerging from a divorce that they did everything to prevent, such persons have resolved with fierce intensity to rebuild their battered homes with a union that honors Christ from the first day to the last. Now, years later, such couples exhibit that sturdy devotion to each other and to their children that is the hallmark of an exemplary Christian home. Can there be any doubt that the latter, despite a history of divorce, is far more qualified *by marriage* for the diaconate than the former?

But some will reply: Why not limit our leaders only to those who qualify on *both* counts, that is, to those whose marriages bear powerful witness to a Christian home *and* who have been married only once? Obviously this is the safest course, and for that reason has long been followed by many churches, including our own. Yet it may be asked whether such a policy does not at times deny leadership to the church that it sorely needs. In our region one thinks of the incalculable influence for good on Baptist life provided by Southwestern Seminary in Fort Worth, Texas. That institution was uniquely the offspring of its first president, B. H. Carroll, a towering spiritual and theological giant who almost single-handedly made the school possible. But B. H. Carroll was divorced as the result of a failed teenage marriage at the time of the Civil War.[11] Perhaps Southwestern Seminary could have happened apart from Carroll, but history suggests that God did not so intend. We shudder to think of the consequences if Carroll had been barred from ministerial office for a lifetime and denied his colossal contribution because of a fifteen-year-old bride who abandoned him after two weeks!

The issue, however, runs deeper than the practical wisdom of utilizing valuable leadership that may be stronger precisely because of, rather than in spite of, domestic adversity. Is any person really "qualified" for office by *all* the standards summarized in the pastoral letters? To take only one example, our text is but half of 1 Timothy 3:12, which continues, "leading their children and their own households well" (author's translation). If the latter clause were applied as strictly as some want to apply the former, it would bar to ordination anyone with a delinquent child not submissive to parental discipline. All of us can think of deacons' families in which there is a sound "one-and-only" marriage between husband and wife but a tragic rupture caused by rebellion between loving parents and a prodigal child. Ironically, some who want to be most rigid on the divorce phrase, claiming that we somehow "dilute" the Bible by ever making an "exception," are the very ones who overlook or even show tender compassion to those with wayward children. The point, of course, is not to enlarge the area of exclusion but to strive for consistency of application.

When we do so, and determine to take the biblical criteria seriously, there is no way to pretend that any church leader has been true for a lifetime to all of the stated qualifications. Indeed, it is hard enough for those in their most spiritually mature years to honor these guidelines day by day. The early church faced this problem far more acutely than we. Many of its members were converted from paganism without benefit of even minimum moral foundations. In discussing the "unrighteous" of his world, Paul named "the immoral…idolaters…adulterers…sexual perverts…thieves…the greedy…drunkards…revilers… robbers"—but then added: "And such were some of you." (1 Cor. 6:9–11). The only way for him to deal with this sordid past was with a doctrine of transforming grace that declared, "If any one is in Christ, he is a new creation; the old has passed away; behold, the new has come" (2 Cor. 5:17). To be sure, there is an historical continuity by which one accepts responsibility for the past (1 Cor. 7:17–24). But balancing this is a divine discontinuity by which one is freely forgiven of the burdens of the past.

Here we come to the deepest issue of all: Does our contemporary practice balance fidelity and freedom, law and grace, judgment and mercy, constraint and compassion? Grace does not flourish best in a climate of caution. The Everlasting Mercy is restless with the strictures of safety. Without hedging on our ideals or compromising our witness, do we want to say by the leaders we choose to represent us that a person's past may contain something that Christ cannot overcome? Saul of Tarsus ravaged the flock of God like a wild beast (Gal. 1:13); yet, after Christ changed all of that, Paul insisted on his right to be equal with any leader in the church (Gal. 2:6–10). Why? Because the old Paul was now dead, crucified with Christ (Gal. 2:20). If that kind of change can happen to a persecutor, liberating him to fulfill the most important leadership role in the history of Christianity, can it not happen also to divorcees, freeing them to serve as Christ shall lead his people to determine?

SERMON: Women in Church Leadership

One of the most significant developments in recent years is the changing role of women in our society. Many are entering vocations traditionally reserved for men. Several women in our congregation hold key executive and professional positions in our city. Increasingly comprehensive legislation is guaranteeing women's legal rights to equal opportunities for employment and the protection of women from discrimination and harassment. Beyond the workplace, women are finding their voice as significant contributors to the political process and are searching for personal fulfillment in ways that affirm their dignity and equality as members of the human family.

This remarkable ferment raises the unavoidable question of whether women will also play new roles in the life of the church. For example, in recent years more and more of you have submitted the names of women members for consideration as deacons, so much so that the deacon nominating committee has asked me to address the matter from the pulpit, since, in our long history, women have not heretofore served in that capacity. Again, we have received an inquiry from one of our women members finishing seminary as to whether we would be open to ordaining her to the gospel ministry, something that, as far as I know, has not been done by any Baptist church in Louisiana. Doubtless many divergent viewpoints on these questions compete within our congregation and need to be resolved. Such resolution should come not by voting our attitudes on current social trends, but by a careful study of God's Word and its relevance for our life as a church today. This sermon seeks to move us in that direction.

I. The Imperatives of the Biblical Witness

The Bible does not paint a pretty picture of the place that a woman occupied in the ancient world. We need not be squeamish, however, about acknowledging her low estate even within Scripture, an estate often revealed in the practices of concubinage and polygamy. The issue for us is not how much progress was actually achieved during the millennium covered by biblical literature, but whether God chose that often deplorable situation in which to disclose his ultimate intention for woman. In the Bible we find real rather than ideal social conditions, in some respects better but in other respects worse than those which obtained elsewhere. What this means is that God did not necessarily pick out the most advanced society in which to work. God was willing to deal with a sometimes progressive and a sometimes regressive situation in the world. Such a realization offers the hope that our wayward world may yet have a chance for divine guidance even in those cultures in which women are still brutally exploited.

How may we determine the distinctive contours of biblical faith and locate the center around which that faith coheres? The focal point is clearly Christ and all that he means for the life of humanity. But the reality of Christ is best understood when set in the context of a redemptive drama stretching from creation to consummation. Three realities taken together unify biblical faith because, in them as nowhere else, divine truth from beyond history most clearly impinges upon the whole of God's redemptive history. It is from this threefold perspective that woman may be viewed both in the light of the painful realities of this world and in the light of the perfected realities of the world to come.

Woman and Creation. The oldest and in many ways the most comprehensive biblical witness to the place of woman as defined by creation appears in Genesis 2:4b–25. There we meet the male in his solitude as an incomplete creation: it was "*not good* that the man should be alone" (2:18a, emphasis added). When no other living creature could be found to fill that void (2:19–20), God fashioned woman to be a companion "corresponding" to him (literally: "a helper according to what is in front of him;" that is, a kind of mirror image of his humanity). When man was presented with his "opposite number," he immediately rejoiced to discover that in her he now had both otherness (i.e., community) and sameness (i.e., "bone of my bones / and flesh of my flesh," 2:23), a relationship that he could never sustain with the animals. So necessary was each to the other that their attachment was to transcend every other loyalty, even the blood tie between parent and child (2:24). Just as a piece of paper, by its nature, has two sides, so humanity, by its created nature, has two genders. Neither the male nor the female alone, but only the two of them together as "one flesh," constitute and complete what it means generically to be human.

Because this account depicts woman as having been created *after* man, *from* man, and *for* man, some have seen in its concept of complementary companionship a theology of female subordination. Neither this text nor Genesis 1:26–31 has any hint of that. "God created man in his own image," creating "male and female" concurrently (1:27). Gender differentiation was inherent in God's design for humanity from the outset: the female was not an accident, an afterthought, or an expedient. A paradoxical singularity and plurality of being ("God created *him*; male and female he created *them*," 1:27) corresponded to or "imaged" a similar reciprocity in God's being ("Let *us* make man…*he* created him/them," 1:26–27). We, like God, were meant to be a fellowship within ourselves, though our human nature is defined by gender, while God's is defined by the Trinity.

Jesus, of course, was the supreme interpreter of creation theology within the Bible (Mt. 19:3–9/Mk. 10:2–12). In response to a question regarding the rights of a husband to divorce his wife, he identified the Mosaic legislation of Deuteronomy 24:1–4 as an effort to deal with "hardness of heart," but, over against that, set the "beginning of creation" (Mk. 10:6) when "it was not so" (Mt. 19:8). It is significant that Jesus attributed to sin the male dominance seen so clearly in the unfair divorce laws of his day. By contrast, he based his positive understanding of gender differences on a fusion of the key elements in Genesis 1:27 and 2:24, thereby acknowledging both the unity and the primacy of these passages. For him, God had "joined together" two equal partners as "one," thereby ruling out not only the male prerogative of divorce but any other form of unfaithfulness by either partner that would weaken the marriage bond (Mk. 10:11–12).

Unlike Jesus, Paul did have occasion to refer to the subordination of woman rooted in Genesis 3:16 (cf. 1 Cor. 11:3–9; 14:34; Eph. 5:22–24; 1 Tim. 2:11–15). In so doing, however, he was careful to maintain the unity and equality of the sexes in the creative purpose of God (1 Cor. 11:11–12; Eph. 5:28–33; and, by implication, 1 Cor. 6:16). Insofar as Christians still lived "in the world," in a fallen creation subjected to futility and bondage (Rom. 8:20–21), male dominance and female subjection were ever-present realities that could not be ignored lest social chaos erupt and Christianity be branded as a libertine escapist movement. But insofar as they now lived "in the Lord," these cultural restrictions were already transcended. In the eyes of the world, women at worship could be completely misunderstood if they did not keep silent (1 Cor. 14:34; 1 Tim. 2:11), whereas in the eyes of faith these same women were free to pray and prophesy and even to teach (1 Cor. 11:5; Titus 2:3).

Woman and Christ. For the Bible, the meaning of the Christ was uniquely incarnated in the historical ministry of Jesus. It is striking that his message nowhere included references to circumcision, that distinctively male rite of initiation from which Jewish women and female proselytes were excluded. In place of this ancient practice that had assumed such importance in first-century Judaism (Eph. 2:11), Jesus focused on faith as the basis of one's standing before God. This immediately put women, as well as foreigners, on equal footing with Jewish males (Mk. 5:34; Mt. 8:10). Moreover, he demanded that women make their own personal commitment to him even if it shattered the solidarity of the family circle (Mt. 10:34–6; Lk. 12:51–3). In response, women formed a special band that accompanied him from Galilee, several of whom were so prominent that their names have become a part of the gospel record (Lk. 8:2–3). "The fact that women followed Jesus is without precedent in contemporary Judaism."[12]

Examples of the ways in which women became an integral part of Jesus' ministry might be multiplied. In contrast to Jewish parallels, both his parables and his miracles often dealt tenderly with women. He talked to them in public (Jn. 4:27) and made friends of them in the home (Lk. 10:38–42). No wonder they were the last at the cross in courage (Mt. 27:55–56), the first at the tomb in compassion (Mk. 16:1). The important point to grasp here is the theological reality underlying this remarkable pattern. Albrecht Oepke provides a clue: "Jesus is not the radical reformer who proclaims laws and seeks to enforce a transformation of relationships. He is the Saviour who gives Himself especially to the lowly and oppressed and calls all without distinction to the freedom of the Kingdom of God."[13]

That is why the apostle Paul could affirm, in the clearest expression of his Christ-centered faith: "there is neither male nor female; for you are all one in Christ Jesus" (Gal. 3:28). Viewed historically, behind that claim lay the important role of women in the founding of the church (Acts 1:14; 2:17; 12:12), in the spread of the missionary movement (Acts 16:13–15;

17:4, 12, 34; 18:18, 26), and in positions of leadership and service (Rom. 16:1, 3, 6, 12, 15). But viewed theologically, here is not merely the claim that in Christ the "male and female" duality of creation has been redeemed from its corruption by sin, but also that in the life of the body of Christ (3:27) it has actually been transcended. The children of God who live by a faith (3:26), which expresses itself in baptism (3:27a), have thereby been "clothed" with a Christ-identity (3:27b) that supersedes racial, social, and sexual identities.

Woman and the Consummation. During the ministry of Jesus, the Sadducees sought to snare him with a particularly offensive illustration of levirate marriage to seven successive brothers (Mt. 22:23–33/Mk.12:18–27/Lk. 20:27–40), on which basis they asked, "In the resurrection whose wife will she be?" (Mk. 12:23), hoping thereby to justify their rejection of the future life by ridiculing its premises. In his response, "when they rise from the dead, they neither marry nor are given in marriage, but are like angels in heaven" (Mk. 12:25), Jesus exposed a basic fallacy: his opponents had not reckoned with "the power of God" to fashion an order so completely different from earth that it need not perpetuate any of earth's ambiguities. Since the angels were in the heavenly court prior to creation, they must be nonflesh creatures without gender. When the husbands and wives of earth exchange their physical bodies for spiritual bodies (1 Cor. 15:44), they leave the earthly institution of marriage behind.

Paul entertained a similar view, which helps to explain one of the most puzzling passages in his letters: "The appointed time has grown very short; from now on, let those who have wives live as though they had none...For the form of this world is passing away" (1 Cor. 7:29–31). The apostle was aware that, sooner than most realize, the whole order to which marriage belongs would terminate—whether at the end of world history through the return of Christ, or at the end of each individual's personal history through death—and therefore now was the time to prepare for that impending heavenly existence. This could be done neither by divorce (7:27) nor by separation or sexual restraint (7:3–5), but by practicing an "undivided devotion to the Lord" (7:35). The intensity of Paul's commitment to the world beyond was remarkable indeed: so clearly did the Age to Come loom on his spiritual horizon that he was ready for it to reshape the most intimate relationships of earthly life.

When we put all of the relevant passages together, they coalesce into a coherent perspective that sets human sexuality into a "saving history" framework. Both Jesus and Paul recognized three distinct "ages" or stages in the relationship of male and female:

1. The Old Age, in which "hardness of heart" led to male dominance, female subjection, unfaithfulness, and exploitation.
2. The Messianic Age, in which Christ makes possible a realization of the original intention for man and woman in the created order, namely an equality of reciprocal loyalty, fidelity, and support.
3. The Age to Come, in which our earthly relationships will be transcended and our unity-in-reciprocity will be fulfilled, not by oneness with the opposite sex, but by a perfect oneness with God-in-Christ.

This biblical way of stating its perspective on woman may be applied most relevantly in two respects. Historically, we may ask where the church in our generation wishes to be located on this salvation timetable. Shall we revert once more to the Old Age, as if woman had not been punished enough, and seek new ways to keep her in subjection? Or shall we take seriously the fact that Christ has come and liberated both male and female from their age-long strife to new possibilities of mutual respect and caring? Indeed, dare we push our spirits to the boundary where time itself shall be no more to go beyond a careful equality and mutuality of the sexes to a realm of pure spiritual adventure in Christ where gender matters not at all? These same questions may also be asked personally as I decide just how far I am willing to recapitulate in my own experience the age-long quest to regain "Paradise Lost" and see woman as she was meant to be, the indispensable "otherness" without whom my humanity is incomplete, and by truly finding her to discover beyond us both that essential humanity that lives both now and forevermore with "undivided devotion to the Lord."

II. Gender Equality in the Life of the Church

It really does not matter if we are "for" gender equality in our church unless it makes a difference in the effectiveness with which we minister. Our challenge is to prove by the health of our congregation that we can do God's work better when we utilize the contributions of male and female alike without restriction. Since there is not time to discuss the many ways that our life together is enriched by encouraging the full participation of women on the same basis as men, let me select only three areas to illustrate how men and women can work together in a partnership of equals as servants of Christ.

The Initiative of God. Baptists have always based the authorization for ministry not on apostolic succession, but on the call of God. When an early Christian group called Judaizers insisted that one must follow their ancient traditions—that is, embrace circumcision, Sabbath observance, and temple sacrifice—to become a Christian, God kept running ahead of this restrictive theology and saving Gentiles *before* they embraced these Jewish practices. When, for example, Peter was criticized for baptizing the uncircumcised Cornelius (Acts 10:1–48), his defense was that God had validated the centurion's conversion by filling him with the Holy Spirit quite apart from meeting any of the conditions the Judaizers imposed (Acts 11:1–18).

Note carefully the key principle that Peter learned from this experience: "If then God gave the same gift to them as he gave to us when we believed in the Lord Jesus Christ, who was I that I could withstand God?" (Acts 11:17). Here is a situation in which theology was being challenged to catch up with experience. For centuries, pious Jews had believed that Scripture was telling them to circumcise every male convert, a practice that became urgently important to them in the first century when they felt threatened with extinction through cultural assimilation. But now a new day had dawned when their understanding of what God had *said* was being reinterpreted by what God had actually *done!* This explains why circumcision, a dominant practice throughout the Old Testament, was dropped almost immediately in the New Testament, never again to become a restriction limiting Gentile participation in the Christian movement.

Baptists today face the same situation in regard to women as Peter did in regard to Gentiles. For generations we were rooted in the soil on farms or as laborers and shopkeepers in the cities. In that social system, men did the "public" work while women stayed at home. Thus it was only natural for men to exercise leadership in the churches. But now all of that has changed. Many of our Baptist women are in the workplace, where equal employment opportunities are mandated by law. Years ago, very few women indeed heard God's call to minister, except perhaps in a very different culture on some foreign field. After all, back then they could not even gain admission to a Baptist seminary to receive the training needed for such service. Today, when all the educational opportunities available to men are also open to women, when women are assuming leadership roles in every other vocation, when there is a chronic shortage of qualified male candidates for ministry, is it any wonder that more women are hearing and heeding God's call to ministry?

Baptists place a high priority on personal religious experience. If a young man steps forward and declares with clarity and conviction that God has called him to the ministry, we are almost certain to ordain him after examination by a council of mature church leaders. How, then, can we do otherwise if a young woman steps forward, if her testimony is radiant with an impelling sense of God's call, if her understanding of Baptist faith and practice is sound and sensible, if she is willing to prove the sincerity of her dedication through years of sacrificial preparation, if her abilities are equal or superior to those of many male ministers? With Peter we must ask, Who are we to hinder the freedom of God to call whom he will? Dare we limit his grace by our inherited traditions? Let us learn to rejoice rather than to resist when God is ready to do a new thing in our midst.

A Representative Ministry. Turning now from the divine to the human side of the equation, Baptists began as a lay movement, and that of necessity because ordination was then controlled by the state church. For this reason we emphasize the priesthood of every believer rather than viewing the ministry as some "official" group with a special status denied to other members. We take seriously the promise of Acts 2:17–18, that God's Spirit is now available to all, whether they be male or female, young or old, master or servant. It is in the power of the Spirit that every Christian ministers, whether it be through prophesy, seeing visions, or dreaming dreams. As the entire book of Acts makes clear, it is not by ordination but by spiritual empowerment that God's work is done in our world.

Then why do Baptists set apart ministers and deacons by ordination? Clearly they are meant to lead as representatives of the entire ministering membership. The requirements of the democratic process demand some such arrangement. Obviously a congregation of several thousand members, as was the case from the beginning at Pentecost, cannot conduct its business as a committee of the whole. And so, manageable groups, such as the Twelve and the Seven, soon began to function on behalf of the larger body (Acts 6:1–6). In the first century, it was customary for such leadership groups to be exclusively male, since women had virtually no legal rights or public role in society.

Today, however, the situation is very different. Not only are women enfranchised in society, but many of them function as heads of household. For years the argument was made that women could have influence in a male-led church through their husbands, but this assumption ignores not only the rising number of women who have no husband because they are single, divorced, or widowed, but also those women whose husbands are either not Christian, inactive, or in another church. Let us be both honest and practical: Is there an all-male clergy or diaconate anywhere that can claim to understand and minister to the deepest needs of the half or more of our members who are female? Of equal seriousness: what does it say about *all* Christians being a priesthood of believers if there are *no* women serving as priests in the leadership of the church?

It is neither candid nor consistent for Baptists to give women utterly crucial spiritual responsibilities on the one hand, but deny them any status and recognition on the other hand. For example, women have long done more than their share of Bible teaching in the Sunday school, have supported our vast missionary enterprise with limited help from the men, and have provided virtually all of the leadership for our children and youth during the most formative years of their spiritual development. Functionally, women have been performing many of the most important ministries of the church while, formally, most of the status implied by ordination has been handed out to men. To refuse to correct this imbalance is to perpetuate a "put down," as if women were somehow spiritually inferior to men.

The Sharing of Gifts. In addition to our emphasis on grace, by which we affirm our willingness to let God give what he will even before we are ready to receive it, Baptists have placed equal stress on the importance of faith, by which we mean that our response is also a crucial component in the divine-human encounter. The sovereign grace of God does not leave us passive but rather frees us to participate gladly in the new thing that God is doing. To limit or exclude women from leadership roles strikes at the heart of this understanding of faith, for we do not decide whether to be male or female; rather, we find ourselves fashioned into one or the other by the reproductive process that God has established for human procreation. The ultimate danger here is to assign a negative value to something that God has done in which we have no choice.

In place of arbitrary restrictions that would deny women certain opportunities for service simply because of their gender, let us magnify the freedom of each person to share fully such spiritual gifts as he or she has been given. Women obviously have a special sensitivity to the needs of other women, particularly in such areas as pregnancy, child care, and homemaking. What male, whether he be minister or deacon, could possibly be as effective as a female in helping women deal with such intimate crises as infertility, miscarriage, or menopause? Women also need a spiritual sisterhood to see them through such traumas as divorce or widowhood or their own approaching death. But this ministry by women should not be limited to other women. Precisely because of their gender, women have their own distinctive expectations of worship, ways of witnessing, theological perspectives, ethical concerns, and styles of leadership. Their approaches are not necessarily better than those more typical of men. But they are different because of their rootage in feminine experience, and thereby likely to be both relevant to the female half of the church and broadening to the male half of the church.

Today, the Christian faith finds itself facing awesome challenges that will require the most courageous and creative leadership of which we are capable. To put it plainly, we are going to need all of the help we can get, whether from clergy or laity. If so, then why respond with one hand tied behind our back by limiting women with spiritual gifts from serving in any leadership position? If, in Christ and in his body, there really is "neither male nor female" (Gal. 3:28), can we not work toward the kind of church in which each of us, whether a man or a woman, may experience the full potential that our gender offers us for spiritual fulfillment?

Preaching to the Power Structure

Most preaching is intensely personal, either to the individual or to the congregation. In Shreveport, which has often been called "the buckle on the Bible Belt," any application beyond that was often viewed with suspicion as an expression of the "social gospel." This kind of reductionism failed to recognize that the New Testament gospel is not only personal and social, but even cosmic in scope (Col. 1:16–17; Eph. 3:9–10). Because of a strong tradition of evangelistic preaching in Shreveport churches, many of our pulpits paid little or no attention to the responsibility of Christians to contribute to the common good, such as the well-being of the city in which we lived.

This general neglect of the civic agenda confronted me as pastor with an acute problem for at least two reasons. First, a great number of prominent local leaders were in our membership. At the governmental level this included a United States senator, representatives in the Louisiana Legislature, a city commissioner, and veteran members of both the federal and state judiciary. The editors of both daily newspapers and one of the publishers belonged to the church, as did the owners of a network television station. Leaders in every phase of business and professional life were well represented, as were many arbiters of the city's social and cultural life. Volunteer work was highly regarded by our members, a number of whom sat on multiple boards of organizations responsible for contributing to the quality of life of all our citizens. Collectively, all of this involvement represented an enormous stewardship, but there was little awareness of how the Christian faith might guide in the discharge of such responsibilities.

Second, near the time of my arrival in Shreveport the need for new civic initiatives was given added urgency by virtue of several disturbing trends. The dominant economic driver in Shreveport had long been the oil and gas industry, which was then in steady decline. It was a feast-or-famine business that made fortunes for some while bankrupting others. In the former category, a few families held tightly to a large amount of inherited wealth. This wealth, unlike earned wealth, had resulted in a good bit of inbred elitism that was indifferent to the plight of the less fortunate. Civic philanthropy was at a low level. Bright young adults were moving away to Dallas and Houston for lack of entré into a rigid social structure. The metropolitan area was Balkanized by class distinctions into four quadrants. The civil rights struggle had left a legacy of distrust between ethnic groups. Warning flags were flying everywhere, but my well-positioned parishioners were doing very little to meet the challenge.

For our congregation, Independence Sunday (the Sunday nearest July 4) was a prime time to treat civic concerns. In 1976 we had celebrated our country's bicentennial with a rousing display of patriotic fervor. Thus I used Independence Sunday in 1977 to balance this national emphasis with a local focus. My sermon strategy was threefold: (a) to define the crisis for those in denial regarding the seriousness of what was happening all about us; (b) to sketch a biblical theology of the city for those content to exclude urban concerns from the Christian agenda; and (c) to urge a fresh commitment to work for the common good, especially on the part of those who seemed to be excessively preoccupied with their own social status. You will readily see from the attached sermon how these purposes were pursued.

Having been in Shreveport less than two years when the sermon was preached, my expectations regarding results were modest indeed. I had hoped that the sermon would open a dialogue with several of the civic leaders in the congregation regarding ways to bring Christian insights to bear on many of the problems that our city faced. Little could I know that the sermon would be printed in the next Sunday's newspaper and become the subject of intense discussion both in the media and throughout the city for months to come. Looking back, I now understand the two main reasons for this unexpected response much better than I did when I stood to preach. The first is that Shreveport was far more ready, even overdue, for a catharsis than I could have possibly known. The second is that casting the sermon in a strategic mode made it more useful to a host of others outside our congregation, as yet unknown to me, who longed to take off the blinders and attack the urban blight that had given us a case of what came to be called "Shreveportitis."

There is not space or need to trace here the many "outworkings" of this one sermon. A small sampling might include the following: It mobilized the ministers of our metropolitan churches for a concerted effort to arouse their influential members to action. It put me in touch with a creative minority in every area of the city willing to be catalytic of a better climate in our urban life. It put me before a host of organizations working on various aspects of the larger agenda such as civic clubs, the Junior League, the Committee of 100, the Chamber of Commerce, the current class of Leadership Shreveport, and the local colleges and universities. It led to the establishment of a Social Justice and Peace Committee that brought together a "coalition of the concerned" to work on better race relations. Jesus once told how sowing the seed of the word can lead to a hundredfold harvest (Mk. 4:14, 20). That does not happen very often, but this was one time that it did.

SERMON: Shreveport at the Crossroads

Shreveport is a city in crisis. Although a litany of our woes is regularly recited in the public media, let me draw together some basic ingredients in our present predicament for your fresh consideration.

I. The End of an Era

The State of Louisiana provides the larger context in which the struggle of Shreveport must be set. Here the story is one of disconnection, depletion, and deprivation. Caught in a fratricidal political conflict that cleaves the state into competing regions, Shreveport rules its northwest corner in splendid isolation, still after all these years without the life-giving arteries of a North-South expressway or a Red River waterway. Once the crude oil capital of the state, Shreveport has seen its prime industry shift during the postwar years first to South Louisiana and then even farther away into the waters of the Gulf of Mexico. Dependent since the days of Huey Long on severance tax revenues from petroleum extraction to underwrite nearly half the state's budget, Louisiana has watched its known reserves decline throughout this decade, with experts ominously predicting that gas and oil wells could be pumped dry within five to fifteen years. Until major replacement revenues can be found from other sources, the prospect is bleak for any improvement in essential government services, such as education, which are now near the bottom nationally in per capita expenditures.

Here at home, our city was tested recently in a national survey that rated its quality of life "substandard" (the lowest of five categories) and ranked Shreveport seventieth among eighty-three medium-sized metropolitan areas in America (population 200,000 to 500,000).[14] Immediately, even before the results of the study were available for careful scrutiny, our town fathers cried with indignation that we had been judged unfairly by a computer using obsolete data. Just as quickly the matter was forgotten. Once the report did arrive, its results turned out to be based, not on fuzzy speculations, but on 123 carefully weighted "quality-of-life" factors involving economic, political, environmental, health-education, and social components. Nor is there any evidence that the results were skewed by using 1970 data, which, because of the decennial national census, provide the most adequate facts available. Doubtless Shreveport has made progress since the beginning of this decade, but there is no indication that it surpasses the progress made by other cities with which we must be compared.

In fact, in one area the intervening years have been particularly unkind to our fair city, that of governmental leadership. We need no computer to tell us that the "quality of life" at City Hall has declined precipitously during this decade! In swift succession two members of our congregation were propelled into public service in the aftermath of emergencies that were not without embarrassment, while another heads a citizen's panel that has lodged stinging criticisms of shortsightedness in the prudent management of pension funds and other fiscal resources. Brooding over all this confusion, unmentioned but not forgotten, looms the larger-than-life tragedy of George D'Artois. To be sure, the picture is not all dark, but any light that we can now see must be etched with a dimension of disgrace.

The upshot of it all is a subtle mood of attrition, a nagging hunch that our city is being diminished rather than enhanced. The sense of loss is all about us: our leaders are languid; our downtown is drooping; our spirits are sagging. Most of all, we mourn the exodus of our people. A recent article in *Fortune* depicted a map of the Sunbelt, which showed that "every state in the region except Louisiana gained on balance from migration during the first half of the Seventies."[15] All of the parishes in Shreveport's Standard Metropolitan Statistical Area were colored as losers. Commented a local journalist after musing on that map: "The fact that the numbers are going somewhere else is symptomatic of a general recognition that something is wrong here."[16]

II. The Enduring Norm

Does Christianity have anything to say to the plight of our city? Many of its most avid believers would answer strongly in the negative. To them, the gospel deals almost exclusively with personal salvation and so is directed primarily to individuals and to their relations within the church. Any talk about God-and-city smacks of a now discredited "social gospel" advocated by "liberals" in the early decades of this century. Better to leave such things to the politicians so as to keep the sacred and secular realms clearly distinct.

Despite the popularity of this view in a time of intense privatism, the plain fact is that it simply does not do justice to significant dimensions of our faith. The Bible is full of explicit teachings on the cities of its day. So numerous are those scriptural references that we have time to select only the most important example, Jerusalem, as an illustration for our discussion. The three great epochs in its destiny provide a typology by which to understand and evaluate any city, including Shreveport, in the light of the purposes of God.

1. The first significant phase in Jerusalem's history from a biblical perspective was its choice to serve as a unifying center for the people of

God (1 Kings 11:13). A pagan city had long existed on the site (Judg. 19:10–12) when David wrested it from the Jebusites (2 Sam. 5:6–10; 1 Chr. 11:4–9) and made it the capital of his kingdom. Lying between Israel and Judah in the territory of Benjamin, it belonged to none of the twelve tribes but was a common possession of them all. In subsequent centuries, as the Jews scattered in every direction, Jerusalem remained the one focal point to which their loyalties turned (e.g., Ps. 87, 122, 137). Because the one true God dwelt in the temple there, Jerusalem was supremely set apart as a city open to all of the authentic aspirations of the world, a beckoning mountain to which all peoples could flow in their quest for justice and peace (Isa. 2:2–5; Mic. 4:1–5).

Here we discover the foundations for a biblical definition of what any true city should be. Pagan towns are tribal in character; as such, they are designed to protect and to prosper a particular race or clan. The one true God is no local deity but a universal Lord. Thus God's cities bring together many tribes and nations, thereby fashioning strangers separated by birth and blood into fellow citizens of one new community of humankind. Shreveport was once a pagan site like the Canaanite Jebus, inhabited by the Caddo Indian tribe and thus narrowly exclusive in character. Then came the sojourners who had migrated from "Egyptian" bondage in Europe, possessed by a faith that made possible here a new kind of city, one open to pilgrims from every wilderness, alike only in the desire to order their common life by the dictates of justice and peace.

2. In the second phase of her biblical history, however, Jerusalem faltered in fulfilling its God-given design. David's successor, Solomon, was lured into idolatry by his multiple marriages, thereby compromising the strength of the people's allegiance to one universal God. As the city reverted to fragmenting competition between pagan cults, divine wrath was kindled (2 Kings 23:26–27), which soon allowed the monarchy to be divided and then to be devastated by its enemies. Despite this painful lesson, which reduced Jerusalem to ruins for more than a generation (586–520 B.C.E.), the city was in danger of making the same fatal mistake during the ministry of Jesus. This time the idolatry came not from pagan neighbors but from an inward disposition to exclude the rest of the world (i.e., the "Gentiles") from their city by making God the Lord only of the Jewish race. When at last the temple on Mount Zion became a fortress from which to kill outsiders, rather than "a house of prayer for all the nations" (Mk. 11:17), divine wrath fell with such finality that Jerusalem forfeited its place as a city in the purposes of God (Mt. 23:37–38).

This grim chapter tells us that the same Lord who is the "builder and maker" of cities with foundations of faith (Heb. 11:10) is also the judge and destroyer of cities that no longer welcome the sojourner from afar, that close their gates to a stranger such as Abraham, who "went out not knowing where he was to go" (Heb. 11:8). History is littered with the wreckage of once-proud cities that shut their doors to surprises, turning inward until they were suffocated by a self-imposed claustrophobia. Shreveport is not exempt from this fearful judgment. Jesus uttered woes against specific cities, Chorazin and Bethsaida, for their refusal to change in the face of a New Age dawning before their very eyes (Mt. 11:20–24; Lk. 10:13–15). God will do no less to Shreveport if we worship the idolatrous god of the status quo.

3. But judgment was not the last word for Jerusalem. Instead, it was the crucible in which tragedy was pounded into the substance of hope. Paul knew that if "the present Jerusalem" was in slavery, "the Jerusalem above" is free, "and she is our mother" (Gal. 4:26). Isaiah (1:26–27) and Ezekiel (40:1—48:35) anticipated the outlines of that archetypal city from afar. But the early Christians realized that they had already "come to…the city of the living God, the heavenly Jerusalem" (Heb. 12:22). Even now, John of the Apocalypse could see "the holy city, new Jerusalem, coming down out of heaven from God" (Rev. 21:2). John described with unforgettable imagery the metropolis of his dreams (Rev. 21:1–22:5). As the Bible ends, the dialectic of urban failure and fulfillment reaches its ultimate expression, first with a terrifying dirge over fallen Babylon (Rev. 18:1–24), symbolic of all the pagan cities of history, then with a celebration of that celestial city whose "gates shall *never be shut*" (Rev. 21:25, emphasis added) and whose architect is the One who declares, "Behold, I make all things *new*" (Rev. 21:5, emphasis added).

What this vivid language seeks to express is the conviction that cities, like the citizens within them, can also be redeemed! God intends to save persons both in their individuality and in their collectivity. Cities do not have to become enslaved by the strictures of their culture. They can choose to model themselves after the "Jerusalem above" and become truly "free cities" into which shall be brought "the glory and the honor of the nations" (Rev. 21:26). Always we face the awful temptation to be like Babylon, proud and powerful on the outside but already condemned and dead on the inside. Shreveport could succumb and go the way of once-mighty Rome in the time of Augustine, or it could resolve to foreshadow that "City of God" which is our sure habitation in this world and in the world to come.[17]

III. The Present Challenge

Now that we have sketched a biblical framework against which to measure the cities of earth, we may ask what can be done to insure not just the survival but the spiritual vitality of Shreveport in the years to come.

From the theological critique of Jerusalem just attempted, we see that the crucial issue is one of openness and freedom. Will Shreveport become a "tribal" town of closed groupings based on race and class and kin? Or will it summon the faith to rise above such idolatrous paganism by serving the one universal Lord who calls all nations and peoples to dwell together in justice and peace within the City of God?

In large measure the answer to that question will be determined by the quality of leadership that emerges to meet the present crisis. "Politics" is the art of fashioning an authentic *polis* (the Greek word for "city"). That task must be entrusted in no small part to those fitted for it by training, resources, opportunity, and esteem. For its size, Shreveport has a splendid "Establishment" with more than enough education, wealth, leisure, and reputation to get the job done. But does this elite possess the requisite attitudes—indeed, the sturdy faith—to build a New Jerusalem on the banks of the Red River?

My misgivings come at the point of a classic French concept, *noblesse oblige,* which affirms that "nobility (or rank or station) imposes obligations." This is but a specialized application of the biblical imperative, "To whom much is given, of him will much be required" (Lk. 12:48). Having paid close attention to this "gifted" group for nearly two years, I am afraid that many within its number now follow the opposite philosophy that "rank confers privilege." Too many of our potential leaders who already have enough money seem concerned only about how to make more of it! Jesus once called for a drastic reordering of priorities by asking what it would profit a man if he gained the whole world but lost his own soul (Mt. 16:26; Mk. 8:36; Lk. 9:25). We may address that wisdom to those among us with an inordinate itch for prosperity by asking, "What shall it profit a man if he makes money to spare but loses the city in which to enjoy it?"

The problem is not that the names of our nobility seldom appear on the ballot. Very few are needed to run for public office, but those few who do offer themselves need to be like the tip of an iceberg, undergirded by and representative of an informed and committed Establishment willing to forfeit voluntarily some of its fastidiousness and get its hands dirty building a better place to live. There is a rich literature on the city that many of our gifted business leaders know nothing about. I suggest that the time has come for informal study groups to spring up in executive suites all over the city, for out-of-town business trips to include shop-talk with creative city planners, for dormant committees in civic clubs to be replaced by task forces that complete action projects; in short, for the talented people of this town to escalate the seriousness with which they contribute to the determination of its destiny.

My guess is that most have heard this plea to the Establishment in almost exclusively masculine terms, which is, in itself, a problem since fully half or more of our citizenry belong to the opposite sex. The "model" of political responsibility for women in Shreveport is entirely too passive, too prim, too demure. Somewhere the tradition has arisen that the role of the male nobility is to make money and of the female nobility is to give parties. Surely there is no place on the face of the earth where ladies can dress up more elegantly and entertain more enchantingly than in Shreveport! Nor is this pastime any less worthy than the pursuit of honest gain by the men. The issue, rather, is one of priorities and proportion. If officeholders think that half of the electorate is concerned only with social amenities, then all that they will do for them is drink an occasional cup of tea. But if they know that these women are aware both of the political agenda and of their ability to influence it, if they are forcibly reminded that these women will both vote their convictions at the polls and urge others to do so, then an entirely new climate of expectations is created that significantly lifts the quality of their performance.

Our male and female nobility expend enormous resources of time and money on those recurring rituals by which the social pecking order is regulated and reaffirmed. Since these gala events have at times drawn the ire of Baptist preachers, usually because of their dancing and drinking, let me here indicate that I think they serve a harmless and perhaps even useful function. A clearly identified and institutionalized establishment may be needed to provide stability in a time of excessive social upheaval. My observation is, however, that the "first families" of Shreveport are already well known. Except for minor adjustments to accommodate a very few, such as a new commanding general at Barksdale, their constituency seldom changes. It is not a little ironic that a power structure so static goes to such lengths to belabor what is already obvious to everyone. If this sort of thing could be cut in half, with equal energy and effort going into urban revitalization, I strongly suspect that everybody would be just as happy and that those needing social recognition would get all of it they deserve.

Since, in the Bible Belt, the ministry occupies a special niche in the Establishment, let me conclude this critique of our local leadership with a look at the Shreveport clergy. Measured by depth of concern, height of vision, or breadth of involvement, the ministerial contribution leaves much to be desired. With a few outstanding exceptions, most of us have not acted ecumenically, denominationally, or unilaterally to do anything significant about our city as a whole. It is not that we have tried and failed, which might be commendable enough; it is rather that we have not even put the real issues on our agenda! It is true that Baptists are often hesitant in this area because of the strong localism in their church polity. But we have scarcely begun to channel the contributions even of our own individual congregations in building a better Shreveport.

IV. The Way Ahead

I have concentrated here on the "movers and shapers" of our city because of their heavy responsibility to provide leadership in the days just ahead. But all of us may rightly ask what we can do to meet the present malaise. I have two specific suggestions. First, let us work to overcome the excessive fragmentation that has compartmentalized our city into isolated enclaves. You have heard me call repeatedly this year for a metropolitan rather than a neighborhood outlook, but that commitment is slow in coming. Although our historic role as a *First* Baptist Church is to serve the entire area, just now we find ourselves rather cozily ensconced on the south slope of Mount Zion! But we cannot build a twenty-foot wall around South Highland-Pierremont-Spring Lake and call that our city. Instead, we must reach out and get deeply involved in what is happening to the North and West as well as at the center of our metropolis.

A second suggestion is to beware of the ideological trap that is being set as a result of our regional devotion to the word *conservatism*. When that term is used to refer to the preservation of our most cherished values, it is precious indeed and worthy of all acceptance. But when it becomes the codeword for a reactionary defense of the status quo, it needs to be just as emphatically rejected as a misreading of reality. Cherished values do not change, but circumstances do. We are simply sticking our heads in the sand not to recognize it. The Rodessa oil fields have changed. The Queensborough community has changed. The headquarters of Texas Eastern and United Gas have changed. We must build a Shreveport responsive to the realities, not of yesterday, but of tomorrow, and in so doing we dare not be impeded by a misplaced clinging to the term "conservatism."

Yes, Shreveport is at the crossroads, just as Jerusalem was on that day when Jesus looked down from the Mount of Olives, saw the Holy City in its true condition, and "wept over it" (Lk. 19:41). He cared *that much*, not just for individuals, but for a *city*! And when we learn his costly compassion, when his tears become our tears, there is hope for the redemption of our city.

Notes

Preface

[1]"Church Leaders Emphasize Motivation, But Struggle with Strategy," The Barna Update, February 27, 2006, http://www.barna.org. For this understanding of strategic leadership, see George Barna, *A Fish Out of Water: 9 Strategies Effective Leaders Use to Help You Get Back into the Flow* (Nashville: Integrity, 2002), 37–63.

[2]James P. Wind and others, "The Leadership Situation Facing American Congregations," an Alban Institute Special Report, September, 2001, http://www.alban.org/leadership.asp, with a useful bibliography on pp. 16–17.

[3]L. Gregory Jones and Susan Pendleton Jones, "Pivotal Leadership," *Christian Century* (September 12–19, 2001): 25, report on how Duke Divinity School is using a $10 million Lilly grant to develop "a highly select group of promising church leaders." Thus far, Lilly has awarded at least $92.7 million to colleges to encourage students to consider a career in ministry, $81 million to theological schools for congregational ministry and youth-oriented programs, and $3.2 million in annual grants to pastors for its National Clergy Renewal Program.

[4]Donald A. Schön, *The Reflective Practitioner* (New York: Basic Books, 1983). See also his *Educating the Reflective Practitioner: Toward a New Design for Teaching and Learning in the Professions* (San Francisco: Jossey-Bass, 1987).

[5]Charles B. Templeton, *Life Looks Up* (New York: Harper & Brothers, 1955), 116–17.

Chapter 1: Strategic Preaching in Contemporary Homiletics

[1]William Toohey and William D. Thompson edited *Recent Homiletical Thought: A Bibliography, 1935-1965* (Nashville: Abingdon Press, 1967), listing 446 books, 1,081 articles, and 610 theses and dissertations, for a total of 2,137 entries. A sequel edited by A. Duane Litfin and Haddon W. Robinson, *Recent Homiletical Thought: An Annotated Bibliography, Volume 2, 1966-1979* (Grand Rapids: Baker, 1983), covered 238 books, 1,371 articles, and 289 theses and dissertations, for a total of 1,898 entries. Since 1976, bibliographic coverage has been provided by *Homiletic: A Review of Publications in Religious Communication,* which first appeared annually (vols. 1-4, 1976-79) and then semiannually (vols. 5 ff, 1980-present) under the joint sponsorship of the Academy of Homiletics and the Religious Communication Association. Through the winter of 2005 (vol. 30, no. 2), 2,449 items had been reviewed.

[2]The Academy of Homiletics is surveyed periodically to determine which textbooks are most widely used by teachers of preaching. For a summary of results with interpretation, see H. Barry Evans, "Survey Results: Books for Preachers," *Homiletic* 5, no. 1 (1980): 1–4; Donald F. Chatfield, "Textbooks Used by Teachers of Preaching," *Homiletic* 9, no. 2 (1984): 1–5; and Alyce M. McKenzie, "Homiletical Grammars: Retrospect and Prospects," *Homiletic* 26, no. 2 (2001): 1–10.

[3]Henry Grady Davis, *Design for Preaching* (Philadelphia: Fortress Press, 1958); George E. Sweazey, *Preaching the Good News* (Englewood Cliffs, N.J.: Prentice-Hall, 1976); Fred B. Craddock, *Preaching* (Nashville: Abingdon Press, 1985); David G. Buttrick, *Homiletic: Moves and Structures* (Philadelphia: Fortress Press, 1987); Clyde E. Fant, *Preaching for Today,* rev. ed. (New York: Harper & Row, 1987). According to McKenzie, "Homiletical Grammars," ten new textbooks appeared between 1985 and 1989 "as attempts to consolidate the best of the field (3), but, since then, "the days of the lone star textbook, standing above the others, used by one and all are past. In its place is a much broader menu, one that includes a growing number of enormously helpful, specialized contributions" (10).

[4]Buttrick, *Homiletic,* 230–33.

[5]Sweazey, *Preaching the Good News,* 23–24, 74–75, 115.

[6]Craddock, *Preaching,* 37–41.

[7]William H. Willimon and Richard Lischer, eds., *Concise Encyclopedia of Preaching* (Louisville: Westminster John Knox Press, 1995). For an overview, see Steven Reagles, "Interview with Richard Lischer and William Willimon," *Homiletic* 20, no. 2 (1995): 15–21.

[8]Willimon and Lischer, *Concise Encyclopedia of Preaching,* vii–ix.

[9]This is evident in his many writings, none more so than in those books coauthored with Stanley Hauerwas, such as *Resident Aliens: Life in the Christian Colony* (Nashville: Abingdon

Press, 1990), and *Where Resident Aliens Live: Exercises for Christian Practice* (Nashville: Abingdon Press, 1996).

[10]Richard Lischer, *The Preacher King: Martin Luther King, Jr., and the Word that Moved America* (New York: Oxford, 1995). This "rhetorical biography" was named the Outstanding Book of 1995–96 by the Religious Speech Communication Association, *Homiletic* 21, no. 2 (1996): 57.

[11]John S. McClure, *Other-wise Preaching: A Postmodern Ethic for Homiletics* (St. Louis: Chalice Press, 2001). The historical section is on pp. 67–132. The verdict by Chopp is cited on the back cover of the book by the publisher.

[12]McClure, *Other-wise Preaching*, 130–32. Note all references to "hegemony, hegemonies, hegemonic" in the Index, 169–70.

[13]These contemporary trends are well summarized by O. C. Edwards Jr., *A History of Preaching* (Nashville: Abingdon Press, 2004), 703–73.

[14]Leadership provides the underlying rationale for the standards by which the Association of Theological Schools accredits the Master of Divinity degree. The purpose of the degree is to prepare ministers "for general pastoral and religious *leadership* responsibilities in congregations and other settings" (A.1). Instruction in biblical, historical, and theological studies "shall be conducted so as to indicate…their significance for the exercise of pastoral *leadership*" (A.3.1.1.3). Personal and spiritual formation "includes concern with the development of capacities—intellectual and affective, individual and corporate, ecclesial and public—that are requisite to a life of pastoral *leadership*" (A.3.1.3). A primary goal of the program is "capacity for ministerial and public *leadership*," to which an entire standard is devoted (A.3.1.4). See *ATS Bulletin 46*, Part 1 (Pittsburgh: The Association of Theological Schools in the United States and Canada, 2005): 193–97, italics added.

[15]For an example of such prodding, note the recurring emphasis on leadership in the comments of the executive director of The Association of Theological Schools in the United States and Canada, "Seminaries and the ecology of faith: An interview with Daniel Aleshire," *Christian Century* (February 3-10, 1999): 110–23.

[16]Kenneth L. Woodward, "Heard Any Good Sermons Lately?" *Newsweek* (March 4, 1996): 50.

[17]For a concise overview of the various approaches, see Paul Scott Wilson, *Preaching and Homiletical Theory*, Preaching and Its Partners (St. Louis: Chalice Press, 2004).

[18]H. Shelton Smith, *In His Image, But …: Racism in Southern Religion, 1780-1910* (Durham, N.C.: Duke University Press, 1972), 129. On this issue see Eugene D. Genovese, *A Consuming Fire: The Fall of the Confederacy in the Mind of the White Christian South* (Athens: University of Georgia Press, 1998); and Mark A. Noll, "The Bible and Slavery," in *Religion and the American Civil War*, ed. Randall M. Miller, Harry S. Stout, and Charles Reagan Wilson (New York: Oxford University Press, 1998), 43–73. Noll has set his detailed essay in a broader context in *America's God: From Jonathan Edwards to Abraham Lincoln* (New York: Oxford University Press, 2002), 365–445, and in *The Civil War as a Theological Crisis* (Chapel Hill: University of North Carolina Press, 2006).

[19]On protology, see Ronald L. Numbers, *The Creationists* (New York: Alfred A. Knopf, 1992). On eschatology, see Paul Boyer, *When Time Shall Be No More: Prophecy Belief in Modern American Culture* (Cambridge: Harvard University Press, 1992).

[20]John A. Broadus, *On the Preparation and Delivery of Sermons*, new and rev. ed., ed. Jesse Burton Weatherspoon (Nashville: Broadman, 1944), xiii. Without in any way minimizing the importance of the Bible—the author himself being equally famous as a professor both of New Testament and of Preaching—Broadus devoted the bulk of his treatment to such matters as structure (arrangement, construction, order, sequence), function (explanation, argument, illustration, application), and style (clarity, energy, elegance, imagination).

[21]The rhetorical paradigm has enjoyed something of a comeback in recent years. This is due in part to the popularity of "literary" preachers, such as Frederick Buechner, *Telling the Truth: The Gospel as Tragedy, Comedy, and Fairy Tale* (New York: Harper and Row, 1977), who employed categories such as comedy and tragedy to illumine what might be called "an aesthetic of preaching," and David G. Buttrick, *Homiletic: Moves and Structures* (Philadelphia: Fortress Press, 1987), esp. 40–43, the most scholarly textbook on homiletics in this generation. Buttrick represents in part a return to "Christian rhetoric" in its detailed analysis of sermonic "moves" and "modes." On the

importance of the rhetorical dimension despite a Barthian critique, see James F. Kay, "Reorientation: Homiletics as Theologically Authorized Rhetoric," *Princeton Seminary Bulletin,* new series, 24, no. 1 (2003): 16–35. For a defense of preaching as rhetorical art and act, see Lucy Lind Hogan and Robert Reid, *Connecting with the Congregation: Rhetoric and the Art of Preaching* (Nashville: Abingdon Press, 1999). For a brief survey of recent trends in developing an aesthetic homiletic see Cas Vos, "The sermon as a work of art," *The Expository Times* 116, no. 11 (2005): 371–73.

[22]For a critique see Neil Postman, *Amusing Ourselves to Death: Public Discourse in the Age of Show Business* (New York: Viking, 1985); on electronic preaching, see chapter 8, "Shuffle Off to Bethlehem," 114–24.

[23]W. K. Wimsatt Jr. and M. C. Beardsley, "The Intentional Fallacy," *Sewanee Review,* vol. 54 (1946): 468–88; reprinted without notes in W. K. Wimsatt, *The Verbal Icon: Studies in the Meaning of Poetry* (Lexington: University Press of Kentucky, 1954), 1–18.

[24]In his influential study of early Christian rhetoric, Amos N. Wilder, *The Language of the Gospel: Early Christian Rhetoric* (New York: Harper & Row, 1964), 20, pointed out that apostolic preaching was a "new utterance" different from classical rhetoric in that it "was not only the spoken word but personal address; it was not only in the indicative mode but in the imperative; it was not only in the third person but in the second and the first; it was not only a matter of declaration but of dialogue."

[25]Harry Emerson Fosdick, "Personal Counseling and Preaching," *Pastoral Psychology* 2, no. 22 (1952): 11–15. Fosdick did not write a book on preaching, and this brief article hardly does justice to his actual pulpit practice. For an overview of the issue with reference to several full-length scholarly works, see Robert Moats Miller, *Harry Emerson Fosdick: Preacher, Pastor, Prophet* (New York: Oxford, 1985), 333–78.

[26]A fresh thrust was given to congregational studies by James F. Hopewell, *Congregation: Stories and Structures* (Philadelphia: Fortress Press, 1987).

[27]African-American preaching has long been highly participatory, with the congregation functioning as a partner in proclamation. See Henry Mitchell, *Black Preaching* (Philadelphia: Lippincott, 1970), and *The Recovery of Preaching* (New York: Harper & Row, 1977). For bibliography see Robert R. Howard, "African American Preaching: A Bibliography," *Homiletic* 23, no. 2 (1998): 21–23; 25, no. 1 (2000): 25–30; 26, no. 1 (2001): 1–4.

[28]Most of the works thus far on women and preaching treat the preacher, but implicit in many of the analyses is the role of gender in responding to the sermon. For a comprehensive bibliography see Robert R. Howard, "Women and Preaching: A Bibliography," *Homiletic* 17, no. 2 (1992): 7–10; 18, no. 1 (1993): 34–36; 19, no. 1 (1994): 28–30; 20, no. 1 (1995): 7–10; 22, no. 1 (1997): 27–29; 26, no. 1 (2001): 4–7. For reflections on this literature, see Richard L. Thulin, "Because of the Woman's Testimony ...," *Homiletic* 21, no. 1 (1996): 1–6.

[29]Michael E. Williams, "Toward an Oral/Aural Homiletic," *Homiletic* 11, no. 1 (1986): 1–4.

[30]Roger E. Van Harn, *Pew Rights: For People Who Listen to Sermons* (Grand Rapids: William B. Eerdmans, 1992), 14. See now his *Preacher, Can You Hear Us Listening?* (Grand Rapids: William B. Eerdmans, 2005). On the importance of the listener in the preaching event, see John S. McClure and others, *Listening to Listeners: Homiletical Case Studies* (St. Louis: Chalice Press, 2004); and Ronald J. Allen, *Hearing the Sermon: Relationship/Content/Feeling* (St. Louis: Chalice Press, 2004), the first two volumes in a four-part series called "Channels of Listening."

[31]Randolph introduced the title and approach in a lecture at Princeton Theological Seminary during the founding meeting of the North American Academy of Homiletics in 1965. The title deliberately paralleled the New Hermeneutic, which was then beginning to influence the theology of preaching, especially through the work of Gerhard Ebeling. See James David Randolph, *The Renewal of Preaching* (Philadelphia: Fortress Press, 1969); compare James Randolph, *The Renewal of Preaching in the 21st Century* (Babylon, N.Y.: Hanging Gardens Press, 1998), which contains three parts: (1) brief critiques of Randolph's work by David Buttrick, Paul Scott Wilson, and Lucy Rose, followed by a substantial introduction to his 1969 work by Robert Stephen Reid; (2) a reprint of *The Renewal of Preaching;* and (3) comments by Randolph both on the influence of his 1969 work and on the future of his emphasis in the 21st century. From Ebeling came an emphasis on the word of faith as a language-event, hence on what the sermon *does* for the hearer and not just on what it *says* to the hearer. On the work of Ebeling related to preaching, see Gerhard Ebeling, *Word and Faith* (Philadelphia: Fortress Press, 1963), *The Problem of Historicity*

in the Church and Its Proclamation (Philadelphia: Fortress Press, 1967), and *God and Word* (Philadelphia: Fortress Press, 1967). For an introduction, see James M. Robinson and John B. Cobb Jr., eds., *The New Hermeneutic,* New Frontiers in Theology, vol. 2 (New York: Harper & Row, 1964). For a summary, note Randolph's introduction to Ebeling's *On Prayer: Nine Sermons* (Philadelphia: Fortress Press, 1966), 1–36.

[32]Fred B. Craddock, *As One Without Authority: Essays on Inductive Preaching* (Enid, Okla.: Phillips University Press, 1971), and *Overhearing the Gospel* (Nashville: Abingdon Press, 1978). The enduring value of these volumes is illustrated by the reissue of both in revised and expanded editions by Chaice Press, the former in 2001 and the latter in 2002.

[33]Richard L. Eslinger, *A New Hearing: Living Options in Homiletical Method* (Nashville: Abingdon Press, 1987), 13–14. The notion of a "paradigm shift" should not imply that this "move to listeners" is an entirely new development in homiletical history. Rather, it is better viewed as the renewal of an emphasis that has reoccurred in various periods of church history but received fresh impetus in late twentieth century. See Beverly Zink-Sawyer, "'The Word Purely Preached and Heard': The Listeners and the Homiletical Endeavor," *Interpretation* 51, no. 4 (1997): 342–57.

[34]For an insightful survey of this development, see Robert Stephen Reid, "Postmodernism and the Functions of the New Homiletic in Post-Christendom Congregations," *Homiletic* 20, no. 2 (1995): 1–13. Reid interprets the shift historically as a move from the philosophical rhetoric of Aristotle designed to convey knowledge through ideas to the sophistical rhetoric of Isocrates designed to move listeners through the persuasion of opinion. The understanding of preaching as "creating an experience for listeners" is based on the inductive approach of Craddock.

[35]John S. McClure, *The Roundtable Pulpit: Where Leadership and Preaching Meet* (Nashville: Abingdon Press, 1995); Lucy Atkinson Rose, *Sharing the Word: Preaching in the Roundtable Church* (Louisville: Westminster John Knox Press, 1997); Leonora Tubbs Tisdale, *Preaching as Local Theology and Folk Art* (Minneapolis: Fortress Press, 1997).

[36]John S. McClure, "Conversation and Proclamation: Resources and Issues," *Homiletic* 22, no. 1 (1997): 1.

[37]Ibid., 5. The Levinas reference is to *Totality and Infinity* (Pittsburgh: Duquesne University Press, 1969).

[38]McClure, "Conversation," 5, strengthens this insight with "an incipient process-relational theology of the Word" in which "the Word of God is not an ontological category, it is a relational reality. It is not static, essential, and conclusive; it is dynamic, emergent, and disclosive…[T]he Word is closely related to the communal *reality* it seeks to provoke."

[39]Ibid., 5–6.

[40]McClure, *The Roundtable Pulpit*, 48–94.

[41]In his sequel to *The Roundtable Pulpit*, entitled *Other-wise Preaching: A Postmodern Ethic for Homiletics* (St. Louis: Chalice Press, 2001), McClure moves well beyond the assumptions of the New Homiletic in seeking to lay the historical and epistemological foundations for a homiletic concerned, not only to hear and empower the marginalized, but to champion their "other-ness" by radically deconstructing to the point of erasure the hegemonic discourse of the establishment (131). While I applaud his desire to include "strangers" in the homiletical conversation, I am not sure that these outsiders should be spared "the most rigorous ideological suspicion" (102), which McClure would direct primarily toward insiders. Nor am I sure that advocates of this approach, most of whom are guaranteed lifetime academic employment and salary as tenured professors in endowed chairs funded mainly by the captains of capitalism, can achieve that radical vulnerability or "ego martyring" (127) necessary to enter into solidarity with, and speak for, the socially oppressed and the religiously disenfranchised. This dense but profound prolegomenon to a philosophy of homiletics deserves far more attention than can be devoted to its intricate arguments in this book.

[42]Elton Trueblood, *The Company of the Committed* (New York: Harper & Brothers, 1961), 68–72.

[43]In making comments of this kind I am not implying that preaching should in any way minimize the personal needs of individuals. Rather, I am trying to correct a perceived imbalance caused by isolating the individual from those communal purposes that animate the life of the church. I suspect that this has happened primarily because the dominance of the pastoral care movement in the past generation focused attention on therapeutic approaches rather than on

leadership approaches to preaching. For example, Gary D. Stratman's *Pastoral Preaching* (Nashville: Abingdon Press, 1983) includes an extensive annotated bibliography dominated by works on the pastor as caregiver, but almost none on the pastor as leader. Because of the prevailing seminary culture in the turbulent sixties and seventies, many preachers trained in that generation simply assume that "pastoral preaching" means "pastoral *care* preaching" rather than "pastoral *leadership* preaching." If the church is a fellowship (*koinōnia*), then listeners are not just a collection of diverse individuals seeking to have their needs met but are a body of believers united by the Holy Spirit who seek to share their spiritual resources with one another because they experience the deepest realities of life "in common."

Chapter 2: A Biblical-Theological Framework for Strategic Preaching

[1]For the context of this development, see James M. Robinson, ed., *The Beginnings of Dialectical Theology* (Richmond, Va.: John Knox Press, 1968), 9–30, with the key essay by Friedrich Gogarten, "Between the Times," 277–82. The modern developments are further described by James D. Smart, *The Divided Mind of Modern Theology: Karl Barth and Rudolf Bultmann, 1908-1933* (Philadelphia: Westminster Press, 1967), esp. 74–75, 107–09, 131–32, 178–79. The motto *Zwischen den Zeiten* became the title of a journal published by Barth, Gogarten, and Thurneysen from 1923 to 1933.

[2]Joachim Jeremias, *The Lord's Prayer,* Facet Books: Biblical Series—8 (Philadelphia: Fortress Press, 1964), 32, esp. n. 27.

[3]James D. G. Dunn, *The Theology of Paul the Apostle* (Grand Rapids: William B. Eerdmans, 1998), 461–98.

[4]Rudolf Bultmann, *Theology of the New Testament* (London: SCM, 1952–55). See esp. Part 4, chap. 7, sec. 58, found in vol. 2, 155–202.

[5]Ibid., 1: 101.

[6]Jürgen Moltmann, *Theology of Hope: On the Ground and Implications of a Christian Eschatology* (New York: Harper & Row, 1967), 162.

[7]Sandra Hack Polaski, *A Feminist Introduction to Paul* (St. Louis: Chalice Press, 2005), 86–87.

[8]E. J. Tinsley, *The Imitation of God in Christ* (Philadelphia: Westminster Press, 1960), 31–49.

[9]See Eduard Schweizer, *Lordship and Discipleship,* Studies in Biblical Theology, no. 28 (London: SCM, 1960), 11–21; Gerhard Kittel, "*akoloutheo …,*" in *Theological Dictionary of the New Testament* (Grand Rapids: Wm. B. Eerdmans, 1964), 1: 210–16; Tinsley, *The Imitation of God in Christ,* 100–17. More generally, see Richard N. Longenecker, ed., *Patterns of Discipleship in the New Testament* (Grand Rapids: William B. Eerdmans, 1996).

[10]Martin Hengel, *The Charismatic Leader and His Followers* (Edinburgh: T. & T. Clark, 1981), 5.

[11]Schweizer, *Lordship and Discipleship,* 20.

[12]Ibid., 21.

[13]Albert Schweitzer, *The Quest of the Historical Jesus,* 3rd ed. (London: Adam and Charles Black, 1954), 401.

[14]Tinsley, *The Imitation of God in Christ,* 168–71.

[15]Ernst Käsemann, *The Wandering People of God: An Investigation of the Letter to the Hebrews* (Minneapolis: Augsburg, 1984), 22–24.

[16]Augustine, *On Christian Doctrine,* trans. D. W. Robertson Jr., The Library of Liberal Arts (New York: Liberal Arts Press, 1958), 121, 134. Italics added.

[17]The concept of movement is receiving renewed attention in contemporary homiletical discussion. The emphasis is well summarized in Eugene L. Lowry, *The Sermon: Dancing the Edge of Mystery* (Nashville: Abingdon Press, 1997), 15–28. Note, for example, the role of movement in the "form-sensitive sermon" of Mike Graves, *The Sermon as Symphony: Preaching the Literary Forms of the New Testament* (Valley Forge: Judson Press, 1997), 12–14, 21–22. Also suggestive is the concept of "plotted mobility" in the work of David Buttrick, *Homiletic: Moves and Structures* (Philadelphia: Fortress Press, 1987), 9–17, 285–93, and "On Doing Homiletics Today," in *Intersections: Post-Critical Studies in Preaching,* ed. Richard L. Eslinger (Grand Rapids: William B. Eerdmans, 1994), 95–97.

[18]Moltmann, *Theology of Hope,* 95–229.

[19]For an effort to move beyond thinking of Christ "statically, as one person in two natures," but instead "to grasp him dynamically, in the forward movement of God's history with the world"

(xiii), see Jürgen Moltmann, *The Way of Jesus Christ: Christology in Messianic Dimensions* (New York: Harper Collins, 1990).

[20]For the exegetical details of this understanding, see Markus Barth, *Ephesians,* The Anchor Bible, vol. 34A (Garden City, N.Y.: Doubleday, 1974), 484–96.

[21]Gilbert Murray, *Five Stages of Greek Religion,* 3rd ed. (Garden City, N.Y.: Doubleday Anchor, 1955), 119. Murray entitled his fourth stage "The Failure of Nerve" (119–65).

[22]Peter Gay, *The Enlightenment: An Interpretation* (New York: Alfred A. Knopf, 1969), 2: 3.

[23]Ibid., 2: 12.

[24]Standard surveys include J. B. Bury, *The Idea of Progress: An Inquiry into Its Origin and Growth* (New York: Dover, 1987 reprint of the 1932 edition); John Baillie, *The Belief in Progress* (New York: Charles Scribner's Sons, 1951). For a recent sober assessment, see Anthony O' Hear, *After Progress: Finding the Old Way Forward* (New York: Bloomsbury, 1999). The high tide of secular optimism stretched from the Napoleonic Wars to the Great War (1815–1914).

[25]On the fiendish ability of the twentieth century to mock the pretensions of the European Enlightenment, see Paul Johnson, *Modern Times: The World from the Twenties to the Eighties* (New York: Harper & Row, 1983); Robert Conquest, *Reflections on a Ravaged Century* (New York: W. W. Norton, 2000).

[26]Jacques Ellul, *Hope in Time of Abandonment* (New York: Seabury, 1973), 13. For an update of Ellul's diagnosis see Marva J. Dawn, *Unfettered Hope: A Call to Faithful Living in an Affluent Society* (Louisville: Westminster John Knox Press, 2003), 1–60.

[27]Ellul, *Hope in Time of Abandonment,* 8.

[28]Wolfhart Pannenberg, *Metaphysics and the Idea of God* (Grand Rapids: William B. Eerdmans, 1990), 96.

[29]Ellul, *Hope in Time of Abandonment,* 248.

[30]Ibid., 249.

[31]Dietrich Bonhoeffer, *The Cost of Discipleship,* rev. ed. (New York: Macmillan, 1959), 35–47.

[32]Wendell Berry, *Life Is a Miracle: An Essay Against Modern Superstition* (Washington: Counterpoint, 2000), 12, 55–58, 130–31.

[33]Jean Bethke Elshtain, "Beyond Traditionalism and Progressivism, or Against Hardening of the Categories," *Theology Today* 58, no. 1 (2001): 7. This entire essay (4–13) is a vigorous jeremiad against all forms of ideological utopianism that fail to take human fallenness seriously. Elshtain has worked out these concerns more fully in *Who Are We? Critical Reflections and Hopeful Possibilities* (Grand Rapids: William B. Eerdmans, 2000), but her journal article focuses the issues more sharply, partly because of the two responses that follow (14–27).

[34]Dawn, *Unfettered Hope,* 183–99.

[35]Glenn Tinder, *The Fabric of Hope: An Essay,* Emory University Studies in Law and Religion (Atlanta: Scholars Press, 1999), 201.

[36]Ibid., 202.

[37]Frank Kermode, *The Sense of an Ending: Studies in the Theory of Fiction* (New York: Oxford University Press, 1967).

[38]Tinder, *The Fabric of Hope,* 175.

[39]Alfred North Whitehead, *Modes of Thought* (New York: Macmillan, 1938), 233.

[40]Daniel Jenkins, *The Strangeness of the Church* (Garden City, N.Y.: Doubleday, 1955), 38.

[41]Ranier Maria Rilke, *Letters to a Young Poet,* trans. Stephen Mitchell (New York: Random House, 1984), 84.

[42]Gerhard Delling, *Worship in the New Testament* (Philadelphia: Westminster Press, 1962), 10.

[43]Samuel Stennett, "On Jordan's Stormy Banks," refrain, *Baptist Hymnal* (Nashville: Convention Press, 1975), #521.

[44]Herman Melville, *Moby Dick: Or, The Whale* (New York: Modern Library, 1950 rep. of 1851 ed.), 38–39. "What could be more full of meaning?—for the pulpit is ever this earth's foremost part; all the rest comes in its rear; the pulpit leads the world…Yes, the world's a ship on its passage out, and not a voyage complete; and the pulpit is its prow" (39).

[45]For a sustained theological meditation on this theme, see Moltmann, *Theology of Hope,* who depicts faith as a "straining after the future" (19) because "the believer is not set at the high noon of life, but at the dawn of a new day at the point where night and day, things passing and things to come, grapple with each other" (31). For his latest and most systematic exposition of eschatological doctrine, see Jürgen Moltmann, *The Coming of God: Christian Eschatology* (Minneapolis: Fortress Press, 1996), on which, see Richard Bauckham, ed., *God Will Be All in All:*

The Eschatology of Jürgen Moltmann (Edinburgh: T & T Clark, 1999). On the relevance of hope in the new millennium, see Richard Bauckham and Trevor Hart, *Hope against Hope: Christian Eschatology at the Turn of the Millennium* (Grand Rapids: William B. Eerdmans, 1999); Gerhard Sauter, *What Dare We Hope? Reconsidering Eschatology* (Harrisburg, Pa.: Trinity Press International, 1999); Miroslav Volf and William Katerberg, eds., *The Future of Hope: Christian Tradition Amid Modernity and Postmodernity* (Grand Rapids: William B. Eerdmans, 2004).

Chapter 3: A Hermeneutic of Strategic Preaching: Biblical

[1]William J. Webb, *Slaves, Women & Homosexuals: Exploring the Hermeneutics of Cultural Analysis* (Downers Grove, Ill.: InterVarsity Press, 2001), 30–66. For an aggressive rejection of this approach as contradicting the Reformation principle of *sola Scriptura* and nullifying the moral authority of the New Testament, see Wayne Grudem, "Should We Move Beyond the New Testament to a Better Ethic?" *Journal of the Evangelical Theological Society* 47, no. 2 (2004): 299–346. Although raising a number of useful cautions about possible misuses of Webb's methodology, Grudem fails to address the central question of whether the New Testament itself expected the Holy Spirit to be a source of continuing revelation that would supplement and enrich the revelation that the followers of Jesus had thus far apprehended (Jn. 16:12–15). Reading Webb and Grudem in tandem illustrates some of the differences between dynamic and static approaches to Scripture, which is a concern of this chapter. For a more balanced discussion of the issue, with attention to the work of Webb, see I. Howard Marshall, *Beyond the Bible: Moving from Scripture to Theology*, Acadia Studies in Bible and Theology (Grand Rapids: Baker Academic, 2004), with helpful responses by Stanley E. Porter and Kevin J. Vanhoozer.

[2]Webb, *Slaves, Women & Homosexuals*, 37–38, 44–45.

[3]For a study of Pauline texts as establishing trajectories, see Sandra Hack Polaski, *A Feminist Introduction to Paul* (St. Louis: Chalice Press, 2005). Note the references to "trajectory" in the Subject Index, 158.

[4]Webb, *Slaves, Women & Homosexuals*, 66, who expounds on this summary sentence, 57–66.

[5]Anthony C. Thiselton, *The First Epistle to the Corinthians: A Commentary on the Greek Text*, The New International Greek Testament Commentary (Grand Rapids: William B. Eerdmans, 2000), emphasizes both the strategies of Paul in appealing to his readers and the subsequent adaptation of these strategies throughout church history. See the many references in the Index of Subjects under the entries on "Rhetoric, rhetorical strategy" and on "Posthistory of texts."

[6]This connotation is nicely captured in the German word *Umwelt* meaning "environment, milieu." The prepositional prefix *um* means "round about" or "around," and *welt* means "world," hence the compound literally means "the world that is around us."

[7]This simplistic approach has two weaknesses: (a) the fallacy of a timeless message, as if truth had an eternal kernel with an historical husk; (b) the fallacy of a timeless world, as if events do not really change the course of history and introduce fundamentally new situations. It is difficult, if not impossible, to protect either assumption from an implicit gnosticism inimical to biblical realism.

[8]Three multi-volume Bible encyclopedias are standard at this time. The most extensive, and in many ways the most demanding, is *The Anchor Bible Dictionary*, ed. David Noel Freedman in six large volumes (New York: Doubleday, 1992). No less scholarly but perhaps more useful to the pastor is *The Interpreter's Dictionary of the Bible*, ed. George Arthur Buttrick in four volumes (New York: Abingdon Press, 1962), which should be used with a Supplementary Volume, ed. Keith Crim (Nashville: Abingdon Press, 1976). The most conservative of the three is *The International Standard Bible Encyclopedia*, ed. Geoffrey W. Bromiley in a completely rewritten four-volume edition replacing the original five-volume edition of 1915 (Grand Rapids: William B. Eerdmans, 1979). See also The *IVP Bible Background Commentary New Testament*, ed. Craig S. Keener (Downers Grove, Ill.: InterVarsity Press, 1993); The *IVP Bible Background Commentary Old Testament*, ed. John H. Walton, Victor H. Matthews, and Mark W. Chavalas (Downers Grove, Ill.: InterVarsity Press, 2000); and the *Archaeological Study Bible*, ed. Donna L. Huisjen (Grand Rapids: Zondervan, 2005).

[9]Particularly good on background is *Harper's Bible Dictionary*, ed. Paul J. Achtemeier (San Francisco: Harper & Row, 1996). Quite recent is *Eerdman's Dictionary of the Bible*, ed. David Noel Freedman (Grand Rapids: William B. Eerdmans, 2000). Unusually helpful for our purposes

is the *Dictionary of New Testament Background*, ed. Craig A. Evans and Stanley E. Porter (Downers Grove, Ill.: InterVarsity Press, 2000), which "attempts to situate the New Testament and early Christianity in its literary, historical, social and religious context" (p. ix). It forms the sequel to a three-volume series that also contains many valuable entries on setting: *Dictionary of Jesus and the Gospels*, ed. Joel B. Green and Scot McKnight (Downers Grove, Ill.: InterVarsity Press, 1992); *Dictionary of Paul and His Letters*, ed. Gerald F. Hawthorne and Ralph P. Martin (Downers Grove, Ill.: InterVarsity Press, 1993); and *Dictionary of the Later New Testament & Its Developments*, ed. Ralph P. Martin and Peter H. Davids (Downers Grove, Ill.: InterVarsity Press, 1997). The Old Testament parallel series has two volumes completed: *Dictionary of the Old Testament Pentateuch*, ed. T. Desmond Alexander and David W. Baker (Downers Grove, Ill.: InterVarsity Press, 2003) and *Dictionary of the Old Testament Historical Books*, ed. Bill T. Arnold and H. G. M. Williamson (Downers Grove, Ill.: InterVarsity Press, 2005). The entire set reflects the growing methodological sophistication and theological appreciation of conservative evangelical scholars in studying the historical rootage of Scripture.

[10]Close attention to setting is characteristic of *The Anchor Bible Commentaries* because of the influence of W. F. Albright and D. N. Freedman in conceiving the series. The same is increasingly true of the *Word Biblical Commentary* as it nears completion (e.g., the three-volume work of David E. Aune on Revelation). The more classical approach typical of German scholarship is on display in *Hermeneia: A Critical and Historical Commentary on the Bible*, although many of these volumes will likely prove to be too technical for most pastors.

[11]This fourfold typology of social factors is used by Gerd Theissen, *The Social Setting of Pauline Christianity: Essays on Corinth* (Philadelphia: Fortress Press, 1982), 28–40.

[12]See, for example, Rainer Albertz, *A History of Israelite Religion in the Old Testament Period*, trans. John Bowden, 2 vols. (Louisville: Westminster John Knox Press, 1994); Philip J. King and Lawrence E. Stager, *Life in Biblical Israel*, Library of Ancient Israel, ed. Douglas A. Knight (Louisville: Westminster John Knox Press, 2001); Philip F. Esler, ed., *Ancient Israel: The Old Testament in Its Social Context* (Minneapolis: Fortress Press, 2006); Paula McNutt, *Reconstructing the Society of Ancient Israel*, Library of Ancient Israel, ed. Douglas A. Knight (Louisville: Westminster John Knox Press, 1999); and Victor H. Matthews and Don C. Benjamin, *Social World of Ancient Israel 1250–587 BCE* (Peabody, Mass.: Hendrickson, 1993). Compare *Dictionary of Biblical Imagery*, ed. Leland Ryken, James C. Wilhoit, Tremper Longman III (Downers Grove, Ill.: InterVarsity Press, 1998).

[13]See Lester L. Grabbe, *Priests, Prophets, Diviners, Sages: A Socio-Historical Study of Religious Specialists in Ancient Israel* (Valley Forge, Pa.: Trinity Press International, 1995); Joseph Blenkinsopp, *Sage, Priest, Prophet: Religious and Intellectual Leadership in Ancient Israel*, Library of Ancient Israel, ed. Douglas A. Knight (Louisville: Westminster John Knox Press, 1995); Stephen L. Cook, *Prophecy and Apocalypticism: The Postexilic Social Setting* (Minneapolis: Fortress Press, 1995); John J. Collins, ed., *The Encyclopedia of Apocalypticism* (New York: Continuum, 1998); Greg Carey, *Ultimate Things: An Introduction to Jewish and Christian Apocalyptic Literature* (St. Louis: Chalice Press, 2005).

[14]For a small sampling of foundational works in these areas, see J. G. Gager, *Kingdom and Community: The Social World of Early Christianity* (Englewood Cliffs, N.J.: Prentice-Hall, 1975); Gerd Theissen, *Sociology of Early Palestinian Christianity* (Philadelphia: Fortress Press, 1977); A. J. Malherbe, *Social Aspects of Early Christianity*, 2nd ed. (Philadelphia: Fortress Press, 1983); Wayne A. Meeks, *The First Urban Christians: The Social World of the Apostle Paul* (New Haven: Yale University Press, 1983); B. J. Malina, *The New Testament World: Insights from Cultural Anthropology* (Atlanta: John Knox Press, 1981); *The Social World of Jesus and the Gospels* (New York: Routledge, 1996). For more-recent works, see R. J. Banks, *Paul's Idea of Community* (Peabody, Mass.: Hendrickson, 1994); J. H. Elliott, *Social-Scientific Criticism of the New Testament* (London: SPCK, 1995); C. Osiek, *What Are They Saying About the Social Setting of the New Testament?* (New York: Paulist, 1992); B. W. Winter, *Seek the Welfare of the City: Christians as Benefactors and Citizens* (Grand Rapids: Eerdmans, 1994). A great deal of concisely summarized information as well as carefully selected bibliography is found in Evans and Porter, eds., *Dictionary of New Testament Background*.

[15]Wayne A. Meeks, "A Hermeneutics of Social Embodiment," *Harvard Theological Review* 79 (1986): 176–86. Reprinted in Wayne A. Meeks, *In Search of the Early Christians: Selected*

Essays, ed. Allen R. Hilton and H. Gregory Snyder (New Haven: Yale University Press, 2002), 185–95. For the way in which Meeks came to this hermeneutic that builds on the work of Hans W. Frei and George A. Lindbeck, see his autobiographical "Reflections on an Era," xi–xxviii.

[16]John McIntyre, "Analogy," *Scottish Journal of Theology* 12 (1959): 2.

[17]Henry Barclay Swete, *The Gospel According to St. Mark* (Grand Rapids: Wm. B. Eerdmans, 1951, rep. of the 3rd ed. in 1913).

[18]A. E. J. Rawlinson, *St Mark,* Westminster Commentaries (London: Methuen, 1925); B. Harvie Branscomb, *The Gospel of Mark,* The Moffatt New Testament Commentary (London: Hodder and Stoughton, 1937); Vincent Taylor, *The Gospel According to St. Mark* (London: Macmillan, 1952).

[19]Eduard Schweizer, *The Good News According to Mark* (Richmond: John Knox Press, 1970); William L. Lane, *The Gospel According to Mark,* The New International Commentary on the New Testament (Grand Rapids: William B. Eerdmans, 1974); Hugh Anderson, *The Gospel of Mark,* New Century Bible (Greenwood, S.C.: Attic Press, 1976); Robert A. Guelich, *Mark 1—8:26,* Word Biblical Commentary 34A (Dallas: Word, 1989); Mary Ann Talbert, *Sowing the Gospel: Mark's World in Literary-Historical Perspective* (Minneapolis: Fortress Press, 1989); B. J. Malina and R. L. Rohrbaugh, *Social-Science Commentary on the Synoptic Gospels* (Minneapolis: Fortress Press, 1992); Robert H. Gundry, *Mark: A Commentary on His Apology for the Cross* (Grand Rapids: Eerdmans, 1993); Pheme Perkins, "The Gospel of Mark," *The New Interpreter's Bible* 8 (Nashville: Abingdon Press, 1995), 507–733; B. M. F. van Iersel, *Mark: A Reader-Response Commentary,* JSNTSup 164 (Sheffield: Sheffield Academic Press, 1998); Craig A. Evans, *Mark 8:27—16:20,* Word Biblical Commentary 34B (Nashville: Thomas Nelson, 2001).

[20]Ulrich Luz pioneered this approach in his work on Matthew. See his *Matthew in History: Interpretation, Influence, and Effects* (Minneapolis: Fortress Press, 1994), 2–4, 23–38; and *Matthew 1—7: A Commentary* (Minneapolis: Augsburg, 1989), 95–99. It has also been used as space permitted by Thiselton, *The First Epistle to the Corinthians,* esp. xvii, 196. Blackwell is currently publishing a commentary series dedicated to the history of reception. For example, see David M. Gunn, *Judges,* Blackwell Bible Commentaries (Oxford: Blackwell, 2005), and InterVarsity Press has almost completed its 28-volume *Ancient Christian Commentary on Scripture,* ed. Thomas C. Oden. On the general background of *Wirkungsgeschichte* in the hermeneutical work of Hans-Georg Gadamer and Paul Ricoeur, as well as in the literary work of "reception theory" and "reader-response criticism," see Anthony C. Thiselton on "Communicative Action and Promise in Hermeneutics" in *The Promise of Hermeneutics,* ed. Roger Lundin, Clarence Walhout, and Anthony C. Thiselton (Grand Rapids: William B. Eerdmans, 1999), 133–239. A summary by Thiselton is in his *New Horizons in Hermeneutics* (Grand Rapids: Zondervan, 1992), 516–23. On the philosophical foundations, with particular attention to the concepts of "horizon" and "foregrounding," see Hans-Georg Gadamer, *Truth and Method,* 2nd rev. ed. (New York: Crossroad, 1989), 300–307. For a brief introduction to "reception theory" as it relates to reading the Bible, see David S. Katz, *God's Last Words: Reading the English Bible from the Reformation to Fundamentalism* (New Haven: Yale University Press, 2004), x–xvi.

[21]Ulrich Luz, *Matthew 8—20: A Commentary,* Hermeneia—A Critical and Historical Commentary on the Bible (Minneapolis: Fortress Press, 2001), 372.

[22]On the eschatological connotation of Matthew 5:17, see W. D. Davies, *Christian Origins and Judaism* (Philadelphia: Westminster Press, 1962), 44.

[23]The formula with citation is found in Matthew 1:22–23; 2:15; 2:17–18; 2:23; 4:14–16; 8:17; 12:17–21; 13:35; 21:4–5; 27:9–10. Citations are implied but not given in Matthew 26:54, 56. The complete formula is found in John 12:38–40; 13:18; 15:25; 19:24, 36. A partial formula with either the citation or the term for fulfillment implied is found in John 1:23; 2:17; 6:31, 45; 7:42; 12:14–15; 17:12; 19:28. On the formula quotations, see W. D. Davies and Dale C. Allison Jr., *A Critical and Exegetical Commentary on the Gospel According to Saint Matthew* (Edinburgh: T. & T. Clark, 1997), 573–77.

[24]Johann Perk, *Handbuch zum Neuen Testament: Alttestamentliche Parallelen* (Angermund: Julius Nüttgens, 1947) counts 2,688 uses of the Old Testament in the New Testament. While some are little more than literary allusions, the very fact that the Old Testament was the Bible of the early church meant that most usages reflect a serious theological engagement with the text, often in an effort to show how the understanding of the text is enriched when approached from a Christian perspective.

[25]John 14:15–17; 14:25–26; 15:26–27; 16:5–11; 16:12–15.

[26]For numerous examples of this hermeneutic at work in the Fourth Gospel, see William E. Hull, "John," *The Broadman Bible Commentary*, vol. 9, ed. Clifton J. Allen (Nashville: Broadman, 1970), 204. In a more detailed treatment in *Anatomy of the Fourth Gospel: A Study in Literary Design,* New Testament: Foundations and Facets (Philadelphia: Fortress Press, 1983), R. Alan Culpepper traces how in John much is only "implicit," especially the misunderstandings, irony, and symbolism that remain to be clarified, either by the narrator or by the reader, after the event. Note esp. 34–43, 61–70, 149–202.

[27]C.F.D. Moule, "Fulfilment-Words in the New Testament: Use and Abuse," *New Testament Studies* 14 (1967–68): 294, points out that the meaning "fill" or "complete" in the sense of "filling to capacity" is at the root of the biblical words for fulfillment. One task of strategic preaching is to fulfill the potentiality of a text.

Chapter 4: A Hermeneutic of Strategic Preaching: Contemporary

[1]Clyde E. Fant Jr. and William M. Pinson Jr., *20 Centuries of Great Preaching* (Waco: Word, 1971), 13 vols.

[2]Ibid., 1:v.

[3]The historian Leopold von Ranke (1795–1886) gave classic expression to this emphasis when he wrote that he only wanted to explain the past as it actually happened (*wie es eigentlich gewesen*). See his "Preface to the History of the Latin and Teutonic Nations," in *The Varieties of History,* ed. F. Stern, 2nd ed. (London: Macmillan, 1970), 57, discussed on 55–62.

[4]Krister Stendahl, "Biblical Theology, Contemporary," *The Interpreter's Dictionary of the Bible,* ed. George Arthur Buttrick (New York: Abingdon Press, 1962), 1:419–20.

[5]For an exposition and critique, see Anthony C. Thiselton, *The Two Horizons: New Testament Hermeneutics and Philosophical Description with Special Reference to Heidegger, Bultmann, Gadamer, and Wittgenstein* (Grand Rapids: William B. Eerdmans, 1980), references in the Index of Subjects under "Fusion of horizons" and "Horizon."

[6]Historians and theologians use different criteria to evaluate their findings, the former focused on fact and the latter on faith. But the preacher must somehow fuse their findings in the act of proclamation or be left with a message that has no rootage in lived history, thus compromising its call to incarnational realism.

[7]Tania Oldenhage, *Parables for Our Time: Rereading New Testament Scholarship after the Holocaust,* American Academy of Religion Cultural Criticism Series (New York: Oxford University Press, 2002).

[8]Ibid., 51–59. See Joachim Jeremias, *The Parables of Jesus* (London: SCM, 1954), 120–26. The quotation cited is found in the summary conclusion on page 126. This English translation is of the third German edition of 1954, which incorporated extensive revisions of the second German edition of 1952. However, there are no significant changes in this section, or in the conclusions based on it, from the first German edition of 1947 to the sixth German edition of 1962 on which the revised English edition of 1963 is based.

[9]Although Oldenhage does not directly accuse Jeremias of anti-Semitism, the implicit charge lies close to the surface in her confessional style of writing. I spent the 1962–63 academic year on sabbatical leave studying with Professor Jeremias in Göttingen and know only too well both of the agonizing circumstances under which his book on the parables was written and of the enormous courage which he displayed in opposing the National Socialist policy on the so-called Jewish Question despite pro-Nazi views held by prominent theological faculty in Göttingen. It is regrettable that Oldenhage did not balance her presentation of Jeremias with reference to his forthright preaching in the University Church when the Nazis were present listening to every word.

[10]Oldenhage, *Parables for Our Time,* 69, quoting Elisabeth Schüssler Fiorenza and David Tracy, "The Holocaust as Interruption and the Christian Return into History," *Concilium* 175 (1984): 83.

[11]The problem is accentuated by the large number of free-standing seminaries where neither faculty nor students have intimate daily contact with those working in other disciplines, such as modern history, psychology, and sociology, whose job is to study trends in contemporary life. Sad to say, even some divinity schools related to comprehensive universities neglect the opportunity to engage their faculty and students in the full range of intellectual concerns represented across the campus.

[12]Most such treatments look at contemporary life through homiletical lenses, searching only for those features of the modern world that obviously merit a sermon (e.g., doubt, despair, loneliness, corruption). Approached in this fashion, the resulting portrait is almost always incomplete, distorted, and pessimistic. Methodologically, it is better to begin with the modern world as it is struggling to understand its own reality before highlighting those features that may deserve a pulpit response.

[13]The semi-annual review journal *Homiletic,* which has been available since 1976, contains a brief section in most issues called "Human Sciences and Culture," which provides three or four entries on modern life of interest to scholars in the Academy of Homiletics. However, almost none of the works cited are written to help pastors or to relate preaching to the contemporary world.

[14]W.R. Inge, *Diary of a Dean: St. Paul's 1911-1934* (New York: Macmillan, 1950), 12.

[15]Dietrich Bonhoeffer, cited by Heinrich Ott, *Theology and Preaching* (Philadelphia: Westminster Press, 1965), 12.

[16]Alexis de Tocqueville, *Democracy in America,* trans. Henry Reeve as revised by Francis Bowen and ed. Phillips Bradley (New York: Alfred A. Knopf, 1945). A somewhat more "conservative" or literal translation is by Harvey C. Mansfield and Delba Winthrop, eds. (Chicago: University of Chicago, 2000). The most recent edition is translated by Arthur Goldhammer (New York: Library of America, 2004). For the background of this landmark study, see James J. Schleifer, *The Making of Tocqueville's Democracy in America* (Chapel Hill: University of North Carolina Press, 1980); and Richard Reeves, *American Journey: Traveling with Tocqueville in Search of Democracy in America* (New York: Simon and Schuster, 1982). On the life of the author, see André Jardin, *Tocqueville: A Biography* (New York: Farrar, Strauss, and Giroux, 1988).

[17]Taylor Branch, *Parting the Waters: America in the King Years, 1954-1963* (New York: Simon & Schuster, 1988); *Pillar of Fire: America in the King Years, 1963-65* (New York: Simon & Schuster, 1998); *At Canaan's Edge: America in the King Years, 1965-1968* (New York: Simon & Schuster, 2006). Note the Exodus terminology in the wording of all three titles.

[18]A convenient guide to the riches of Southern studies is provided by three one-volume encyclopedias: David C. Roller and Robert W. Twyman, eds., *The Encyclopedia of Southern History* (Baton Rouge: Louisiana State University Press, 1979); Charles Reagan Wilson and William Ferris, eds., *Encyclopedia of Southern Culture* (Chapel Hill: University of North Carolina Press, 1989), with a multi-volume revision and expansion underway; Samuel S. Hill, ed., *Encyclopedia of Religion in the South,* 2nd ed. (Macon: Mercer University Press, 2005).

[19]To cite but two ministerial examples in a vast field: Robert Moats Miller, in *Harry Emerson Fosdick: Preacher, Pastor, Prophet* (New York: Oxford University Press, 1985), shows how his subject's life was a prism refracting every hue of American culture throughout the first half of the twentieth century. Marshall Frady and William Martin have told the story of Billy Graham in such a way that it illumines the interaction of neo-evangelicalism and American culture throughout the second half of the twentieth century. See Marshall Frady, *Billy Graham: A Parable of American Righteousness* (Boston: Little, Brown, 1979); and William Martin, *A Prophet with Honor: The Billy Graham Story* (New York: William Morrow, 1991).

[20]James A. Hopewell, *Congregation: Stories and Structures,* ed. Barbara G. Wheeler (Philadelphia: Fortress Press, 1987).

[21]Begun in 1987, the Congregational History Project has produced a two-volume work edited by James P. Wind and James W. Lewis, *American Congregations* (Chicago: University of Chicago Press, 1994). Vol. 1, *Portraits of Twelve Religious Communities,* contains a collection of "critical historical portraits of a broad variety of American congregations" (p. 3), which attempts "to clarify the strategic position of the congregation on the borderline between the public and private spheres of American life" (p. x). Vol. 2, *New Perspectives in the Study of Congregations,* contains eight essays on congregations in relation to their context, their traditions, and their leadership written by eight of the sixteen senior scholars who participated in the Congregational History Project seminar.

[22]Nancy Tatum Ammerman with Arthur E. Farnsley II and fifteen others, *Congregation & Community* (New Brunswick, N.J.: Rutgers University Press, 1997). This is primarily a study of the ways in which changes in nine American communities have affected two focal congregations selected for study in each of these settings. For methodological orientation see Nancy T. Ammerman, Jackson W. Carroll, Carl S. Dudley, and William McKinney, eds., *Studying*

Congregations: A New Handbook (Nashville: Abingdon Press, 1998); Carl S. Dudley and Nancy T. Ammerman, *Congregations in Transition: A Guide for Analyzing, Assessing, and Adapting in Changing Communities* (San Francisco: Jossey-Bass, 2002).

[23]For a first effort to relate congregational studies to theological education, with special reference to the work of James F. Hopewell, see Joseph C. Hough Jr. and Barbara G. Wheeler, eds., *Beyond Clericalism: The Congregation as Focus for Theological Education* (Atlanta: Scholars Press, 1988).

[24]The narrative element is emphasized in virtually all studies of the Bible as literature by scholars such as Robert Alter, Frank Kermode, and Northrop Frye. Of especial importance on the neglect of a realistic reading of the narrative element since the Enlightenment is Hans W. Frei, *The Eclipse of Biblical Narrative: A Study in Eighteenth and Nineteenth Century Hermeneutics* (New Haven: Yale University Press, 1974).

[25] The literature is enormous. Karl Barth gave impetus to a movement that includes such theologians as Stanley Hauerwas, George Lindbeck, James W. McClendon, George W. Stroup, Ronald Thiemann, and Terrence W. Tilley.

[26]Representative of the extensive literature are Edmund A. Steimle, Morris J. Niedenthal, and Charles L. Rice, *Preaching the Story* (Philadelphia: Fortress Press, 1980); Eugene L. Lowry, *The Homiletical Plot: The Sermon as Narrative Art Form,* expanded edition (Louisville: Westminster John Knox Press, 2001); Richard A. Jensen, *Telling the Story* (Minneapolis: Augsburg, 1980). For an insightful critique see Richard Lischer, "The Limits of Story," *Interpretations* 38, no. 1 (1984): 26–38.

[27]Stephen Toulmin, *Cosmopolis: The Hidden Agenda of Modernity* (New York: Free Press, 1990), 75–76.

[28]For a theological essay on how memory operates in community, see Charles R. Pinches, *A Gathering of Memories: Family, Nation, and Church in a Forgetful World* (Grand Rapids: Brazos, 2006).

[29]Hopewell, *Congregation*, 19–32.

[30]Northrop Frye, *Anatomy of Criticism* (Princeton: Princeton University Press, 1957), 158–239. Hopewell applied this typology to the stories told around his hospital bed as he battled terminal cancer, *Congregation*, 57–65.

[31]In many ways, Hopewell's work on the four worldview categories is the most stimulating section of his book, with considerable diagnostic potential for understanding the underlying religious outlook of a congregation. The terminology, however, is almost certain to be confusing. By "Canonic" he means a traditional or authoritarian approach to religion, i.e., submission to and reliance on some received standard of truth. By "Gnostic" he refers neither to ancient Gnosticism nor to contemporary New Age movements. Rather, for Hopewell, Gnostic refers to intuitive and holistic ways of grasping ultimate reality. By "Charismatic" he does not mean the Pentecostal movement but an intense spirituality open to an invasive sense of the supernatural. By "Empiric" he means an objective realism willing to tolerate a high degree of ambiguity (doubt) in the search for truth. Writing in the early 1980s, Hopewell illustrated his categories from national television personalities: Jerry Falwell as Canonic, Robert Schuller as Gnostic, and Oral Roberts as Charismatic. Lacking a prominent pulpit representative of the Empiric, I would suggest the "lay preacher," Bill Moyers.

[32]Hopewell, *Congregation*, 114. These four themes are applied to three congregations, 119–38.

[33]Ibid., 87–93.

[34]Ibid., 93–99. The instrument is provided in an appendix, 203–10.

[35]Leonora Tubbs Tisdale, *Preaching as Local Theology and Folk Art* (Minneapolis: Fortress Press, 1997).

[36]Ibid., 1–30.

[37]Ibid., 31–55. The concept of "local theology" is from Robert Schreiter, *Constructing Local Theologies* (Maryknoll, N.Y.: Orbis, 1985).

[38]For Tisdale's methodology, see Ibid., 56–90.

[39]Tisdale, *Preaching as Local Theology and Folk Art,* emphasizes that "preaching as local theology," i.e., the sermon rooted in the church's story, "is not only proclaimed 'to' but also 'out of the midst' and 'on behalf of' a local faith community" (41). For an example of how laypersons can help write the story, see Nora Gallagher's account of her life over a twelve-month period at

Trinity Episcopal Church, Santa Barbara, California, published as *Things Seen and Unseen: A Year Lived in Faith* (New York: Alfred A. Knopf, 1998).

[40]R.H. Charles, "The Book of Jubilees," *The Apocrypha and Pseudepigrapha of the Old Testament* (Oxford: Clarendon, 1913), 2:36–37. Compare O.S. Wintermute, "Jubilees," *The Old Testament Pseudepigrapha*, ed. James H. Charlesworth (New York: Doubleday, 1985), 2:87.

[41]See Ephesians 2:11. This language, which made circumcision a prime boundary marker of group identity, roots in an ancient Hebrew practice of referring to pagan nations such as the Philistines as "uncircumcised" (Judg. 14:3; 15:18;1 Sam. 14:6; 17:26, 36; 31:4; 2 Sam. 1:20; 1 Chr. 10:4).

[42]Adolf Schlatter, *The Church in the New Testament Period* (London: S.P.C.K., 1955), 59.

[43]Dom Gregory Dix, *Jew and Greek: A Study in the Primitive Church* (London: Dacre, 1953), 54.

[44]Daniel Boyarin, *A Radical Jew: Paul and the Politics of Identity* (Berkeley: University of California Press, 1994), 36. This book deals from beginning to end with the issues raised for Jews by Paul's treatment of circumcision, thus affording Christians a chance to understand better both sides of the struggle, which is almost impossible to grasp when reading only the work of other Christians. Note also the somewhat speculative sequel by Boyarin, *Border Lines: The Partition of Judaeo-Christianity* (Philadelphia: University of Pennsylvania Press, 2005). For a stimulating comment on Boyarin's earlier work, including his book *Carnal Israel*, see John Dominic Crossan, *The Birth of Christianity: Discovering What Happened in the Years Immediately After the Execution of Jesus* (San Francisco: HarperSanFrancisco, 1998), xx–xxvii.

[45]For a comprehensive history, see David H. Bennett, *The Party of Fear: From Nativist Movements to the New Right in American History* (Chapel Hill: University of North Carolina Press, 1988).

[46]For a summary, see Ibid., 253–66, in which the relevant bibliography is cited in the endnotes.

[47]Glen Jeansonne, *Gerald L.K. Smith: Minister of Hate* (New Haven: Yale University Press, 1988). For the broader context, see Leo P. Ribuffo, *The Old Christian Right: The Protestant Far Right from the Great Depression to the Cold War* (Philadelphia: Temple University Press, 1983).

[48]On religious terrorism, see especially the works of Mark Juergensmeyer, who edited *Violence and the Sacred in the Modern World* (London: Frank Cass, 1991), and has authored *The New Cold War? Religious Nationalism Confronts the Secular State* (Berkeley: University of California Press, 1993), and *Terror in the Mind of God: The Global Rise of Religious Violence* (Berkeley: University of California Press, 2000). For a provocative effort to probe the biblical and theological roots of religious intolerance, see Regina M. Schwartz, *The Curse of Cain: The Violent Legacy of Monotheism* (Chicago: University of Chicago Press, 1997). For an introduction to the foundational work of René Girard on *Violence and the Sacred* (Baltimore: Johns Hopkins Press, 1977), see Gil Bailie, *Violence Unveiled: Humanity at the Crossroads* (New York: Crossroad, 1995).

[49]On the ambivalent attitudes toward circumcision in contemporary American Judaism that remarkably reprise the first-century situation see Jon D. Levenson, "The New Enemies of Circumcision," *Commentary* (March 2000): 29–36. For a critical study of modern American circumcision in light of its historical roots in Judaism, see Leonard B. Glick, *Marked in Your Flesh: Circumcision from Ancient Judea to Modern America* (New York: Oxford, 2005).

[50]Broadly speaking, "New Right" religion in America has two main wings: (a) the *evangelical* wing, which, in its more mature form, is sensitive to the dangers of nativism and therefore opposed to the "parochializing" of Christianity (Calvin and Wheaton, Billy Graham, *Christianity Today*); (b) the *fundamentalist* wing, which has deep roots in some of the more extreme forms of nativism (e.g. the Christian Crusade of Billy James Hargis) that have continued to find expression in the Moral Majority of Jerry Falwell, the Christian Coalition of Pat Robertson, and the Christian Reconstructionism of R. J. Rushdoony and Gary North. Tensions between the two groups continue to deepen within both the New Right movement and its favored Republican Party, with no resolution in sight. The literature is enormous. For a balanced treatment, see William Martin, *With God on Our Side: The Rise of the Religious Right in America* (New York: Broadway Books, 1996).

[51]The allusion is to Wayne Meeks' "hermeneutics of social embodiment" discussed in chapter 3. Meeks correctly recognizes that biblical texts sought to move the communities that they addressed toward a "social embodiment" or distinctive kind of communal life. Thus the hermeneutical task is not completed until the text finds a "fitting" social embodiment among those whom it addresses

today. However, he does not explore the kind of leadership needed for the text to achieve these societal results. More generally on the "social embodiment" of the sermon, see Arthur Van Seters, ed., *Preaching as a Social Act: Theology and Practice* (Nashville: Abingdon Press, 1988).

Chapter 5: A Homiletic of Strategic Preaching: Preparation

[1] *The Book of Common Prayer and Administration of the Sacraments and Other Rites and Ceremonies of the Church* (New York: Church Hymnal Corp, 1979), 19–33.

[2] In a widely used minister's manual, James W. Cox provides a conflated "church and civic calendar" with only a selection of important observances, yet for the United States there are 89 different emphases mentioned on ninety different days. Even though this calendar provides more emphases than can be managed in only fifty-two weeks, I would agree that all of the more important options should be kept in mind when making hard choices. See James W. Cox, ed., *The Minister's Manual: 2006* (San Francisco: Jossey-Bass, 2005), 2–3.

[3] Jonathan Swift, *Gulliver's Travels* (New York: Oxford University Press, 1977, based on the 1735 ed.), Part 1, Chapter 1.

[4] Adapted from Matthew Arnold phrase, "Who saw life steadily, and saw it whole," in "Sonnet. To a Friend" in *The Strayed Reveller and Other Poems* (1849).

[5] Abraham Lincoln, First Inaugural Address, March 4, 1861. Cited in *Abraham Lincoln: Speeches and Writings, 1859-1865* (New York: The Library of America, 1989), 224.

[6] For example, Charles R. Swindoll, *Growing Strong in the Seasons of Life* (Portland, Oreg.: Multnomah, 1983) describes winter as a season of reverence, spring as a season of renewal, summer as a season of rest, and autumn as a season of reflection. John Killinger applies the concept to ministers in *Christ in the Seasons of Ministry* (Waco: Word, 1981). For a comprehensive historical approach to what might be called the concept of seasonality, see Michael Kammen, *A Time to Every Purpose: The Four Seasons in American Culture* (Chapel Hill, N.C.: University of North Carolina Press, 2004). Gary Schmidt and Susan M. Felch have edited a useful series of anthologies on the seasons: *Winter: A Spiritual Biography of the Season* (Woodstock, Vt.: SkyLight Paths, 2003); *Spring: A Spiritual Biography of the Season* (Woodstock, VT: SkyLight Paths, 2006); *Summer: A Spiritual Biography of the Season* (Woodstock, Vt.: SkyLight Paths, 2005); *Autumn: A Spiritual Biography of the Season* (Woodstock, Vt.: SkyLight Paths, 2004).

[7] Karl Rahner, *Faith in a Wintry Season: Conversations and Interviews with Karl Rahner in the Last Years of His Life,* ed. Paul Imhof and Hubert Biallowons, trans. Harvey D. Egan (New York: Crossroad, 1990), esp. 5, 189–200. For an extended meditation on Rahner's insight, see Martin E. Marty, *A Cry of Absence: Reflections for the Winter of the Heart* (San Francisco: Harper & Row, 1983).

[8] Adapted from William E. Hull, "Agenda for Preaching—I," *Church Chimes,* The First Baptist Church in Shreveport, Louisiana, January 17, 1981, 3.

[9] John S. McClure, *The Roundtable Pulpit: Where Leadership and Preaching Meet* (Nashville: Abingdon Press, 1995); Lucy Atkinson Rose, *Sharing the Word: Preaching in the Roundtable Church* (Louisville: Westminster John Knox Press, 1997); Leonora Tubbs Tisdale, *Preaching as Local Theology and Folk Art* (Minneapolis: Fortress Press, 1997).

[10] McClure, *The Roundtable Pulpit,* 7.

[11] Ibid., 7.

[12] Ibid., 58.

[13] John A. Broadus, *On the Preparation and Delivery of Sermons,* rev. Jesse Burton Weatherspoon (Nashville: Broadman Press, 1944), 50–58.

[14] Ibid., 55.

[15] This approach stimulated by the building of the Berlin Wall in 1961 was enlarged into a series of sermons that became the basis for a book, *Beyond the Barriers* (Nashville: Broadman Press, 1981).

[16] Representative examples of recent critiques that are generally sympathetic to lectionary preaching despite a candid acknowledgment of its limitations are William H. Willimon, "The Lectionary: Addressing the Gains and Losses in a Homiletical Revolution," *Theology Today* 58, no. 3 (2001): 333–42, and C. Clifton Black, "Journeying through Scripture with the Lectionary's Map," *Interpretation* 56, no. 1 (2002): 59–72, with additional critiques referenced in the footnotes.

[17] For a brief but instructive survey see John Reumann, "A History of Lectionaries: From the Synagogue at Nazareth to Post-Vatican II," *Interpretation* 31, no. 2 (1977): 116–30.

¹⁸For a brief sketch of this later history, see Peter C. Bower, ed. , "Introduction," in *Handbook for the Common Lectionary* (Philadelphia: Geneva, 1987) 15–40; and Horace T. Allen Jr., "Introduction: Preaching in a Christian Context," in *Handbook for the Revised Common Lectionary,* ed. Peter C. Bower (Louisville: Westminster John Knox Press, 1996), 1–24.

¹⁹Marion Soards, Thomas Dozeman, and Kendall McCabe, *Preaching the Revised Common Lectionary: Year C* (Nashville: Abingdon Press, 1994), 1:9. This regrettable rhetoric is found in an introductory section on "Why We Use the Lectionary," which is reprinted virtually unchanged in all four volumes of this series.

²⁰Karen B. Westerfield Tucker, "Lectionary Preaching," in *Concise Encyclopedia of Preaching,* ed. William H. Willimon and Richard Lischer (Louisville: Westminster John Knox Press, 1995), 306, argues that the kind of "idiosyncrasies" that need to be counteracted are those "forced readings when a text or texts are chosen ad hoc to address a specific topic or occasion." But why should a reading be "forced" when it is "chosen ad hoc" rather than when it is prescribed? I would argue just the opposite: preachers are more likely to force a meaning on a text when they find it in a lectionary and have no idea why it was chosen than when they search the Scriptures until they find the text that most clearly and powerfully addresses the need they are seeking to meet. To Westerfield Tucker, this exercise of "the preacher's subjectivity and selectivity" would somehow not allow "the message of the scripture to take rightful precedence over the message of the preacher." But why set up this dichotomy between the two messages when what we are after is a fusion of the two that maintains the biblical balance between Word and Spirit as agents of revelation?

²¹There are 23,144 verses in the Old Testament, and 7,957 in the New Testament, for a total of 31,101 in the Bible without the Apocrypha, or an average of 200 verses per week for 156 weeks. I have never seen an exact count of how many verses are included in the Revised Common Lectionary, but the three weekly readings plus the Psalm selection typically include 35–40 verses, which means that the three-year cycle of Sunday readings contains some 18–20 percent of the total verses in the Bible.

²²For two insightful articles in this area, see Gerard S. Sloyan, "The Lectionary as a Context for Interpretation," *Interpretation* 31, no. 2 (1977): 131–38, and Lloyd R. Bailey, "The Lectionary in Critical Perspective," *Interpretation* 31, no. 2 (1977): 139–53. However, these critiques have become increasingly dated as the Common Lectionary and Revised Common Lectionary took steps to address some of their concerns.

²³Assuming an average of twenty verses per week devoted to the Old Testament reading and the Psalm, this would total 3,120 verses in three years, which is only 13 percent of the verses in the Hebrew Bible.

²⁴We do not have space here to give this problem the attention that it deserves. Sloyan, "The Lectionary as a Context for Interpretation," 138, comments on "the overall absence of biblical robustness" in the lectionary: "Congregations are being protected from the insoluble mystery of God by a packaged providence, a packaged morality, even a packaged mystery of Christ." Bailey, "The Lectionary in Critical Perspective," 150, follows James A. Sanders, "Hermeneutics," sec. 8e, *Interpreter's Dictionary of the Bible Supplementary Volume,* (Nashville: Abingdon Press, 1976), 406, in viewing the irreconcilable elements in Scripture as a reflection of the "ambiguity of reality" that guards against "theologically based imperialism in the present." Willimon, "The Lectionary," 336, remarks that "troublesome, incongruous, even threatening verses that challenge our systems of value are frequent victims of the lectionary's attempt to tidy up a passage." Richard B. Hays, *First Corinthians,* Interpretation: A Bible Commentary for Teaching and Preaching (Louisville: John Knox Press, 1997), shows repeatedly how the RCL omits those passages that reflect the nitty-gritty of church life in Corinth and thus obscures the nature of the problem with which Paul was dealing. See esp. pp. 63, 64, 88, 99, 171, 172, 191, 193, 249, 281, 293.

²⁵This contention was advanced in a difficult but path-breaking manifesto by Walter Wink, *The Bible in Human Transformation: Toward a New Paradigm for Biblical Study* (Philadelphia: Fortress Press, 1973). The discerning reader will recognize that, in the criticism of pastoral "subjectivism" by lectionary advocates, I hear echoes of the "objectivism" characteristic of the scholarly guild against which Wink inveighs.

²⁶The Greek construction, which differs from that used to introduce the mention of apostles, prophets, and evangelists earlier in the verse, suggests that the phrase "pastors and teachers" refers to one distinct ministry rather than two and so could be translated "teaching pastors." On the minister as educator see Ronald J. Allen and Clark M. Williamson, *The Teaching Minister* (Louisville: Westminster John Knox Press, 1991).

[27]Bower, "Introduction," in *Handbook for the Common Lectionary,* 29–30.

[28]Leonora Tubbs Tisdale, *Preaching as Local Theology and Folk Art* (Minneapolis: Fortress Press, 1997), 101.

[29]To illustrate: As regards selection, none of the letters to the seven churches in Revelation 2–3 is included anywhere in the lectionary. As regards sequence, the key parables that might be included in a series are scattered over three years depending on the synoptic gospel in which they are found. As regards schedule, such passages as the Ten Commandments and the Beatitudes are concentrated on one Sunday rather than being spaced over the several Sundays needed for detailed treatment.

[30]The latest revision of the lectionary contains more continuous readings than ever before, particularly during Ordinary Time; however, none of these cover an entire book. In fact, not a single book of the Bible is included without omissions in the lectionary even when counting both Sunday and weekday readings over a three-year period. To grasp the sketchy nature of its coverage, consult the "Index of Scripture Readings" in Bower, *Revised Common Lectionary*, 275–92.

[31]For this study I consulted five anthologies that are ecumenical in scope and thus not tied to a denominational tradition that might support or neglect the lectionary. By far the most extensive is the thirteen-volume work of Clyde E. Fant Jr. and William M. Pinson Jr., *20 Centuries of Great Preaching* (Waco: Word, 1971). Others include Andrew W. Blackwood, compiler, *The Protestant Pulpit: An Anthology of Master Sermons from the Reformation to Our Own Day* (New York: Abingdon Press, 1947); James W. Cox, ed., *The Twentieth Century Pulpit* (Nashville: Abingdon Press, 1978 and 1981), 2 vols.; John F. Thornton and Katharine Washburn, eds., *Tongues of Angels, Tongues of Men: A Book of Sermons* (New York: Doubleday, 1999); and Michael Warner, ed., *American Sermons: The Pilgrims to Martin Luther King, Jr.* (New York: Library of America, 1999). In most cases there is no indication of how these sermons were prepared. However, the ways in which most of them use Scripture seem to indicate that very few were shaped by the lectionary.

Chapter 6: A Homiletic of Strategic Preaching: Presentation

[1]For a narrative rather than analytical treatment of these central categories, see the novel by Eliyahu M. Goldratt and Jeff Cox, *The Goal: A Process of Ongoing Improvement*, 2nd rev. ed. (Croton-on-Hudson, N.Y.: North River Press, 1992).

[2]Susan V. Hull, "In Focus: Worship This Sunday," Circular Congregational Church in Charleston, South Carolina, October 11, 1994, 2.

[3]Susan V. Hull, "In Focus: Worship This Sunday," Circular Congregational Church in Charleston, South Carolina, August 23, 1994, 2.

[4]David W. Hull, "First Thoughts," *The Messenger,* First Baptist Church in Huntsville, Alabama, vol. 57, no. 16, April 21, 2005, 1.

[5]Professionally trained church musicians will have a thorough familiarity with the musical resources available for use in worship. Lay volunteers without this background may find helpful for hymn selection such reference works as Thomas B. McDormand and Frederic S. Crossman, *Judson Concordance to Hymns* (Valley Forge: Judson Press,, 1965); and Donald A. Spencer, compiler, *Hymn and Scripture Selection Guide* (Valley Forge: Judson Press,, 1977). For help with the more classical anthem literature, see James Laster, compiler, *Catalogue of Choral Music Arranged in Biblical Order* (Metuchen, N.J.: Scarecrow, 1983).

[6]On the importance of the visual, not only in the artifacts of worship, but in the rhetoric of the sermon, see Jolyon P. Mitchell, *Visually Speaking: Radio and the Renaissance of Preaching* (Louisville: Westminster John Knox Press, 1999). This book points out how pictures now dominate our cognitive processes as a result of television, thus radio speakers have learned to present their material in ways that enable listeners to imagine the message in pictorial terms. Preachers need to become more skillful in speaking visually rather than abstractly to the congregation. In Shreveport, I was encouraged to do this, not only because of the ubiquitous presence of television in the lives of our members, but because for several years my messages were interpreted to our deaf congregation, in which the use of picture-language is all-important to the translation process.

[7]See chapter 5, p. 78.

[8]I am pleased to report that the capital campaign was approved and oversubscribed, the proposed facilities constructed, and the enlarged programs for preschool children launched with a minimum of dissension, which quickly dissipated as a consensus formed regarding the need to give higher priority to the spiritual development of the young in their early formative years. This sermonic effort played only a modest part in shaping such a positive outcome, as is usually the

case with only one sermon, but what little influence it had did contribute directly to the strategic thrust of the church at this point in its ongoing story.

⁹A Baylor University survey named the twelve "most effective preachers" in the English-speaking world. For a report, see Kenneth L. Woodward, "Heard Any Good Sermons Lately?" *Newsweek* (March 4, 1996): 50–52.

¹⁰For a listing of the 100 "Persons of the Century," see *Time* (June 14, 1999). The special issues are dated April 13, 1998 (Leaders and Revolutionaries); June 8, 1998 (Artists and Entertainers); December 7, 1998 (Builders and Titans); March 29, 1999 (Scientists and Thinkers); and June 14, 1999 (Heroes and Icons).

¹¹Judith M. Gundry-Volf, "Between Text and Sermon: Mark 9:33–37," *Interpretation* 53, no. 1 (1999): 57–61.

¹²Ibid., 59.

¹³Children's Defense Fund, "Moments in America for Children," http://www.childrensdefense.org/moments.aspx . The sermon cited statistics as of February 1999, which have been updated here to November, 2005.

¹⁴"Suffer the Little Children," *Time* (October 8, 1990): 41. Since the sermon was preached, child abuse has, if anything, continued to escalate. One thinks immediately of the pedophile scandal in the Roman Catholic priesthood, of pre-teen boys conscripted to commit atrocities in Sierra Leone's civil war, and of preschool girls being repeatedly raped in the brothels of Cambodia.

¹⁵Charles Whitfield, *Healing the Child Within* (Florida: Health Communications, Inc., 1987); John Bradshaw, *Homecoming: Reclaiming and Championing Your Inner Child* (New York: Bantam Books, 1990).

¹⁶Julia Cameron, *The Artist's Way: A Spiritual Path to Higher Creativity* (New York: G. P. Putnam's Sons, 1992). Note the index entries under "artist child within."

Chapter 7: The Pastor as a Strategic Leader

¹James MacGregor Burns, *Leadership* (New York: Harper & Row, 1978), 2. For an overview of the vastness of the subject, see the 1,182 page work of Bernard M. Bass, *Bass & Stogdill's Handbook of Leadership: Theory, Research, and Managerial Applications,* 3rd ed. (New York: Free Press, 1990). For a concise literature review of twenty-four leadership theories that emerged in the twentieth century, see Stephen R. Covey, *The 8th Habit: From Effectiveness to Greatness* (New York: Free Press, 2004), 352–58. On the relevance of leadership for pastoral service, see Robert J. Banks and Bernice M. Ledbetter, *Reviewing Leadership: A Christian Evaluation of Current Approaches* (Grand Rapids: Baker Academic, 2004).

²John W. Gardner once wrote of "The Antileadership Vaccine" with which "we are immunizing a high proportion of our most gifted young people against any tendencies to leadership." Anyone who has taught ministerial students in a theological school over many years is well aware of the effectiveness of that inoculation. See John W. Gardner, "The Antileadership Vaccine" (New York: Carnegie Corporation of New York, 1965), 9, reprinted from the 1965 Annual Report.

³The creative juxtaposition of these examples was suggested by the introduction to "Historical Views of Leadership" in *The Leader's Companion: Insights on Leadership Through the Ages,* ed. J. Thomas Wren (New York: Free Press, 1995), 45–47. Relevant excerpts from the eight examples cited are provided on pp. 53–80.

⁴For an insightful analysis, see Matthew J. Price, "After the Revolution: A Review of Mainline Protestant Clergy Leadership Literature Since the 1960s," *Theology Today* 59, no. 3 (2002): 428–50.

⁵H. Richard Niebuhr, *The Purpose of the Church and Its Ministry: Reflections on the Aims of Theological Education* (New York: Harper & Row, 1956), 90, shrewdly remarked that "as the polity of all the churches…has been modified in the direction of the political structures of…the United States, so the institutional status and authority of the ministry are being modified in the direction of the democratic type of political, educational, and economic executive or managerial authority. In this situation the temptation of ministers to become business managers is balanced by the opposite temptation to maintain the kind of status and authority their predecessors enjoyed in more hierarchically ordered society."

⁶Ibid., 79–94.

⁷Henri J. M. Nouwen, *The Wounded Healer: Ministry in Contemporary Society* (Garden City, N.Y.: Doubleday, 1972). Note also his sequel, *In the Name of Jesus: Reflections on Christian Leadership* (New York: Crossroad, 1990).

⁸Representative of those who have expressed concern for the excessive individualism and social fragmentation characteristic of American religion during the last forty years are Robert N. Bellah and others, *Habits of the Heart: Individualism and Commitment in American Life* (Berkeley: University of California Press, 1985); Robert Wuthrow, *After Heaven: Spirituality in America since the 1950s* (Berkeley: University of California Press, 1998); Robert D. Putnam, *Bowling Alone: The Collapse and Revival of American Community* (New York: Simon & Schuster, 2000).

⁹Some students of leadership root these paradigm shifts in generational differences, attributing a preference for the executive model to the "Greatest Generation" (born 1901–24) and the "Silent Generation" (born 1925–42), due in part to the influence of World War II, while attributing a preference for the enabling model to the "Boomer Generation" (born 1943–64) and the "Generation X-ers" (born 1965–81) due in part to the social upheaval of the sixties. On this understanding the assumption is often implicit that the executive paradigm with its respect for formal authority is dying as the older generations pass off the scene, to be replaced by the enabler paradigm as the younger generations take their place. See Jay A. Conger, "How Generational Shifts Will Transform Organizational Life," in *The Organization of the Future,* ed. Frances Hesselbein, Marshall Goldsmith, and Richard Beckhard (San Francisco: Jossey-Bass, 1997), 17–24. I would observe that authoritarian patterns of leadership often have a great attraction for upwardly mobile young adults, hence the popularity of the earlier paradigm is not likely to wane for the foreseeable future as Conger predicts.

¹⁰David Brooks, "Lions and Foxes," *The Atlantic Monthly* 290, no. 3 (2002): 28.

¹¹Ibid., 30.

¹²Rosabeth Moss Kanter, *Confidence: How Winning and Losing Streaks Begin and End* (New York: Crown Business, 2004) defines confidence as the expectation of a positive outcome that a leader creates in others.

¹³Note the perceptive comments of Anthony B. Robinson, "Power Outage: When Leaders Don't Lead," *Christian Century* (October 18, 2003): 9-10. On Robinson's general approach to leadership, see his *Transforming Congregational Culture* (Grand Rapids: William B. Eerdmans, 2003).

¹⁴For the thesis that the fellowship (*perichōrēsis*) of the three persons of the Trinity models the kind of community that we are called to incarnate in the church, see George Cladis, *Leading the Team-Based Church: How Pastors and Church Staffs Can Grow Together into a Powerful Fellowship of Leaders* (San Francisco: Jossey-Bass, 1999), 1–29.

¹⁵On team-based leadership, see George Barna, *The Power of Team Leadership: Achieving Success Through Shared Responsibility* (Colorado Springs: WaterBrook Press, 2001).

¹⁶Gifford Pinchot, "Creating Organizations with Many Leaders," in *The Leader of the Future: New Visions, Strategies, and Practices for the Next Era,* ed. Frances Hesselbein, Marshall Goldsmith, and Richard Beckhard (San Francisco: Jossey-Bass, 1996), 25, quoting Lao Tsu, "When actions are performed without unnecessary speech, the people say, 'We did it ourselves.'"

¹⁷On the importance of lay leadership training see Leith Anderson, *Leadership That Works: Hope and Direction for Church and Parachurch Leaders in Today's Complex World* (Minneapolis: Bethany House, 1999), 39–40.

¹⁸H. Richard Niebuhr, *Christ and Culture* (New York: Harper & Brothers, 1951).

¹⁹Rick Warren, *The Purpose-Driven Church: Growth Without Compromising Your Message and Mission* (Grand Rapids: Zondervan, 1995).

²⁰Peter F. Drucker, *The New Realities* (New York: Harper & Row, 1989), *Post-Capitalist Society* (New York: HarperBusiness, 1993), and *The Ecological Vision: Reflections on the American Condition* (New Brunswick, N.J.: Transaction, 1993).

²¹Burt Nanus, *Visionary Leadership: Creating a Compelling Sense of Direction for Your Organization* (San Francisco: Jossey-Bass, 1992). This book provides the conceptual foundations for a type of workshop pioneered by Nanus, which he calls a vision retreat. See Burt Nanus, *The Vision Retreat: A Facilitators Guide* (San Francisco: Jossey-Bass, 1995), and *The Vision Retreat: A Participant's Workbook* (San Francisco: Jossey-Bass, 1995).

[22]On this broader hermeneutical and even epistemological use of "ecology," see Peter F. Drucker, "Afterword: Reflections of a Social Ecologist," in *The Ecological Vision: Reflections on the American Condition*, 441–57. On "ecology" as perception rather than conception, see Drucker, *The New Realities*, 255–64.

[23]On the many ways that, "for several centuries now, we have disembodied the faith and dismembered (that is, individualized) the church," see Rodney Clapp, *Border Crossings: Christian Trespasses on Popular Culture and Public Affairs* (Grand Rapids: Brazos, 2000), 14 and *passim*.

[24]Warren Bennis, *On Becoming a Leader* (Reading, Mass.: Addison-Wesley, 1989), 13–37.

[25]Ibid., 73–100. On the practice of innovative learning, see Peter F. Drucker, *Innovation and Entrepreneurship* (New York: Harper & Row, 1985), 19–140.

[26]Adapted from Bennis, *On Becoming a Leader*, 45.

[27]James MacGregor Burns, *Leadership* (New York: Harper & Row, 1978), 19–20.

[28]Bennis, *On Becoming a Leader*, 44–49.

[29]Ibid., 45.

[30]Adapted from Robert G. Cope, *Opportunity from Strength: Strategic Planning Clarified with Case Examples*, ASHE-ERIC Higher Education Report No. 8 (Washington: Association for the Study of Higher Education, 1987), 4. For a summary of "representative statements on leadership and management," see Stephen R. Covey, *The 8th Habit*, 360–64.

[31]On discerning significant changes in one's context for ministry see chapter 4, pp.49–50.

Chapter 8: The Priority of Purpose in Strategic Leading

[1]The theological justification for a both/and rather than an either/or approach to these polarities is based on the biblical conviction that God's dealings with his people in the past provide a paradigm of his promised future. Thus, for example, his final redemption will be a new exodus foreshadowed by the original exodus from Egypt. Supremely, the triumphant Lord of the Parousia will be the same Jesus who first came in lowly flesh.

[2]On the connections between Luke 1—2 and Acts 1—2, see Raymond Brown, *The Birth of the Messiah*, new updated edition (New York: Doubleday, 1993), 242–43.

[3]Richard Belward Rackham, *The Acts of the Apostles*, Westminster Commentaries (London: Methuen, 1901), 43.

[4]One way to communicate these purposes in popular fashion was suggested to me by the First Baptist Church, Tulsa, Okla., in its weekly newsletter of June 13, 2002. Adapted to the terminology used here, the purposes might be described as: Worship: Growing Taller; Outreach: Growing Larger; Nurture: Growing Deeper; Fellowship: Growing Warmer; Service: Growing Broader; Support: Growing Stronger.

[5]On ministry systems, see Peter L. Steinke, *Healthy Congregations: A Systems Approach* (Herndon, Va.: Alban Institute, 1996).

[6]On the importance of purpose in preaching, see Jay E. Adams, *Preaching with Purpose: The Urgent Task of Homiletics* (Grand Rapids: Zondervan, 1982). Adams offers a number of useful suggestions about how to make preaching more purposeful, but does not relate this emphasis to the leadership task of the pastor in making the congregation itself more purposeful. In the idiom of this study, the overall thrust of his approach is not very strategic.

[7]The periodic evaluation of pastoral performance, if conducted properly, can contribute to the self-evaluation of the church, but this is seldom the case. See Jill M. Hudson, *When Better Isn't Enough: Evaluation Tools for the 21ˢᵗ-Century Church* (Herndon, Va.: Alban Institute, 2004).

[8]For an insightful look at this failing in the business world, see Jim Collins, *Good to Great: Why Some Companies Make the Leap...and Others Don't* (New York: HarperBusiness, 2001), esp. 65–89.

[9]All of these techniques and others are discussed at length in the vast literature on the Quality Movement. For applications to church life, see Walther P. Kallistad and Steven L. Schey, *Total Quality Ministry* (Minneapolis: Augsburg, 1994), esp. 78–92; Norman Shawchuck and Gustave Roth, *Benchmarks of Quality in the Church: 21 Ways to Continuously Improve the Content of Your Ministry* (Nashville: Abingdon Press, 1994). For general orientation, see Ezra Earl Jones, *Quest for Quality in the Church* (Nashville: Discipleship Resources, 1993).

[10]I owe this analogy to my son, David W. Hull, in his presentation to a Doctor of Ministry seminar that I was teaching at Beeson Divinity School of Samford University on January 10, 2003.

[11]William M. Easum, *The Complete Ministry Audit: How to Measure 20 Principles for Growth* (Nashville: Abingdon Press, 1996), 5.

[12]George H. Gallup Jr. and D. Michael Lindsay, *The Gallup Guide: Reality Check for 21ˢᵗ Century Churches* (Loveland, Colo.: Group, 2002).

[13]Thomas G. Bandy, *Facing Reality: A Congregational Mission Assessment Tool* (Nashville: Abingdon Press, 2001).

[14]Ibid., 11.

[15]Bandy has written two books to undergird the approach in *Facing Reality,* both of which should be studied before utilizing the assessment tool. See Thomas G. Bandy, *Moving Off the Map: A Field Guide to Changing the Congregation* (Nashville: Abingdon Press, 1998), and *Kicking Habits: Welcome Relief for Addicted Churches* (Nashville: Abingdon Press, 1997). With the latter, use Thomas G. Bandy, *Coming Clean: A Study Guide for Kicking Habits* (Nashville: Abingdon Press, 2001), which is also an introduction to *Facing Reality.*

[16]For an example of their joint efforts, see William W. Easum and Thomas G. Bandy, *Growing Spiritual Redwoods* (Nashville: Abingdon Press, 1997).

[17]Easum, *The Complete Ministry Audit.* For an overview, see Easum's *The Church Growth Handbook* (Nashville: Abingdon Press, 1990). Easum issued *The Complete Minstry Audit,* 2d ed. (Nashville: Abingdon Press, 2006) too late to be used in this study.

[18]For additional information see the Easum, Bandy, and Associates Web site (www.easumbandy.com).

[19]Randy Frazee, *The Christian Life Profile* (Arlington, Tex.: Creative Leadership Ministries, 2001). The author developed the tool for use in the Pantego Bible Church, which he served until recently as senior pastor (see www.pantego.org). For more information on securing copies as well as related products and resources, contact Christian Life Profile, 2134 Bay Cove Court, Arlington, TX 76013-5201, e-mail CLP@pantego.org. For background, see Randy Frazee, *The Connecting Church: Beyond Small Groups to Authentic Community* (Grand Rapids: Zondervan, 2001), 39–106, and www.TheConnectingChurch.com.

[20]Gallup, as quoted in Frazee, *Christian Life Profile,* 7.

[21]For a foundational introduction, see Christian A. Schwarz, *Natural Church Development: A Guide to Eight Essential Qualities of Healthy Churches,* 4th ed. (St. Charles, Ill.: ChurchSmart Resources, 2000). On the application of this approach, see Christian A. Schwarz and Christoph Schalk, *Implementation Guide to Natural Church Development* (St. Charles, Ill.: ChurchSmart Resources, 1998). On the conceptual underpinnings, see Christian A. Schwarz, *Paradigm Shift in the Church: How Natural Church Development Can Transform Theological Thinking* (St. Charles, Ill.: ChurchSmart Resources, 1999). Other materials are appearing regularly, especially in the NCD Discipleship Resources series, for which contact the publisher, ChurchSmart Resources, 3830 Ohio Avenue, St. Charles, IL 60174, e-mail: customerservice@churchsmart.com. For a critique, see George G. Hunter III, "Examining the 'Natural Church Development' Project," *The Pastor's Guide to Growing a Christlike Church* (Kansas City, Mo.: Beacon Hill Press of Kansas City, 2004), 105–14.

[22]The cost of one survey for the pastor and thirty surveys for active laity, plus NCD computer processing with a report on minimum factors and an implementation guide, was $150.00 as of 2006. The questionnaires may be processed internally by the church if its representative attends an NCD Basic Training event to obtain the CORE software (which is regularly upgraded to include findings from ongoing research).

[23]Max DePree, *Leadership Is an Art* (New York: Doubleday, 1989), 9.

[24]Peter F. Drucker, *The Five Most Important Questions You Will Ever Ask About Your Nonprofit Organization: Participant's Workbook* (San Francisco: Jossey-Bass, 1993), 11–16.

[25]Rick Warren, *The Purpose Driven Church: Growth Without Compromising Your Message & Mission* (Grand Rapids: Zondervan, 1995), and *The Purpose Driven Life: What on Earth Am I Here For?* (Grand Rapids: Zondervan, 2002).

Chapter 9: The Vitality of Vision in Strategic Leading

[1]Chapter 2, p. 28.

[2]Rainer Maria Rilke, *Letters to a Young Poet,* trans. Stephen Mitchell (New York: Random House, 1984), 84.

[3]Laura Lee, *Bad Predictions* (Rochester Hills, Mich.: Elsewhere Press, 2000).

[4]Leonard Sweet, *Sweet's Soul Café* 2, nos. 6 and 7 (1996): 9.

[5]Rolf Jensen, *The Dream Society: How the Coming Shift from Information to Imagination Will Transform Your Business* (New York: McGraw-Hill, 1999), 20.

[6]Translation cited by Martin E. Marty, "Resurrection," *Christian Century* (April 20, 2004): 47.

[7]Andrew Marvell, "To His Coy Mistress," *The Complete Poems*, ed. Elizabeth Story Donno (New York: Penguin Books, 1985), 51.

[8]Robert K. Merton and Elinor Barber, *The Travels and Adventures of Serendipity: A Study in Sociological Semantics and the Sociology of Science* (Princeton, N.J.: Princeton University Press, 2004).

[9]Stephen Nachmanovitch, *Free Play: Improvisation in Life and Art* (Los Angeles: Jeremy P. Tarcher, 1990); Robert Lowe, *Improvisation, Inc.: Harnessing Spontaneity to Engage People and Groups* (San Francisco: Jossey-Bass/Pfeiffer, 2000).

[10]Thomas R. Hawkins, *The Learning Congregation: A New Vision of Leadership* (Louisville: Westminster John Knox Press, 1997). This is an emphasis developed especially by Peter M. Senge, *The Fifth Discipline: The Art and Practice of the Learning Organization* (New York: Doubleday/Currency, 2006).

[11]Burt Nanus, author of a standard work on visioning in the business world entitled *Visionary Leadership: Creating a Compelling Sense of Direction for Your Organization* (San Francisco: Jossey-Bass, 1992), has had good results with a vision retreat. See his *The Vision Retreat: A Participant's Workbook* (San Francisco: Jossey-Bass, 1995) and *The Vision Retreat: A Facilitator's Guide* (San Francisco: Jossey-Bass, 1995).

[12]Reggie McNeal, *The Present Future: Six Tough Questions for the Church* (San Francisco: Jossey-Bass, 2003), 103. This debriefing could include such questions as: "What impressions did they form? Did people speak to them? Did the service make sense? Did they feel that they stuck out in the crowd? Was signage adequate? Did they encounter God? Were they inspired, challenged, and uplifted? What do they think the church is most interested in? Would they recommend the church to their friends? Would they come back if they were not paid to?" (p. 103).

[13]There are rich resources for understanding the centrality of risk in the creative process. The theme is set in the context of world history by Daniel J. Boorstin's trilogy, *The Discoverers: A History of Man's Search to Know His World and Himself* (New York: Random House, 1983); *The Creators: A History of Heroes of the Imagination* (New York: Random House, 1992); and *The Seekers: The Story of Man's Continuing Quest to Understand His World* (New York: Random House, 1998). The biblical witness is unsurpassed on this point, especially as regards the prophets, Jesus, and Paul, all of whom plumbed the depths of failure in ways that were catalytic of some of the greatest breakthroughs the human spirit ever experienced. There is no way to put the cross at the center of the Christian faith without developing a theology of failure that is at once both tragic and triumphant.

[14]C. S. Lewis, *The Weight of Glory and Other Addresses,* rev. and exp. , ed. Walter Hooper (New York: Macmillan, 1980), 3–4.

[15]Martin Luther King Jr., as quoted in Veronica Zundel, comp., *Eerdmans' Book of Famous Prayers* (Grand Rapids: William B. Eerdmans, 1983), 122.

[16]Robert D. Dale, *To Dream Again* (Nashville: Broadman Press, 1981). The title is taken from a poem by Charles A. Lindbergh (p. 148).

[17]C. H. Dodd, *The Apostolic Preaching and Its Development* (London: Hodder & Stoughton, 1936).

[18]Ibid., 74–77.

[19]In addition to Ibid., 21, see C. H. Dodd, *According to the Scriptures: The Sub-structure of New Testament Theology* (London: Nisbet, 1952).

[20]Chapter 3, pp. 38–41.

[21]Norman Perrin, *Rediscovering the Teaching of Jesus* (New York: Harper & Row, 1967), 39–43.

[22]Dodd, *Apostolic Preaching,* 33.

[23]For details, see W. D. Davies, *Torah in the Messianic Age and/or the Age to Come,* Journal of Biblical Literature Monograph Series, VII (Philadelphia: Society of Biblical Literature, 1952);

"Matthew 5:17, 18," *Christian Origins and Judaism* (Philadelphia: Westminster Press, 1962), 31–66.

[24]Albert Schweitzer, *The Teaching of Reverence for Life,* trans. Richard and Clara Winston (New York: Holt, Rinehart and Winston, 1965).

[25]The Roman Catholic Church has led in developing a unified ethic on multiple issues relating to the sacredness of life. In the United States, important preparatory work was done by Joseph Cardinal Bernardin in the 1980s, on which see Thomas G. Fuechtmann, ed., *Consistent Ethic of Life* (Kansas City, Mo.: Sheed & Ward, 1988). The climax of this emphasis came with the 1995 papal encyclical of John Paul II, *Evangelium Vitae* ("The Gospel of Life"), which gave rise to the popular distinction between a "culture of life" and a "culture of death."

[26]"Born Again Christians Just as Likely to Divorce as Are Non-Christians," *The Barna Update,* September 8, 2004, www.barna.org.

[27]For a typology of untruth, see Sissela Bok, *Lying: Moral Choice in Public and Private Life* (New York: Pantheon, 1978).

[28]Clarence Jordan, *The Cotton Patch Version of Hebrews and The General Epistles* (New York: Association Press, 1973), 35.

[29]A standard bibliography on theological education for ministry has 283 entries on pastoral care but none on leadership: Heather F. Day, *Protestant Theological Education in America: A Bibliography,* ATLA Bibliography Series, no. 15 (Metuchen, N.J.: Scarecrow Press, 1985), 468, 470.

[30]This is a restatement of the "customer satisfaction" principle that is at the heart of the Quality Movement.

[31]On prayer as eschatological, see Joachim Jeremias, *The Lord's Prayer,* Facet Books: Biblical Series-8 (Philadelphia: Fortress Press, 1964), 16–33. "Jesus grants to them, as the children of God, the privilege of stretching forth their hands to grasp the glory of the consummation, to fetch it down, to believe it down, to pray it down—right into their poor lives, even now, even here, today" (p. 27).

[32]Cited by Donald G. Miller, *Fire in Thy Mouth* (New York: Abingdon Press, 1954), 17.

[33]Henry F. Lyte, "Abide with Me," stanza 2, *Chalice Hymnal,* ed. Daniel B. Merrick (St. Louis: Chalice Press, 1995), no. 636.

[34]Johnson Oatman Jr., "Higher Ground," stanza 1, *The Baptist Hymnal,* ed. Wesley L. Forbis (Nashville: Convention Press, 1991), no. 484; John T. Benson Jr., "I Shall Not Be Moved," refrain, (1950).

[35]William J. Bouwsma, "Christian Adulthood," *Daedalus* 105, no. 2 (1976): 77–92, shows that central to the Christian understanding of transformation was the notion that the essence of adulthood is the capacity for growth, the willingness to change, the openness to risk.

Chapter 10: Strategic Planning to Implement Mission

[1]For a stinging indictment of strategic planning as practiced by professionals in the field, see Henry Mintzberg, *The Rise and Fall of Strategic Planning: Reconceiving Roles for Planning, Plans, Planners* (New York: Free Press, 1994). Because of the importance of his critique, I have included a summary of his contentions as an appendix to this chapter.

[2]Ephesians 4:17 in Eugene H. Peterson, *The Message: The New Testament in Contemporary English* (Colorado Springs: Navpress, 1993), 407.

[3]H. Beecher Hicks Jr., *Preaching Through a Storm* (Grand Rapids: Zondervan, 1987). This book contains case studies of sermons preached through this crisis. Each chapter begins with a "prologue" that describes the context in which the sermon was born. This is followed by the sermon itself, then by an "epilogue" in which Hicks reflects on the impact that the sermon had in the life of the congregation. These sermons illustrate what might be called strategic preaching when under fierce attack.

[4]Mintzberg, *Rise and Fall,* 201–2.

[5]Ibid., 201–9.

[6]In its broad outlines, this model is indebted to the 10-step Strategic Decision Engine methodology presented and interpreted by Michael G. Dolence and Donald M. Norris, "Using Key Performance Indicators to Drive Strategic Decision Making," in *Using Performance Indicators to Guide Strategic Decision Making,* ed. Victor M. H. Borden and Trudy W. Banta, New Directions

for Institutional Research, no. 82 (San Francisco: Jossey-Bass, 1994), 63–80. While written for higher education, this approach is readily adaptable to churches.

⁷The use of KPIs is not yet common in church strategic planning. They are, however, of growing importance in higher education, from which they may be readily adapted to congregational use. In addition to the Borden and Banta essays cited in the previous note, see Gerald Gaither, Brian P. Nedwek, and John E. Neal, *Measuring Up: The Promises and Pitfalls of Performance Indicators in Higher Education,* ASHE-ERIC Higher Education Report No. 5 (Washington: George Washington University Graduate School of Education and Human Development, 1994); Barbara E. Taylor, Joel W. Meyerson, and William F. Massy, *Strategic Indicators for Higher Education: Improving Performance* (Princeton: Peterson's Guides, 1993).

⁸One such manual is by the veteran consultant, Lyle E. Schaller, who has now put his tools for congregational analysis into a book, *The Interventionist,* with the descriptive subtitle: "A conceptual framework and questions for parish consultants, intentional interim ministers, church champions, pastors considering a new call, denominational executives, the recently arrived pastor, counselors, and other intentional interventionists in congregational life" (Nashville: Abingdon Press, 1997).

⁹On scenario-building, see Peter Schwartz, *The Art of the Long View* (New York: Doubleday/ Currency, 1991). For a survey of the current state of the practice, see *Future Research Quarterly* 17, no. 2 (2001): 5–85.

¹⁰Dolence and Norris, "Using Key Performance Indicators," 64. On the cross-impact analysis, see pp. 68–69, 72. It is particularly effective to conduct this Delphi technique as a group process using networked computers that instantly report and rank results, thereby identifying the priorities of the group as the basis for further discussion.

¹¹Edmund Burke, *Reflections on the Revolution in France,* cited with helpful comments by Martin E. Marty, *Context* 19, no. 22 (1987): 2–3.

¹²On the distinction, see Robert H. Waterman Jr., *Adhocracy: The Power to Change,* The Larger Agenda Series (Knoxville: Whittle Direct Books, 1990).

¹³Peter M. Senge, *The Fifth Discipline: The Art and Practice of the Learning Organization* (New York: Doubleday/Currency, 2006). For an application to the church, see Thomas R. Hawkins, *The Learning Congregation: A New Vision of Leadership* (Louisville: Westminster John Knox, 1997).

¹⁴Senge, *The Fifth Discipline,* especially in the chapter on "The Leader's New Work," 317–40.

¹⁵Warren Bennis ended his study of leadership with "ten factors for the future," a helpful set of insights that overlap mine at several points. The main difference is that Bennis based his list on experiences with business leaders while I based my list on experiences with church leaders. See Bennis, *On Becoming a Leader* (Reading, Mass.: Addison-Wesley, 1989), 191–201.

¹⁶Senge stresses a systems approach to leadership in *The Fifth Discipline.* See especially the many entries on "systems" in the Index, 443.

¹⁷Cited in Senge, *The Fifth Discipline,* 210.

¹⁸This is a major theme in Bennis, *On Becoming a Leader,* esp. 26–30, 95–100, 116–17, 143–54, 194–96.

¹⁹Chapter 10, p. 168, n. 1.

²⁰Mintzberg, *Rise and Fall,* 321.

²¹Henry Mintzberg, Bruce Ahlstrand, and Joseph Lampel, *Strategy Safari: A Guided Tour Through the Wilds of Strategic Management* (New York: Free Press, 1998), ix.

²²Mintzberg, *Rise and Fall,* 4.

²³Ibid., 294–303.

²⁴Aaron Wildavsky, *Speaking Truth to Power: The Art and Craft of Policy Analysis* (Toronto: Little, Brown, 1979), 129, cited in Mintzberg, *Rise and Fall,* 189.

²⁵Ibid., 319.

²⁶Ibid., 175.

²⁷Ibid., 276–78.

²⁸Ibid., 325.

²⁹Ibid., 333. For more on the need for both strategizing and planning, see pp. 329, 361–67, 393.

³⁰I fully recognize that some individuals are more gifted by temperament and training to be strategists, others to be planners. This explains the separate vocations—indeed the two different

cultures—that are common in the business world. Psychological tests designed to identify preferred leadership styles often reveal these differences. For example, those who score high on the "dominance" and "influence" sections of the Personal Profile System are more likely to excel at strategizing, while those who score high on the "steadiness" and "conscientiousness" or "compliance" sections are more likely to enjoy planning. For a religious application, see Ken Voges and Ron Braund, *Understanding How Others Misunderstand You* (Chicago: Moody, 1995) with *Workbook* (Moody, 1994). Likewise, those in the red and green quadrants of the Birkman profile usually show a greater aptitude for strategizing, those in the yellow and blue quadrants for planning. See Roger Birkman, *True Colors* (Nashville: Thomas Nelson, 1997).

Chapter 11: The Relevance of Strategic Preaching

[1]For a swift survey of these themes, see Andrew Delbanco, *The Real American Dream: A Meditation on Hope* (Cambridge, Mass.: Harvard University Press, 1999).

[2]Alexis de Tocqueville, *Democracy in America*, trans. and ed. Phillips Bradley (New York: Alfred A. Knopf, 1945), 2:318, from the Second Part, Fourth Book, chapter 6 entitled, "What Sort of Despotism Democratic Nations Have to Fear." For alternative translations, see the editions by Harvey C. Mansfield and Delba Winthrop, *Democracy in America* (Chicago: University of Chicago Press, 2000), 663; and by Arthur Goldhammer, *Democracy in America* (New York: Library of America, 2004), 818.

[3]Robert D. Putnam, *Bowling Alone: The Collapse and Revival of American Community* (New York: Simon & Schuster, 2000). The bulk of the book is on "the collapse" (pp. 15–363), whereas "the revival" is treated briefly and tentatively at best (pp. 367–414).

[4]Robert Wuthnow, *Loose Connections: Joining Together in America's Fragmented Communities* (Cambridge, Mass.: Harvard University Press, 1998).

[5]Putnam, *Bowling Alone,* 183–84.

[6]For a convenient summary of recent statistical research with useful commentary on its interpretation, see Putnam, *Bowling Alone,* 65–79, with abundant documentation provided by the endnotes, 451–55.

[7]For a popular summary of the research, see Bob Amietana, "Statistical Illusion," *Christianity Today* (April 2006): 85–88.

[8]Putnam, *Bowling Alone,* 73. See Wade Clark Roof, *A Generation of Seekers: The Spiritual Journeys of the Baby Boom Generation* (San Francisco: HarperSanFrancisco, 1993), and *Spiritual Marketplace: Baby Boomers and the Remaking of American Religion* (Princeton, N.J.: Princeton University Press, 1999).

[9]On the growth of media-based spirituality as a substitute for congregation-based involvement, see Phyllis A. Tickle, *Re-Discovering the Sacred: Spirituality in America* (New York: Crossroad, 1995), and *God-Talk in America* (New York: Crossroad, 1997).

[10]E. M. Forster, *Howards End* (New York: Penguin Books, 2000), 159. On the difficulty of forming authentic relationships, see Laura Pappano, *The Connection Gap: Why Americans Feel So Alone* (New Brunswick, N.J.: Rutgers University Press, 2001).

[11]Although not directly cited, this entire section is informed by the work of Robert Bellah and collaborators in *Habits of the Heart: Individualism and Commitment in American Life* (Berkeley: University of California Press, 1985), especially its treatment of "Sheilaism," which views faith as "just my own little voice" (p. 221). For an update of Bellah's views, see his "The Protestant Structure of American Culture: Multiculture or Monoculture?" *The Hedgehog Review* 4, no. 1 (2002): 7–28, with critical responses, pp. 29–48.

[12]Putnam, *Bowling Alone,* makes frequent use of the concept throughout his book as indicated by the Index (pp. 535–36), but describes it most clearly on pp. 19–25, 287–95.

[13]Ibid., 289.

[14]For a somewhat similar idea of the equitable distribution of "spiritual capital," developed independently of Putnam, see the intriguing thesis of Robert William Fogel, *The Fourth Great Awakening & the Future of Egalitarianism* (Chicago: University of Chicago Press, 2000), 1–14, 202–15.

[15]R. Paul Stevens and Phil Collins, *The Equipping Pastor: A Systems Approach to Congregational Leadership* (Bethesda, Md.: Alban Institute, 1993), xix.

[16]*The Oxford English Dictionary* devotes eighteen large columns to its treatment of the word *self-* as a prefix, followed by sixty columns of specific compounds. The numerous citations provide

a telling commentary on the pervasiveness of this usage. See the Second Edition prepared by J. A. Simpson and E. S. C. Weiner (Oxford: Clarendon Press, 1991), 14: 907–33.

[17]The term is regularly used for "psychology's deep commitment to narcissism, egoism, self-worship, the individual, isolated self," in Paul C. Vitz, *Psychology as Religion: The Cult of Self-Worship*, 2nd ed. (Grand Rapids: William B. Eerdmans, 1994), xi.

[18]The primary works are Christopher Lasch, *The Culture of Narcissism: American Life in an Age of Diminishing Expectations* (New York: W. W. Norton, 1978), and *The Minimal Self: Psychic Survival in Troubled Times* (New York: W. W. Norton, 1984). These themes also recur in Lasch's *The True and Only Heaven: Progress and Its Critics* (New York: W. W. Norton, 1991), and *The Revolt of the Elites* (New York: W. W. Norton, 1995).

[19]Bellah et al., *Habits of the Heart*, 71–75.

[20]Delbanco, *The Real American Dream*, 103.

[21]Erich Fromm, "The Present Human Condition," *The American Scholar* 25, no. 1 (1955–56): 30.

[22]Fromm, "The Present Human Condition," 30, adds: "Man has transformed *himself* into a commodity, experiences his life as capital to be invested profitably; if he succeeds in this, he is 'successful,' and his life has meaning; if not, 'he is a failure.' His 'value' lies in his salability…" Lasch, *The Culture of Narcissism*, 59, makes the same point by saying, "What a man *does* matters less than the fact that he has *made it*" (italics added).

[23]The literature is enormous. A mature mediating work from historical and philosophical perspectives is Charles Taylor, *Sources of the Self: The Making of the Modern Identity* (Cambridge, Mass.: Harvard University Press, 1989). A brief popular summary of his central concerns is Taylor, *The Ethics of Authenticity* (Cambridge, Mass.: Harvard University Press, 1992). An overview from a psychological perspective is provided by Walter Truett Anderson, *The Future of the Self: Inventing the Postmodern Person* (New York: Tarcher/Putnam, 1997), esp. 1–63. Representative of postmodern views are Kenneth J. Gergen, *The Saturated Self: Dilemmas of Identity in Contemporary Life* (New York: BasicBooks, 1991); and Robert Jay Lifton, *The Protean Self: Human Resilience in an Age of Fragmentation* (New York: BasicBooks, 1993).

[24]On modern expressions of Gnosticism, see the idiosyncratic but insightful work of Harold Bloom, *The American Religion: The Emergence of the Post-Christian Nation* (New York: Simon & Schuster, 1992), supplemented by his *Omens of Millennium: The Gnosis of Angels, Dreams, and Resurrection* (New York: Riverhead Books, 1996). On the gnostic shaping of contemporary selfhood, see Carl A. Raschke, *The Interruption of Eternity: Modern Gnosticism and the Origins of the New Religious Consciousness* (Chicago: Nelson-Hall, 1980), supplemented by his *The Bursting of New Wineskins: Reflections on Religion and Culture at the End of Affluence*, Pittsburgh Theological Monograph Series, no. 24 (Pittsburgh: Pickwick Press, 1978). On the enduring characteristics of Gnosticism both ancient and modern, see Hans Jonas, *The Gnostic Religion: The Message of the Alien God and the Beginnings of Christianity* (Boston: Beacon Press, 1958); and Ioan P. Couliano, *The Tree of Gnosis: Gnostic Mythology from Early Christianity to Modern Nihilism* (San Francisco: HarperSanFrancisco, 1990).

[25]A very amorphous and heterogeneous movement that, consistent with its own claims, has never achieved either stability or continuity as a historical force, but has had pervasive influence on the American religious mindset. The movement has roots in Theosophy, Spiritualism, Astrology, Human Potential, Holistic Health, Native American, and Zen traditions. More serious advocates include Theodore Roszak, Joseph Campbell, Ken Wilbur, Matthew Fox, and Jacob Needleman. Popularizers offering here-today-and-gone-tomorrow bestsellers include Deepak Chopra, Marilyn Ferguson, John Gray, Barbara Hubbard, Arianna Huffington, Shirley MacLaine, Marlo Morgan, James Redfield, Neale Donald Walsch, and Marianne Williamson. For a descriptive listing of 334 phenomena and the personalities associated with the movement, see J. Gordon Melton, *New Age Encyclopedia* (Detroit: Gale Research, 1990).

[26]Philip J. Lee, *Against the Protestant Gnostics* (New York: Oxford University Press, 1987).

[27]See Anthony C. Thiselton, *Interpreting God and the Postmodern Self: On Meaning, Manipulation and Promise* (Grand Rapids: William B. Eerdmans, 1995), 121–26.

[28]Warren Bennis, *On Becoming a Leader* (Reading, Mass.: Addison-Wesley, 1989), 13–37.

[29]Chapter 4, pp. 50–56.

[30]Jonas, *The Gnostic Religion*, 68.

[31]Typical of the hubris was Knight Kiplinger, *World Boom Ahead: Why Business and Consumers Will Prosper* (Washington: Kiplinger Books, 1998); Peter Schwartz, Peter Leyden, and Joel Hyatt, *The Long Boom: A Vision for the Coming Age of Prosperity* (Reading, Mass.: Perseus Books, 1999); James K. Glassman and Kevin A. Hassett, *Dow 36,000: The New Strategy for Profiting from the Coming Rise in the Stock Market* (New York: 1999). Notable exceptions to the trend were Jeremy J. Siegel, *Stocks for the Long Run* (New York: McGraw-Hill, 1998); and Robert J. Shiller, *Irrational Exuberance* (Princeton, N.J.: Princeton University Press, 2000).

[32]On probability theory as a guide to life, see Amir D. Aczel, *Chance: A Guide to Gambling, Love, the Stock Market, and Just About Everything Else* (New York: Thunder's Mouth Press, 2004).

[33]For multiple illustrations, see Glenn Collins, "Playing It Fast and Loose with Lady Luck," *The New York Times,* December 10, 2000.

[34]Ginia Bellafante, "The Lucky Thirteen," *Time* (August 10, 1998): 62–64.

[35]Craig Lambert, "Trafficking in Chance," *Harvard Magazine* (July-August 2002): 34.

[36]George F. Will, "Electronic Morphine," *Newsweek* (November 25, 2002): 92.

[37]Paul Weiler, cited by Lambert, "Trafficking in Chance," 34.

[38]Popular reports of the craze include Kevin Conley, "The Players," *The New Yorker* (July 11 and 18, 2005): 52–58; Brad Stone, "Going All in for Online Poker, *Newsweek* (August 15, 2005): 40–41.

[39]Adam Wolfson, "Life Is a Gamble," *The Wall Street Journal,* August 14, 1998.

[40]Jackson Lears, "Gambling for Grace," *The New Republic* (May 29, 2000): 37. This review article summarizes some of the main contentions in his *Something for Nothing: Luck in America* (New York: Viking, 2003), which is well summarized in his "Luck and Pluck in American Culture," *Chronicle of Higher Education,* January 24, 2004, B-15.

[41]Gerhard Friedrich, *Theological Dictionary of the New Testament,* ed. Gerhard Kittel (Grand Rapids: William B. Eerdmans, 1964), 2: 731–32.

[42]See chapter 3, p 38.

[43]James E. Block, *A Nation of Agents: The American Path to a Modern Self and Society* (Cambridge: Belknap Press, 2002), 22.

[44]These reflections on intentionality are indebted particularly to the insightful comments of Rollo May, *Love and Will* (New York: W. W. Norton, 1969), 223–45.

[45]Ibid., 181–222.

[46]The phrase was used by Gilbert Murray to characterize the pessimism, even morbidity, of the Hellenistic Age in *Five Stages of Greek Religion* (Garden City: Doubleday Anchor Books, 1955), 3–4, 119–65.

[47]May, following the phenomenologist Edmund Husserl, emphasizes that intentionality is an epistemology (May, *Love and Will,* 225–28). He concludes: "Cognition, or knowing, and conation, or willing, then go together. We could not have one without the other. This is why commitment is so important. If I do not *will* something, I could never *know* it; and if I do not *know* something, I would never have any content for my willing" (230).

[48]May, *Love and Will,* 228.

[49]Ibid., 229.

[50]Ibid., 224.

[51]Ibid., 242-43.

[52]See chapter 2, pp. 15–16.

[53]Albert Schweitzer, *The Quest of the Historical Jesus: A Critical Study of Its Progress from Reimarus to Wrede,* 3rd ed. (London: Adam & Charles Black, 1954), 401.

[54]The concept of "thick description" was popularized by Clifford Geertz in *The Interpretation of Cultures* (New York: Basic Books, 1973). For an application to congregational life see Leonora Tubbs Tisdale, *Preaching as Local Theology and Folk Art* (Minneapolis: Fortress, 1997), 58–77.

[55]I suggest two ways to probe this characteristic feature: (1) trace the sayings of Jesus on "it is necessary" (Greek: *dei*) in the synoptics and (2) on "the hour" that has not yet come (Greek: *hora*) in John. More generally, the "I-sayings" in the gospels point to the enormous vitality of the willpower of Jesus, even in the face of bitter controversy, yet without any trace of arrogance or fanaticism, a sure sign of mature intentionality.

[56]John E. Biersdorf, "A New Model of Ministry," in *Creating an Intentional Ministry,* ed. John E. Biersdorf (Nashville: Abingdon, 1976), 35–37.

Chapter 12: Case Studies in Strategic Preaching

[1]The concept of "presiding metaphor" is based on the work of Robert B. Heilman, especially in *This Great Stage* (Baton Rouge: Louisiana State University Press, 1948); and *Magic in the Web: Action and Language in Othello* (Lexington: University of Kentucky Press, 1956).

[2]The literature on the *Titanic* is so enormous as to constitute a library within itself. At the time of initial sermon preparation, I found most helpful the popular treatment by Walter Lord, *A Night to Remember* (New York: Henry Holt, 1955), soon to be supplemented by his sequel, *The Night Lives On* (New York: William Morrow, 1986). Of course, in recent years the story of the Titanic has gained almost a cult following as a result of James Cameron's blockbuster movie of 1997. On the role of the *Titanic* in modern mythology, see Steven Biel, *Down with the Old Canoe: A Cultural History of the* Titanic *Disaster* (New York: W. W. Norton, 1996). Of the many books spawned by the latest wave of publicity, I have found most helpful for further study the careful work of Daniel Allen Butler, *"Unsinkable": The Full Story of RMS* Titanic (Mechanicsburg, Pa.: Stackpole Books, 1998) and have used it for the information that follows.

[3]For examples of artwork that express the religious significance of the nautical metaphor, see an issue on the theme of "The Sea," *Weavings* 14, no. 2 (2001).

[4]Useful in that regard are such passages as Psalms 36:6; 42:7; 77:19; 95:5; and 130:1.

[5]Information about the *Carpathia* compiled and paraphrased from sources cited in note 2.

[6]Information about the *Californian* compiled and paraphrased from sources cited in note 2.

[7]James Rowe, "Love Lifted Me," stanza 1, *Baptist Hymnal* (Nashville: Convention Press, 1975), no. 462. On its composition in the spring of 1912, see William J. Reynolds, *Companion to Baptist Hymnal* (Nashville: Broadman, 1976), 107.

[8]Chapter 8, p. 131.

[9]Jim Collins, *Good to Great: Why Some Companies Make the Leap…and Others Don't* (New York: Harper Business, 2001), 41.

[10]The *Revised Standard Version* read "married only once" in the text of its New Testament edition of 1946 and its full Bible edition of 1952, but soon shifted back to "husband of one wife," which it had originally carried as a footnote. The *New Revised Standard Version* of 1989 reinstated the rendering "married only once." The *Revised English Bible* also reverted to the translation "husband of one wife."

[11]J. B. Cranfill, compiler, *Sermons and Life Sketch of B. H. Carroll* (Philadelphia: American Baptist Publication Society, 1908), ix; J. Dee Cates, "B.H. Carroll: The Man and His Ethics," unpublished doctoral dissertation (Ft. Worth: Southwestern Baptist Theological Seminary, 1962), 15–16. Carroll married in 1861, when he was eighteen, to a bride who was fifteen. After two weeks she refused to live with him, claiming she did not love him. In 1862, he enlisted in the Confederate Army and, while serving, gave his brother consent to sue and win a divorce on grounds of adultery. Records show that she remarried on the day following the divorce. Carroll was converted and joined a Baptist church in 1865, being ordained to the gospel ministry in the following year. Also in 1866 he married Ellen Bell and, after her death, married Hallie Harrison in 1899.

[12]Werner Foerster, *Palestinian Judaism in New Testament Times* (Edinburgh: Oliver and Boyd, 1964), 127.

[13]Albrecht Oepke, *Theological Dictionary of the New Testament,* ed. Gerhard Kittel (Grand Rapids: William B. Eerdmans, 1964), 1:784.

[14]Ben-Chieh Lin, *Quality of Life Indicators in the U.S. Metropolitan Areas, 1970* (Kansas City: Midwest Research Institute, 1975), 23–35, 54–55.

[15]Gurney Breckenfeld, "Business Loves the Sunbelt (and Vice Versa)," *Fortune* (June 1977): 134.

[16]Stanley Tiner, "How Long Must Louisiana Wait," *Shreveport Journal*, June 10, 1977.

[17]Aurelius Augustine (354–430 C.E.) wrote *The City of God* between 413–426 C.E. in the dark days following the sacking of Rome by Alaric.

Author Index

Cope, Robert G., 260 n. 30
Couliano, Ioan P., 266 n. 24
Covey, Stephen R., 258 n. 1, 260 n. 30
Cox, James W., 255 n. 2, 257 n. 31
Craddock, Fred B., 3, 4, 10, 242 nn. 3,
    4(chap. 1), 245 n. 32
Cranfill, J. B., 268 n. 11
Crim, Keith, 248 n. 8
Crossan, John Dominic, 254 n. 44
Crossman, Frederic S., 257 n. 5
Culpepper, R. Alan, 251 n. 26

D

Dale, Robert D., 262 n. 16
Davids, Peter H., 248–49 n. 9
Davies, W. D., 250 nn. 22, 23; 262 n. 23
Davis, Henry Grady, 3, 242 n. 3(chap. 1)
Dawn, Marva J., 247 nn. 26, 34
Day, Heather F., 263 n. 29
Delbanco, Andrew, 195, 265 n. 1,
    266 n. 20
Delling, Gerhard, 247 n. 42
DePree, Max, 140, 261 n. 23
Dix, Dom Gregory, 59, 254 n. 43
Dodd, C. H., 158, 262 nn. 17, 18, 19, 22
Dolence, Michael G., 263 n. 6, 264 n. 10
Dozeman, Thomas, 256 n. 19
Drucker, Peter, 118; 140; 259 n. 20; 260
    nn. 22, 25; 261 n. 24
Dudley, Carl S., 252–53 n. 22
Dunn, James, 15, 246 n. 3

E

Easum, William M., 139, 261
    nn. 11, 16, 17, 18
Ebeling, Gerhard, 244 n. 31
Edwards, O. C., Jr., 243 n. 13
Elliott, J. H., 249 n. 14
Ellul, Jacques, 25, 247 nn. 26, 27, 29, 30
Elshtain, Jean Bethke, 247 n. 33
Esler, Philip F., 249 n. 12
Eslinger, Richard L., 10, 245 n. 33,
    246 n. 17
Evans, Craig A. 248–49 nn. 9, 14;
    250 n. 19
Evans, H. Barry, 242 n. 2(chap. 1)

F

Fant, Clyde E., 3; 43; 242 n. 3(chap. 1); 251
    nn. 1, 2; 257 n. 31
Farnsley, Arthur E. II, 252 n. 22
Felch, Susan M., 255 n. 6
Ferris, William, 252 n. 18

Fiorenza, Elisabeth Schüssler, 44, 251 n. 10
Foerster, Werner, 268 n. 12
Fogel, Robert William, 265 n. 14
Forster, E. M., 192, 265 n. 10
Fosdick, Harry Emerson, 9, 244 n. 25
Frady, Marshall, 252 n. 19
Frazee, Randy, 139, 140, 261 nn. 19–20
Freedman, David Noel, 248 nn. 8, 9
Frei, Hans W., 253 n. 24
Friedrich, Gerhard, 267 n. 41
Fromm, Erich, 195, 266 nn. 21, 22
Frye, Northrop, 53, 253 nn. 24, 30
Fuechtmann, Thomas G., 263 n. 25

G

Gadamer, Hans-Georg, 250 n. 20
Gager, J. G., 249 n. 14
Gaither, Gerald, 264 n. 7
Gallagher, Nora, 253 n. 39
Gallup, George, Jr., 140, 261 nn. 12, 20
Gardner, John W., 258 n. 2
Gay, Peter, 24, 247 nn. 22, 23
Geertz, Clifford 267 n. 54
Genovese, Eugene D., 243 n. 18
Gergen, Kenneth J., 266 n. 23
Girard, René, 254 n. 48
Glassman, James K., 267 n. 31
Glick, Leonard B., 254 n. 49
Gogarten, Friedrich, 15, 246 n. 1
Goldhammer, Arthur, 252 n. 16,
    265 n. 2
Goldratt, Eliyahu M., 257 n. 1
Grabbe, Lester L., 249 n. 13
Graves, Mike, 246 n. 17
Green, Joel B., 248–49 n. 9
Grudem, Wayne, 248 n. 1
Guelich, Robert A., 250 n. 19
Gundry, Robert H., 250 n. 19
Gundry-Volf, Judith, 105, 258 nn. 11, 12
Gunn, David M., 250 n. 20

H

Hart, Trevor, 247–48 n. 45
Hassett, Kevin A., 267 n. 31
Hauerwas, Stanley, 242 n. 9
Hawkins, Thomas R., 262 n. 10,
    264 n. 13
Hawthorne, Gerald F., 248–49 n. 9
Hays, Richard B., 256 n. 24
Heilman, Robert B., 268 n. 1
Hengel, Martin, 246 n. 10
Hicks, H. Beecher, Jr., 169, 263 n. 3
Hogan, Lucy Lind, 243–44 n. 21

Scripture Index